T0340330

The Organization of Craft Work

This edited book focuses on the organization and meaning of craft work in contemporary society. It considers the relationship between craft and place and how this enables the construction of a meaningful relationship with objects of production and consumption. The book explores the significance of raw materials, the relationship between the body, the crafted object and the mind, and the importance of skill, knowledge and learning in the making process. Through this, it raises important questions about the role of craft in facing future challenges by challenging the logic of globalized production and consumption.

The Organization of Craft Work encompasses international analyses from the United States, France, Italy, Australia, Canada, the UK and Japan involving a diverse range of sectors, including brewing, food and wine production, clothing and shoemaking, and perfumery. The book will be of interest to students and academic researchers in organization studies, marketing and consumer behaviour, business ethics, entrepreneurship, sociology of work, human resource management, cultural studies, geography, and fashion and design. In addition, the book will be of interest to practitioners and organizations with an interest in the development and promotion of craft work.

Emma Bell is Professor of Organisation Studies at The Open University, UK.

Gianluigi Mangia is Professor of Organization Studies at the University of Naples Federico II, Italy, and Head of Department of Management, Organizations and Human Resources at the Scuola Nazionale dell'Amministrazione (SNA) in Rome, Italy.

Scott Taylor is Reader in Leadership and Organization Studies at University of Birmingham, UK.

Maria Laura Toraldo is a Postdoctoral Research Assistant and Lecturer at the Università della Svizzera italiana (USI), Lugano, Switzerland.

Routledge Studies in Management, Organizations and Society

This series presents innovative work grounded in new realities, addressing issues crucial to an understanding of the contemporary world. This is the world of organised societies, where boundaries between formal and informal, public and private, local and global organizations have been displaced or have vanished, along with other nineteenth-century dichotomies and oppositions. Management, apart from becoming a specialized profession for a growing number of people, is an everyday activity for most members of modern societies.

Similarly, at the level of enquiry, culture and technology, and literature and economics can no longer be conceived as isolated intellectual fields; conventional canons and established mainstreams are contested. **Management, Organizations and Society** addresses these contemporary dynamics of transformation in a manner that transcends disciplinary boundaries, with books that will appeal to researchers, students and practitioners alike.

Recent titles in this series include:

Counterproductive Work Behaviors
Understanding the Dark Side of Personalities in Organizational Life
Aaron Cohen

Relational Research and Organisation Studies
Charlotte Øland Madsen, Mette Vinther Larsen, Lone Hersted and Jørgen Gulddahl Rasmussen

Organisational Space and Beyond
The Significance of Henri Lefebvre for Organisation Studies
Edited by Sytze F. Kingma, Karen Dale, and Varda Wasserman

The Organization of Craft Work
Identities, Meanings, and Materiality
Edited by Emma Bell, Gianluigi Mangia, Scott Taylor, and Maria Laura Toraldo

The Organization of Craft Work

Identities, Meanings, and Materiality

Edited by Emma Bell, Gianluigi Mangia,
Scott Taylor, and Maria Laura Toraldo

Routledge
Taylor & Francis Group

NEW YORK AND LONDON

First published 2019
by Routledge
711 Third Avenue, New York, NY 10017

and by Routledge
2 Park Square, Milton Park, Abingdon, Oxon, OX14 4RN

Routledge is an imprint of the Taylor & Francis Group, an informa business

First issued in paperback 2019

Library of Congress Cataloging-in-Publication Data
A catalog record for this book has been requested

ISBN: 978-1-138-63666-8 (hbk)
ISBN: 978-0-367-35548-7 (pbk)

Typeset in Sabon
by Out of House Publishing

Contents

Figures

Tables

Contributors

Jane Andrew is an educator and researcher working at the University of South Australia in the School of Art, Architecture, and Design, where she is Director of Match Studio, an interdisciplinary research and professional practice studio that supports students' transition from university to work. She is also co-convenor of The Art & Design of Health & Wellbeing research and innovation cluster, and Research Associate with Susan Luckman on the Australia Research Council funded *Crafting Self* project. Jane's early career as a designer-maker, together with her role as Executive Director of Craftsouth (now Guildhouse), inspired her teaching and research career that focuses on the contribution 'creative capital' makes to economic development.

Emma Bell is Professor of Organisation Studies at the Open University, UK. Her approach to understanding management critically explores meaning-making in organizations. Key themes include change and organizational loss, learning and the production of management knowledge, and spirituality in organizations. In addition to publishing her research in journals, she is (co-)author of the following books: *Reading Management and Organization in Film* (2008), *Business Research Methods* (2015) and *A Very Short, Fairly Interesting and Reasonably Cheap Book about Management Research* (2013). Emma is a past Chair of the Critical Management Studies Division of the Academy of Management and joint Editor-in-Chief of *Management Learning*.

Richard K. Blundel is Professor of Enterprise and Organisation at the Open University, UK. He has examined growth and innovation in craft-based firms, including cheesemakers, boatbuilders, furniture designer-makers and brass musical instrument manufacturers, and has a particular interest in the relationship between craft and environmental sustainability. Richard's work is published in journals such as *Entrepreneurship & Regional Development, Enterprise & Society, Industry & Innovation and The Journal of Small Business*

Management. He has contributed to *The Oxford Companion to Cheese* (Oxford University Press, 2016), and is co-author of Exploring Entrepreneurship (2nd edition) (Sage, 2017).

Stefano Consiglio is Professor in Business Organisation at the University of Naples, Federico II, in the Department of Economics, Management and Institutions. A former vice-president of Human Sciences and Director of the Department of Sociology, he currently coordinates the specialization course in Organisation and Management of Cultural and Environmental Heritage at the University of Naples, Federico II. He is a member of the governing board of the Italian Academy of Business Administration and Management (AIDEA). His research interests focus on business management, human resource management, innovation, and enterprise creation.

Nada Endrissat is a research professor at the Business School of Bern University of Applied Sciences, Switzerland. Her research interests include identities, spaces and practices of work in aesthetic capitalism, including craft work, work on social media, and co-working. Her research has been published in *Human Relations, Organization Studies, Journal of Business Research and Leadership*, among others.

Deirdre Figueiredo MBE is Director of Craftspace, a leading craft development organisation and creative producer. Craftspace commissions exceptional, world-class contemporary craft and champions makers to take an active role in civil society. It connects creative practice with diverse communities of interest and place through a range of activities and partnerships. These include touring exhibitions, cross-artform productions and participatory projects. www.craftspace.co.uk

Fiona Hackney is Professor of Fashion Textiles Theories, University of Wolverhampton, UK. Fiona has research interests in craft and design history, specifically dress and fashion culture, interwar print media, co-production, and social design. Recent publications include: The Power of Quiet: Re-Making Amateur and Professional Textiles Agencies, *Journal of Textile Design, Research & Practice* (2016). She has headed up a number of Arts & Humanities Research Council Connected Communities projects, most recently Designing a Sensibility for Sustainable Clothing (S4S) and Maker-Centric: building place-based, co-making communities.

Robin Holt is Professor in the Department of Management, Philosophy and Politics at Copenhagen Business School, Denmark. He has just written a book *Judgment and Strategy* (Oxford University Press) and is writing two further books, one on craft, strategy, and technology, the other on entrepreneurship and desire. He was co-editor of the journal *Organization Studies* 2013–2017.

Doreen Jakob is a ceramic artist and Honorary Research Fellow at the University of Exeter, UK. Her academic research is noted for the critical enquiry she brings to questions of arts and economic development, shaped through her interdisciplinary background in sociology and economic geography. Her research has focused on the creative industries, creative entrepreneurship, arts and cultural funding, festivalization, place branding, urban development, and the experience economy. In recent years Doreen has extended her arts practice, establishing herself as a ceramic artist in Durham, North Carolina, USA, selling work through her studio name Doora, specializing in clay and fabric arts.

Maria Karampela is Lecturer in Marketing at the University of Strathclyde Business School, Scotland. Her research interests include branding and international marketing strategies, with particular focus on micro and small-medium firms. Her current research focuses on how embeddedness in local, regional, and sectoral network structures and relations facilitates micro-firms' growth.

Chris Land is Professor of Work and Organization at Anglia Ruskin University, UK. His research explores the relationship between economic value and substantive values in management, work, and organization. He has published on ethical values in fashion branding, the commercialization of 'friendship' as a commodity, and the commodification of knowledge by academic publishers. His current research examines the valorization of craft in the brewing industry, and the work involved in establishing the authenticity of a 'craft' product. His writing has been published in journals including *Organization Studies, Human Relations, Organization, Sociology, The Sociological Review, Capital & Class,* and *ephemera.*

Susan Luckman is Professor of Cultural Studies in the School of Creative Industries at the University of South Australia. She is the author of *Craft and the Creative Economy* (Palgrave Macmillan 2015), *Locating Cultural Work: The Politics and Poetics of Rural, Regional and Remote Creativity* (Palgrave Macmillan 2012), and co-editor of *The New Normal of Working Lives: Critical Studies in Contemporary Work and Employment* (Palgrave 2018), *Craft Economies* (Bloomsbury 2018), and *Sonic Synergies: Music, Identity, Technology and Community* (Ashgate 2008).

Gianluigi Mangia is Professor of Organization Studies at the University of Naples Federico II, Italy, and Head of the Department of Management, Organizations and Human Resources at the Scuola Nazionale dell'

Amministrazione (SNA) in Rome, Italy. He has worked as Visiting Scholar at Cardiff Business School, Warwick Business School and London School of Economics in the UK. His research interests are around power and resistance in organizations, and more recently on organizational research methods. His research has been published in international journals such as *Organizational Research Methods* and *Nonprofit and Voluntary Sector Quarterly*, and he has been a contributor to international edited volumes published by Palgrave-Macmillan and Routledge. He is a board member of the European Group for Organizational Studies (EGOS).

Blake Mathias is Assistant Professor in the Department of Management and Entrepreneurship, Indiana University, USA. He has been involved in numerous entrepreneurial ventures, including owning businesses in the assisted living, hardware, and construction industries, and thoroughly enjoys working with students as they develop their ventures. Blake's research interests are at the intersection of psychology and entrepreneurship, focusing on entrepreneurial decision-making and identity. He has published work in *the Journal of Business Venturing, Strategic Management Journal, Journal of Management, Organizational Research Methods, Strategic Entrepreneurship Journal, Journal of Business Ethics*, and authored several book chapters. He has twice received the National Federation of Independent Business award for the best conference paper at the Babson College Entrepreneurship Research Conference.

Jana Milovanović is a cultural anthropologist specializing in itinerant communities, grass-root practice, sustainability, and ethical marketing. Her broad experience includes working with communities of Roma, circus travelers, Irish travelers, asylum seekers, and refugees. Since 2011 she has been director of Terra Vera Association.

Claus Noppeney is a researcher and consultant working at the intersection of economy and culture, creativity and business, organizing and aesthetic practices. Since 2009, he has been Professor at Bern University of Applied Sciences, Switzerland, catalyzing interdisciplinary collaboration. In 2014, he initiated Scent Culture Institute, a hub for projects on smelling in culture, business, and society.

Laura Onions is an artist and educator based in the English West Midlands, teaching Fine Art at the School of Art, University of Wolverhampton. Her research interests include community-engaged practice and feminist approaches to education, exploring diffractive methodologies and notational spaces for painting, teaching, and writing. www.lauraonions.com

Robert Ott is Associate Professor in the School of Fashion at Ryerson University, Toronto, Canada. Robert is currently pursuing a Ph.D. at the School of Business, University of Leicester, UK, investigating the resurgence of craftsmanship in contemporary fashion systems with a focus on bespoke tailoring and shoemaking. He holds a master's degree in the Management of Technology and Innovation and an undergraduate degree in Fashion Design, Apparel Production Management, both from Ryerson. In addition, Robert is Director of the Fashion Zone, an incubator for fashion-inspired start-ups, and Director of The Suzanne Rogers Fashion Institute, a fellowship program for upcoming Canadian fashion designers.

Juho Pesonen is the head of e-tourism research at the University of Eastern Finland, Centre for Tourism Studies. He received his doctorate from University of Eastern Finland Business School in 2013 with a focus on online tourism marketing. Juho has been involved with tourism research since 2009 and has managed and worked in several national and international tourism research and development projects and networks. His main research interests are in digital tourism marketing, destination marketing and development, sustainable tourism, and rural and nature-based tourism.

Ann Rippin is an academic quilter, recently retired from the Department of Management, University of Bristol, UK, where she was Reader in Management. Her research interests included the aesthetics of organization and alternative research methodologies, including the use of textiles. She was co-editor of *Culture and Organisation* and the Chair of the Standing Conference on Organizational Symbolism.

Gavin Rogers is an artist, lecturer, and community arts practitioner. He has particular interest in how the city and art making can improve people's aspiration and well-being. He enjoys working in the mediums of sculpture, conversation, walking, and video, and actively takes part in arts-based conferences, exhibitions, and events.

Jennifer Smith Maguire is Associate Professor of Marketing in the University of Leicester School of Business, UK, and a member of the University's Research Institute for Cultural and Media Economies (CAMEo). Jennifer's research focuses on processes of cultural production and consumption in the construction of markets, tastes, and value. She has published her research in such journals as *Journal of Consumer Culture*, and *Consumption, Markets & Culture*, and is the author of *Fit for Consumption: Sociology and the Business of Fitness* (Routledge, 2008), editor of *Food Practices and Social Inequality* (Routledge, 2018), and co-editor of *The Cultural Intermediaries Reader* (Sage, 2014).

Shelby J. Solomon completed his Ph.D. in Strategic Management at Louisiana State University, USA, in 2017. Shelby researches oppositional market categories, alternative entrepreneurial types, and critical theory. His research has been published in a number of academic outlets including the *Journal of Business Venturing*. He is an active member of the Southern Management Association and the United States Association for Small Business and Entrepreneurship. Shelby is currently Assistant Professor of Management at Roger Williams University, where he enjoys teaching students business strategy through the use of hands-on activities.

Neil Sutherland has now taken the not-so-obvious career progression of teaching and writing about the theory and practice of organizations, after spending his formative years touring across the world in DIY punk bands. He currently works as Senior Lecturer at University of the West of England, UK. He is particularly interested in understanding 'alternatives' to current problematic systems. This started with looking at leaderless activist groups, and now encompasses a range of areas including craft industries, gender studies, and consultancy practice.

Scott Taylor is Reader in Leadership & Organization Studies, Birmingham Business School, University of Birmingham, UK. His current research centers on feminist analysis of women's experiences of work and organization, in craft brewing and British politics, and critical perspectives on corporate social responsibility. With collaborators, he has published research on people management in small organizations, training and development, work/life balance, and organizational death. Scott is Associate Editor for *Organization* and Section Editor for *Journal of Business Ethics,* and sits on the editorial board of *Academy of Management Learning & Education.*

Nicola J. Thomas is Associate Professor in Cultural and Historical Geography at the University of Exeter, UK. She has developed a body of work around craft geographies, situating contemporary and 20th- century craft practice within the broader creative economy. Her approach addresses the intersection of material, historical, cultural, social, political, and economic contexts through an exploration of craft makers' livelihoods and the spatial dimension of their labor. Her research always attends to the historicity of cultural production and consumption, bringing a historical sensitivity to critical understandings of the cultural and creative economy.

Maria Laura Toraldo is a post-doctoral researcher at the University of Lugano, Switzerland. Maria Laura's research interests include the relationship between individual and collective identities and the production and interpretation of organizational culture within and across organizations. In her research on craft work, she is interested in how businesses build brand identities based on authenticity in craft. Maria Laura has also conducted studies on methodological issues surrounding the process of research, such as knowledge creation and interpretation during the practices of research. Her research has been published in international journals, including *Organizational Research Methods, Organization Studies, Culture and Organization,* and *Nonprofit and Voluntary Sector Quarterly.*

Sheena J. Vachhani is a senior lecturer in Management at the Department of Management, University of Bristol, UK. Her work centers on embodiment, ethics, and feminist activism, and she has written on craftivism and vinyl collecting. She has published in scholarly journals such as *Organization Studies; Work, Employment and Society* and *Organization.* She is also an associate editor for *Gender, Work and Organization.*

Nadine Waehning is Lecturer in Marketing at York St John University, York Business School, UK. Her Ph.D. from Hull University is on the topic of consumer motives to purchase regional products and how this is influenced by cultural value differences. Her current research interests are in consumer motives, internationalization of micro-firms and SMEs, and how network structures and relations facilitated growth, with a current focus on the craft-beer industry.

Yutaka Yamauchi is Associate Professor at the Graduate School of Management, Kyoto University. He obtained his Ph.D. in Management from UCLA Anderson School and worked as a researcher at Xerox Palo Alto Research Center (PARC) prior to joining the GSM in 2010. He conducts research in various service settings including restaurants, bars, and apparel stores, typically by using video-recordings to analyze interactions from the ethnomethodological standpoint. He is also Fellow at the Institute on Asian Consumer Insight, Nanyang Technological University, Singapore, and a board member of the Society for Serviceology.

Introduction
Understanding Contemporary Craft Work

Emma Bell, Maria Laura Toraldo, Scott Taylor and Gianluigi Mangia

The concept of craft is central to understanding work and organizations. Commentaries on the values associated with craft, and how they have been eroded by capitalism and globalization, underpin classic theories of organization including Taylorism and Marxism, and inform key organizational concepts such as deskilling (Braverman 1974) and McDonaldization (Ritzer 1995). The endurance and recent flourishing of craft as a way of thinking about work invites consideration of how it has been understood historically, as well as how it is practiced and managed today. This edited volume therefore focuses on the organization of craft work. It considers the importance of craft as a way of understanding work and as a source of cultural meaning.

It is usual at the start of a book such as this to set out what we mean by craft work. However, craft is not a pre-given category that is open to precise delimitation. It is therefore important to avoid 'pedantic semantics' (Miller 2010) in the pursuit of a definition of craft work where a single definition does not exist. Hence we approach craft interpretively, as a phenomenon that is culturally and socially constructed, the result of agreed-upon patterns of action and language that are the outcome of social relations. Consequently, craft continually emerges and is inextricably linked to the socio-cultural, economic and historical conditions of its production. We also need to consider the structural conditions within which craft work is located (Giddens 1984), including state policy frameworks and wider economic and political conditions that contribute towards the current moment in which craft is celebrated, or even fetishized.

Crafted things are assumed to be made with love and care (Rowley 1997). The beauty that is accrued by such crafted objects is understood to be *haptic*, arising from touch, *optic*, related to sight, and *cognitive*, related to concepts, ideas and suggestions (Smith 1997). Combined with these aesthetic values, craft (unlike art) is characterized by the making of functional objects that serve a useful purpose (Becker 1978). In contrast to automated processes of production where there is a high level of certainty and standardization about the outcome, the objects of craft work cannot be accurately predetermined. This is what British designer and woodworker David Pye (1995) refers to as the 'workmanship of risk'.[1] Craft work involves celebrating the imperfections associated with the execution of thought by hand (Ullrich 2004). The realization of these values is understood to depend on the experience of the maker, whose 'virtuoso' skills (Becker 1978) are the result of continuous practice. Acquired virtuosity involves the body as well as the mind of the craft worker, in using raw materials, tools and techniques to make things. In so doing, notions of craft problematize the longstanding Cartesian dualism that elevates the rational, disembodied mind and separates it from the body. These values are important in providing the foundations that inform the organization of contemporary craft work.

Craft is also a discourse that contributes to the social world and our identities within it (Phillips & Hardy 2002; see Luckman 2015a). Viewing craft in this way focuses attention on the embodiment and enactment of craft discourses through historically and socially situated talk and texts. These discourses are used to personalize relationships between producers and consumers. The mockumentary film '*How to Sharpen Pencils*'[2] features an 'artisanal pencil sharpening business' owner. As well as demonstrating the mundane task of how to sharpen pencils, the pencil sharpening businessman demonstrates 'traditional sharpening tools' (i.e. a knife), and an elaborate display tube into which the sharpened pencil is placed to be shipped to the customer, together with a detailed record of when, where and how and by whom the pencil was sharpened. Through parodying the discourses of craft, this text draws attention to their popularity and pervasiveness. Such texts thereby provide insight into how the meaning of craft work is constructed, brought into being and contested.

The remainder of this introduction focuses on the contestation that surrounds the meaning and practice of contemporary craft work organization. Through exploring the nature of this contestation, we introduce three enduring organizational themes which, we suggest, enable understanding of how craft work is organized: identities, meanings and materiality. By tracing the historical significance of each of these themes, we show how they enable understanding of the revival of craft work as a way of thinking about production and consumption. We conclude this introduction by briefly summarising the chapters that comprise the rest of the book.

Contestation in Craft Work Organization

In the past decade, there has been a flourishing of the term 'craft' to refer to a wide range of products and services (Freyling 2011; Luckman 2015a). The language of craft is invoked by a wide range of organizations, from long established family businesses to eco-friendly pop-up enterprises. In fashionable districts of cities across Europe, North

America and Australasia, there can be found numerous examples of small, independent, artisanal businesses making bespoke, handmade, handcrafted, small-batch products in order to appeal to the tastes of craft-conscious, elite professional consumers. These organizations claim that the things they sell are made with love, care and attention to detail.

A key source of meaning which attributions of craft share relies on distancing and differentiating products from mass-manufactured, globalized, mechanized processes of industrial production. This dichotomy is based on the implicit assumption that craft values and practices have been eroded as a consequence of the separation of mental and manual tasks caused by the mechanization and division of labour under Fordism and Taylorism which resulted in deskilling and alienation. Craft work is thereby represented as an antidote to dominant twentieth-century organizing principles of modernist, mechanized industrial production and mass consumerism which, in the nineteenth century, resulted in the 'death of the Artisan Republic' as a moral and political force (Hanlon 2016).

Yet global multinational corporations are also laying claim to craft work. An example is provided by IKEA, the world's largest furniture retailer, which recently introduced a handmade product collection.[3] The collection includes handwoven textiles, pottery and handmade paper products, produced by artisans in rural areas of Thailand. Objects are advertised as unique, produced respecting local traditions and communities. IKEA's craft range is a departure from the organization's core brand and purpose, which is modelled on the principles of McDonaldization – efficiency, predictability, calculability and non-human technology (Ritzer 1995). In so doing it highlights the contested meaning which surrounds craft. This raises the question of whether craft can be distinguished according to the outputs and attributes of products that are 'handmade' or 'handcrafted' on a small scale, or from the spaces, processes and relationships that entangle the maker in the world (Popp & Holt 2016). If the former, then the scale of making and the type of organization that is engaged in craft work is less significant. If the latter, more philosophically and ethically informed perspective is taken, then companies like IKEA may be understood as cynically co-opting craft simply to sell more stuff.

The contested nature of craft work is driven by ideological concerns (Becker 1978), including a desire to find alternatives to global capitalist models of production and consumption (Parker et al. 2014). The pursuit of alternative ways of organizing craft work has led to innovative approaches to business financialization, such as crowdfunding campaigns. For example, UK craft beer company BrewDog has developed a means of raising capital through its 'Equity Punks' scheme, now in its fourth iteration. Consumers are invited to pledge cash to the company in exchange for community and membership benefits and an implicit prospect of profiting from owning a 'share' in the company. A sense of community is maintained with 'shareholders' through regular email contact and an online members' area. The ideology on which this alternative financial model draws is inspired by countercultural rhetoric (Frank 1997), as expressed in the BrewDog Manifesto: '*We are on a mission to make other people as passionate about great craft beer as we are. We bleed craft beer. This is our true North. We are uncompromising. If we don't love it, we don't do it. Ever. We blow shit up. We are ambitious, we are relentless, we take risks…*'.[4]

But while businesses such as this might seem to be using craft ideology in a way which enables alternatives to conventional shareholder capitalism, the tenuous nature of these logics is also evident. In 2017 BrewDog failed to raise sufficient equity in a US-based crowdfunding round and turned to a conventional venture capital firm to make up the shortfall needed to complete a new brewery and retail facility. The promotion of an ideology of craft as a radical alternative to corporate capitalism was transformed overnight into a relatively conventional approach to business organization. This suggests craft ideologies are just another iteration of the countercultural 'artistic critique' that emerged in the 1960s and 1970s. While craft work appears to enable liberation from the inauthentic, managerial spirit, ultimately its fate appears always to be co-optation by capitalism (Boltanski & Chiapello 2005).

Examples like this, and the commercial growth that craft appears to enable, have contributed to instances of backlash. A recent McDonald's marketing campaign represents artisanal coffee as slow, unnecessarily complicated and expensive, an indulgence more oriented towards satisfying the 'hipster'[5] maker than the person buying it. This provides the basis for contrast with the ostensibly straightforward, reasonably priced, reliable coffee at McDonald's.[6] Backlash is also associated with 'fake' or inauthentic use of craft. For example, Mast Brothers is a successful artisanal chocolatier headquartered in Brooklyn, New York. The company makes 'bean to bar' chocolate, a term that refers to a chocolate making process where the producer retains control at every stage, from sourcing the cocoa beans to the finished wrapped bar. Founded by two bearded 'hipster' brothers from Iowa, the self-taught chocolatiers describe themselves as dedicated to 'meticulous craftsmanship'. Mast Brothers set up their New York chocolate factory in 2007. Since then the company has grown into a global business, with stores in London and Los Angeles.

In 2015 Mast Brothers were the focus of complaints that alleged they had not always made chocolate from scratch. Instead the brothers were accused by chocolate industry insiders of purchasing mass-produced chocolate from a well-known French manufacturer and remelting it. It appeared that the success of Mast Brothers was founded on sophisticated marketing and beautiful packaging, rather than skilful making from raw ingredients from a known source.[7] The inauthenticity of these organizational practices was further emphasized through the fact that customers were able to visit the Mast Brothers Williamsburg factory to witness the chocolate-making process. Such 'staged scenes of making that give consumers direct access to the site of production' (Dudley 2014: 104) are relatively common in craft work organizations. Yet they can also be read as a form of Disneyization (Bryman 2004) which transforms craft into an 'experience' or staged performance that bears little resemblance to actual practices or experiences of making.

Rather than avoiding the manipulative intent (Thrift 2008) associated with 'the artificially constructed world of typical corporate communi-cation' (Schroeder 2012: 129), such examples emphasize that craft discourses are being used precisely to convey an image that belies the reality of production. Despite producers' claims of 'honesty' 'transpar-ency' and 'integrity', and the apparent visibility of craft making, such organizational practices generate an 'authenticity paradox' (Guthey & Jackson 2005) that exposes the organization's chronic *lack* of authen-ticity. This is related to the seductive cultural nostalgia that surrounds craft discourses (Luckman 2015a) which encourages articulation of a romantic desire to return to a former way of life that was more stable, secure and meaningful.

Craft work is thus a complex and contested activity where meaning and value is shaped by historical, sociocultural and economic conditions. The purpose of this volume is to explore these multiple, contested meanings in a range of organizational contexts. In the following section, we take the resurgent contemporary popularity of craft as an opportunity to investi-gate the meaning of craft work as a material practice and reflect upon the organizational identity work that these discourses enable.

Why Craft, Why Now?

The widespread revival of craft in the twenty-first century tells us some-thing about the current *zeitgeist*, or spirit of the times. Specifically, the current craft revival channels *fin de siècle* cultural fears that the nature and meaning of work, and what can be achieved through it, is fundamen-tally changing. Craft work discourses are associated with questioning industrial capitalism in periods of rapid change. This can be seen from the late-nineteenth and early-twentieth century Arts and Crafts Movement in the UK, Europe and the USA. This was underpinned by philosophies developed through art critic John Ruskin's (1909) political economic cri-tique of mechanized industrial development in England, and the destruc-tion of landscape and people that it wrought. Led by public advocates such as William Morris, who sought progressive social reform in the UK based on opposition to mass production and the pursuit of alternatives to alienated labour (Greenhalgh 1997; Krugh 2014), the Movement was associated with an antimodernist sentiment which questioned the logic of scientific and technological progress as the basis for living a good life. Such historical precedents as this are echoed within the current craft revival by authors such as Sennett (2008), who argues that the desire to do a job well is an enduring feature of the human condition. This forms an aspect of a wider cultural positioning of craft work as a means of overcoming worker alienation (Crawford 2009) and challenging consumerism (Luckman 2015a).

The craft revival is also related to predictions about the future of work, particularly the likely impact of technological developments in robotics and computing and the anxieties that stem from this. Such developments are hailed as a threat to the need for human labour, judgment and interaction in many jobs. This includes white-collar knowledge work which, it is argued, is becoming drained of its cognitive and creative elements (Crawford 2009; Sennett 2012), as well as manual jobs (Brynjolfsson & McAfee 2014). Ocejo (2017: 133) argues that certain traditional, low-status manual occupations, such as bartending, distilling, barbering and butchery, have come to occupy a special place in the new economy as symbols of a traditional era that represents the 'epitome of hipster culture'. These occupations are experienced not as a form of downward mobility by their predominantly male, middle-class occupants, but as a calling or vocation that relies on a 'sense of craft' based on technical skill and the ability to understand and communicate 'specialized knowledge' (p.135). As Crawford argues, there is considerable appeal in 'tangible work that is straightforwardly useful' such that not only is it economically viable, but for many people it provides a 'greater sense of agency and competence' than other jobs 'officially recognized as "knowledge work"' (p.5). Craft work can thereby be interpreted as a reaction against technological advances that call into question the presumed naturalness of the human body in organizations.

This spirit has generated a revival of craft in popular culture. In the UK, TV series such as *The Great Pottery Throw Down* and *The Great British Sewing Bee* combine cultural nationalism and nostalgia for a former era when things were made by hand, locally and imperfectly, in the home or in combined home-work spaces. In Austria, a recent exhibition entitled 'Handicraft: Traditional Skills in the Digital Age'[8] at the Museum for Applied Arts in Vienna highlighted a further aspect of interest in craft as embodied making. This is fueled by the rise of global online crafting communities such as the Maker Movement or the Do-It-Yourself network. In its more radical form this has given rise to 'craftivism', a social practice that relies on making things which speak to contemporary social, environmental and political issues, often through participatory, community-based projects. The utilization of craft as a source of resistance, protest and transformation (Greer 2014; Black & Burisch 2014) echoes former meanings of the term as an ungovernable power (Dormer 1997), especially in relation to women and work (Wolfram Cox & Minahan

2007)[9]. However, the extent to which the current craft revival is genuinely socially progressive, especially in relation to gender, is one of the questions that this volume seeks to address.

The revival of craft is also linked to economic conditions and the current geopolitical climate. The craft revival is shaped by new forms of populist politics driven by fears about migration and work. These political discourses focus on postindustrial regions such as the North American 'rustbelt', LaTrobe Valley in Australia, Southern Italy, Wales or the North-East of England. These communities have been adversely affected by disinvestment in, and offshoring of, industry such as mining or steelmaking due to globalization (Strangleman 2017). Craft work provides an opportunity through which policy-makers and politicians in the UK have sought to rebuild communities and create employment (Jakob & Thomas 2015). In some cases, this involves returning to and resurrecting sites and buildings that were used to make things in the past, such as in the recent regeneration of a Victorian cotton mill in Manchester in the UK to produce luxury yarn for domestic and overseas markets.[10]

This leads us to a further aspect of the craft revival which concerns its potential role in the development of more sustainable economies (Luckman 2015a). Embedded practices of local making in place are often contrasted with globalized, environmentally damaged, masculinized societies (Wolfram Cox & Minahan 2007). This alternative economy of craft work organization is closely associated with eco-localism and place-based approaches to production and consumption which attempt to address the intertwined crises of climate change and 'peak oil' (Ganesh & Zoller 2014). The importance of place within craft work discourses is captured by the notion of 'provenance', tracing objects to the places and people who made them. The presence of craft discourses in such contexts reflects a desire to move away from continuous, conspicuous consumption, in-built obsolescence (Packard 1963) and disposability, towards the development of local and virtual networks that foster mutually reinforcing patterns of production and consumption. This aspect of the craft revival chimes with contemporary notions of 'peak stuff',[11] 'voluntary simplicity' and 'degrowth' by ascribing value to a life based on constrained production and consumption of material objects as the basis for enhanced subjective wellbeing (Curry 2011). Examples of craft practices associated with alternative economies include 'post-growth fashion', which draws on the idea of 'craft of use', involving creative, ingenious and resourceful adaptation of garments in ways that are satisfying to self and others (Fletcher 2016). The priority within such practices of making is *usership*, rather than *ownership,* as a source of pleasure and delight.[12]

At the same time, the inherently contradictory nature of the craft revival means the term also operates as a marker of wealth and class, enabling a form of conspicuous consumption based on the value of embodied labour. Luxury brands such as Italian fashion label Salvatore Ferragamo use the terms 'craft' and 'handmade' as markers of taste and distinction (Bourdieu 1984) that attribute 'honorific value' (Veblen 2009[1899]) to crafted objects in a way which enables consumers to distinguish themselves from others (Simmel 1957). Data collected by one of us as part of a recent fieldwork project about craft work in the UK confirms this: managers suggest that the appeal of handmade shoes and bicycles offers wealthy global elites a way of differentiating themselves through the connoisseurship of knowing where and how things are made and how their quality is measured (Dudley 2014) in a world where even luxury brands are ubiquitous and provide insufficient distinction. This aspect of the craft revival directly contracts the use of the term to indicate pursuit of more sustainable approaches to production and consumption. Rather, and as Simmel reminds us, 'the attraction of' crafted objects will continue to 'desert the present article just as it left the earlier one' (*ibid*: 556).

Craft Work and Organization Studies: Identities, Meanings and Materiality

Understanding contemporary craft work organization relies on cross-disciplinary engagement between academic disciplines. Consistent with this notion, the chapters in this book are written by researchers in the fields of marketing, strategy, entrepreneurship and organization studies, working alongside human geographers, cultural studies scholars and researchers in fashion and design, and craft practitioners. Before engaging in this cross-disciplinary conversation, we consider how organization studies contributes towards understanding craft work. Our discussion relates to three themes – identities, meanings and materiality.

Identities

The theme of identities relates to the role of craft in 'people's subjectively construed understandings of who they were, are and desire to become' (Brown 2015: 20). Several of the chapters in this book show how identities are being shaped by prevailing craft discourses. This includes consideration of how craft work discourses are used by individuals to construct a coherent sense of self, as well as by organizations, to construct an identity that appeals to members and consumers. Embodied and aesthetic identities of craft workers are increasingly being mobilized in the marketing of crafted and handmade products. These representations of craft workers are a form of aesthetic labour (Warhurst & Nickson 2009) that involves incorporation of employees' physical selves into the brand (Land & Taylor 2010).

The identity work involved in craft organization draws on narratives (Czarniawska 1998) through which workers and consumers seek to account for their lives and actions. Meaning is also constructed through marketing which explains the role of craft workers in processes of making, often accompanied by beautiful images of craft work and craft workers' bodies. Hence the meaning of craft work is constructed through consumption of the craft worker and their visual representation, as much as the crafted object itself. The virtual sphere is an important locale in the construction and circulation of stories of making. For example, online craft-selling platform Etsy creates connections between makers and consumers and gives consumers the opportunity to own objects that possess a story.[13] American crowdfunding websites for creative projects like Indiegogo and Kickstarter also draw on stories to provide meaning, placing emphasis on the life narratives of creative workers who use the sites to seek funding for their projects. A key feature of craft worker identity narratives concerns their entrepreneurial nature; Etsy defines sellers as 'empowering, flexible entrepreneurs'.[14] This positions craft work as a project of the enterprising self, in an era when worker identity is less stable (du Gay 1996). Craft work is thus an identity practice that is characterized by entrepreneurial risk-taking (Dudley 2014) as a way of carving out alternatives to mainstream employment (Crawford 2009) by branding the self in a context of increased economic precarity.

The building of craft work identities based on entrepreneurial subjectivity also relies on eroding the boundaries between work and leisure and co-opting the home as a site of capitalism (Luckman 2015b). The significance of the home as a place of craft work has a long history in the gendering of craft work identities (Callen 1984; Wolfram Cox & Minahan 2007). The development of industrial capitalism in the nineteenth century positioned craft work as a domestic, community-based, small-scale activity which was the domain of women (Greenhalgh 1997). It was only after the growth of industrial organization that the organization of activities such as brewing (Thurnell-Read 2014) and pottery making (Whipp 1985) were taken out of the home and into large factories. Under these conditions, the production of beer became increasingly masculinized, as companies employed only men and advertising was targeted at male industrial workers (Thurnell-Read 2014). Recent fieldwork by one of us suggests that contemporary craft discourses introduce possibilities for women to reshape established gender identities associated with craft brewing. As Luckman (2015a) argues, the craft revival is associated with the rise of home-based flexible employment as a neoliberal, pragmatic response to structural organizational inequalities that continue to systematically disadvantage women in formal workplaces. Yet the gendering of craft work is complex and often conflicting, with some writers suggesting that the craft revival offers male workers and consumers a means of redressing the so-called 'crisis' of masculinity (Crawford 2009; Ocejo 2017). Hence, it is our contention that the gendering of craft work and the power relations reinforced through this warrant greater critical scrutiny.

Craft work identities are also constructed within groups, networks and communities. Previous research into communities of practice focused on how knowledge is exchanged and collectively shared (Cook & Yanow 1993), including through conversation (Orr 1996). Communities of craft are based on work that is not conductive to standardized procedures and involves physical experimentation (Orr 1996). Tacit and embodied knowledge are important resources in craft making that can be diffi-cult to articulate through material and transferrable practices such as codes or expressed procedures (Toraldo et al. 2016). Craft knowledge is acquired through intimate physical engagement with objects and relies on perceptions and aesthetic subtleties, as a means of becoming accomplished in processes of making or doing. This is related to the idea of sharing by doing or acting (Castillo 2002; Hakanson 2007) and notions of embodied learning (Willems 2018). We therefore need to understand how knowledge operates within contemporary craft work organizations and the role of communities of practice in enabling this.

Meanings

The second theme through which organization studies can contribute to understanding craft work concerns its role a source of social and individual meaning. A key question that the craft revival raises is 'what kind of work makes life worth living?' (Dudley 2014: 6). Meaning is central to understanding craft work as a way of making a living and a way of being (Terkel 1974). Contemporary craft discourses appeal to the desire for meaning in work by positioning labour as a source of existen-tial or metaphysical meaning, as well as a way of making a living. This seductive notion recalls the Marxist ideal of un-alienated labour through which workers can exercise the full extent of their humanity in a self-determining context (Marx 2000: 379ff.). Craft discourses offer an anti-dote to modernist organization which is associated with the removal of meaning from work through the implementation of managerial logics of instrumental rationality (Thompson 1963) and worker deskilling (Braverman 1974).

The meaning of craft is also related to the concept of enchantment. The notion of enchantment refers to an experience that produces a sense of the mysterious, magical or imagined (Taylor & Bell 2011). Weber (1993) argued that modernity, rationality and science entail a process of disen-chantment, whereby all aspects of life are experienced and understood as more knowable and manageable and therefore less mysterious. He predicted that enchantment would ultimately be eradicated through the growth of modernism and the rise of instrumental rationality, eventually denuding social and cultural life of the potential to generate meaning. The meaning of craft work is continually being mobilized and negotiated by producers and consumers via a set of complex social relations (Endrissat et al. 2015). This relies on a cultural production process wherein emotional meaning is positioned as central to acts of production (Thurnell-Read 2014) and consumption (Meamber 2014). Craft producers and consumers report their 'love' for objects or express great enthusiasm for making and buying them (Endrissat et al. 2015).

Craft may therefore be understood as providing meaning through enchantment, as the basis for a form of re-enchantment in public life. This involves endorsement of a moral perspective that positions work as central to the maintenance of meaning (Suddaby et al. 2017). These authors argue that the craft resurgence implies that enchantment has not been completely rationalized out of existence. They suggest this is related to global economic shifts, including the 2008 global financial crisis, which has provoked a move towards craft work as a more viable form of commerce (Suddaby et al. 2017). However, it must be remembered that this discourse is enacted within existing structural conditions, especially those related to ownership of the means of production.

Materiality

Our third theme relates to the importance of *materiality* in understanding craft work organization. Despite attempts to rationalize organized work in ways which imply the denial or removal of the body, we suggest that embodied signifiers of craft, in the form of the hand and the eye, remain as important symbolic presences in manufacturing and other types of organized work. The development of practice-based theories in organization studies draws attention to materiality, practices and embodiment, in contrast to cognition, as a way of explaining social action and order (Sandberg & Tsoukas 2016). Practice theory thereby provides a valuable basis for understanding craft work as a set of embodied practices, actions, materials and objects associated with making. This way of thinking challenges scientifically rational accounts of organization in favour of theories of organization that draw on the philosophy of Wittgenstein, Merleau-Ponty and Heidegger to account for our entwined relationship with matter. Recent development of new materialist thinking (Fox & Alldred 2017) furthers our understanding of the entangled nature of materiality through a relational epistemology that challenges traditional binaries of human/non-human, social/natural, mind/body in ways which destabilize conventional subject/object relations in organizational theory. It draws attention to the lively materiality of physical matter (Bennett 2010) and human interactions with it, as unable to be measured simply in terms of commodity exchange (Dudley 2014).

The practice turn in organization studies also chimes with the renewed focus on the body as a subject of study in disciplines like sociology (Shilling 2007). Shilling suggests that the reason the body is an absent presence within sociology is because the discipline has focused predominantly on industrial structures and processes. Hence, it has tended to overlook relationships between nature and culture, which are the predominant concern of anthropology. This is not to say that social theorists like Marx and Weber were uninterested in the body. However, they assumed that capitalism and the structural and cultural forces associated with it, alienated social actors from their embodied selves (Shilling 2007). Similar arguments can also be made in the context of organization studies.

For Shilling, it is important that the body is not understood as a surface phenomenon that is inscribed upon (Foucault 1979); instead he uses the idea of bodily techniques to explore the *body pedagogics* through which the embodied subject is constituted within a culture. This is consistent with Wacquant's (2005: 446) sociology *from* the body which promotes the ethnographic study of bodily craft as the 'sociocultural competency residing in pre-discursive capacities that illuminate the embodied foundation of all practice'. As well as having methodological implications for how we study craft work in a way which generates understanding of these features, such an approach focuses attention on the *visceral* nature of craft work organization as a lived and felt experience. The focus on materialities of craft work builds on existing research in organization studies, related to aesthetics as well as to the body, which highlights the importance of sensory knowledge as the basis for organizational coordination and learning (Strati 2007; Hindmarsh & Pilnick 2007). The tactility of craft work intersects with creativity in a way which is productive of memory and affective relationships with objects (Vachhani 2013). This presents exciting opportunities for the study of embodied practices of material engagement in craft work organization.

Crafting this Book

By bringing together the contributors to this book to write about craft, we too are engaged in a form of craft work that results in the making of an object. For us, and we suspect for other researchers and academic writers, publishing a journal article is a qualitatively different experience that does not evoke the same responses as arise from crafting a book. The love that we have for books, and their role in nurturing our spiritual growth (Kiriakos & Tienari 2018), is an indication of their importance as a craft resource in academic work. We hope that this book is read as a demonstration of craft work.

This book seeks to develop an understanding of the diversity of craft work organization. Through the contexts and cultures covered, consisting of Japan, United States, Italy, UK, Australia and France, the authors draw attention to the importance of place, space and time in situating craft work. Their analyses encompass craft work in a diverse range of contexts and sectors, from beer, sushi and winemaking, to crafting handmade shoes, silk ties and bespoke perfumery. We see it as significant that many of the contributors represent craft visually, perhaps because photographs and pictures can sometimes capture the embodied, sensory, aesthetic and emotional qualities of craft better than words (Bell & Davison 2013).

Robin Holt and Yutaka Yamauchi's chapter explores the potential of nostalgia to return to a lost past via craft. Their chapter advances the notion that craft activities are imbued with emotional meanings which appear as a collective reaction to mass-produced objects. Taking the case of traditional sushi bars, the authors posit that sushi is a craft product that recreates the past; nostalgia for a lost past is thus present in the experience of sushi, which reproduces the qualities of traditional Japanese craft. Similarly, Solomon and Mathias also touch on aspects related to the meaningfulness associated with craft work. Through in-depth interviews with craft entrepreneurs in America, the authors argue that increasingly routinized, and depersonalized corporate jobs have paved the way for the emergence of craft entrepreneurship in the US. This is not just a way of making a living but also a way of being and feeling that is anchored in the local context and tradition. The interplay between craft, authenticity and cultural legitimacy is object of analysis in Jennifer Smith Maguire's chapter. She focuses on the concept of authenticity associated with wine products, showing how the term operates to establish the legitimacy of consumption. Her chapter provokes questions around the use of craft as marker of taste to promote alternative forms of (elite) consumption.

Susan Luckman and Jane Andrew illustrate the dynamics of home-based work within ccontemporary craft economy. This chapter describes the work of women engaged in self-employed craft work as a way of overcoming the obstacles of managing family/motherhood and work in traditional organizations. The authors explore the ramifications of home-based work on women's identity and draw implications related to the precarity of self-employment and work-life balance. Based on a longitudinal study of niche perfumery, Nada Endrissat and Claus Noppeney's chapter connects to craft ideology and explores the inevitable ambiguity of craft products in contemporary capitalism. The authors question whether craft offers a radical alternative to the big perfume industry or a superficial modification to consumerist culture. Maria Laura Toraldo, Stefano Consiglio and Gianluigi Mangia's chapter focuses on organizational identity in craft work and the role of place, local history and tradition. Using the case study of an elite tie-maker in the Italian city of Naples, they show how the firm relies on collective memories based on local history and place to construct a distinctive organizational narrative. Chris Land, Neil Sutherland and Scott Taylor's chapter explores several themes associated with contemporary craft work, including the authenticity of artisanal products, cultural nostalgia toward a pre-industrial age, and the use of anachronistic gendered ideals in marketing craft products. Their chapter focuses on the craft beer industry, revealing a hyper-masculine culture and demonstrating how a pre-industrial, feminized craft became a male-dominated practice.

Nadine Waehning, Maria Karampela and Juho Pesonen provide an investigation into the definition of craft, revealing ambiguities inherent in craft terminology. With reference to craft beers, the authors explore consumers' interpretation of the term 'craft', focusing on what 'authentic' means to them. Through their analysis, they shed light on the contested meaning of the craft label and reflect on the practical implications for the craft brewing industry. Nicola Thomas and Doreen Jakob address timely questions about local regeneration, specifically of rural areas, through the practice of craft. The authors look at the role of regional craft guilds in the South-West of Britain and reveal the importance of membership within such associations. Employing the notion of 'community of practice', they argue that being part of a guild offers opportunities to local makers by enhancing their skills and abilities and attributing a mark of distinction to their work. Robert Ott continues this theme, through analysis of bespoke shoemaking in Canada. He emphasizes the contingent nature of craft work and its organization, drawing on Niklas Luhmann's arguments on objects in the world, to show the centrality of uncertainty to this way of making.

Ann Rippin and Sheena Vachhani's chapter takes the form of a dialogue on craft where the authors engage in a conversation on the potentiality of craft as a source of resistance. Craft is here indicated as a social progressive force and the authors unpack the concept of craftivism – a form of craft-based 'gentle resistance' – which represents a central resource for challenging organizational oppression and exploitation. Together, the authors reflect on the subversive potential of craft in contrast to the commodification of academic work. Hackney et al.'s chapter takes a similar position to several other chapters in this volume with regard to the relevance of history, tradition and cultural context; however, they take a distinctive approach in discussing craft heritage as a resource for creation of a sense of community. Written by authors involved in the Maker-Centric project, a project to revitalize local areas through hand-making, the authors argue that the craft practice is a valuable means for engaging communities and working on issues related to diversity and inclusion.

The concluding chapter in this edited collection provides a short reflective commentary on the state of craft work organization. Richard Blundel's historically informed analysis focuses on the role of the past in defending and promoting craft practice and describes how organizations can make use of this history today.

A final thought to end on, and one reinforced by several chapters in this volume, concerns the elusiveness of craft work organization. In this book, craft is characterized as a *practice* (e.g. Hackney et al.; Jakob & Thomas), an *object* (e.g. Endrissat and Noppeney), an *aesthetic ideal* (e.g. Smith Maguire), and a *profession* (e.g. Solomon and Mathias). Yet, as these chapters further demonstrate, there are certain commonalities in the understanding of craft work – objects are 'made by hand', characterized by authenticity, and consumer choice is informed by judgements based on taste, rather than determined purely by economic logic. We believe that the richness and diversity that characterizes craft work organization, including differences in scale and size (from the home-making studio described by Luckman et al. to the family-based medium sized tie-maker described by Toraldo et al.), and variety of sectors and locales (from Holt and Yamauchi's illustration of Japanese craft sushi, to the Canadian hand-made shoes described by Ott), make craft discourses highly eclectic and at the same time very specific as a way of thinking about organization. This eclecticism enables new ways of thinking about organization, while its specificity enables a sense of craft work that endures.

Acknowledgment

Front cover photograph of glassmaking from the With Love Project,[15] which documents the work of people who do things with passion and purpose. © Rob Evans. Reproduced with permission and thanks.

Notes

1 We take the view that even if not etymologically gender-specific, the use of such gendered language as 'craftsman' reinforces the idea that women are marginal. We therefore use gender-neutral terms apart from in direct quotes.
2 'How to Sharpen Pencils' (2013) by Pricefilms https://vimeo.com/60718161 [accessed 7 April 2017]
3 See www.ikea.com/my/en/catalog/categories/collections/34659/ [accessed 2 June 2017]
4 See www.brewdog.com/about/culture [accessed 9 February 2018]
5 Hipster is a term that is used to refer to usually well-educated, middle-class urban gentrifiers (Ocejo, 2017).
6 See McDonald's corporate YouTube channel: www.youtube.com/watch?v=Kra1eWAiKvE [accessed 9 February 2018]
7 https://qz.com/571151/the-mast-brothers-fooled-the-world-into-buying-crappy-hipster-chocolate-for-10-a-bar/ [accessed 7 April 2017]
8 See www.mak.at/handicraft [accessed 9 February 2018]

9   This can be contrasted with former iterations of craft discourses such as the Arts and Crafts Movement, which reproduced and reinforced a prevailing patriarchal ideology that restrained women (Callen, 1984). Leaders of that movement failed to question the positioning of women as domestic, passive, and necessarily focused on reproductive labour.

10 Cotton Spinning to return to Greater Manchester, BBC News, 2 December 2015 www.bbc.co.uk/news/uk-england-manchester-34984504 [accessed 7 April 2017]

11 Will Hutton 'If having more no longer satisfies us, perhaps we've reached "peak stuff"?', 31 January 2016, *Guardian* www.theguardian.com/commentisfree/2016/jan/31/consumerism-reached-peak-stuff-search-for-happiness [accessed 7 April 2017]

12 'A Conversation on Craft Culture' with Kate Fletcher and Susan Luckman, CAMEo Research Institute for Cultural and Media Economies, University of Leicester, UK, 9 November 2016.

13 The art and craft of business, 4 January 2015, *The Economist* www.economist.com/news/business/21592656-etsy-starting-show-how-maker-movement-can-make-money-art-and-craft-business [accessed 19 April 2017]

14 Etsy. (2013) Redefining Entrepreneurship: Etsy Sellers' Economic Impact. https://blog.etsy.com/news/files/2013/11/Etsy_Redefining-Entrepreneurship_November-2013.pdf [accessed 9 February 2018]

15 www.withloveproject.co.uk/ [accessed 9 February 2018]

References

Becker, H.S. (1978) Arts and crafts. *American Journal of Sociology*, 83(4): 862–89.

Bell, E. & Davison, J. (2013) Visual management studies: empirical and theoretical approaches. *International Journal of Management Reviews*, 15(2): 167–184.

Bennett, J. (2010) *Vibrant matter*. Durham, NC: Duke University Press.

Black, A. & Burisch, N. (2014) In M.E. Buszek (Ed.) *Extra/ordinary: craft and contemporary art*. Durham, NC: Duke University Press, pp. 204–221.

Boltanski, L. & Chiapello, E. (2005) *The new spirit of capitalism*. London: Verso.

Bourdieu, P. (1984) *Distinction: a social critique of the judgement of taste*. London: Routledge.

Braverman, H. (1974) *Labor and monopoly capital: the degradation of work in the twentieth century*. New York: Monthly Review Press.

Brown, A.D. (2015) Identities and identity work in organizations. *International Journal of Management Reviews*, 17(1): 20–40.

Bryman, A. (2004) *The Disneyization of society*. London: Sage.

Brynjolfsson, E. & McAfee, A. (2014) *The second machine age: work, progress and prosperity in a time of brilliant technologies*. New York: Norton.

Callen, A. (1984) Sexual division of labour in the Arts and Crafts Movement. *Woman's Art Journal*, 5(2): 1–6.

Castillo, J. (2002) A note on the concept of tacit knowledge. *Journal of Management Inquiry*, 11(1): 46–57.

Cook, S. & Yanow, D. (1993) Culture and organizational learning. *Journal of Management Inquiry*, 2(4): 373–390.

Crawford, M.B. (2009) *Shop class as soulcraft: an inquiry into the value of work*. New York: Penguin.

Curry, P. (2011) *Ecological ethics*. Cambridge: Polity Press.

Czarniawska, B. (1998) *A narrative approach to organization studies*. Thousand Oaks, CA: Sage.

Dormer, P. (1997) The salon de refuse? In P. Dormer (Ed.) *The culture of craft: status and future*. Manchester: Manchester University Press, pp. 2–16.

Dudley, K.M. (2014) *Guitar makers: the endurance of artisanal values in North America*. Chicago: University of Chicago Press.

du Gay, P. (1996) *Consumption and identity at work*. London: Sage.

Endrissat, N., Islam, G. & Noppeney, C. (2015) Enchanting work: new spirits of service work in an organic supermarket. *Organization Studies*, 36(11): 1555–1576.

Fletcher, K. (2016) *Craft of use: post-growth fashion*. London: Routledge.

Foucault, M. (1979) *Discipline and punish: the birth of the prison*. New York: Vintage Books.

Frank, T. (1997) *The conquest of cool*. Chicago: University of Chicago.

Freyling, C. (2011) *On craftmanship: towards a new Bauhaus*. London: Oberon.

Fox, N.J. & Alldred, P. (2017) *Sociology and the new materialism: theory, research, action*. London: Sage.

Ganesh, S. & Zoller, H. (2014) Organizing transition: principles and tensions in eco-localism. In M. Parker, G. Cheney, V. Fournier & C. Land (Eds.) *Routledge companion to alternative organization*. Abingdon: Routledge, pp. 236–250.

Giddens, A. (1984). *The constitution of society*. Cambridge: Polity.

Greenhalgh, P. (1997) The history of craft. In P. Dormer (Ed.) *The culture of craft: status and future*. Manchester: Manchester University Press, pp. 20–52.

Greer, B. (Ed) (2014) *Craftivism: the art of craft and activism*. Vancouver: Arsenal Pulp Press.

Guthey, E. & Jackson, B. (2005) CEO portraits and the authenticity paradox. *Journal of Management Studies*, 42(5): 1057–1082.

Hakanson, L. (2007) Creating knowledge: the power and logic of articulation. Industrial and Corporate Change, 19(6): 51–88.

Hanlon, G. (2016) *The dark side of management: a secret history of management theory*. Abingdon: Routledge.

Hindmarsh, J. & Pilnick, A. (2007) Knowing bodies at work: embodiment and ephemeral teamwork in anaesthesia. *Organization Studies*, 28(9): 1395–1416.

Jakob, D. & Thomas, N. (2017) Firing up craft capital: the renaissance of craft and craft policy in the UK. *International Journal of Cultural Policy*, 23(4): 495–511.

Kiriakos, C.M. & Tienari, J. (2018) Academic writing as love. *Management Learning*. https://doi.org/10.1177/1350507617753560

Krugh, M. (2014) Joy in labour: the politicization of craft from the Arts and Crafts movement to Etsy. *Canadian Review of American Studies*, 44(2): 281–301.

Land, C. & Taylor, S. (2010) Surf's up: work, life, balance, and brand in a New Age capitalist organization. *Sociology*, 44(3): 395–413.

Luckman, S. (2015a) *Craft and the creative economy*. Houndmills, Basingstoke: Palgrave Macmillan.

Luckman, S. (2015b) Women's micro-entrepreneurial homeworking: a magical solution to the work-life relationship. *Australian Feminist Studies*, 30(84): 146–160.

Marx, K. (2000) *Karl Marx: selected writings*, edited by David McLellan, 2nd edition. Oxford: Oxford University Press.

Meamber, L. (2014) Cultural production and consumption of images in the marketplace. In Bell, E., Warren, S. & Schroeder, J. (Eds.) *The Routledge companion to visual organization*. Abingdon: Routledge, pp. 96–115.

Miller, D. (2010) *Stuff*. Cambridge: Polity.

Ocejo, R. (2017) *Masters of craft: old jobs in the new urban economy*. Princeton: Princeton University Press.

Orr, J. (1996) *Talking about machines: an ethnography of a modern job*. Ithaca, NY: Cornell University Press.

Packard, V. (1963) *The waste makers*. Harmondsworth: Penguin.

Parker, M., Cheney, G., Fournier, V. & Land, C. (2014) (Eds.) *Routledge companion to alternative organization*. Abingdon: Routledge.

Phillips, N. & Hardy, C. (2002) *Discourse analysis: investigating processes of social construction*. Qualitative Research Methods Series 50. London: Sage.

Popp, A. & Holt, R. (2016) Josiah Wedgwood, manufacturing and craft. *Journal of Design History*, 29(2): 99-119.

Ritzer, G. (1995) *The McDonaldization of society*. Thousand Oaks, CA.: Pine Forge Press.

Rowley, S. (1997) Introduction. In Rowley, S. (Ed.) *Craft and contemporary theory*. St Leonards, AU: Allen & Unwin, pp. xiv–xxvi.

Ruskin, J. (1909) *Unto this last and other essays on art and political economy*. London: Dent.

Sandberg, J. & Tsoukas, H. (2016) Practice theory: what it is, its philosophical base, and what it offers organization studies. In R. Mir, H. Willmott & M. Greenwood (Eds.) *Routledge companion to philosophy in organization studies*. Abingdon: Routledge, pp. 184–198.

Schroeder, J. E. (2012) Style and strategy: snapshot aesthetics in brand culture. In C. McLean, P. Quattrone, F-R. Puyou & N. Thrift (Eds.) *Imagining organisations: performative imagery in business and beyond*. London: Routledge, pp. 129–151.

Sennett, R. (2008) *The craftsman*. London: Penguin.

Sennett, R. (2012) *Together: the rituals, pleasures and politics of cooperation*. London: Penguin.

Shilling, C. (2007) Sociology and the body: classical traditions and new agendas. In C. Shilling (Ed.) *Embodying sociology: retrospect, progress and prospects*. Oxford: Blackwell/The Sociological Review, pp. 1–18.

Simmel, G. (1957) Fashion. *American Journal of Sociology*, 62(6): 541–558.

Smith, T. (1997) Craft, modernity and postmodernity. In Rowley, S. (Ed.) *Craft and contemporary theory*. St Leonards, AU: Allen & Unwin, pp. 18–28.

Strangleman, T. (2017) Deindustrialisation and the historical sociological imagination: making sense of work and industrial change. *Sociology*, 51(2): 466–482.

Strati, A. (2007) Sustainable knowledge and practice-based learning. *Management Learning*, 38(1): 61–77.

Suddaby, R., Ganzin, M. & Minkus, A. (2017) Craft, magic, and the re-enchantment of the world. *European Management Journal*, 35(3): 285–296.

Terkel, S. (1974) *Working: people talk about what they do all day and how they feel about what they do*. New York: Random House.

Taylor, S. & Bell, E. (2011) The promise of re-enchantment: organizational change and the spirituality at work movement. In Boje, D., Burnes, B. & Hassard, J. (Eds.) *The Routledge companion to organizational change*. London: Routledge, pp. 569–579.

Thompson, E.P. (1963) *The making of the English working class*. London: Victor Gollancz.

Thrift, N. (2008) The material practices of glamour. *Journal of Cultural Economy*, 1(1): 9–23.

Thurnell-Read, T. (2014) Craft, tangibility, and affect at work in the microbrewery. *Emotion, Space & Society*, 13: 46–54.

Toraldo, ML., Islam, G. & Mangia, G. (2016) Modes of knowing: video research and the problem of elusive knowledge. *Organizational Research Methods*, 1–28.

Ullrich, P. (2004) Workmanship: the hand and body as perceptual tools. In A.M. Fariello, & P. Owen (Eds.) *Objects and meaning: new perspectives on art and craft*. Lanham, MD: Scarecrow Press, pp. 198–215.

Vachhani, S. J. (2013) (Re)creating objects from the past – affect, tactility and everyday creativity. *Management and Organizational History*, 8(1): 91–104.

Veblen, T. (2009[1899]) *The theory of the leisure class*. Oxford: Oxford University Press.

Wacquant, L. (2005) Carnal connections: on embodiment, apprenticeship, and membership. *Qualitative Sociology*, 28(4): 445-474.

Warhurst, C. & Nickson, D. (2009) "Who's got the look?" Motional, aesthetic and sexualized labour in interactive services. *Gender, Work and Organization*, 16(3): 385–404.

Weber, M. (1993) *The sociology of religion*. Boston: Beacon Press.

Whipp, R. (1985) Labour markets and communities: an historical view. *Sociological Review*, 33(4): 768–791.

Willems T. (2018) Sensing and sensing the railways: a phenomenological view on practice-based learning. *Management Learning*, 49(1), p. xx.

Wolfram Cox, J. & Minahan, S. (2007) Stitch'nBitch: cyberfeminism, a third place and the new materiality. *Journal of Material Culture*, 12(1): 5–21.

1 Craft, Design and Nostalgia in Modern Japan

The Case of Sushi

Robin Holt and Yutaka Yamauchi

Nostalgia

On encountering the West midway through the nineteenth century, Japan was diverted, reluctantly, from the long-travelled, twisting paths that it had been following into its own interior for centuries. These westernising forces came embodied in the black ships of Commodore Matthew Perry. As well as troops, they were carrying letters from the US government insisting (as was the way with this enthusiastic, upstart nation) that it be allowed to establish trading ports along the Japanese coast. After much procrastination (or so it seemed from a Western point of view) the Shogunate acceded, and the islands changed irrevocably. For one, the political turmoil that ensued overturned the Shogunate and enacted the country of Japan. The destinies of different dynastic prefectures that had historically gathered in little more than loose alignments became braided in increasingly tighter and more intricate patterns. As the ports were established and grew in size and wealth, new political and social structures also emerged in an attempt to administer them. Without any explicit design the islands found themselves acting together.

The form this administration took was, on the surface at least, quiescent: rather than resist trade, the Japanese were collectively undertaking to excel in it. They did, and what began as a gradual and stylistic absorption became, over time, explicit and heavily managed. Denizens of the shogunates were forcibly and even violently converted into a loyal citizen body (*shimin*) (Ivy 1995: 10–11) and a policy of military-backed, aggressive regional expansion sought to secure resources and markets for a growing industrial base organized by an increasingly visible central government. The shameful and deadly failures of some of these centralizing and expansionist policies during WWII seemed only to serve to put the populace on notice to redouble their efforts, 'encouraged' yet again by pressure from the USA. The citizens' zeal for manufacturing seemed endless. They were diligent, industrious and governed by 'cradle to grave' career systems characterized by levels of micro-management that would have held Frederick Taylor and Henry Ford in rapturous awe. They also became eager customers, participating in cycles of ownership, use and disposal with seemingly few qualms about deleterious psychological, social and environmental effects. Western ways had beaten them into a new shape, and they were now beating the West hands down.

Nowhere has the mimetic rush to materialize and commodify life been more pronounced than in the gridded, neon-lit streets of Tokyo; an entire urban setting has become high on lines of production and consumption, a floating world no more. From inside this huge space (there does not seem to be an outside) the change to an entirely commercialized lifestyle seems complete. Like Kafka's story *Metamorphosis,* however, this change is not at all a natural or easy one. The human being has become something very different, at first perhaps a little embarrassed and unsure, but then increasingly aware of how new, powerful movements become possible. Cities like Tokyo are testimony to this affective sense of power. And yet, just as in Franz Kafka's *Metamorphosis,* where Gregor Samsa, despite becoming insect-like, retains and indeed intensifies an anxious concern for his earlier human selfhood, Japan's commercial grab carries remains braided with traditional style. The transforming and then hardening to the rhythm of managed productiveness has been a process of absorption, not wilting exposure. Foreign influence changed the body of Japan into something more physically powerful and agile, yet rather than change completely, this material productiveness and global economic presence has perhaps served to further insulate the nation's traditional and almost unique sense of soul and sentiment. Japan has westernized, but in a Japanese way. It is because of this persisting sense of distinctiveness that Japan has seemed well able to absorb the ironies of its own commitments. Western brands can be obsessed over and brandished joyously, but more as one might fetishize anything exotic: their attractiveness lies in them being 'at a distance', much as the smell of grass meadows remains sufficiently alien to throw a poetising city dweller into bucolic reverie. The same goes for the Western politics of individuality and liberalized markets, or Western dress and entertainments, all of which have been enthused over and adopted in some ways, but always with a twist, and sometimes under an inscrutable gaze.

The impress of the new millennium (a handy, Western epochal marker) has witnessed further change in this complex relationship with itself, as many in Japan have begun to realize their prowess in manufacturing and consuming mass-produced objects does not equate to a meaningful life. A collective anxiety has become palpable. Perhaps chastened by the experience of often heedless commercial development, and certainly now in awe of sublime natural forces, Japanese people are looking to what went before all this economic productiveness. Why did they want to be 'Number 1'? As rapidly and totally as Japan has industrialized, it has also become suspicious of its experience – the sheer pace of development has meant the old ghosts and gods have not had enough time to die, they linger still in the shadows and ceremonies and subcultures that permeate the digitized and mechanized patterns of thought and action.

There is, amongst some, nostalgia for what lay behind the belching smoke from Perry's iron-clad, US naval vessels beached off Okinawa in 1853. What is imagined is a time when seasonal rhythms and the moon and sun were more apparent, when organized activity, feeling and thought were communally governed, working smoothly, uncomplainingly, and somehow in touch with natural things. Inwardly the nation is being reminded of what has been lost and how their culture might have been different. Nostalgia does this: something is felt to be at stake and a loss has already occurred. The argument goes something like this: what is being lost is the connexion to the 'old ways' by which the country was distinct, unique even (Ivy 1995: 10). The lack of distinctiveness caused anxiety amongst a people who economically were becoming very successful, but only through excelling in practices that were not, fundamentally, felt to be their own. One way of alleviating this anxiety is by nurturing intense affection for substitutes that recreate the past. These recreations are stories and so always beholden to narrative form: they appear only in being continually retold, and are nothing outside of the telling. The passion for craft is one such substitute, and in Japan its stories are being forever told and retold.

Craft and Design

It is an easy association to bring craft alongside cultural and national identity and to find in its exponents a respectful and enhancing embodiment of the old ways. Easy, but in Japan at least, not simple, because in Japan the narratives of craft have so often been kneaded with the imaginaries created in branded design. Take one example amongst so many: the coloured splashes of the Japanese designer and artist Takashi Murakami that float over the fine-grained skins used to make Louis Vuitton bags. Japanese imagination meets Western heritage under the commercially managed imprint of a global design house. The quality of the leather and stitching is of minimal interest; the look governs, and the projection of status predominates. In all this representation the craft seems to get lost. Murakami, a passionate advocate for craft, is playing with the language of design, and perhaps even lamenting its pervasiveness. The gently ironic, cartoon bubbles whose impossibly uniform, bright colour pull the objects they adorn slightly out of place, also keep them there as things to be fetishized. Design concerns the projection of ideas and feelings through representation, whereas craft involves embodied work, which cannot be represented. Craft, then, is practice in which what is being done and made constitutes its own purposive structure, without need for an elaborate representational 'superstructure'. It is quieter than design, looser in conscious direction, and perhaps less in thrall to the idea of being distinct and noticeable. Craft is about things, whereas design is about objectified things, or objects.

For David Pye, this difference between design and craft constitutes a form of hierarchy: designers could never specify a certain material or form, or elaborate on an idea, without craftwork having first laid the groundwork and experimented with available possibilities. This groundwork seems to require a form of connexion back to nature. Craft accentuates this awareness of nature by revealing its essence. It is not the natural material itself, but the skilfully worked material, the wood that has been nurtured, sawn, dried, planed, sanded, oiled and then worked and worked into something rare, revealed and accentuated. Form is similarly an attentive accentuation of what is found, yielding lines, planes and volumes of light and dark that pull maker and user alike into an entire world.

In coupling history and nature within itself craft gives voice to an inherent rather than consciously designed sense of truth and beauty. It is not something about which people can agree using rational arguments; rather, they accede respectfully and expertly. It is not as if, says Pye (1968/ 2002: 18), thingly materials or forms exist in their own right. You do not just find useable clay, lacquer, metal ore or wood: those who work with them must bring out the promise that lies latent in such materials. Nor is form to be found in templates, dies, patterns and stamps, for these too are formed by attending to the materials' qualities. Craft is the working and forming of things from out of the possibilities thrown up by materials. It is work in which the outcome is under constant risk, depending as it does on the judgment, care and dexterity of the worker. Contrary to mass production and machine manufacture, craft preserves and works with the possibility of failure, and it is in this dark space that a sense of human complicity and responsibility for what becomes a distinct and distinctive thing takes root. In short, craft craves and needs risk, whereas design can and often does reach for certainty (Popp & Holt 2016; Pye 1968/ 2002: 20–21). Murakami's Louis Vuitton bags have both, but the craft is managed into near non-existence by processes of quality control and financial accounting, or it becomes a represented object thrown onto the busy, noisy surfaces of a marketing campaign.

The craft for which the Japanese are developing a nostalgia is more that of risk than design; the pre-industrialized exposure to material form and purposive structures to which the skill of the worker must be brought under the impress of lengthy apprenticeships, habituated generational expectations and rigorously embodied ceremony. These processes of training in making and use ameliorate but never eliminate the risk, for without uncertainty what is created has no life of its own, and it is in the encounter with and maintenance of such a distinction that craft generates its peculiar hold. To be things of craft the pots, knives, umbrellas, theatrical performances or food are created with the possibility that they could have been otherwise. In this they are quietly unique, albeit often in very ordinary ways. This goes for all craft, irrespective of its place. In Japan, however, the capacity to imagine the ways of the past by absorbing and creating with risk seems to be gathered as a ritualistic riposte to its commercialization that few other cultures seem to match in its intensity. Moreover, whilst in the wake of the Western Renaissance civilization was equated with the separation of the social and the natural, and the human from the animal, the Japanese world view has never really worked on pushing such anthropological divisions. An electricity pylon is much like a tree, and eagles will perch on both under a common sky. This further leaves the country prone to, and animated by, the narratives afforded by craft.

For some exponents of Japanese craft, it is a process of imagining oneself back into the past, and into nature, in order, then, to act anew: a looking back into what is lost in order then to project forward. Here is one of its most persuasive exponents, Junichorō Tanizaki (1933/1991: 9):

> Had we invented the phonograph and the radio, how much more faithfully they would reproduce the special character of our voices and our music. Japanese music is above all a music of reticence, of atmosphere. When recorded, or amplified by a loudspeaker, the greater part of its charm is lost. In conversation, too, we prefer the soft voice, the understatement. Most important of all are the pauses. Yet the phonograph and radio render these moments of silence utterly lifeless. And so we distort the arts themselves to curry favour for them with the machines. These machines are the inventions of Westerners, and are, as we might expect, well suited to the Western arts. But precisely on this account they put our own arts at a great disadvantage.

And as for amplification, so for paper, photography, toilets, eating implements, glass making and candlelight. The lost Japan for which Tanizaki feels almost constant pangs of nostalgia is one of mellowness and opaque mystery whose inscrutable character is given heft by pensive acceptance of life's patinas. In contrast, presumably, the Westerner is a bellicose, assertive, logocentric, neophiliac wanting only distinction. Leaving aside the quaint racism, and accepting that Tanizaki was writing at a time when Japan had yet to fully display its own vicious brand of assertiveness by laying waste to vast stretches of China (1937), or entering WWII with attacks on the United States, Singapore and Malaya (1941–1942), there is something to be learned from Tanizaki's affections for the quiescent, sober and sensitive forms of crafting around which Japanese character might be purposively ordered.

Take a traditional house. Its palely coloured walls are made with softening paper (*shōji*), dried clay and richly grained woods that absorb and gather a light so indirect as to be stripped of its luminosity. The floors are strewn with mats of woven straw (*tatami*) whose gently astringent smell and firm yield underfoot announce themselves as equals to any human presence. The alcove (*tokonoma*) holds a vase, stem and scroll whose pale union yields utterly to their paler burnished surrounds. The eating areas are alive with pots glazed in mannered imperfection stacked neatly next to lacquerware bowls painted in liquid darkness that comes to life in the occasional flicker of an oil lamp. And the eaves cast shadows over a balcony as a peony made heavy by late spring rain might hang over neatly tended grass.

The craft involved in making these homely things is as apparent as the things themselves and it appears in use, not representation. The mats, walls and bowls are created for everyday life, throwing themselves into the thrown condition in which the Japanese people live out their day-to-day lives – mats for sitting, walls for privacy and bowls for eating. Here all is as it is, and the craft remains equipment to be used thoughtlessly and instrumentally. Yet Tanizaki's nostalgia evokes something more grounded than these things being just well-made tools for use. There is an attention to style and disposition that extends way beyond the presence of things. Indeed what is there physically is of far less importance than the relations that are thereby sustained, so long as the things are made well. The traditional house is made the way it is to live with its surroundings: this is how it becomes a whole, as do those who come and go across its threshold. The threshold is itself a space, and is often extended in repetition through porches, so that the distinction between inside and outside becomes vague, the one giving onto the other in muted contact rather than occluding separation, the affect being one of the transience rather than presence.

Figure 1.1 Temple

Many traditional buildings in Japan share this avoidance of solid distinction, giving voice to an impermanence and intangibility that Tanazaki (1933/1991: 46) finds evoked beautifully in a traditional song of the countryside: 'the brushwood we gather stack it together, it makes a hut; pull it apart, a field once more'. The song line acknowledges the impermanence of all things and yet celebrates the human capacity for making that is integral to their preservation. Buildings fall into nature and occupants into the building and the entwinement gives voice to a rootedness and connectivity in which any sense of a subject manipulating objects to serve preconceived interests becomes as faint as the wisps of mist that evaporate in morning sun. The risk comes in allowing nature into the house whose apparent simplicity has very little to do with the stripped-back, tidy and efficient designs favoured by Western rationalism and its obsession with the new. Where in the West simplicity can embody a turning away from nature and history and towards designs organized according to efficient principles of doing more with less, there is in Tanizaki's ideas of simplicity an exposure to the variety and subtlety of nature that can be brought forth in sustained attention to being with things.

Kenya Hara argues it is the capacity of Japanese craft to sustain these risky relationships that lend it distinction. These relations are embodied ones, and attain a richness and density of expression when they are unspoken. The representing word is overwhelmed by a historically embalmed slew of symbolic associations to which the entire expressive body of the Japanese is devoted. By way of example, Hara (2015a) talks of the *komainu* that stand in the doorway of Shinto shrines, a pair of dogs whose facial expressions show an open-mouthed exhaling (*Ah*) on the right and a closed inhaling in the left (*Un*). As a basic pairing they are emblematic of the unspoken breathing in which the body touches the immaterial, the unspoken giving and receiving of understanding by which spirit moves through the world, and through the body that in receiving also gives forth. Hara (2015a: 16) talks of its being an immediate, sometimes overwhelming and entirely relational way of understanding, but also one open to surprise, so at one and the same time there is clarity and opacity, directness and indirectness, the settlements of the known and thrill of the unknown. The *komainu* symbolize unspoken direct communion on the one hand, and anticipation of the unknown on the other, showing understanding itself to be a threshold process in which the expected and unexpected meet.

This meeting of the unexpected, however, is hard won. One cannot simply breathe in and out, one has to learn, be apprenticed, and the apprenticeships in Japanese craft are arduous, especially if the narrative of craft remains steeped in an enervating 'respect' for the old ways. The apprenticeships are long and apparently pointless, and the right to become an acknowledged master is hard earned; nothing comes without discipline. There can be a deep conservatism here, especially in those practices which put a premium on the security of tradition and which find that rituals and formalities constitute their own meaning, freed from the expressive and hence risky influence of active and experimental users.

Often (and certainly for Tanizaki) the intricacies of such craft are deemed impenetrable to outsiders, especially foreigners, who are often seen as incapable of appreciating the mysteries of such a refined and subtle indigenous culture. Thus, nostalgia can induce a quiet and depleting xenophobia in which the making and using of things can only end in hollowed-out, ossified performative expressions as bloodless as the white masks and makeup of *kabuki* theatre. If craft is to connect its makers and users to what lies beyond them, it necessarily touches what is other to itself, and things carry vividness only insofar as their presence touches what they are not, and against which they might maintain their distinction. All forms of craft make things in relation to what is deeply familiar and therefore also foreign. They can do so with joy and so increase the affective capacity in the relational cycles of making and using. Or they can do so in sadness, denuding the capacity to feel until it shrivels into a pastiche of its own aspiration. This is also an aspect of the risk of which Pye speaks.

So, to risk a brief summary, we have suggested that if craft involves the presence of risk, then in Japan this is constituted in: acknowledging the fleeting impermanence of things, in the creation of relations between the human maker and user that extend into a wider exposure to nature and history, and finally in submission to disciplinary regimes of training that demand apprentices loosen themselves from a sense of individual pre-eminence. In all three aspects there is an association of mastery with humility and experiment, one that is both encouraged but also imperilled by the nostalgic call for the impossible restoration of lost tradition.

Sushi

It is to these aspects of Japanese craft (the fleeting, relationality, discipline) that we bring *o-sushi* or sushi. Sushi is the serving of raw fish on a softly packed ball of slightly salted, vinegared rice. The rice has to be warm and it is renewed constantly as it becomes cold. When sushi is served it must be in the perfect condition. Variants on this basic form include the use of vegetables, fried tofu, and omelette. *Nori maki* has become the main variant of this basic form, in which the rice, fish and other ingredients are themselves wrapped in sheets of pressed seaweed. The fish is raw but also worked on, sometimes quite extensively. For example, Tokyo-style, *Edomae* sushi involves 'work' that is done to the ingredients, e.g., salting fish to extract moisture, adding *umami* by lining it on top of dried kelp and sometimes fermenting fish to soften the texture and condense the flavour. Plain fresh fish is not considered a good match with the rice. In fact, for *Edomae-zushi*, the rice is said to be the main protagonist and fish is worked on to match the rice. Other styles involve less mediation, but there is always marinating, mixing, pickling and steeping involved somewhere. Once made and presented, the traditional way of eating sushi is to hold sushi directly with the fingers, not chopsticks.

For contemporary Japanese, the word 'sushi' implies a scale of provision and experience: at one end we have traditional sushi bars and the other mechanized, conveyor belt sushi. Traditionally there was a sushi place in each neighbourhood. Most of them were reasonably priced although sushi was always considered to be the food for special occasions. These mid-range sushi bars have now largely disappeared. In their place have come chains and franchises running conveyor belt sushi restaurants. Their convenience and lower price make them increasingly popular, with many offering two pieces of sushi for JPY100. Most of these companies have factories in China where globally sourced fish are mechanically prepared, packaged and shipped. Employees in the sushi bar simply open the vacuum-packaged fish and put them on top of robot-made rice. In addition to changing the way sushi is prepared, these companies are also innovating with new kinds of sushi, involving cheese, meats, roasts and even fried potatoes.

The traditional sushi bars maintain a sense of distance from such brash commercialization, and it is here that the word craft might still apply. For 'craft' read 'cost,' with a typical visit costing between JPY20,000 and

Figure 1.2 Conveyor Belt with Sushi

JPY40,000 per person. Though traditional in form, many bars are new, and like their conveyor belt brethren are becoming popular. Some offer wine to match sushi and others combine sushi with *kaiseki*, which is a menu-based, meal-style cooking. Many magazines and books write features on these sushi bars, further feeding an ever-present discourse around sushi. Though polar opposites in the manner of preparation and eating, even the most efficient and cheap mass-produced sushi still shares in and relies on this discourse. Customers use the traditional sushi and the whole sushi culture as a reference point in talking about and experiencing this popularized version. For example, when people say to others, "I had sushi for lunch today," they do not forget to add, "It was the rotating one, though", as if at some other juncture they would be trying the more traditional, pricier version.

Although categorially sushi is associated with restaurants and as a style of cuisine, at least in the traditional places it is considered to be a distinct craft. Sushi chefs are called *shokunin*, the same word used for a craftsperson of other kinds. They are said to apprentice, *shugyo*, with a master, *oyakata*. In this they contrast with kinds of chef in Japan, for example chefs practising the Kyoto-style cuisine called *kaiseki*, which consists of ten or more dishes of a variety of ingredients, preparation techniques and plates. These chefs are called *ryorinin* and are much closer to the image of Western-style chefs. In contrast, sushi *shokunin* focus on an apparently simple, stripped-back form of trade in which skill comes through the repetition of making and eating relatively standard forms of food using long-established techniques and ingredients.

The Fleeting

In sushi what is made is made to disappear, at least to be physically reconstituted at the very moment of its coming to fruition. It comes and then goes in a brief but somehow beguiling life: it is made to die and be remade in cycles of learned and disciplined expression by which the dispositions, values and styles of a culture become sedimented and channelled into something almost archaic. The customer is to eat the piece of sushi in one bite; biting it in half or leaving some is not acceptable, and it is to be eaten within seconds after the chef serves it in front of them.

This is because sushi is most perfect at the time of making and then quickly gets dry. Similarly, the rice is packed softly so that air remains between grains of rice. If the sushi is left too long, the rice is pressed down by the fish on top of it and loses the sense of lightness imparted by the *shokunin*. The rice, as Roland Barthes (1970/1982: 12) notices "can be defined only by a contradiction of substance; it is at once cohesive and detachable; its substantial destination is the fragment, the clump, the volatile conglomerate".

Figure 1.3 Sushi

The smell too is an important consideration in the craft. Customers are told not to use perfume, which would contaminate the subtle aromas of sushi that the *shokunin* attempts to gather at the moment of making. The temporary nature of the things is palpable: the smells are elusive, the lifting of the rice little more than a pause, the lucent pull of the sliced fish is caught in a glimpse. The sushi is there and then not there, in one mouthful it is present and absent. Customers are therefore given only a short moment to savour it. Their discipline comes in a respect for what is offered to them, fleetingly, and for what allows itself to be prepared, carefully. Both those preparing and eating the food are themselves plaited with a temporal experience of confronting and being complicit with the demise of what has been painstakingly created, which is treated as a living thing, receptive to its climate and carrying its own subtleties, and even surprises. Because the piece of sushi is 'alive', its taste cannot be entirely controlled, there is space enough for nature to do its own work.

Just as the form that each piece of sushi takes carries with it its own demise, so the presence of the *shokunin* too is minimal. He (it is nearly always a 'he') brings the rice, seaweed and fish into a culinary coherence that reveals his sensitivity to the tastes and aesthetic form inherent in the ingredients. The *shokunin* does not impose this form upon the ingredients but lets it emerge, according to the nature of what is before him, which he then works on. In some ways it is akin to what Hara (2015b) calls 'ex-forming', the pulling away of any explicit, known design in order to let what is not known, and hence risky, come through. In this way the fish, crab or prawn evoke the forms they took when alive, the rice grains remain together yet distinct enough to be their comestible themselves. So the skill of preparing comes in emptying out any aggrandizing individuality: the *shokunin* learn to attend to and reveal the forms they discover latent within the ingredients, forms whose latticework can be shared by the calligrapher and dancer. This is also why the sushi bar is always plain and lit without distracting lights. It is made of white cypress wood. Like the wood in many traditional buildings it serves a functional, social and symbolic purpose. It is not easy to find an immaculate cypress that is long enough to span the long counter in one piece. There is no decoration, only the plain wood, its pale grain giving itself as a backdrop to the carefully made pieces of fish, rice and vegetable. The food itself carries an inscrutable depth and suggestiveness that is denuded by decoration and excessive colour. The sushi is there because it allows itself to be there. The presence of the expert is minimal, and this is his expertise.

The same minimalism goes for the equipment and the preparation, serving and eating space. The kitchen behind the bar can get quickly cluttered if not attended to continually. The *shokunin* constantly cleans the cutting board and knives. Knives can easily get stained and need to be wiped and dried constantly, and are constantly being sharpened and polished with a stone that gradually reduces them to invisibility. The knife is the dominating implement, indeed really the only one when it comes to preparation: the minimalist space reflects a minimalist style of cooking. In being cut, rolled and pressed, but not heated, sushi sits between the raw (nature) and the cooked (culture) in an equivocal way. Those of us weaned on these distinctions so painstakingly distilled from the cultural myths analysed by ur-structuralist Claude Lévi-Strauss ought to be able to place food on this symbolic scale of cultural sophistication. Sushi gives the lie to this imperialist science. In being rigorously formed and eaten with disciplinary awareness, pieces of sushi lean towards being 'cultural'. The aesthetic attentiveness to detail and quality means that what began as simple street food can now exemplify the height of civilized sophistication. According to Tanizaki: "It has been said of Japanese food that it is a cuisine to be looked at rather than eaten. I would go further and say that it is to be meditated upon". To look upon the food is to sense the refinement in skill and manners by which it has been realized. Yet at the same time, because it is considered 'alive', sushi is also related to as a very natural thing, untainted by the overbearing attentions of conscious human design.

In meditating upon a piece of sushi (but not for long), the uncultured qualities of nature (the raw) are also experienced. Here sushi gives off nothing other than what is found in nature, its life, which is given over in democratic fragmentation, one piece amongst many, like souls – without hierarchy, *Ah-Un*.

Relational

The space for eating sushi matters not simply for the preparation and eating of the food but because it is where the customers and *shokunin* form a gathering. It is typically a small, frugal-looking space. People sit and lean at the bar, gossip and share everyday news. The chef is part of curating the conversation as well as preparing the creation of food. In this, sushi becomes almost an essential form of craft, coming as it does as an entire ensemble of minutely managed moments, some ceremonial and entirely emptied of any obvious purpose, but all of which cohere into cycles of conversational, culinary and ritualistic exchange.

Before and after the making and eating, apprentices attend to preparing and serving areas, cleaning up and sweeping the floor and getting to know the space itself, its rhythms and how interactions occur. The space is integral to the cooking. There is little hiding away, just cycles of training, preparation, serving, eating and engaging. In a French kitchen, for example, you wait for the magic to appear from hidden depths, whereas sushi is about the open and clear present unfolding in public,

Figure 1.4 Sushi Bar

where what is made is, almost uniquely in the context of craft, done in the very same moments of its being used.

As well as the bars allowing people to relate to one another, sushi itself places humans in relation to nature. Seasonal fluctuations, for example, are very apparent: indeed, the small bar might be said to be an entire world of shifting climatic patterns. Even when fish can be caught in a wider time frame, there is a limited time during which each fish is particularly tasty, often to do with how much fat has been accumulated. The Japanese fetishize firstlings; they desire the foremost, the earliest: bonitos in April, young spotted shads in July, and crabs in November. Prices soar for these nascent rarities. The location from which fish come from is another topic often discussed at sushi bars. Tuna from *Oma* in the northern part of Japan is considered best. So are mackerel from Oita, arch shells (*Akagai*) from Yuriage, and Japanese cockles (*Torigai*) from Kyoto. So, whilst the sushi bar is closed off from the street, it remains intimate with broader patterns of natural and economic change – customers and chefs are intimately aware of how animals and plants emerge from seasonal shifts, and respect them for being such. The universal availability of food has not as yet been imported into the sushi bar, at least not into those espousing a level of craft, which move sympathetically with the seasons, and also sensitively with the market.

Just as sushi touches wider nature, so it also forms a bond between the rural and urban, and across all classes of people. Here is Tanazaki again, commenting on the preparation of sushi:

> I learned of the dish from a friend who had been to Yoshino and found it so exceptionally good that he took the trouble to learn how to make it – but if you have the persimmon leaves and salted salmon it can be made anywhere. You need only remember to keep out every trace of moisture, and to cool the rice completely. I made some myself, and it was very good indeed. The oil of the salmon and the slight hint of salt give just the proper touch of seasoning to the rice, and the salmon becomes as soft as if it were fresh – the flavour is indescribable, and far better than the sushi one gets in Tokyo. I have become so fond of it that I ate almost nothing else this summer. What impressed me, however, was that this superb method of preparing salted salmon was the invention of poor mountain people. Yet a sampling of the various regional cuisines suggests that in our day country people have far more discriminating palates than city people, and that in this respect they enjoy luxuries we cannot begin to imagine.

The cities are now more porous to rural influence than when Tanazaki was writing, and the rural definitely more exposed to urban encroachment, and both are exposed to international styles. These porous boundaries expose sushi to the risk of dilution to cater for foreign tastes, but on the plus side to experimental developments that can only come by remaining in touch with what lies beyond its treasured orthodoxy.

Discipline

There is obvious discipline in the preparation of sushi, and given the length and repetitive nature of the apprenticeships in cleaning the bar and preparing the food some might say the repetition is somewhat gratuitous. The chefs embody a neat filigree of technique that demands extreme attentiveness. They have spent years here, and during the early years they barely get to touch the food, spending more time with a sweeping brush and detergents than with chopping boards and ingredients. As apprentices they learn by endlessly preparing the rice, each iteration constituting nothing more that the difference of its being the next in a long sequence through which conscious rule-following becomes thoughtless expertise, then it's the eggs for the omelettes, then the rolling of seaweed. Again and again.

It is easy to trace the lineage of the master–apprentice relations by which a *shokunin* comes into being; some have more than one master in their career and, in turn, top *shokunin* can be responsible for producing a large cohort of successful disciples. In following the master, some will inherit the name of the master's business as a whole, or in part. It is rare that *shokunin* open multiple sushi bars at the same time. Most of them have one place, and it is they who do the making. So, unlike other restaurants, it is also rare that the master chef is absent and thus just a brand. As in most crafts, the touch of the maker matters, it carries an aura, and the maker presides over the creation of the whole thing. There is no sense in which the *shokunin's* skill will fit with the wider divisions of labour and specialization prevalent in the production of conveyor-belt sushi. Customers expect to see the chef *in situ* doing the making whenever they visit. When they have to travel, they shut up shop and take a financial hit. Their reputation is what matters, and their physical presence is integral to that.

And that presence is often exhausting. A critical part of the *shokunin's* work is to procure fish in the central market, *Tsukiji*. They wake typically at 5 a.m. and visit the market every day. They do this after keeping the bar open until late at night. If they do not make themselves present in the market, they lose credibility among the fish-brokers who auction off fish specifically for certain *shokunin*, and do so on the basis of long-established, trusting relationships and knowing the kind of fish that is preferred. If the relationship is a strong one, the broker will bend over backwards to get the necessary fish, even at high prices, meaning any profit for him is minimal or even negative. In the end, the quality and the relationship will endure hand in hand, with broker and *shokunin* each looking to the other.

As well as requiring the devotion of most waking hours, the discipline also tends toward the conservative. Like many other craftspeople, sushi chefs do not do bricolage all that well; indeed, it is often deemed déclassé. Using available materials to improvise something that works is just not good enough. From the beginning to the end, they have a duty to perfect the process. If they have not procured the fish of the quality they demand of themselves, they do not offer it to customers. The same goes for all other ingredients. The types or forms of sushi are also typically the same year on year, season on season, week on week.

Slight modifications, however, are allowed, even encouraged. *Shokunin* will modify the preparation techniques for each fish, for example, by plunging the fish in vinegar a few seconds longer or altering the way they slice the fish block and pack rice, depending on the customer, whom they constantly observe during each visit and over multiple visits. And customers tend to be loyal habitués of one establishment, and are also typically disciplined in behaving in the right way and developing a knowledgeable relationship with what they are eating. It is not uncommon for *shokunin* to test customers, especially newer ones, by posing a difficult question and observing how the customer responds. For instance, as soon as a customer is seated, a *shokunin* might ask them what they would like to drink. This is done before explaining what is available. Some say that beer is not the right drink for sushi because it does not go well with raw fish. While many people prefer sake, some say that sake is made of rice and conflicts with the rice in sushi. A few people recommend eating sushi with green tea. There is nothing hard and fast about any of this, deliberately so, because then it becomes a matter of judgment, which implies involvement, knowledge and hence, also, ignorance.

Because in *okonomi* – as you like – style there is no written menu provided, customers are required to know what fish would be appropriate to order in which order. There is often heated debate as to the order of sushi one should pick. People seem to agree that they should begin with leaner fish like red snapper and flounder, move to strong-flavoured fish like tuna and mackerel, and end with rolls and then with sweet sushi like sea eel and omelette. Some sushi bars have a glass case in front of the customers so they can look. Still, it is not easy to determine the name of the fish by looking at it and many sushi bars store fish in wooden cases. Customers then need to know what fish is in season. Customers are not supposed to ask for help either. A typical 'joke' goes like this: When a customer asks, "What do you recommend?" the chef replies, "We don't have anything that we don't recommend", or more tersely "There is no recommendation. Please let me know what you want". Newer and less experienced customers might hesitate, perhaps aware they are being tested, but unsure how. More generally, there is a public image that sushi bars, notably traditional ones, are scary places to visit and *shokunin* are often said to be tetchy. Given the customers are not informed of the prices of each piece of sushi and are only given the bill after completing the meal, this reputation is in many ways well grounded: novices have to force themselves to learn and it is not made easy for them. Customers should gain experience of the craft in order to become proper customers. The expertise extends from acquiring the manners and rituals to developing the palate to discern differences in flavour. So, in consumption as well as production, comes a care for the right combinations and their order, a deliberate and disciplined eschewal of considering cost, and a willingness to experience the risk of getting it wrong.

Three Aspects as One

This emphasis on consuming correctly shows the interconnected nature of the three aspects of craft: it is nigh on impossible to isolate one, or to ascribe dominance to it. Demanding appreciation from those eating the food and partaking of the ritual establishes rings of increasing exclusivity into which customers attempt to place themselves, the inner circle being that which is deemed most intensely appreciative of and sensitive to the subtleties and niceties of the ephemeral, risky thing being placed before them. The sense that there are different customer circles also leaves space for myths to perpetuate, such as the *shokunin* allegedly using discretion to alter prices from customer to customer depending on their disciplinary skill and familiarity. Customers who eat constitute the craft of sushi as readily as the *shokunin*, though always in a position of subservience. Some customers actually consider themselves as apprentices to a sushi master. They try to frequent a particular sushi bar so that they taste the subtle difference from month to month as well as can gain the trust of the master. In becoming experts, they can also develop increasingly uneasy feelings about novice customers who almost inevitably behave inappropriately. A kind of snobbery begins to creep in as those customers who cannot bring the craft of sushi to fruition become an annoyance for those who are 'at one' with it.

And so, one wonders what these loyal, long-standing customers might make of a new and sizable group of relatively young customers calling themselves *Sushi Otaku* or 'sushi geeks'. The word *otaku*, which started in Japanese comics and animation, is often negatively perceived, and they have adopted the term somewhat ironically. Being passionate about sushi, these newer customers actively develop their taste by acquiring multiple experiences and discussing their taste with peers. There is no sense of them being from an elite, and their style and skill breaks the standard structural reading of taste offered by the likes of Bourdieu (1997). Of course, many customers of traditional sushi bars are from conservative and often elite strata of society, yet these new *otaku's* taste is equally if not more refined, and their background can be from anywhere; they do not exhibit a transposable *habitus*, and instead have converted the tradition of sushi into an amateur subculture entirely devoted to craft (Hennion 2007a; 2007b). They have confidence in their taste for and knowledge of sushi, they have eaten sushi more than anybody else and have the most distinguished palate of nearly any customer, but at the same time depreciate themselves and refuse to be associated with wider social and cultural categorizations

Here sushi is being used as much as a compensation for being uprooted from the culture and tradition as a nostalgic enforcer. There is no attempt to recover loss (whilst still keeping hold of the sense of loss). Rather, sushi expertise becomes a mobile signifier of self-reliance, a symbolic condition of sophistication being used by those forced to compete and develop their own identifies (Boltanski & Chiapello 2005). There is anxiety here still, but it comes from a lack of felt connexion to the old ways. In this, these *sushi otaku* embody a threat to the stratified veneration of traditional crafts, and by extension to the elites who sustain such orthodoxy. For example, one writer associated with upper-class gourmets and close to a well-known author, Shotaro Ikenami, who was also known as a gourmet, has accused them of being addicted to information about sushi gleaned from the internet rather than being real sushi customers (Shigekane 2009: 228–229). This new class is hard to deal with. They seem to have absented themselves from society and history in a similar manner to the long-venerated timeless folk (*minzoku*) of myth who preserve the essence of Japan against the onslaught of global capitalism (Ivy 1995: 18), yet they have precisely the reverse effect, appropriating a craft in such a way as to abide in their own self-willed atmosphere. Rather than use the nostalgia for craft to resist and absorb the modern, these *sushi otaku* are its upshot, and here the affect of craft is not to linger with the old ways, but to suggest new ones. And some *shokunin* are taking note, acknowledging that these *sushi otaku* are acquiring a discipline and fine taste from which might emerge sources of innovative play. Newer *shokunin* are creating sophisticated sushi that matches *sushi otaku*'s taste; for instance, the newer style sushi is typically smaller in size and lighter in taste than traditional sushi, which sometimes could be rough, expressing the old, stubborn *shokunin*'s own strong taste.

Back to Nostalgia

Our foray into sushi finds craft a delightfully elusive phenomenon. What we have hazarded as the defining qualities of Japanese craft are all faithfully reproduced in sushi. There is care for social relations in the gathering force of which fish-brokers, master chefs, apprentices, customers and critics are configured as a commons shared by generations before them. Nature too is made very apparent, with many sushi bars being run to the structure of seasonal almanacs of what to eat when, why and how. There is also the discipline necessary not only to make things well and uniquely and absorb the risk of them failing, but also to consume them appropriately. It is not only makers who must learn. And finally, there is the mannered acceptance of and even delight in the evanescent: whatever approaches perfectibility also touches on its own dissolution, and in small pieces of sushi such harmonic intimacy between form and its dissolution finds a beguiling expression.

Yet considering sushi as craft has also thrown up some interesting anomalies. Its rejuvenation has been very much a function of growing popularity amongst newer customers, including internationally, seduced by marketing and the branding of fast food versions: the conscious manipulation of an idea has led them into a practice that consciously resists such representations. So, far from being antithetical to its craft, in the case of sushi large-scale mechanization has been its midwife. This widening of the customer base has also disturbed the traditional alliance between the appreciation of craft and a long-standing cultural elite, certainly in Japan. By becoming passionate about the food, and dedicated to learning more, a subculture has emerged that has used the tradition as a resource to articulate a form of cultural confidence and independence; conservatism is being used against itself to enchant an otherwise obedient life (Suddaby et al. 2017). For the *Sushi Otaku* the disciplined, relational and intangible aspects of craft become the medium in which an emancipatory force might be realized, albeit one steeped in consumption. Their aesthetic and culinary performance disturbs the standard narratives afforded by craft insofar as a nostalgic sense of loss is subsumed by an excitement for raw aesthetic, culinary and social gain.

We began the chapter suggesting craft can be understood as a peculiarly effective narrative whose affective force is carried by nostalgia for a lost past. Craft absorbs and in turn feeds the experiences of longing. Craft, so the narrative is told and retold, is a conduit back to how it was. Here the past is only available as a story of the kind in which Tanizaki excels when he muses on how technology might have looked had the Japanese influence been stronger. This reverie invokes a sense of the past that cannot be considered to form any part of what historians call evidence. There are no events to check or patterns to trace. Rather, the role of the story is to evoke a verisimilitude that is necessarily vague, and which evokes a feeling of loss and longing. It is this feeling of yearning for what lies at the other side of an ungraspable distance, and not the past as such, which is the real object of sentimental concern (Illbruck 2012: 144). This feeling is being produced in the stories to which craft has traditionally been integral and in which it has been complicit, and which, in the vagueness articulated throughout its discipline, relationality and intangibility, allow such sentiment to flourish. The reluctance of the elite gourmet classes and master *shokunin* to embrace the *sushi otaku* can be read as an urge to preserve this vagueness and hence sentiment for longing, a feeling of which they are the self-regarding stewards. They and their ilk are steeped in the ineffable sensitivity to the 'old ways' embodied by craft, but only suggestively in nuances that cannot be heard unless one is disposed to hear by birth and bearing.

So, with sushi we have three narratives woven as threads into a story. First we have a slightly Luddite reading of craft as a conduit to the integrity and dignity of the 'old ways'. Second comes a reading of craft being venerated as an instinctual, collective reaction by those who have sentimentalized experiences of longing and loss. This sentimentality is necessary because without it adherents have to then confront the suspicion that there is, indeed, no place to call an origin or 'home' to which they, as persons and a whole people might somehow return. Stuck on a feeling in this way, the *Sushi Otaku* also acknowledge in their actions the impossibility of retrieving the past and its spirit, but do so more joyously, allowing themselves to be prompted by an intense interest in craft. This is the third reading, in which the re-imagination of the past through craft affords exponents an emancipatory presence in the present whose spatial home is the sushi bar itself, to which one can arrive, albeit only ever in a spirit of care for its continual rebuilding, visit after visit. These *shokunin* who respond to this emerging subculture also move from the first and second to the third reading of their craft, willing to explore the possibility of difference that comes in the repetition of attempts at creating things steeped in qualities of relationality, discipline and the fleeting.

References

Barthes, R. (1970/1982) *The Empire of Signs*. New York: Noonday Press.

Boltanski, L., & Chiapello, E. (2005) *The New Spirit of Capitalism*. London: Verso.

Bourdieu, P. (1984) *Distinction: A Social Critique of the Judgement of Taste*. Cambridge, MA: Harvard University Press.

Hara, K. (2015a) The Origins of Japanese Design. In R. Menegazzo & S. Piotti (Eds.) *Wa: The Essence of Japanese Design*. London: Phaidon.

Hara, K. (2015b) *Ex-formation*. Zurich: Lars Müller

Hennion, A. (2007a) Pragmatics of Taste. In Mark D. Jacobs & Nancy Weiss Hanrahan (Eds.) *The Blackwell Companion to the Sociology of Culture*. Oxford, UK: Blackwell Publishing, pp. 131–144

Hennion, A. (2007b) Those Things That Hold Us Together: Taste and Sociology. *Cultural Sociology*, 1(1): 97–114.

Holt, R. & Popp, A. (2016) Josiah Wedgwood, Manufacturing and Craft. *Journal of Design History*, 29(2): 99–119

Illbruck, H. (2012) *Nostalgia*. Evanston, IL: Northwestern University Press.

Ivy, M. (1995) *Discourses of the Vanishing: Modernity, Phantasm, Japan*. Chicago: University of Chicago Press.

Pye, D. (1968/2002) *The Nature and Art of Workmanship*. Bethel, CT.: Cambium Press.

Shigekane, A. (2009) *Common Knowledge and Uncommon Knowledge about Sushi (Sushi Ya No Joshiki, Hijoshiki)*. Tokyo: Asahi Shimbun Publications.

Suddaby, R., Ganzin, M., & Minkus, A. (2017) Craft, Magic and the Re-enchantment of the World. *European Management Journal*, 35(3): 285–296.

Tanizaki, J. (1933/1991) *In Praise of Shadows*. London: Vintage.

2 Crafted in America
From Culture to Profession

Shelby Solomon and Blake Mathias

Introduction

> I truly like making ham and bacon. So I figure I am one lucky hill-
> billy and I am going to enjoy it. I have friends who are professionals.
> Some are just blue-collar workers that I know of that hate every day
> they go to work. How lucky am I that I don't hate what I do, that
> I enjoy work?
>
> (Appalachian Country Ham)

Companies such as Ford and McDonalds were built in America.
These organizations contributed not only to the division of labor
and highly routinized work but also inspired critical thinkers such as
Antonio Gramsci and George Ritzer to coin terms such as Fordism and
McDonaldization to describe mechanized processes among organizations
worldwide (Gramsci 1971/1934; Ritzer 1983). In today's post-industrial
society, much of American labor is centered on heavily bureaucratic and
depersonalized white-collar work (Crawford 2009). That is, most of the
work is conducted in offices where jobs involve systems of rule-following
that limit worker autonomy, creativity, and competency. Within this
modern arrangement of labor, workers are often rewarded and promoted
for their ability to follow rules and act as team players—because the
work is so depersonalized, technical skill is difficult to assess and subsequently given little credence in distinguishing good workers from poor
workers.

However, in America (and much of the developed world), a growing
population of entrepreneurial firms eschews many principles of industrial production and traditional labor practices. These entrepreneurs take
a craft or artisan approach to operating their firm. This trend, which
has experienced a significant resurgence in America (McCracken 2006;
The Economist 2014), highlights a marked break from the path of strict
adherence to administrative rationality that has dominated American
businesses in recent decades.

This brand of entrepreneurship is distinct from classical entrepreneurship in that entrepreneurs run firms with an eye toward serving their need for creative expression by creating products intended to be of high quality and made unique by involved production techniques (Crawford 2009; Fauchart & Gruber 2011; Mathias & Smith 2016; Menger 1999). Thus, creativity and technical prowess are the primary metrics of a craft entrepreneur's competence. Whereas, classical entrepreneurship is conceptualized by materialist values that prioritize the entrepreneur's needs for growth, efficiency, and the accumulation of wealth (Gartner 1990). As the intended motivations of craft entrepreneurship center on creative expression, quality, and human involvement, they conflict with much of the conventional wisdom of traditional management and entrepreneurship. Specifically, many concepts tied to conventional managerial or administrative logic, such as assembly lines or relying on quantitative measures of success (e.g., efficiency, profits, or accounting ratios), are often thought to compromise attributes of craft (e.g., creativity, production involvement, and quality) (Braverman 1974; Ritzer 1983). Moreover, the abstract attitudinal measures of worker desirability used by modern firms such as emotional intelligence or team-building skills are similarly unrelated to creating organizations conducive to producing outcomes tailored to the ideals of craft (Crawford 2009).

Craft entrepreneurship has grown and expanded across many industries in America. For example, craft beer consumption has more than doubled in the time span from 2010 to 2014 (Brewers Association 2014). The craft coffee industry has experienced similar growth, with daily consumption of specialty coffee doubling from 2008 to 2014 (Specialty Coffee Association of America 2014). Craft sentiments and entrepreneurs have also found growth within trades such as handcrafted soap, craft butchery and sustainably raised livestock, and handcrafted furniture (FiBL & IFOAM 2016; McGuinley 2016; Sherman 2012). Therefore, American craft entrepreneurship has grown exponentially, with few signs of slowing. In addition, America arguably represents the largest country—both in geographical size and population—that has embraced the craft movement. Given its vastness, America contains distinct cultural differences across regions and gives unique meaning to the term "localness" as it relates to craft; accordingly, the US context has unique theoretical implications for our understanding of craftwork.

The purpose of this chapter is to further elaborate on craftwork and craft entrepreneurship in the context of America. To date, the topic of craft entrepreneurship has received little mainstream American academic attention, which perhaps is driven by America's history and affinity for profit- and growth-oriented entrepreneurs (e.g., Isenberg 2010; Smith 1967; Smith & Miner 1983). The purpose of this chapter is to further elaborate on this growing brand of craft entrepreneurship that has taken root in America. In elaborating on craft entrepreneurship in America, we seek to answer the research question of "What drives and inspires individuals in America to pursue a craft-based entrepreneurial career?" In answering this research question, we contribute to our understanding of American craft entrepreneurship in three ways. First, we highlight themes that lead American craft entrepreneurs to abandon taking a traditional career path and toward a career in craftwork. Second, we illustrate how being an American and affiliated with a particular cultural region or identity (e.g., being Cajun or Appalachian) inspires craft entrepreneurs to produce a particular product or employ a specific means of production. Third, we discuss how craft entrepreneurs assess the state of the American craft category. To achieve these aims and further explore craft entrepreneurship in America, we leverage an American sample of 35 in-depth interviews with craft entrepreneurs in addition to 24 corresponding online biographies.

Field Study

We took an inductive, qualitative approach to explore American craft entrepreneurship. We made use of two data sources—interviews and online biographies—in the present study to answer our research question. First, we identified the market for consumables (e.g., food, drink, soap) as a broad industry sector that would allow us to narrow our search for craft entrepreneurs. We targeted the consumables market because of the high level of growth and craft activity that has taken place within segments of this market, such as craft beer, specialty coffee, whole animal butchery, and handcrafted soap (Brewers Association 2014; FiBL & IFOAM 2016; Sherman 2012; Specialty Coffee Association of America 2014). After selecting a specific market from which to sample, we then began to interview individual craft entrepreneurs. See Table 1 for a summary of the sample of entrepreneurs.

After interviewing each craft entrepreneur, we also collected his or her online biography. However, we found that 11 of the craft entrepreneurs did not have a website with a corresponding personal bio. Hence, we were only able to match 24 of the biographies to the original sample of 35 entrepreneurs. This additional data was used to triangulate the findings and add robustness to the study. We inductively analyzed the online biographies along with the data obtained during the primary interviews. We conducted all the semi-structured interviews, typically face-to-face and at the entrepreneur's place of business. On average, each interview lasted approximately one hour, but the interviews varied in duration from 23 minutes to 1 hour and 49 minutes. The interviews started with questions such as, "Can you tell me your story as to how you got into doing what you do now?" As the interviews unfolded, we asked more probing questions based on the substance of the previous discussion, such as "What would you say motivated you to start up this business?" or "Why do you think customers are so interested in your products?"

Table 2.1 Summary of the Sample of Entrepreneurs

Firm Type	Age	Firm Age	Previous Career Field	Region
Acadian Country Coffee Roaster	67	5	Commercial Pilot	Deep South
Acadian Country Coffee Roaster	unknown	5	N/A	Deep South
Appalachian Country Ham	67	41	Education	Appalachia
Appalachian Distillery	68	2	Restaurant Management	Appalachia
Artisan Sandwiches	52	1	Life Coach	Deep South
Back Country Butcher	50	18	HR Manager	Deep South
Beer & Silk Soap	54	5	Business Administration	Deep South
Boucherie Bucher	42	7	Oil and Gas	Deep South
Boutique Bath, Body, and Candles	49	18	Sales	Texas
Cajun Brewery	53	8	Military	Deep South
Cajun Coffee Roaster	31	10	N/A	Deep South
Charcuterie Restaurant	30	3	Nursing	Deep South
Coconut Oil Body Products	39	1	Airlines	Texas
Cold Pressed Juice	33	3	N/A	Deep South
College Coffee Roaster	53	27	Counseling	Deep South
Consumer-Supported Agrarian	48	8	Healthcare	New England
Craft Sausage House	33	4	Real-estate	Texas
Cutting Edge Cold Brew Coffee	26	1	Finance	West Coast
Goat's Milk Soap	41	3	N/A	Deep South
Kombucha	32	3	Real estate	Deep South
Monastic Soap	67	16	N/A	Mid-West
Mustard & Condiments	61	4	N/A	Deep South
New Mexican Coffee Roaster	51	12	Education	Southwest
Po-boy Restaurant	68	23	Grocery Store	Deep South
Raw Granola Bars	30	2	N/A	Deep South
Mountain Region Coffee Roaster	35	3	Tech Industry	Rocky Mountains
San Francisco Butcher	49	6	N/A	West Coast
Shenandoah Region Meatpacking	59	8	Landscape Design	Mid-Atlantic
Southern Coffee Roaster	46	97	N/A	Deep South
Studio Artist Soap	59	3	N/A	Southwest
Sustainable Coffee Roaster	39	7	Fabricator	Appalachia
Technical Coffee Roaster	60	15	Environmental Protection	Appalachia
Tennessee Coffee Roaster	64	19	Bartender	Appalachia
Thai Coffee Importer	27	3	Education	Appalachia
Umpqua Region Meat	51	2	Grocery Store	West Coast

Findings

Upon conclusion of the data collection and analysis, we found three distinct higher-order themes emerged from the data, which spoke directly to the topic of American craft entrepreneurship. First, we observed craft entrepreneurs often held corporate jobs but realized they were "not meant for traditional employment," and subsequently left their corporate careers. Second, we discovered that craft entrepreneurs' draw from their unique regional American culture to inspire their craft approach to their business. Third, we found craft entrepreneurs perceived America was undergoing a craft revolution and were highly optimistic about the future of American craftwork.

Not Meant for Traditional Employment

We found many American craft entrepreneurs felt traditional corporate employment was not for them. That is, numerous craft entrepreneurs started off their career in corporate America but soon discovered that they did not enjoy the work enough to sustain them long-term. Note in Table 1 that many of the craft entrepreneurs previously held corporate jobs that were highly dissimilar from their future craft endeavors. Moreover, this finding is consistent with prior work that suggests that many individuals make mid-career transitions as they grapple with finding a job that truly matches their identity (Crawford 2009; Ibarra 2002). The quote below illustrates the mid-career professional turned craft entrepreneur archetype.

> I fall into the category of mid-career professionals who made a major leap and transferred into a completely different way of life, which is not an uncommon thing. I believe in the small craft entrepreneur line of work. I grew up in Pittsburgh, but I lived many places. I got an undergraduate degree in biology from Marie College out in Portland Oregon, and I have a master's in landscape architecture from Harvard University's graduate school of design, and then spent 20 years working for a large private consulting business.
>
> (Shenandoah Region Meatpacking)

We found many professionals pursued a mainstream career path to do the "responsible thing" that provided for their family and yielded potentially high earnings (Arcidiacono, Holtz, & Kang 2012). Recently, many individuals have been dissuaded from craft or trade work, as knowledge work has come into fashion as the most prestigious form of employment throughout much of the world (Crawford 2009). However, this has led many individuals into jobs that do not match their identity and causes them to either endure an unfulfilling life or attempt to make a mid-career shift to something that is more consistent with "who they are." This situation is well articulated in the quote below, where a now successful craft sausage entrepreneur discusses his college and early adulthood experience.

> I just felt like that was [a] very responsible thing to do [go into finance and real estate]. When I was in college there was a sausage cart on the street called the [redacted], and that is where the initial idea came from…I used my degree as a commercial real estate broker and almost immediately realized that was not what I wanted to do, but was faced with the same question that all twenty-somethings people are faced with, which is "What to do with my life," which should be a really easy question, but it is a shockingly difficult one. And so this idea that I had back when I was in college this kind of kept popping up, but I kept suppressing it and started saying that is a dumb thing to do.
>
> (Craft Sausage House)

Others made the mid-career transition because of the global financial crisis of 2008. The trend of making a mid-career transition from corporate work to entrepreneurship during the economic downturn was rather common in America (Fairlie 2013). When the global financial crisis hit America, many firms closed their doors and went out of business, or laid off large numbers of workers, which left many unemployed. The surplus of unemployed workers found it difficult to find employment elsewhere and many came to see entrepreneurship as a viable alternative. During the data collection effort, we interviewed several individuals who were part of this forced exodus from the corporate world. For example, in the quote below a kombucha (fermented tea) entrepreneur discusses how he had become very successful in real estate at a young age but lost it all during the recession when the housing market collapsed. Furthermore, the event caused him to re-evaluate his role in corporate America and enter the world of craft because the corporate world had failed him. Following the great financial crisis and housing market collapse, many Americans questioned the institution of corporate America (Langman 2013; Shrivastava & Ivanova 2015)

> Every dollar I made [as a real estate project manager] I reinvested into a rental property, and 2008 hit…2009 things got really bad… Like I was 25 and I had a bunch of property—I bought my first place at 19. I was really happy and proud and then that day I woke up and didn't have any property. It was devastating… I kind of went through this dark period in my life. I really enjoy starting things from scratch and it failed. You know I tasted failure, horrible failure, it is not fun to have a place ripped out from underneath from you. So when things hit rock bottom, I got into bar and restaurant consulting. I would

bartend on the side and make extra money and just do what I could, really, just to get myself back on my feet, I started to really experiment with flavors and kinds of things and I discovered this talent of combining stuff and making things that taste good.

(Kombucha Brewery)

For other craft entrepreneurs, a specific event, such as a critical work situation or a major life event, caused them to question their role in corporate America. These events led them to recognize their mortality, which triggered them to re-evaluate their career path. As such, specific life events led individuals to question their passion for their career, or the events made the possibility of failure more salient and caused individuals to re-evaluate their work (Vaitenas & Wiener 1977). For example, in the following quote, a *boucherie* butcher entrepreneur discusses how he began to re-evaluate his life after his younger brother died, which led him to take on an iconoclastic attitude and pursue a career in craft butchery.

I experienced a tragedy when I was 26. I had a younger brother that passed away, and I really feel like…I had a desire…I think because of that tragedy I realized how little bit of control I really had with life in general. And the more I looked, the more I found I didn't have really any control, and I was part of the system, I was working in the oil field, I had a 9 to 5. And at some point, I just threw my hands up in the air and gave up on it all, I didn't want to contribute into that system anymore, and I think that was the beginning of me having that attitude.

(*Boucherie* Butcher)

Craft entrepreneurs may come from a variety of backgrounds and operate a variety of different types of craft firms upon making the transition. However, a common theme is that craft entrepreneurs recognize traditional employment in corporate America is not for them. We found that becoming disenchanted with their current career path or seriously affected by a significant life or historical event often guides individuals toward a career in craft entrepreneurship. Thus, many craft entrepreneurs realize they cannot be true to themselves and continue with their career in corporate America. For additional quotes that further articulate and illustrate this phenomenon, see Table 2.

Craftwork Inspired by Unique Cultural Experiences

Similar to other research on career selection, we found cultural values and identity also influence craft entrepreneurs in regard to the products they produce and their means of production (Brown 2002; Ibrahim, Ohnishi, & Wilson 1994). As our interviews spanned multiple geographical

Table 2.2 Illustrative Data on Traditional Employment in Corporate America

American	Not Meant for Traditional Employment
Craft Sausage House	I don't think it was the autonomy, I think it was that… as a commercial real estate broker I was incredibly autonomous actually…it was a passion, you want to feel like your life has purpose and a huge part of your life is your job and there was a void there for me and for whatever reason I sort of had this calling to get into the restaurant business and make food the right way and so that also became a big driving force…
Charcuterie Restaurant	I actually growing up thought I wanted to be a nurse, so I tell this story back in spring it was back in 2008 at this time I was in nursing school at the Lake…I was taking care of this patient at the hospital and I was in charge of him and I was the only nurse in his room at the time…one particular day his monitor just started going flat, he flat lined and like I said I was the only nurse in his room at the time and I kind of blanked out…I was pretty embarrassed of myself and probably took 2 or 3 seconds to realize (A) I don't have an action plan, (B) I am not going to do anything, so I need to (C) go find the next closest nurse to go take care of this guy and so I ran out of the room to go find a nurse and eventually we got back and he was ok. And after that experience it kind of made me reevaluate if nursing was the direction that I really wanted to go in…
Artisan Sandwiches	Owning my own time was a big deal it is really one of the things I've finally pegged after figuring out why I just couldn't be here [working in corporate America] anymore.
Shenandoah Region Meatpacking	…at the master planning level I helped put some facilities together that were critical for operating the Iraq war, which I was very opposed to from the very beginning—I could see that it was going to be a disaster and left me feeling bad—I just didn't want to keep doing what I was doing. This was around 2007 so there was a bunch of things coming together around that time I was getting my MBA, I was kind of disgruntled with the work I was doing…I was worried about my parents, I was worried about the company I was with because I had a strong feeling about the housing what's about to go through to change, my alarm bells are starting to ring at some of the things I saw…

regions in the US, we found that US craft entrepreneurs relied heavily on regional cultural differences to inspire their work and distinguish it from the work performed in other areas. In other words, craft entrepreneurs may draw inspiration from their family history or culture to produce a craft product or take a craft approach to production that celebrates their unique backgrounds (Paige & Littrell 2002). This process of analyzing one's culture and history and then becoming inspired to pursue a career in the craft category is well illustrated in the quote below. This quote describes how a nascent craft entrepreneur began to analyze his roots, history, and culture after realizing he was not meant to become a nurse. Moreover, this reflection caused him to see that a common theme in his family was hospitality and food, which inspired him to open a charcuterie restaurant.

> I started analyzing my roots, where do I come from, what makes me tick. My grandfather was a mayor, he was a people person, he was the mayor of Houma, Louisiana. He devoted a lot of his business life but most of his political life to the people. My grandmother had a tour business so she would pack people into buses and drive around the country to different venues and just take care of people so it is kind of in my blood and it is in my nature to provide hospitality and I didn't really realize that, until I started re-evaluating what I exactly want to do with my life…food has always been a passion for me, I grew up in the kitchens with my grandparents, my grandmother is an awesome cook.
>
> (Charcuterie Restaurant)

In other cases, individuals became interested in craft because of their exposure to a particular practice or custom at a young age, which then led to their eventual interest in craftwork. Numerous entrepreneurs highlighted this phenomenon, and below are two quotes from two different specialty coffee entrepreneurs that speak to this process. In the first quote, the coffee entrepreneur describes how he grew up on a farm and how that led to his interest in coffee, as conscientious coffee roasters in America typically have a personal relationship with coffee farmers. In the second quote, a Cajun coffee roaster discusses how he associated drinking coffee with his father, whom he deeply admired.

> I grew up on a farm in Blount County Tennessee, which is just south of Knoxville here. So I had a lot of exposure to farming as a young person—so that was a major component of my eventual interest in coffee.
>
> (Sustainable Coffee Roaster)

> When I was a kid I used to drink [coffee]… In the morning, my dad would—we had a bee farm and my dad would go out there with the suit and get the honey from bees and stuff like that—and my dad would also have a garden. And so I was just wanted to do what my dad was doing. So, when I would see my dad wake up in the morning and do the whole crack the egg and drink the egg straight without cooking it, and so I wanted to do the same thing, of course my dad was like, "you're too young for that," but he also drinks

coffee—actually [I] have a coffee pot in here that we used to make coffee with but he would make you coffee. So, I basically just love that, and the connection with my father, and coffee was one of those connections.

(Cajun Coffee Roaster)

Other American craft entrepreneurs found success and inspiration by producing signature products tied to a specific culture or region (e.g., *boucherie* or smoked ham). That is, these American craft entrepreneurs established a firm built around producing a product that had been traditionally produced by individual families and kept in-house or shared within a small community. Cultural products are uniquely suited for the craft category because the tradition of producing the products for personal or community use can preserve the craft aspects of the product. As cultural products are traditionally produced for personal use—their maker typically consumes them. Hence, quality is most important to the maker, such that he or she is not made to consume a subpar product (Marx 2010/1867). Moreover, this is different from products that have long been commercialized, as commercialization incentivizes the maker to maximize profit margins. This profit-oriented incentive may also lead the maker to use lower-quality components in certain areas. Therefore, the cultural products that are brought into market from the craft entrepreneur's background have likely been kept authentic and refined to meet the quality standards of the community or maker rather than to maximize profit. Thus, cultural products are ideal for entrepreneurial craft endeavors, as product authenticity is held in high regard within the craft category (Verhaal, Khessina, & Dobrev 2015; Weber, Heinze, & DeSoucey 2008).

The set of quotes below illustrate two craft entrepreneurs taking products from their specific culture to market as the basis of their entrepreneurial endeavor. These entrepreneurs describe how the products they offer were originally produced and consumed within their communities as a way of life and not traditionally sold on the market. Thus, these owners exemplify how a nascent craft entrepreneur may be inspired by their unique culture as the basis of their firm.

To get an authentic boucherie restaurant is like a contradiction in itself because anyone that was raised with those traditions will not have the money to finance a restaurant or will probably not know people that have that…that want to invest. Because, basically…if you were raised in it—you were probably raised in an impoverished situation, because people who have money wouldn't have been doing it. We did this not because we wanted to be doing it, we did this because we had to…this is how we survived.

(*Boucherie* Butcher)

[Redacted] smoky mountain country hams are slow-cured using salt, brown sugar, and sodium nitrite and typically aged 9–10 months, though hams are available one year and older. This time-honored practice dates back to the era of our forefathers, when the preparation and preservation of meat was a way of life and sustenance.

(Appalachian Country Ham, Bio)

Others found inspiration to pursue craftwork or become craft entrepreneurs because taking a craft approach is most consistent with their unique regional values. Therefore, a craft entrepreneur may be interested in pursuing a craft approach, rather than a profit-focused approach, because it is consistent with the values they took on through their religion, upbringing, gender identity, or ideology. For example, American men may sense that working with their hands is a means through which they may derive their masculinity and subsequently become drawn toward craft ideals, as white-collar work and consumerism may remove individuals from their gender identities (Faludi 1999; Ta 2006). Such concepts are similar to the notion of entrepreneurs taking a particular approach to entrepreneurship based on their social identities (e.g., Fauchart & Gruber 2011). The quotes below illustrate how two craft entrepreneurs were influenced by their rural and/or religious values.

There are people that that is their business—it is to grow and be either acquire or to be acquired. That is not ours—we are country folk—pretty devout Catholics. Our business model is basically just to make people happy, sell enough beer to pay the bills, and reinvest to keep growing.

(Cajun Brewery)

It is funny to think of what we do as new because it is actually old—it is the way that families lived and ate outside of the big cities. This is how people did it. People had a cow. Whether it was for milk or for beef purposes every year, or maybe they had a milk cow and ate the calf or who knows, and almost every family would have a pig out back that they would feed scraps to, and then in the fall they would butcher it, and they have their own smokehouse and they would salt the meat and it was preserved and that is how they were able to keep meat through the fall and winter. So, what we are doing is not new—it seems new to some people because they are so used to going to the grocery store and only buying things wrapped in plastic sitting on Styrofoam, but this is the way it was done for hundreds of years. So, we just feel like it is the natural way of eating.

(Consumer-Supported Agrarian)

In summary, we find individuals' unique regional culture and history often inspires American craft entrepreneurship. Moreover, this inspiration

Table 2.3 Illustrative Data on the Importance of Cultural Inspiration to
Craftwork

American	Inspired by Culture
Cajun Brewery	[Redacted] Brewing was founded on this simple dream—to craft beers that complement the cuisine and lifestyle of Cajuns and Creoles.
San Francisco Butcher, Bio	I have been to some whole animal roast, my father-in-law... my second father-in-law kind of... He is Cuban and I have known him for 20 years and I have been to his Cuban pig roast and I absolutely love it and the whole process, and the family connection, and ironically I was one of the far- removed family members by marriage association, but you know he was trying to bequeath his knowledge onto his sons or daughters but they really had no interest, but I was like "Oh, this is great." So he influenced me... I just love the show that he put on when cooking a pig, and he designed a certain grill for it.
Monastic Soap, Bio	Our Benedictine tradition encourages us to support ourselves by the work of our hands. Soapmaking is one way we carry that tradition into the future.
Appalachian Distillery, Bio	Our mission is deeply rooted in the Old World craft heritage and artisanal Blue Ridge Mountain distilling traditions passed down through generations of immigrants, outlaws and other relatives. Just as the distillers before us, and in keeping with our food backgrounds, [redacted] is committed to using the very best ingredients in each and every one of our exceptional spirits.

may take various forms. Some nascent entrepreneurs may be inspired to pursue a craft approach because of their upbringing and their family history's ties to craftwork (e.g., farming or morning coffee rituals). Other nascent entrepreneurs may be inspired to take a craft approach to bring products tied to their culture, which decree specific craft means of production, to the market. Other entrepreneurs might be predisposed to engage in craftwork because it is consistent with their values, beliefs, or ideologies (e.g., rural values or Catholicism). Finally, given the size and diversity of the US, craft entrepreneurs emphasize their local roots and histories and articulate regional differences to differentiate their products. Thus, US craft entrepreneurship contains an inherently regional component; in addition to *how* something is made, the origins of the craftwork and *where* something is made is also highly valued. See Table 3 for additional quotes that further describe the importance of cultural inspiration to craftwork.

Perceptions of the Future of the American Craft Category

Throughout the interview process, we found American craft entrepreneurs routinely perceived that the craft category would continue to grow and expand throughout America. Additionally, we found craft interviewees saw the scope of this movement take form on both the industry level and on a broader societal level. The quotes below highlight craft entrepreneurs' positive assessment of the craft movement within their specific industries.

> [Being part of a specialty coffee movement] has always been part of my goal and Louisiana has always been a little bit behind when it comes to things like that…I would argue we are about four years behind most people…we are catching up pretty quickly, but we are about four to two years behind. I mean we only had a couple roasters recently in Louisiana—I mean you look at Seattle the coffee shops there and they are on every corner. Now, Louisiana's finally…there's multiple rosters. When we started, there was only like two or three roasters and now there is probably 10, 15, 20, roasters now.
>
> (Cajun Coffee Roaster)

> …with leaps and bounds it [boucherie] has grown. Like the exposure I have gotten and the people who know about what I do…so boucherie went from being something…the boucherie itself went from something that was kind of on its way out—it was just a few old guys that knew what they were doing and that was it. Now it is hip, it is like an "in thing" you know, and it wasn't like that 7 years ago when I started.
>
> (*Boucherie* Butcher)

Other craft entrepreneurs discuss the craft movement at a broader societal level, as they sense they are part of a growing movement that is bigger than just their industry and region. These entrepreneurs sensed that America's values are on a trajectory that places greater importance on self-expression—and that this shift is favorable toward craft-based firms (Roser 2016). The quotes below illustrate how some entrepreneurs sense this growing societal movement reflects a shift in values that aligns with craft production. In the first quote, a craft sausage entrepreneur notes America is in the midst of a craft renaissance, where there is a growing number of craft producers and customers in the market. In the second quote, a craft meatpacking entrepreneur comments that the whole craft movement has been driven by the latest generation of consumers and their desire for goods that meet their qualitative standards.

> There is a renaissance happening. It is one thing if you're a romantic and you want to create a product that is wonderful but if no one wants to buy the product then you're not going to be doing it for that long—and so what you have happening right now is the intersection of both things. You have a desire of a maker community that wants to do that and then there's this consumer base that desires it as well.

And I think that both of those things are growing simultaneously, which is really fueling the whole movement.

(Craft Sausage House)

If you look at demographics and look at the marketing people and how they slice it up, we had the greatest generation, the silent generation, the boomers, gen Y, the millennials... When you hit the millennials, it is like almost geologic, there is just this huge difference in attitudes. They want authenticity, they want closeness to the land. They have a whole host of other things that they look for—if the animal is treated well, are they causing global warming. They look at their food a lot differently. So, if you look at the years going ahead it makes me feel good about where the business is going to be.

(Shenandoah Region Meatpacking)

We found that the craft or artisan movement is perceived by craft entrepreneurs to be alive and well within America; in addition the craft entrepreneurs were pleased with America's current trajectory in placing greater and greater value on craftwork. We find it impressive that this movement has sustained itself, considering that the origins of the craft movement date back to the beginning of the new millennium (Carroll & Swaminathan 2000). Moreover, entrepreneurs and workers within the craft category perceive the craft movement to be only growing in size and momentum, and have confidence regarding the future of the craft category. As such, the current sense of confidence in America's craft category serves to further enhance the entrepreneurs' commitment to their craft-based careers. We also expect that the current sense of confidence and growth in the craft category will help to entice additional nascent entrepreneurs to join the craft category, thereby creating a system of positive feedback. See Table 4 for additional quotes regarding the positive perceptions for the future of the American craft category.

Discussion

We started this research endeavor with the aim of answering the question "What drives and inspires individuals in America to pursue a craft-based entrepreneurial career?" In the end, we find American craft entrepreneurs often follow a general two-stage path in opting for this style of work. First, craft entrepreneurs realize that for some reason they are not meant for traditional work in corporate America. This appears to occur, in part, because they desire more meaningful work and autonomy than they received in their routinized corporate jobs, or they experienced a significant event that led them to rethink their life path. Thus, they perceived that the corporate jobs were inconsistent with "who they were" or "wanted to be." Second, craft entrepreneurs look to their history,

Table 2.4 Illustrative Data on the Perceptions of the Future of Craft

American	Perceptions of the Future of Craft
Mountain Coffee Roaster	I think it is part of a greater specialty food movement, I often will comment that I think specialty coffee is a lot like craft beer and we are like a decade behind them, and before I talk to you today I was talking to a friend of a friend who is talking about starting up a chocolate roastery with like cacao and I would argue that they are probably another decade behind us. I think we are starting to see all kinds of specialty foods. It is kind of part of that movement in my mind the way I picture it. It is sort a part of that movement of farm to cup and people wanting to know where their food is coming from and organic. Like the majority of coffee is definitely not grown in the United States, so I think it's been really easy to just not to pay that much attention to it or not totally understand it and then there has been a lot of people who are like wait no there is so much more to this and doing a conscientious effort to bringing that information to people, and people like it.
Consumer Supported Agrarian	I think people are seeing that because of the ease of getting information through social media... I think that is changing the way people look at their food and I think obviously also the chefs that are out there—their access to products and those type of things... I think we have a generation I don't know if it is the millennials or the end of the Gen Xers but I think they are a lot more socially conscious about where their food comes from and the impact of eating globally...
Shenandoah Meatpacking	...there was just huge pent-up demand for good local meat processing because up until I was born in the 50s and during my lifetime every decade until about 10 years ago plants like ours had been going out of business, they have been losing one or two percent per year across the nation during my entire lifetime up until just a few years before I bought the plant and now they are starting to come back, but that was in part because of the local food movement. Farmers markets started in the 80s and they were growing at 16–17 percent a year for 30 years, but it was all fruits and vegetables. And you really didn't start to see meat in the farmers markets till about 2000, so that is the type of demand that has driven our growth.
Artisan Sandwiches	[In] the 80s...especially in our state...the oil boom and really nationwide in the Reagan years, with crazy big money, and you're paying 50 bucks for an entrée with a pea, a carrot, and a one-and-a-half ounce fillet tenderloin medallion. And those were like the greedy times. When the bottom fell out of the economy that changed things...by necessity you had to change things because the resources changed... people are tired I think of just frivolous waste and unnecessary. They just get more organic in every way food and otherwise and I love it. It fits me very well. It is more casual. It is more meaningful. It is just even hard to describe. It was so gaudy back then, I guess you would call it in general. It is more organic and simple and nice now.

identity, and regional culture for inspiration, as products exported from the entrepreneurs' regional culture to the market are likely to meet the authenticity criteria of the craft market (e.g., Verhaal et al. 2015; Weber et al. 2008). Hence, many American craft entrepreneurs follow a path where they first become dissatisfied with their current employment and then seek to create new employment opportunities by producing goods tied to their personal history, identity, and culture.

In this vein, we see important theoretical implications for American craft entrepreneurship. Specifically, American craft workers' local identity and culture are imbued into their products and organizations—food producers in the South suggest they rely on methods that are "authentically Cajun," butchers from the Mid-Atlantic note their recipes reflect "Appalachian country hams," and brewery owners across the US highlight how they represent the "local brewery" in their respective geographical regions. Put differently, US craft entrepreneurship is not only about producing high-quality products but also involves weaving one's local history and culture into the identity of the organization and its products.

Finally, we found craft entrepreneurs held very positive perceptions about the future of the craft category, as many of the craft entrepreneurs mentioned how pleased they were with how much Americans have begun to value craft and artisan products over the last decade. Moreover, these positive future perceptions of the craft category in America seem to encourage craft entrepreneurs to continue pursuing their work. The bright outlook for America's craft category may also influence other nascent craft entrepreneurs to view craft-based approaches to business as a salient and viable alternative option to traditional business. As such, if the craft category continues to grow and flourish within America it should lure greater numbers of individuals away from traditional careers.

Considering America's growing craft movement and the number of individuals leaving corporate jobs to pursue careers in the craft category (e.g., Brewers Association 2014; FiBL & IFOAM 2016; Sherman 2012; Specialty Coffee Association of America 2014), questions abound as to what this growing category will be like in the future. Anti-Fordist and anti-McDonaldization sentiments appear to have fueled the growth of America's craft category as the American craft movement largely rejects mass production, routinization, and depersonalized work (Gramsci 1971/ 1934; McCracken 2006; Ritzer 1983). However, it will be interesting to see how these craft firms develop and evolve over time to accommodate an ever-growing customer base. As McDonalds and Ford were, at one time, small firms too, if demand for craft products continues to grow, craft ventures will be forced to decide the extent to which they embrace this growth. Whether they eventually grow and evolve into the large depersonalized corporate organizations they oppose or continue to strive for authenticity over profit maximization remains to be seen. In any event, further research is needed and should be dedicated to understanding the evolution of craft businesses and the craft category as a whole, in order to evaluate the extent to which they can sustain themselves as anti-Fordist and anti-McDonaldized organizations.

Similarly, one may question what the craft movement means for the future of work in America. With so many manufacturing jobs leaving America in recent decades, perhaps Americans see the world of craft entrepreneurship as an opportunity to avoid the uncertainties and downsizing that are so prevalent in corporate American manufacturing. Alternatively, some may view craft entrepreneurship as a means through which to bring back American manufacturing and craft work and create jobs for local economies. Although the emergence of American craft work has arguably been a progressive movement, the new political leadership in the United States—with an emphasis on American manufacturing and national protectionist policies—also seems to align with the ideals of craftwork, which value the notion of "locally crafted." It will be intriguing to witness what impact these potential policy changes will have on American manufacturing jobs in the craft category, which have grown significantly in recent years (Komisar 2013; Tuttle 2015). If the craft category continues to grow within America, then the rise of craft may be the answer to sustainably revitalizing the country's manufacturing sector and creating numerous craft-based "plaid-collar" jobs.

References

Arcidiacono, P., Hotz, V. J., & Kang, S. (2012). Modeling college major choices using elicited measures of expectations and counterfactuals. *Journal of Econometrics*, 166(1), 3–16.

Braverman, H. (1974). *Labor and Monopoly Capital*. New York: Free Press.

Brewers Association. (2014). 2014 small & independent U.S. craft brewers' growth in the beer category. Retrieved from www.brewersassociation.org/wp-content/uploads /2015/03/Growth-Small_HR.png.

Brown, D. (2002). The role of work and cultural values in occupational choice, satisfaction, and success: A theoretical statement. *Journal of Counseling & Development*, 80(1), 48–56.

Carroll, G. R., & Swaminathan, A. (2000). Why the microbrewery movement? Organizational dynamics of resource partitioning in the US brewing industry. *American Journal of Sociology*, 106(3), 715–762.

Crawford, M.B. (2009). *Shop Class as Soulcraft: An Inquiry into the Value of Work*. New York: Penguin.

The Economist. (2014, January, 4). The art and craft of business. Retrieved from www.economist.com/news/business/21592656-etsy-starting-show-how-maker-movement-can-make-money-art-and-craft-business.

Fairlie, R. W. (2013). Entrepreneurship, economic conditions, and the great recession. *Journal of Economics & Management Strategy*, 22, 207–231.

Faludi S. (1999). *Stiffed: The betrayal of the American man*. New York: William Morrow.

Fauchart, E., & Gruber, M. (2011). Darwinians, communitarians, and missionaries: The role of founder identity in entrepreneurship. *Academy of Management Journal*, 54, 935–957.

FiBL, & IFOAM. (2016). Organic food sales growth in the United States from 2000 to 2014. In *Statista – The Statistics Portal*. Retrieved from www.statista.com/statistics/196962/ organic-food-sales-growth-in-the-us-since-2000/.

Gartner, W. B. (1990). What are we talking about when we talk about entrepreneurship? *Journal of Business Venturing*, 5, 15–28.

Gramsci, A. (1971). 'Americanism and Fordism', *Prison Notebooks (1934)*. London: Lawrence and Wishart.

Ibrahim, F. A., Ohnishi, H., & Wilson, R. P. (1994). Career assessment in a culturally diverse society. *Journal of Career Assessment*, 2(3), 276–288.

Ibarra, H. (2002). How to stay stuck in the wrong career. *Harvard Business Review*, 80, 40–48.

Isenberg, D. J. (2010). How to start an entrepreneurial revolution. *Harvard Business Review*, 88, 40–50.

Komisar, R. (2013, December, 11). Artisanal manufacturing: Creating jobs to produce things in America again. *Forbes*. Retrieved from www.forbes.com/sites/bruceupbin/2013/12/11/artisanal-manufacturing-creating-jobs-to-produce-things-in-america-again/#4186d5f07350.

Langman, L. (2013). Occupy: A new new social movement. *Current Sociology*, 61, 510–524.

Marx, K. (2010). *Capital, vol. 1 (1867)*. Moscow, RU: Progress Publishers.

Mathias, B. D., & Smith, A. D. (2016). Autobiographies in organizational research using leaders' life stories in a triangulated research design. *Organizational Research Methods*, 19(2), 204–230.

McCracken, G. (2006, November, 6). The artisanal movement, and 10 things that define it. *Cultureby*. Retrieved from http://cultureby.com/2006/11/the_artisanal_m.html.

McGuinley, D. (2016). IBISWorld industry report: Household furniture manufacturing in the U.S. Retrieved from http://clients1.ibisworld.com/reports/us/industry/default.aspx?indid=862.

Menger, P. M. (1999). Artistic labor markets and careers. *Annual Review of Sociology*, 25, 541–574.

Paige, R. C., & Littrell, M. A. (2002). Craft retailers' criteria for success and associated business strategies. *Journal of Small Business Management*, 40(4), 314–331.

Ritzer, G. (1983). The "McDonaldization" of society. *Journal of American Culture*, 6, 100–107.

Roser, M. (2016). Materialism and post-materialism. *OurWorldInData.org*. Retrieved from https://ourworldindata.org/materialism-and-post-materialism/.

Sherman, L. (2012, October, 8). Soap cleans up by raising the bar liquid is getting left behind as consumers seek high-end, crafted solids. *Advertising Age*. Retrieved from http://adage.com/article/news/soap-cleans-raising-bar/237596/.

Shrivastava, P., & Ivanova, O. (2015). Inequality, corporate legitimacy and the Occupy Wall Street movement. *Human Relations*, 68, 1209–1231.

Smith, N.R. (1967). *The entrepreneur and his firm: The relationship between type of man and type of company*. East Lansing, MI: Michigan State University Press.

Smith, N.R., & Miner, J.B. (1983). Type of entrepreneur, type of firm, and managerial motivation: Implications for organizational life cycle theory. Strategic Management Journal, 4(4): 325–340.

Specialty Coffee Association of America. (2014). U.S. specialty coffee consumption report. Retrieved from www.scaa.org/?page=resources&d=statistic-and-reports.

Ta, L. M. (2006). Hurt so good: Fight Club, masculine violence, and the crisis of capitalism. *The Journal of American Culture*, 29, 265–277.

Tuttle, B. (2015, July, 29). 5 great things that beer does for America. Retrieved from http://time.com/money/3976822/beer-jobs-taxes-sales/.

Vaitenas, R., & Wiener, Y. (1977). Developmental, emotional, and interest factors in voluntary mid-career change. *Journal of Vocational Behavior*, 11(3), 291–304.

Verhaal, J. C., Khessina, O. M., & Dobrev, S. D. (2015). Oppositional product names, organizational identities, and product appeal. *Organization Science*, 26(5), 1466–1484.

Weber, K., Heinze, K. L., & DeSoucey, M. (2008). Forage for thought: Mobilizing codes in the movement for grass-fed meat and dairy products. *Administrative Science Quarterly*, 53(3), 529–567.

3 Wine, the Authenticity Taste Regime, and Rendering Craft

Jennifer Smith Maguire

Introduction

The chapter discusses how the taste for authenticity makes craft goods legible *qua* craft. Consumers have a clear desire and willingness to pay a premium for authenticity (Arvidsson 2006; Botterill 2007; Gilmore & Pine 2007; Leigh, Peters & Shelton 2006; Lewis & Bridger 2001; Postrel 2003). Yet, delivering authenticity to consumers is by no means a straightforward task, because authenticity is not a thing unto itself; it does not reside as an inherent property within an object (in the manner of, say, the degree of hardness or opacity). Rather, authenticity is a negotiated, accomplished quality that emerges through judgements, made in relation to taste regimes: evaluative frameworks that typically consist of sets of aesthetic ideals. This chapter focuses on the cultural field of fine wine, for which aesthetic ideals are closely associated with origin, genre, and the process of creation. For fine wine, the taste regime of authenticity involves conventions for the evaluation of provenance—where a thing was made, how, by whom, when, under what conditions. Through examples from the field of fine wine, the chapter explores how this dominant evaluative framework for authenticity overlaps closely with the aesthetic ideals of craft. Those ideals cluster around, on the one hand, a creative and autonomous maker who is equipped with technical skill and specialist know-how and finds meaning in work; and on the other, a physical thing that, variously, evinces dimensions of heritage, tradition, nature, and hand-craftedness (Ocejo 2017; Sennett 2008).

As an introductory illustration, consider the website for Les Artisans du Champagne (http://lesartisansduchampagne.com/), a collective of small-scale *vignerons* (winemakers who grow their own grapes). The website bears all the expected hallmarks of craft. The background image for each page embeds the product in 'the local' and links it to nature: a vineyard in late winter, meticulously pruned, coated in hoarfrost, and glowing in the light of a rosy-fingered dawn. In addition to the vineyards, the *vignerons* are depicted in their physical place of production: walking their chalk caves and underground cellars, and working amidst barrels and tanks.

A section on the artisans' philosophy likens the *vignerons* to artists and alchemists, who 'dare, imagine, experiment and take risks to try and create wines that are authentic, thoroughly truthful and free of artifice'. Each of the 17 *vignerons* comments on what it means to be an artisan; for example, one describes the artisan as 'the link between raw matter and wrought matter. ...[and] knowing the very essence of each grape and each terroir so as to be able to express all their nuances in a bottle'. The website representations highlight various material referents that serve as anchors for judgements of authenticity: the *vignerons*, bottles, vineyards, barrels, *terroir*, grapes, the work itself. Through both indexical and iconic cues (Grayson & Martinec 2004), these representations provide points of attachment for consumers' and producers' judgements of authenticity and self-authentification.

As the Artisans du Champagne website suggests, craft goods are an amalgam in which provenance (context of production) is made available as part of the 'thing' on offer (be that a good, service, experience).[1] Through representations that align with the authenticity taste regime, the craftsperson and the story of making are made available (legible, recognizable) in the representations of the thing. And, in so doing, representations and narratives of provenance render those things as 'craft things'. This chapter thus argues against an essentialist notion of craft. I am concerned with how craft things are embedded within, indeed are inseparable from, the notion of authenticity. To understand the organization of craft requires an understanding of authenticity; craft is a genre of authenticity. What we think of as craft (e.g. craft goods, craft work, craftsperson) is not an essential property of an object, activity, or person, but is the outcome of an evaluation through the lens of authenticity. Craft is an outcome of an exercise of judgement, made in relation to the taste regime for authenticity.

The chapter proceeds by situating craft and authenticity within the broader contemporary context of cultural omnivorousness (Johnston & Baumann 2007; Warde et al. 2008). I then consider omnivorousness and the taste for authenticity in relation to fine wine, a cultural field replete with the hallmarks of craft. To examine how craft is rendered through representation in more detail, I draw on findings from a media analysis of fine wine magazines to elaborate on how particular properties are recurrently disentangled and decoupled from a wine's provenance and framed as legitimate points of attachment for market actors through alignment with the authenticity taste regime. Finally, I consider the limits to the representational rendering of 'any' thing as craft.

Omnivorousness and the Taste for Authenticity

Taste is social. For groups and for societies, notions of 'good taste' and legitimacy tend to reflect the dominant group; tastes are stratified in legitimacy relative to the dominant group's 'good taste' (Bourdieu 1984, 1990). Categories of good taste are not static. Taste conventions are subject to negotiation by groups seeking to improve or defend their social position. Notions of good taste are thus socially and historically specific, changing over time in relation to the relative ascendancy or decline of influence for different groups (socio-economic, generational, or otherwise). Changes in what is considered culturally legitimate taste will also bear the mark of societal changes and technological innovations that impact on the range of things that are available for judgement, and the everyday backdrop against which judgements of taste are made.

Contemporary changes in what is considered good taste are broadly characterized by a breakdown of established boundaries between elite and popular cultural forms. Scholars have dubbed this reformulation of boundaries between the culturally legitimate and illegitimate as 'cultural omnivorousness' (e.g. Peterson & Kern 1996; Peterson 2005). Much of the research on omnivorousness has noted a decline or near-extinction of the 'univorous snob' who would operate narrowly within established categories of elite consumption, and a shift in patterns of discerning consumption towards genre- and boundary-spanning diversity. In place of the snob is the omnivore, with a high diversity of tastes (preferences that cross high/low boundaries), and a high volume of tastes (preferences that span multiple genres). For example, Purhonen et al. (2010), examining Finnish music and literary tastes, find that 40 per cent of Finns report likings that include highbrow, middlebrow and lowbrow musical tastes, and highly educated older women are the most common omnivores. Looking at leisure consumption in the UK, Katz-Gerro and Sullivan (2010) find that the highest levels of economic and cultural capital are associated with the greatest blurring of high and low tastes, and the greatest scale of heterogenous tastes (what they term 'cultural voraciousness'). Omnivorousness is also patterned by gender, such that the greatest gap occurs 'between men with the highest social status and women with the lowest' (Katz-Gerro & Sullivan 2010: 193). Although omnivorousness is found across the class spectrum, it is a taste repertoire that is most concentrated in elites.

Despite the apparent disregard for *established* categories of culturally legitimate tastes, omnivorousness is not a matter of liking everything indiscriminately. Rather, as Warde et al. suggest, 'the omnivore might be a person who is prepared to consider the merits of any cultural artefact or genre, and who is capable of discrimination among them' (2008: 150). As such, scholarly attention has been directed at documenting not only the decline of former elite/low boundaries, but also the emergence of new categories of legitimacy. Recent research has identified a number of evaluative dynamics through which good taste and discernment are performed, including oppositions between old and new/trendy (Bellavance 2008; Taylor 2009), modest and opulent (Daloz

2010; Schimpfossl 2014), cosmopolitan and traditional (Cvetičanin & Popescu 2011), and authentic and mass (Beverland et al. 2008; Johnston & Baumann 2007; Smith Maguire 2016).

Indeed, one could argue that that final opposition—between authentic and mass—has become dominant in contemporary consumer culture, and for omnivores in particular. In their examinations of the field of gastronomy and the attitudes and practices of 'foodies', Johnston and Baumann (2007: 179) suggest that authenticity is a 'near-essential part of the omnivorous...discourse'. The dominance of authenticity within discerning, omivorous consumption is exemplified in the 'New Nordic Cuisine' (NNC), which adheres to the principles of 'purity, freshness, and simplicity; with local, seasonal ingredients from the Nordic terroir; and with a healthy, green, and environmentally friendly profile' (Byrkjeflot et al. 2013: 44). Restaurants in the NNC vein, and the gastronomic media that represents and circulates their global cachet, have drawn credibility from the established currency of Michelin stars, thereby affirming the legitimacy and prestige of impeccable provenance and meticulous sourcing both as guarantors of authenticity and markers of good taste.

Considerable research makes the case that authenticity is a negotiated, accomplished quality that is socially constructed by specific evaluators relative to their particular contexts and goals (Beverland & Farrelly 2010; Cohen 1988; Grayson & Martinec 2004; Grazian 2003; Kirschenblatt-Gimblett 1998; Peñaloza 2000; Zukin 2009). It is the judgement of taste that 'makes' authenticity. Looking across the body of research on consumer attitudes, experiences and evaluations of authenticity, a range of common cues or conventions have been identified. These anchors include economic disinterestedness and anti-commercialism, nature and tradition, the hand-crafted, and the rural and local rather than the mass-produced and industrialized (Beverland 2006; Beverland & Luxton 2005; Fine 2003; Holt 1998; Johnston & Baumann 2007; MacCannell 1989; Sassatelli & Scott 2001; Zukin 2009). These conventions populate the 'taste regime' for authenticity: 'a discursively constructed normative system that orchestrates the aesthetics of practice in a culture of consumption' (Arsel & Bean 2012: 900).

We can thus understand authenticity as a master taste regime for cultural omnivores. The authenticity taste regime provides a framework within which certain things come to seem 'right:' legible, credible, legitimate. Authenticity is rendered—things *become* authentic—through situated evaluation and experience. Just because something is handmade (for example) does not necessarily mean that it will be evaluated or experienced as authentic; taste regimes shape, but do not determine, evaluations and experiences. Herein lies the key connection between authenticity and omnivorousness: the local, traditional, natural or hand-crafted attributes of a thing (conventional expectations of craft goods) are simultaneously a starting point from which to experience a sense of authenticity for the omnivore, and a culturally legitimate basis on which to extend discerning consumption to formerly illegitimate or not-yet-legitimate forms of culture (and thus to perform one's omnivorous good taste).

As much as authenticity might be *experienced* as innately embedded in the item or experience (indeed, mistaking authenticity for actually being 'there' often underpins its pleasure), it is nevertheless subject to individual interpretation and negotiation (Beverland & Farrelly 2010; Grayson & Martinec 2004). Ultimately, authenticity is contingent on the evaluator agreeing that it is 'there'. Judgements of authenticity are not only subject to individual interpretations; they are also, crucially, targeted for strategic mobilization and marketization. While the majority of research focuses on consumers' evaluations of authenticity, some scholars have focused on how evaluations are scripted or channelled through the texts and practices of service workers and other market actors. Such research suggests how particular goods, services and practices are strategically embedded within the authenticity taste regime in order to add economic value (Arnould & Price 1993; Beverland & Luxton 2005; Brown, Kozinets & Sherry 2003; Fine 2003; Johnston & Baumann 2007; Lewis & Bridger 2001; Peterson 1997).

Thus, a critical aspect of rendering things as authentic takes place through representation, before and during the consumer's evaluation and experience of the good or service. Market representations—from tangible forms of marketing communication to intangible service encounters—attempt to selectively 'disentangle' singular elements (McFall 2009) from the entirety of a good/service's context of production; strategically 'decouple' (Beverland & Luxton 2005) those anchors from the non-consonant dimensions of production; and frame the singularized anchors as legitimate 'points of attachment' (McFall 2009) for consumers' desires for authenticity, thus 'mobilizing' their evaluations and behaviour (Miller & Rose 1997). That work of disentangling, decoupling and framing points of attachment is carried out by cultural producers and intermediaries, and given material and communicative form through representations and interactions. While cultural producers and intermediaries can attempt, via marketing communications and service encounters, to 'make' goods and services authentic, ultimately, they are confined, at best, to creating relatively reliable pathways for others' evaluations. Any representation of points of attachment can be subject to a negotiated or oppositional reading (Hall 1980), (mis)translated or (mis)read as ersatz tat, shoddy wares, insincere puffery.

While *any* thing is potentially available for being strategically framed as authentic (if only because every thing has a history of coming into being), *some* things are especially available. If the conventional characteristics of craft are objective attributes of a thing's provenance (e.g. hand-crafting or individual control over the construction process, local materials, specialized techniques, small-scale production, highly variable outputs), then that thing is more likely to have anchors that can be convincingly disentangled, decoupled, and framed as points of attachment for others' evaluations of authenticity. Moreover, in framing those anchors as authentic, representations may also make the thing available to be understood as craft. Craft things become legible as such only through representations shaped and organized by the authenticity taste regime that make provenance (where the thing was made, how, when, by whom) available as a point of attachment. It is because of the simultaneity of provenance—that the 'being made' becomes available as a legible attribute of the thing in the here-and-now—that hand-crafted goods are often understood to not simply bear the marks of the hand that made them (hand-crafted as a physical property of the thing), but also to embody the love, care or motivation of the producer (Fuchs et al. 2015). Without such representations, the passion of the producer, skill of making, raw materials and so forth are not otherwise available or legible; they are hidden behind the façade of the finished product.[2]

I have outlined the wider context of cultural omnivorousness for the taste for authenticity; the strategic, market-making work of rendering goods available for evaluations and experiences of authenticity; and the ways in which the work of disentangling, decoupling and framing may also render some things as craft things. Furthermore, I have argued that craft goods are only legible as such by virtue of representations that have been organized by the authenticity taste regime. I now turn to consider these issues in more detail through the lens of fine wine.

Wine and the Authenticity Taste Regime

The fine wine field exemplifies many of the changes outlined in the previous section with regard to cultural omnivorousness. Historically, hierarchies of prestige in the wine field broadly conflated country of production with quality, resulting in a crude dichotomy of Old World superiority/New World inferiority.[3] While subject to variation and contestation, the Old/New World categorization was nevertheless institutionalized via such mechanisms as pricing conventions, production regulations, wine marketing and wine education (Fourcade 2012; Garcia-Parpet 2008; Schamel 2006). However, the assumed superiority of Old World—and especially French—wine has been eroded since the 1970s, alongside increasing interest in seeking out little-known wine regions (New World and otherwise), obscure or heritage grape varietals, and the use of ancient wine production practices such as the use of amphorae (e.g. Taber 2005). Much of wine's history has involved a quest for increasing the scale, quality and consistency of production and the capacity for wines to be stored and transported without spoilage (Charters 2006). In a seeming reversal of history, 'good taste' in wine now largely operates through a rejection of the mass-produced and the standardized, in favour of the small-scale, highly local and variable. In place of the univorous snob drinking only premier cru clarets, there is the omnivorous wine critic seeking out the authenticity of a red mavrodaphne wine from Kefalonia Greece, or—if the categories of red and white are too predictable—an orange sivi pinot wine from Slovenia's Vipava Valley.

It is commonplace in the fine wine field for particular product properties to be singularized as points of attachment for evaluations of authenticity and quality. For example, a wine's *terroir* and provenance are made available through reference to the soil and climatic conditions of the specific vineyard or region, official designations of origin (e.g. *Appellation d'origine controlée* (AOC) wines), cultural heritage of the region, locally 'unique' styles of production and the personality and philosophy of the winemaker (e.g. Charters 2006; Inglis 2015; Smith Maguire 2013; Vaudour 2002). Furthermore, many small-scale, independent wine producers can legitimately claim that they produce all of their own ingredients, a point of distinction in the craft food and drink market (and a claim that most craft brewers, bakers and distillers cannot make).

The global emergence of natural and 'raw' wines exemplifies the authentic, craft aesthetic in the wine world (Smith Maguire forthcoming). Natural wines are those that are, in the most basic terms, made with minimal chemical and mechanical intervention. Their production is associated with low-yield vineyards in which the use of chemical fertilizers and pesticides, and much of the technology associated with modern-day agriculture, is avoided or outright rejected. This typically results in hand-picking grapes rather than using mechanical pickers, and may extend to using horses and ploughs rather than tractors. This ethos extends to the cellar, where chemical interventions are kept to a minimum, if used at all. For example, naturally occurring yeasts would be common, as would a rejection of the use of sulphur dioxide (a traditional stabilizer/preservative) and other additives. Proponents of natural wines claim that these production parameters result in wines that give the purest possible expression of their place of production, or *terroir*, thereby aligning them with established terms of quality-wine production. For such wines, the discourse of authenticity is linked to the hyperspecification of provenance, and stories of passionate, intrinsically motivated winemakers are as ubiquitous as artisanal, grape-to-glass viniculture.

Nevertheless, as per the wider argument of this chapter, natural wines are not *inherently* craft goods. They must be rendered as such through representation, without which the craft attributes would be unknowable to anyone beyond those who are involved in or directly witness its production, and who thus have indexical anchors for their evaluation of authenticity. More generally, it is not that some wines are authentic and others are not, but that particular product properties are strategically offered as points of attachment for consumers' judgements of taste. The selection, singularization and framing of those points of attachment is shaped by the authenticity taste regime, as the next section explores through the findings from a media analysis of fine wine magazines.

Representing and Rendering Fine Wine

I now turn to findings from an analysis of two leading wine specialist magazines: *Wine Spectator* and *Decanter*. The analysis focused on how good taste is articulated in relation to fine wine in the magazines' editorial and advertising content (Smith Maguire 2016). Over the past four decades, the fine wine field has witnessed a breakdown of former quality distinctions between Old and New World producers. Looking at how both Old and New World wines are represented in the magazines thus offers insight into commonalities and differences within the category of culturally legitimate wines.

While wine consumption has democratized beyond the elite, it remains highly stratified, with *terroir*-driven wines (and their premium price points) aimed primarily at the wealthy. The majority of the magazines' readership[4] are professional/managerial individuals with an average annual income in 2009–10 of approximately US$150,000, whose consumption patterns confirm their high levels of economic and cultural capital. For example, 86 per cent of *Decanter* readers have been on a wine-related holiday and 59 per cent have been on a wine course; 70 per cent of *Wine Spectator* readers have travelled outside of the US in the past three years, and at least 60 per cent claim attending live theatre, museums, and attending wine and food events/festivals as passions and hobbies. Such consumers are more likely both to like wine, and to express culturally omnivorous preferences (by virtue of age and socio-economic status) in which wines they like and how they evaluate those wines.

The analysis of the wine magazines examined how the representations of fine wine align with the taste regime of authenticity, by coding the anchors that had been disentangled, decoupled, and framed as worthy points of attachment for consumer judgements of authenticity. Those anchors were coded in relation to three common legitimacy frames, derived from previous research on common cues for authenticity (e.g. Beverland 2005, 2006; Beverland & Luxton 2005; Fine 2003; Holt 1998; Johnston & Baumann 2007; MacCannell 1989; Sassatelli & Scott 2001; Zukin 2009): transparency (biographic and geographic specificity of production), heritage, and genuineness. The coding identified how frequently these frames were used in the advertising, regular wine columns, and feature articles focused on *terroir*, in relation to what types of anchors, and revealed if there were any significant differences in the representations of Old and New World wines.[5] In general, I was interested in whether there were any echoes of former legitimacy boundaries (through which Old World and especially French wines were assumed to be superior) within an omnivorous discourse that ostensibly eschewed elite/low divides or universalistic categories of cultural inferiority.

In the *Decanter* and *Wine Spectator* samples, the most common legitimation frame was that of transparency, found in 82 per cent of the advertising and 74 per cent of the columns. Through representations of a wine's geographic specificity (via details of the context of production) and biographic specificity (via details of the specific producer), wine magazines perform a crucial function in the construction of legitimacy. The origins for particular wines come to seem known or knowable (Trubeck 2005) and thus trustworthy and credible (Sassatelli & Scott 2001). The heritage frame was found in 35 per cent of the advertising and 39 per cent of the wine columns. There was no significant difference between Old and New World wines in terms of the frequency in advertising representations of the heritage of the winery or brand (the most common material anchor for the heritage frame). By providing visual and textual information on heritage, the wine magazines add value to particular wines through links to tradition, historicism, and an anti-modern nostalgia (e.g. Kirschenblatt-Gimblett 1998; Peñaloza 2000; Zukin 2009). Genuineness was found in just over a quarter of both the advertisements and columns, often in relation to a wine being a 'true' expression of its *terroir* or origins, or to a winemaker being motivated by expressing *terroir* (rather than simply selling a lot of wine). Wines are thus provided with a halo of sincerity, often through juxtaposition with the instrumentality of the mass market (e.g. Beverland et al. 2008; Johnston & Baumann 2007).

On the whole, these findings underscore the omnipresence of authenticity in the construction of cultural legitimacy for wines, but also the centrality of the 'craft' dimensions of wine as material anchors for that legitimacy. The highly local peculiarities of soil, climate, grapes; the generations of accumulated skilled knowledge in the vineyards and cellars; the ethos of giving the purest possible expression of *terroir* and staying true to quality ideals were all common anchors that had been disentangled and decoupled from the mundane, commercial, and industrial aspects of wine production.

A recurrent anchor for all three of these legitimacy frames was the winemaker. Common examples of material anchors for the transparency frame included pictures of, or quotes from winemakers. Advertising for New World wines was much more likely to depict the producer than that for Old World wines was. Similarly, in the feature articles, New World wines were more likely than Old World wines to be discussed with reference to a specific winemaker or winery. However, there was no New World monopoly on the cult of the winemaker: wine columns did not differ with respect to discussions of biographic specificity for Old and

New World wines. The producer was a common material anchor for the legitimacy frame of heritage. The heritage of the winemaker (e.g. being a second- or third-generation winemaker) was far more common in the feature articles for New World wines (much like the differences found in relation to biographic transparency). Finally, the wine producer was the most common anchor for the genuineness frame: 29 per cent of wine columns mentioned the producer's character or philosophy (without a significant difference between representations of Old and New World wines).

An echo of former elite/low divides within the category of good taste thus relates to the maker as an anchor for authenticity and legitimacy, with New World wines more reliant on the winemaker as an indexical and iconic cue. More broadly, the craftsperson or artisan (in this case, the winemaker) is at the centre of the dominant, populist narrative about craft labour as a form of self-actualization and emancipation from the drudgeries of capitalism (Sennett 2008). This popular imaginary is typically inseparable from the celebration of the craftsperson as a heroic figure motivated by passion and skill, and of the craft thing as being uniquely imbued with authenticity. These myths of craft underpin a notion in the minds of consumers that the artisan's love, care, and attention are distilled in the hand-crafted product, leading to a willingness to pay a premium for craft goods (Fuchs et al. 2015). A consumer's choice of the hand-crafted good is the outcome of exercising a preference not only for authenticity and artisanal products, but also for the craft work itself. For example, Fuchs and colleagues (2015) have explored consumers' positive perceptions and valuations of goods that are marketed as handmade. Consumers may perceive the artisan's 'love' as embedded in the thing via the process of handmade production; this affective content then amplifies the emotional bonds experienced with and through the craft good. Yet, in order for that valuation to occur, the craftsperson must be present 'in' the thing, if only through iconic representations that provide a symbolic link to provenance (Grayson & Martinec 2004).

As legitimizing frames within the taste regime of authenticity, transparency, heritage, and genuineness offer a potentially high volume of diverse choices that comply with notions of good taste. All wines potentially have some form of geographic or biographic specificity, a history to their making, and some ideal to which it holds true. Looking across all three authenticity frames suggests the potential of craft attributes, and especially the craftsperson (winemaker), to be a device for the construction of cultural legitimacy and notions of good taste for both Old and New World wines. Yet, there are also differences, with New World wines more reliant on representations of the craft person as an anchor for legitimacy and authenticity. Let us now briefly consider the limits to which *any* thing can be craft.

The Limits of Craft

All wines, by virtue of their provenance, can theoretically be legitimizable through the taste regime of authenticity—even wines once considered beyond the pale. For example, consider a wine review (Beckett 2014: 75) of Turkish wine:

> There was a time when you couldn't have sold a Turkish wine…for love or money…because people would have been embarrassed to put it on the table. These days, however, it seems to be a question of the weirder the wine, the better; and if only one barrel has been made, better still.

Framing the Turkish wine as hand-crafted (one barrel at a time) consecrates it as omnivorous good taste, and affirms the cultural capital of the evaluator (wine writer, reader) who has exercised their capacity to discern quality without recourse to univorous assumptions about Old World wine monopolizing quality production.

Nevertheless, arguing against an essentialist account of craft (and authenticity more generally) requires attentiveness to the limits to which any wine (or any 'thing') can be rendered as craft. Despite the obvious material properties of fine wines that lend themselves to being explicitly labelled as 'craft' products (including traditional methods, limited production, and intensive, skilled effort), the term 'craft wine' has not emerged alongside the other small-scale, provenance-driven, impeccably sourced objects of desire for cultural omnivores, such as craft beer and spirits, artisanal bread and coffee, heirloom vegetables. Hence, perhaps, the annoyance of renowned wine writer Jancis Robinson (2016: np) at the seeming injustice of 'craft' beer and spirit producers capturing consumer hearts and wallets:

> I'm a bit cross. Cross about the word craft. How come all these niche beers and spirits attract the word craft as a prefix that bestows artisan virtue on them whereas no one talks about craft wine?

The answer to Robinson's question—why does no one talk about craft wine?—has at least two dimensions. The first relates to the established legitimacy of aesthetic distance in the exercise of good taste. In his research on taste patterns in French social classes in the 1960s and '70s, Bourdieu (1984) notes the prevalence of a 'disinterested' aesthetic disposition among the dominant group, suggesting its role as a form of cultural capital to perform, defend, or claim social advantage. The ability to adopt and deploy a disinterested stance vis-à-vis cultural experiences—to divorce appreciation from pleasure and sensation, and perform distance from considerations of necessity or compliance with conventions—is revealed as a means of both social positioning and the reproduction of social stratification.

While omnivorousness in the fine wine field may break down the boundary between premier cru claret and Slovenian orange wine as objects of good taste, performances of good taste nevertheless continue to abide by the principle of disinterestedness. The taste regime of authenticity frames a connoisseurial interest in not-yet-legitimate wines, or an intense focus on the pleasurable taste of a wine (both anathema to the 'disinterested' stance as it was adopted by Bourdieu's respondents, but typical especially of the natural wine field) as an omnivore's aesthetic distance *from* univorous snobbism. By the same logic, omnivores must also distance themselves from the faddish (a difficult task when marketers are perpetually trying to co-opt and scale up emergent, 'authentic' cultural forms). Craft as an explicit label is far too 'obvious' to be a credible point of attachment for fine wine intermediaries and intended consumers. When 'craft' is offered as an anchor unto itself (rather than invited as an evaluation through iconic and indexical provenance cues, as it was in the *Decanter* and *Wine Spectator* samples), the label jars with the discerning omnivore's distance from convention. Better to knowingly drink 'bad' wine as an ironic gesture than to appear to have been duped by promotional hype.

As a case in point, the supermarket chain Aldi introduced a range of 'craft wines' in November 2016 (Moore 2016), aimed at millennials and packaged with all the tropes of American craft beer: brown, 50 cl bottles with retro/hipster labels. Such market innovations attempt to capitalize on the perceived consumer demand for craft drinks and 'brands that come across as less profit-driven or less mass-produced' (Mintel 2016: np). The critical reception was mixed:

> Wine critics Charles Metcalf and Fiona Becket also gave the concept the thumbs up, with Becket tweeting that she had recently lamented that supermarkets did not promote craft wines. However *The Telegraphs*'s Victoria Moore said Aldi's "claim to be presenting the first 'craft wines' to a younger audience "don't ring true", adding that the "packaging was the best thing about them". Tim Wilson of the Wilson's Drinks Report agreed. "Craft beer is all about quality and provenance – these wines would seem to fall short on both counts", he said.
>
> (Mileham 2016: np)

A reliance merely on the iconic cues of authenticity poached from another ('lesser') cultural field is problematic. In deploying these tropes as an assertion of craft, without credible provenance cues offered for consumers' discerning evaluation, the Aldi products can be misread as vulgar, populist or fad-led marketing. Just as seemingly *any* thing can be framed as authentic and craft, so too can it be read as *nothing*, in the sense suggested by Ritzer (2007)—social forms that are centrally conceived, controlled and lacking in distinctive content.

Later in the same article, Robinson (2016: np) implies that the second part to an answer to her question has to do with scale of production:

> First-growth red bordeaux may be made in surprising volumes— perhaps 40,000 12-bottle cases a year at Château Lafite, for instance—and has become justifiably, if regrettably, a true luxury product. But the really mass-market brands such as Yellow Tail, Gallo and Blossom Hill are not craft but truly industrial products that sell millions of 12-bottle cases each year.

Despite Robinson's implied essentialist category of 'industrial' wines, even those large-scale wines may attempt to render themselves authentic, by disentangling and decoupling specific anchors to be framed as authentic. This is commonly done through the 'Our Story' or 'About Us' page of web pages (for wines and consumer goods more generally). For example, the Yellow Tail story (www.yellowtailwine.com/our-story/) is of a winery, family-owned for six generations (heritage), located in the small country town of Yenda, Australia (geographic specificity), that continues to uphold the 'family's winemaking philosophy' of wine as something that should be accessible and pleasurable, bringing together friends and family. Similarly, Blossom Hill's story (www.blossomhill.com/our-story) offers biographic specificity via their first winemaker's passionate belief 'that wine should be enjoyed not debated'. In both cases, the wine's genuineness is about holding true to a democratic ethos of conviviality; lifestyle supplants *terroir*. As with Aldi's craft wines, the intended meaning of these stories is likely to be rejected by fine wine intermediaries and connoisseur consumers, but not by those consumers for whom lifestyle is a more resonant point of attachment than provenance for evaluations of authenticity and experiences of self-authentification.

While a craft approach to production may be exemplified by small-scale production wines, it is generally coextensive with fine wines, which may even be relatively large-scale (as Robinson notes in relation to Lafite). Larger-scale fine wines have attributes associated with craft production and authenticity, including traditional methods (albeit requiring extensive decoupling from the mechanization associated with larger-scale production), the peculiarities associated with agricultural raw materials (local and annual variations, unpredictability and the finitude of growing seasons), and the hands-on artisanal interventions of the winemaker (especially, as the media study suggests, for the newly-legitimate wines). Representations of those larger-scale wines must thus provide credible, thick descriptions of their provenance, not only in their own promotional material but also (crucially) confirmed and circulated through specialist media, external quality devices, and the impassioned testimonials of experts, in order to render those attributes as available, legible anchors for consumer evaluations. More generally: evaluations of craft as authentic, legitimate, and desirable will always be contingent and temporary accomplishments. Craft is a product characteristic that will be evaluated as present and credible by *some* market actors working in relation to their specific positions and motivations; thus, because craft is neither objective nor fixed, there will be other actors (with other positions and motivations) and/or the same actors (with changed positions and motivations) who will judge the same product as being not-craft, or being insincere as craft (like Moore and Wilson's evaluations of the Aldi products).

The limits of craft are undoubtedly linked to scale, though not through a simplistic small/large dichotomy. Rather, the limits of craft seem to revolve around the thickness or thinness of provenance. Thin provenance stories—like Aldi's, Yellow Tail's, or Blossom Hill's—provide a veneer of context without making that context a significant part of the thing itself. In Geertz's sense of 'thick description' (1973), in contrast, thick provenance stories not only represent the wine as the thing-in-the-bottle, but also make the context of production seem knowable and available. Iconic cues give the impression of indexicality; the maker's passion seems to be tangible in the thing itself; the quirky minutiae of a wine's biography from grape to glass provide a sense of intimate, insider knowledge. Hence the centrality of stories to the authenticity economy.

Conclusion

In conclusion, I will summarize what the field of fine wine offers to our understanding of how craft goods and markets are organized. First, changes in notions of good taste in the fine wine field underline how consumer understandings of and desires for craft are embedded in larger social patterns. The rise of a culturally omnivorous repertoire of good taste has valorized preferences that cross former elite/low boundaries, and prioritized authenticity as a master taste regime. The value of craft goods is thus linked to much wider developments in consumer culture in fields ranging from food to fashion, home design to automobiles.

Second, and relatedly, by unpacking the non-essentialist character of authenticity, this chapter highlights that craft, too, is the outcome of contingent processes of negotiated evaluation. To understand the organization of craft thus requires an understanding of the motivations that underpin those evaluations, and the differential capacity of goods to furnish consumers with opportunities for the experience of authenticity and the exercise of good taste. Further consideration is needed of how some attributes are repeatedly selected and disentangled over others, how they are framed, and the implications for craft goods to reproduce or challenge existing hierarchies of value. What aspects of the context of production are repeatedly deemed non-consonant with value propositions in the authenticity economy? Whose craftsmanship is repeatedly singularized as a worthy point of attachment, and whose is not? In the field of wine, for example, there is a notable absence of representations of the low-skilled, precarious, and often migrant workers who often form the back-bone of harvesting. Just as others have observed of the narrowly scripted, fetishized way in which the agricultural workers (e.g. coffee growers) of the Global South are packaged for the Western consumer (Bajde 2013; West 2010), further work is required to unpack whose craft work counts as a device for legitimation, and how that affords unequal access to the value chains of the authenticity economy.

Finally, through an analysis of the representations of fine wines, the chapter demonstrates the work of rendering craft *qua* craft. Craft goods may have an 'original,' indexical moment of production (experienced by the maker; witnessed perhaps by a few), but the capacity to circulate in a wider market (regional, national, global) and maintain an identity as 'craft goods' requires the representational work of rendering proven-ance as credible, legible, and available to others who were not there at the moment of creation. If *any* thing can potentially be rendered avail-able as craft, it nevertheless requires the work of intermediaries—filtered through the authenticity taste regime—to selectively disentangle proven-ance properties, decouple them from the entirety of the context of pro-duction (and from non-consonant attributes), and frame those anchors as legitimate points of attachment for others' evaluations of authenticity and craft. The representational work of producers and intermediaries is creative, highly skilled, and reliant on specialist know-how, suggesting how cultural intermediaries might be understood as craftspeople of a sort. Thus, to understand the organization of craft (goods, markets, practices), one must understand the representational work of rendering things available as craft. This entails broadening the view of who is involved in making craft goods, beyond the mythical, lone artisan to include those intermediaries responsible for 'thick' provenance stories, and the consumers on whose evaluations the product property of 'craft' ultimately rests.

Notes

1 The discussion of 'thing' versus 'object' (Latour 2004) is beyond the scope of the chapter; suffice it to note that my preference for the term 'thing' to encap-sulate the variety of phenomena that may be rendered as craft (encounters and experiences; physical creations; spaces and practices of making; makers) reflects my position that craft 'things' are outcomes of socially embedded and contextually contingent processes of evaluation, interaction, negotiation; the essential craft object does not exist.

2 Let us not mistake these representations for actually undoing the masking of the human relations of production that Marx attributes to commodity fetishism. As Binkley (2008) has noted in relation to Feng Shui and the Slow Food movement, such strategic representations offer a fetishized de-fetishization of the commodity form.

3 Old World wines are primarily considered to be those from France, Italy, Spain, Germany and Austria; New World wine producers include Australia, New Zealand, Chile, Argentina, South Africa, the United States and Canada.

4 Information on magazine readership composition was obtained from the magazines' media kits (available online: http://content.yudu.com/A1qxnf/ DecanterMediaInfo/resources/index.htm?referrerUrl=http%3A%2F%2Fwww. decanter.com%2F; www.mshanken.com/winespectator/ws/WSM_Reader11. pdf), which cite various market research sources for the information: NOP 2009 for *Decanter* readership demographics and IPC Media Insight Decanter survey, January 2010 for *Decanter* reader hobbies; and MRI Fall 2010 Survey for *Wine Spectator* readership demographics and Mendelsohn Affluent Study 2010 for *Wine Spectator* reader hobbies.

5 The advertising sample consisted of 124 items (65 from *Decanter*, and 59 from *Wine Spectator*): all full-page or larger advertisements from four 2010 issues each of *Decanter* and *Wine Spectator*, for red and white still and sparkling wine and their producing regions, excluding fortified wine, liquor or non-drinks advertising and duplicates. The wine column sample was constructed by selecting one regular wine columnist from each magazine (James Laube from *Wine Spectator*, Steven Spurrier of *Decanter*); their 2008 and 2010 columns produced 50 items (28 Laube columns, 22 Spurrier columns because *Wine Spectator* publishes three more issues per year than *Decanter*), which were then reduced to a sample of 31, consisting of only those columns that focused explicitly on Old and/or New World wine. The features sample consisted of all features from 2010 issues for which provenance, heritage, *terroir* or regionality were explicitly mentioned in the table of contents description: this produced 12 items. My thanks to the University of Leicester College of Social Science Research Development Fund, and to Liam Voice for his research assistance with the coding.

References

Arnould, E.J. & Price, L.L. (1993) River magic: extraordinary experience and the extended service encounter. *Journal of Consumer Research*, 20: 24–45.

Arsel, Z. & Bean, J. (2012) Taste regimes and market-mediated practice. *Journal of Consumer Research*, 39: 899–917.

Arvidsson, A. (2006) *Brands: meaning and value in media culture*. London: Routledge.

Bajde, D. (2013) Marketized philanthropy: Kiva's utopian ideology of entrepreneurial philanthropy. *Marketing Theory*, 13(1): 3–18.

Beckett, F. (2014) Wine: Fiona Beckett tries some weird but wonderful grapes. *The Guardian Weekend*, 11 October: 75.

Bellavance, G. (2008) Where's high? Who's low? What's new? Classification and stratification inside cultural "repertoires". *Poetics*, 36(2–3): 189–216.

Beverland, M.B. (2005) Crafting brand authenticity: the case of luxury wines. *Journal of Management Studies*, 42(5): 1003–29.

Beverland, M. (2006) The 'real thing': branding authenticity in the luxury wine trade. *Journal of Business Research*, 59: 251–58.

Beverland, M.B. & Farrelly, F.J. (2010) The quest for authenticity in consumption: consumers' purposive choice of authentic cues to shape experienced outcomes. *Journal of Consumer Research*, 36: 838–56.

Beverland, M.B., Lindgreen, A. & Vink, M.W. (2008) Projecting authenticity through advertising: consumer judgments of advertisers' claims. *Journal of Advertising*, 37(1): 5–15.

Beverland, M. & Luxton, S. (2005) Managing integrated marketing communication through strategic decoupling. *Journal of Advertising*, 34(4): 103–16.

Binkley, S. (2008) Liquid consumption: anti-consumerism and the fetishized de-fetishization of commodities. *Cultural Studies*, 22(5): 599–623.

Botterill, J. (2007) Cowboys, outlaws and artists: the rhetoric of authenticity in contemporary jeans and sneaker advertisements. *Journal of Consumer Culture*, 7(1): 105–25.

Bourdieu, P. (1984) *Distinction: a social critique of the judgment of taste*. Cambridge, MA: Harvard University Press.

Bourdieu, P. (1990) *Photography: a middle-brow art*. Cambridge: Polity Press.

Brown, S., Kozinets, R.V. & Sherry, J.F., Jr. (2003) Teaching old brands new tricks. *Journal of Marketing*, 67(3): 19–33.

Byrkjeflot, H., Pedersen, J.S. & Svejenova, S. (2013) From label to practice: the process of creating new Nordic cuisine. *Journal of Culinary Science & Technology*, 11(1): 36–55.

Charters, S. (2006) *Wine & society: the social and cultural context of a drink*. Oxford: Elsevier.

Cohen, E. (1988) Authenticity and commoditization in tourism. *Annals of Tourism Research*, 15: 371–86.

Cvetičanin, P. & Popescu, M. (2011) The art of making classes in Serbia: another particular case of the possible. *Poetics*, 39(6): 444–68.

Daloz J-P. (2010) *The sociology of elite distinction: from theoretical to comparative perspectives*. Basingstoke: Palgrave.

Fine, G.A. (2003) Crafting authenticity: the validation of identity in self-taught art. *Theory & Society*, 32: 153–80.

Fourcade, M. (2012) The vile and the noble: on the relation between natural and social classifications in the French wine world. *The Sociological Quarterly*, 53(4): 524–45.

Fuchs, C., Schreier, M. & van Osselaer, S.M.J. (2015) The handmade effect: what's love got to do with it? *Journal of Marketing*, 79(March): 98–110.

Garcia-Parpet, M-F. (2008) Markets, prices and symbolic value: grands crus and the challenges of global markets. *International Review of Sociology*, 18(2): 237–52.

Geertz, C. (1973) Thick description: toward an interpretive theory of culture. In C. Geertz *The Interpretation of Cultures: Selected Essays*. New York: Basic Books, pp. 3–30.

Gilmore, J.H. & Pine, B.J., II. (2007) *Authenticity: what consumers really want*. Boston: Harvard Business School Press.

Grayson, K. & Martinec, R. (2004) Consumer perceptions of iconicity and indexicality and their influence on assessments of authentic market offerings. *Journal of Consumer Research*, 31: 296–312.

Grazian, D. (2003) *Blue Chicago: the search for authenticity in urban blues clubs*. Chicago: University of Chicago Press.

Hall, S. (1980) Encoding/decoding. In S. Hall, S. Baron, M. Denning, D. Hobson, A. Lowe, & P. Willis (Eds.) *Culture, media, language*. London: Hutchinson, pp. 128–38.

Holt, D.B. (1998) Does cultural capital structure American consumption? *Journal of Consumer Research*, 25: 1–25.

Inglis, D. (2015) On oenological authenticity: making wine real and making real wine. *M/C Journal*, 18(1). Available at http://journal.media-culture.org.au/index.php/mcjournal/article/view/948

Johnston, J. & Baumann, S. (2007) Democracy versus distinction: a study of omnivorousness in gourmet food writing. *American Journal of Sociology*, 113(1): 165–204.

Katz-Gerro, T. & Sullivan, O. (2010) Voracious cultural consumption. *Time & Society*, 19(2): 193–219.

Kirschenblatt-Gimblett, B. (1998) *Destination culture: tourism, museums, and heritage*. Berkeley: University of California Press.

Latour, B. (2004) Why has critique run out of steam?: from matters of fact to matters of concern. *Critical Inquiry*, 30(Winter): 225–48.

Leigh, T.W., Peters, C. & Shelton, J. (2006) The consumer quest for authenticity: the multiplicity of meaning within the MG subculture of consumption. *Journal of the Academy of Marketing Science*, 34(4): 481–93.

Lewis, D. & Bridger, D. (2001) *The soul of the new consumer: authenticity—what we buy and why in the new economy*. London: Nicholas Brealey.

MacCannell, D. (1989) *The tourist: a new theory of the leisure class*. New York: Schocken.

McFall, L. (2009) Devices and desires: how useful is the 'new' new economic sociology for understanding market attachment? *Sociology Compass*, 3(2): 267–82.

Mileham, A. (2016) Is Aldi's 'craft beer-style' wine a game-changer? *The Drinks Business*. Accessed 20 October 2017. www.thedrinksbusiness.com/2016/09/is-aldis-craft-beer-style-wine-a-game-changer/

Miller, P. & Rose, N. (1997) Mobilizing the consumer: assembling the subject of consumption. *Theory, Culture & Society*, 14(1): 1–36.

Mintel. (2016) *Attitudes towards craft alcoholic drinks – UK – February 2016*. Accessed 23 May 2016.

Moore, V. (2016) Aldi attempts to woo millennials and beer lovers with £2.99 'craft wine' range. *The Telegraph*. Accessed 23 May 2016. www.telegraph.co.uk/food-and-drink/news/aldi-attempts-to-woo-millennials-and-beer-lovers-with-299-craft/

Ocejo, R. (2017) *Masters of craft: old jobs in the new urban economy*. Princeton: Princeton University Press.

Peñaloza, L. (2000) The commodification of the American west: marketers' production of cultural meanings at the trade show. *Journal of Marketing*, 64(October): 82–109.

Peterson, R.A. (1997) *Creating country music: fabricating authenticity*. Chicago: University of Chicago Press.

Peterson R.A. (2005) Problems in comparative research: the example of omnivorousness. *Poetics*, 33: 257–82.

Peterson R.A. & Kern, R. (1996) Changing highbrow taste: from snob to omnivore. *American Sociological Review*, 61: 900–907.

Postrel, V. (2003) *The substance of style: how the rise of aesthetic value is remaking commerce, culture, and consciousness*. New York: Harper Collins.

Purhonen, S., Gronow, J. & Rahkonen, K. (2010) Nordic democracy of taste? cultural omnivorousness in musical and literary taste preferences in Finland. *Poetics*, 38: 266–298.

Ritzer, G. (2007) *The globalization of nothing 2*. London: Pine Forge Press.

Robinson, J. (2016) What about craft wine? *Jancis Robinson.com* Accessed 23 May 2017. www.jancisrobinson.com/articles/what-about-craft-wine.

Sassatelli, R. & Scott, A. (2001) Novel food, new markets and trust regimes: responses to the erosion of consumers' confidence in Austria, Italy and the UK. *European Societies*, 3(2): 213–44.

Schamel, G. (2006) Geography versus brands in a global wine market. *Agribusiness*, 22(3): 363–74.

Schimpfossl, E. (2014) Russia's social upper class: from ostentation to culturedness. *The British Journal of Sociology*, 65(1): 63–81.

Sennett, R. (2008) *The Craftsman*. London: Penguin.

Smith Maguire, J. (2013) Provenance as a filtering and framing device in the qualification of wine. *Consumption, Markets and Culture*, 16(4): 368–91.

Smith Maguire, J. (2016) The taste for the particular: a logic of discernment in an age of omnivorousness. *Journal of Consumer Culture*, Online First: 1–18.

Smith Maguire, J. (forthcoming) Natural wine and the globalization of a taste for provenance. In D. Inglis & A-M. Almila (Eds.) *The globalization of wine: the trans-nationalization and localization of production and pleasure*.

Taber, G.M. (2005) *Judgement of Paris: California vs. France and the historic tasting that revolutionized wine*. New York: Scribner.

Taylor, T.D. (2009) Advertising and the conquest of culture. *Social Semiotics*, 19(4): 405–25.

Trubeck, Amy B. (2005) Place matters. In Carolyn Korsmeyer (Ed.) *The taste culture reader: experiencing food and drink*. Oxford: Berg, pp. 260–71. [original material]

Vaudour, E. (2002) The quality of grapes and wine in relation to geography: notions of terroir at various scales. *Journal of Wine Research*, 13(2): 117–41.

Warde, A., Wright, D. & Gayo-Cal, M. (2008) The omnivorous orientation in the UK. *Poetics*, 36(2–3): 148–65.

West, P. (2010) Making the market: specialty coffee, generational pitches, and Papua New Guinea. *Antipode*, 42(3): 690–718.

Zukin, S. (2009) *Naked city: the death and life of authentic urban places*. New York: Oxford University Press.

4 Organising the Home as Making Space
Crafting Scale, Identity, and Boundary Contestation

Susan Luckman and Jane Andrew

Craft SMEs are organised spatially and operationally in diverse and overlapping ways: studio shopfronts; dedicated non-home studios with no public face; artist collectives or formal associations; home studios with some kind of physical shopfront; or strictly via consignment and/or online with no retail presence. Online supply chains and consumer shopfronts, alongside the marketing boon that is social media, have particularly seen exponential growth in the numbers of craftspeople working from home, often from the kitchen table. While homeworking has long been identified as a gendered phenomenon (Jurik 1998: 8), working from home today is a particularly attractive option for women accustomed to paid work, but now also finding themselves with caring responsibilities within the household. But while it is not only women who are fuelling this rise in home-based making and the artisanal economy, women, specifically mothers, are far more likely to be working from home. Drawing upon empirical data generated by a three-year Australian Research Council-funded study of design craft micro-enterprises, in this chapter we will examine the contemporary relationship between craft and meaningful work through the lens of the role of place (space) and time (history) in constructing home-based craft work meanings. What becomes clear is how home-based making impacts professional identity, including how makers negotiate getting other people to 'take them seriously', and how they frequently are required to justify to significant others that their intellectual, emotional and financial investment will one day pay off. All of this is compounded when female makers are working from home as a means by which to realise their desires to be more available to their children, for, as other studies have found – and this is supported by our own research – there is a strong correlation between female self-employment and the presence of children (see Duberley & Carrigan 2012: 630), and thus of the organisation of craft work around the home and family.

The Home as Economic Site of Production

Over the last couple of decades, enabled in no small part by the affordances of digital production and communications technologies, the middle-class

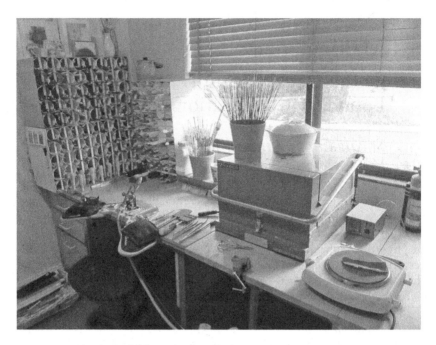

Figure 4.1 The 'Spare Bedroom' as Workplace
Source: Photograph Susan Luckman

home has become a normalised paid work location (Wajcman & Probert 1988), enabling post-Fordist business practices as part of a larger process of the "folding of the economy into society" (Adkins 2012: 621). In this way, the current explosion in women's home-based self-employment is part of wider socio-economic policies and discourses that celebrate entrepreneurialism to enable 'institutionalised individualisation' which, as Beck and Beck-Gernsheim (2002) among others argue, represents an enforced sense of personal responsibility for one's own success or failure in life in the face of the withdrawal of social welfare safety nets and the rise of precarious employment markets (see Luckman 2015). A key trajectory along which this 'extensification' of work across different spaces/scales and times (Jarvis & Pratt 2006) has occurred involves the enrolment into the capitalist marketplace of greater numbers of women via the 'feminisation of finance', which sees the "ordinary and normalised presence of financial capitalism", including its "entrepreneurial subjectivities", in the everyday of the domestic and homelife (Allon 2014: 13). Within the traditional model of capitalist economics as understood by Adam Smith and Karl Marx, the home was previously marked off as the market's 'other', a site frequently "defined in opposition to the economy", with all the gendered presumptions around women's unpaid labour in the home as a given enabling the public economy this gave rise to (Allon 2014: 20). However, the contemporary post-Fordist economy has seen this demarcation collapse with the effect that, as Allon writes, all "the boundaries it presupposes—between life and work, between production and reproduction, between home and market—are almost unrecognisable for most workers today" (Allon 2014: 20).

An emphasis on the aspirational discourses of 'having it all' and 'being your own boss' serve to normalise the financially precarious post-Fordist work practices enabled by the mobilities and 24/7 work affordances of digital technologies. As Gregg has written, the "freedom to work anywhere is the trade-off for constant contactability and the ever-present possibility, if not outright expectation, of work (although the psychological and affective difference between these latter may not vary so very greatly). ... the dominant utopian image is no longer freedom *from* work but freedom *to* work" (2008: 290). But while digital technology has profoundly changed the way, and larger context, within which it occurs, the actual newness of women's working from home can sometimes be somewhat overstated. Even leaving aside the essential work of domestic labour and social (re)production long predominately undertaken by women in the home, it is important to situate current practice within much lengthier histories of home-based craft making which have long seen the home as a primary site for family-based commercial production practices. Certainly, the conventional understanding of paid work as something we 'go out' to a specific office or factory site to do is in fact a recent phenomenon in the Global North, one which is directly traceable back to the major socio-economic upheavals of the Industrial Revolution. Prior to this, while one may 'go out' to tend to fields or undertake other labour in the community, the distance between one's site(s) of work and family space of living tended to be far less, and, indeed, often non-existent.

But despite this history, women's craft production wherever it has been undertaken has had to fight to be seen as more than a 'hobby' (Parker 1984). This image of women's craft as not art and largely amateur is reflected in common references to home-based micro-enterprise as a 'cottage industry'. Consequently, commonly undertaken as a form of homeworking, often part-time and all too frequently for little to no financial reward, craft practice continues to suffer from the long shadow cast by stereotypes of middle-class domestic-based labour being 'not a real job'. But even when money and labour have been traded, the very fact that it is often homeworking means that records of production have historically rarely been kept, further contributing to female craft production's erasure from economic history, and devaluation as 'serious work'. While women have been identified as feeling less empowered than men to take up offers of flexible work arrangements from employers (Gregory & Milner 2009: 8), much of the paid work women have traditionally undertaken in the home has been as self-employed or officially unemployed or in more exploitative working class employment relationships as 'pieceworkers'. In their book on paid labour under-taken in the home, Allen and Wolkowitz further attribute the image of homeworking as a "leisure time activity done for 'pin money' " as respon-sible for the idealised images presented in advertisements directed at housewives, encouraging them to 'turn hobbies into cash' (1987: 60). We find it interesting today to compare this advertising image to its early twenty-first century equivalent: the turn your 'hobby' into cash through 'serious' micro-entrepreneurial self-employment enabled by taking out a bank loan (Bank of Melbourne, Australia) and making sure you have a professional looking website (GoDaddy, United Kingdom). This is where the 'new' of contemporary craft making at home starts to emerge.

Today, contemporary handmade items, sold in galleries, at markets and fairs, and through Etsy-style online retail distribution networks, are positioned as an alternative to mainstream consumer culture (Anderson 2012; Gauntlett 2011; Levine & Heimerl 2008; Luckman 2015). Small, largely home-based handmade businesses are being championed as an answer to industrialisation and unsustainable global value chains – envir-onmentally and in terms of human rights. But the contemporary craft economy also fits in with larger neo-liberal patterns of individualisation of responsibility for one's own economic situation, which offer the high-risk precarity of self-employment as an alternative to more formalised and protected employment. Which, as we have argued elsewhere, serves to mask a new normal of increasing female un- and underemployment (Luckman & Andrew 2018). Indeed, it can become its own vicious circle: the expense of child care often traps makers seeking to scale up in a classic 'catch 22' – to get more time in the studio they often need more child care; to pay for more child care they need more time in the studio to make work.

Couple this with the unfinished business – in 'real world' practice if not policy – of genuinely caregiver-friendly workplaces and cultural practices, and it is no wonder then that we are seeing the recent rise of the figure of the so-called 'mumpreneur' (Duberley & Carrigan 2012; Ekinsmyth 2011; 2012; 2013; 2014; Nel et al. 2010). Ekinsmyth defines 'mumpreneurialism' thus: "Embracing, rather than contesting, the role of 'mother' it is a business practice that attempts to recast the bound-aries between productive and reproductive work" (Ekinsmyth 2011: 104). More than simply a category which encompasses any woman who happens to simultaneously be a mother and small-business entrepre-neur, mumpreneurs explicitly seek to creatively merge the "spacialities of mothering with those of business practice" in order to accommodate and prioritise the former (Ekinsmyth 2011: 105). In short, they are a "group of entrepreneurs whose self-defined rationales and drivers originate pre-dominantly or significantly from the realm of 'reproduction' rather than 'production' " (Ekinsmyth 2011: 104).

Middle-class craft-based 'lifestyle entrepreneurship' is currently experi-encing a moment of growth not only due to the enabling affordances of the internet, but importantly also as a result of persistent and growing social pressures around intensive parenting and a simultaneous lack of profound improvement around more family-friendly formalised employment relationships outside the home. Societal pressures around mothering remain powerful (Pocock 2003: 75; see also Ekinsmyth 2013 & 2014). In such a socio-economic environment, home-based micro-entrepreneurship can be a license to negotiate staying at home in a wider cultural context where, as Hochschild earlier noted, "the role of housewife has lost its allure, [with the effect that] the wives who 'just' stay at home have developed the defensiveness of the downwardly mobile" (Hochschild 1997: 244). As other researchers have noted of the mumpreneurs in their own study, "[b]ecoming self-employed [is] deemed preferable to being perceived as a housewife as it enabled identification with a discourse of intensive mothering, facilitating far greater engagement with children than was possible during previous corporate lives" (Duberley & Carrigan 2012: 629). This is important as it points to what is at stake for all women, not just those relatively privileged enough to make this choice. Moreover, as we shall see shortly in analysing our research findings by drawing upon feminist theorisation around work that is drawn from multiple intersecting disciplinary trajectories, the ongoing demands and expectations upon home-based craft entrepreneurs to be both available parents and successful makers, alongside the unproblematised social expectation that running a home-based business is an ideal way to enable this, gives rise to its own stresses, long hours and feelings of failure for many.

The empirical data informing the rest of this chapter is drawn from a three-year study investigating how online distribution is changing the environment for operating a creative micro-enterprise, and with it, the larger relationship between the public and private spheres. In this project, we recognise that not all handmade micro-entrepreneurs are at the same stage of their career, or have the same origin story. Therefore, this qualitative, mixed methods national research project consists of three parallel data collection activities: semi-structured interviews with established makers; a three-year annual interview monitoring of arts, design and craft graduates as they seek to establish their making careers; and a historical overview of the support mechanisms available to Australian handmade producers. At the time of writing, the project had interviewed 18 peak and/or industry organisations (involving 22 people), 71 Established Makers, and had completed the second round of interviews with Emerging Makers (Year 1/1-Up = 32; Year 2/2-Up = 26). The project employs this phenomenological approach to offer a rich 'insider' perspective on creative micro-enterprise. Semi-structured interviews of this kind are the best tool available for capturing the work/life stories of creative practitioners in their own words. The interviews are all professionally transcribed then thematically coded in NVivo as part of an inductive analysis process.

Spatial Boundary Contestation

Supporting much of the context around family-unfriendly employment as a key driver of the growth of women's home-based self-employment, being able to 'be there' for children, especially but not exclusively while they are young, clearly emerges in our research as one of the key reasons people decide to work from home. But such decisions are not made in a vacuum, and thus represent just one part of the overall negotiations makers engage in, or at least are willing to articulate:

> [I work from home both to be] looking after Miss B and [but also the lack of] affordability of a studio space, it's not viable for me at the moment.
>
> (Female, Established Maker, Queensland)

The spatial tensions implicit in such decision-making, and the trade-offs which are made, are evident in the statements from our research participants who have chosen to no longer work from home:

> I have moved house but I still have my own room as my studio, and what I also did was when I was at Brick and Mortar I started only working from Brick and Mortar on my work days there and I thought that was so excellent. I was so productive because people were watching me and, but … it was a job. I couldn't just walk off and make dinner early, … Or do the washing or anything, even though I really, really try not to do any of that on my days off. … The struggle is real. So since I did that at Brick and Mortar, when I came back home I really tried to contain everything to my office and that's worked out well, because the last time we spoke I said 'oh yeah I work from home and it's all over the house', like the dinner table and coffee table and I've really tried to stop that. …Even though you're at home you sort of [can go], 'okay I'm at work now. The washing can wait'.
>
> (Female, Emerging Maker, South Australia)

> I don't know if there was the background of having a scene that my parents had a space for making or whether it's just the habit you get into of you go somewhere to do what you do but I've always and this is an interesting conversation that I often have with * * * * because she loves having her studio at home and will just go for I don't know, 15 minutes out the back in the studio and does a bit and then comes back in, where I have always preferred to have my studio quite separate and go to the studio, somewhere else where there's not that interference or interruption of the day to day.
>
> (Female, Established Maker, Australian Capital Territory)

[Good things about working from home] no traffic in the morning's wonderful and coming from a job where I spent 1½ hours in traffic every morning, that's the best thing. But there's the, the bad thing is obviously the work/life balance and if I get into a bit of a rut and say I'm not feeling particularly productive it's very easy to lose track of time. It's very easy just to go, I'll unpack the dishwasher or I'll put a load of washing on and for a few months I felt like I wasn't doing any work. And so I got a timer and I started timing how long am I actually sitting at my desk doing work, and I was shocked to find that it was only 5 hours all up when I felt like I was there for 12 hours, because I was working into the evening there, I'm working so hard, I'm working into the evening. And realistically I was thinking, I've got to water some plants, I've got to do this and then it was just like, oh my goodness I'm losing my day. So you, you have to put in some strong boundaries, I'm not good at that at all, that's something I think I will never get my head around. But the perks is I can, I can do anything from home, it's your home, it's, it's nice, it's, it has lots of perks in terms of just, 'what am I going to eat today?' and it's just nice to be in your own surroundings.

(Female, Established Maker, Western Australia)

Plainly, the psychological as well as geographic demarcation offered by going 'out' to work, of having a dedicated work site, be it a solo studio, co-working space, studio shopfront or shared studio/artist run collective is profound. The physical break from the home, however, does not just take away the temptation to catch up on unpaid work tasks; in terms of pull factors people report the (personal as well as financial) value of the networks they enable; the creative stimulation and company offered by working with colleagues; as well as this, as we saw especially in the first interview quote, the Foucauldian self-disciplining of working in a collective space is productive for that maker, who does not yet have children.

It is therefore interesting to note, then, that for other makers still, it is precisely the capacity to control and organise their time flexibly – even if this means also accommodating household tasks or parenting responsibilities – that the majority of the parents, and most of them mothers, we spoke to reported as the key advantage of being able to work from home:

So, [moving my studio back home] means I can manage my time better. So, as far as family/personal life, and business life I can manage that. It's an hour each day of driving [to and from town/studio] and then you've got to pay for parking and so there's lots of pros of being at home, and the disadvantage is only that – the fact that – especially on school holidays … I just need to get away and I can't because they're going to follow me down to the studio – that sort of separation, that's all. That's the only [downside] – oh, and then also the [lack] interaction with the peers – with other creative people.

(Female, Emerging Maker, Tasmania)

...this house when we brought it had a garage which we knocked out a hole in the wall, put some stairs and made it part of the house, there's the laundry, there's [my partner's] computer desk and then there's all my stuff plus a storage room full of stuff. So the process is I get home from taking the kids and then I bring everything up [from storage to the kitchen table]. I madly pour, like it's quite intense just trying to clean the moulds, lay it all out, get it all ready, get my inspiration, work out what it is that I need, try and remember any custom orders which I've stopped taking because I just can't keep up and then I go for it, and then it's four o'clock and I'm trying to get it all downstairs before I go pick up the kids from child care at five, that's two days a week. So that was my method on a Tuesday and a Wednesday when the kids were in child care. On a Monday when **** was at school for a short day, I wouldn't do much pouring, I'd do other bits of stuff and make ear wires or answer emails.

(Female, Established Maker, Tasmania)

Yeah, definitely, because I worked – I set up my studio in the back room of the house initially. So yeah, it was quite handy. Although then, tricky as well, because your work is right there and so as much as you can work around having a kid, it's also there and you run off and just do little bits and pieces here and there. So, home life is not just home life, it's a mish mash of working.

(Female, Established Maker, Tasmania)

All this boundary porosity however requires constant negotiation and policing not just by the makers, but also the adoption of particular understandings about parental availability and spatial rights in the home by other family members, including children:

[The kids are] good – they know mummy's working and then they just piss off. They are so used to that all their life – it's like I will be out in the garden in my shed – I will say I'm going to go and do some work for a couple of hours and I will fit it – I will say you've just to amuse yourself but then I don't push it ... I won't ignore them ... it's part of our household – I fit my work in around everyone else really, but then sometimes it's just like – you have to be at home ... because it's normally about work. Because my husband is really supportive and he's accommodating on my work schedule because sometimes I don't spend all day, every day cleaning the house. Like some days I come here and I am working down the shed and I come up for – I am really disciplined I don't twat up and down. ... I love my work. ... Like somebody asked me once for an interview for something else – I can't remember what it was – and he said what's your ideal day? And I said my ideal day is I never speak to a human being and that

seems really sad but like it's not – my ideal day is walk the kids to school – take the dog for her walk and then go to the shed and just – nobody speak to me – that's my ideal day. So that's what I dream of – peace and quiet – that's it – I just want peace and quiet to make stuff.
(Female, Established Maker, Western Australia)

Conversely, working from home can also limit the potential growth and scaling up of design craft micro-enterprise as the negotiations of having employees working in a domestic environment can be equally fraught:

Yeah, and also now that I have staff. I had one of my staff members coming and working on the kitchen bench and it was just – it wasn't ideal.
(Female, Established Maker, Tasmania)

The physical and mental boundaries afforded by having a studio away from home provide a place and space for negotiations with clients, a sense of professionalism, and for some the ability to emulate the craft industry of a bygone era – for example the following person categorically stated they would not have taken on interns or apprentices when formerly working from home:

I love that [my studio is not] in my house like it used to be. It's a work space. I go there and when I'm there I'm working, and then when I'm home I'm resting; previously when I was working from home I had a real issue with getting in and out of work headspace. So, I don't know, I love that it's – I can just – it's just my space to be creative and to make, and have all my tools out and all those sorts of things. ... Particularly when people wanted to do a commission – wanted to come and talk to me about it [working from home made it difficult to present a professional front]. I used to [say] we have to meet at cafes and things like that which was a bit more difficult, but once I could say, this is my space and – yeah, people like to see your space, I find, a lot.
(Female, Established Maker, New South Wales)

However, it is important to note that precisely for many of the family-friendly and accommodating reasons listed above, business growth is not a focus for action nor indeed even a desire for many makers. In this way, at least, the actions of these mumpreneurs fly in the face governmental desires for creative micro-enterprises and small businesses to operate as akin to start-up companies, providing a proof of concept that can grow in ways that mimic the mythic success stories of traditional entrepreneurism, and answer policy dreams of further employment growth. The desire to not want to get 'too big', despite the rhetoric of entrepreneurialism, is something long noted in other studies of cultural and creative industries. For example, Baines and Robson, UK-based researchers focusing respectively on small enterprise, self-employment, the household and gender; and cultural industries, occupational transitions, self-employment and small-business survival have observed that within culture, arts and the media, "there has been a dramatic increase in self-employment and owner-managed enterprises' (Baines & Robson 2001: 351). But they also note "[t]here is some evidence, however, that a characteristic desire on the part of the self-employed and the small-business owner to be in control and maintain personal independence tends to limit their capacity to be enterprising, and generate new employment, in ways which policymakers wish" (2001: 350; see also Thompson et al. 2009). In our study, this desire manifests frequently around the issue of not wanting to become an employer, with all the responsibilities (legal, economic, personal) that go with this. Concerns over the burdens of employing others are exacerbated for makers who simultaneously fear that this additional business-side work will take them further and further away from the actual making – the thing they love and which they got into this to do in the first place:

> Well I don't know, I think I'd rather just find some Australian outlets first rather than get too taken away. I'm a bit fearful that if my stuff was really popular [and] it started to take off and then I'd become a machine, and it would be like 'oh, what was the point of doing this in the first place?'
>
> (Female, Established Maker, Queensland)

Temporal Boundary Contestation

The geographic policing of space for creative work versus the rest of life is clearly tied up with family and work commitments, compromises and trade-offs over time:

> [Negotiating work/life balance is] yes, very hard particularly because I work from home and I'm not a big TV person so for me I just go, oh I've got a spare 2 hours, I'll just and go do some work, rather than sitting there and not working or relaxing.
>
> (Female, Established Maker, Western Australia)

> [The negative of working from home:] Definitely the lack of structure within your day. It's hard to remember the – keeping to a schedule instead of saying I'll get up at like 9:00 one morning or something. If you feel like you haven't had enough sleep then you just keep sleeping whereas if you had a workshop booked for a certain time then you'd make the effort.
>
> (Male, Emerging Maker, South Australia)

Figure 4.2 At Home, but not 'In the House': The Custom-built Studio Attached to the House as Workplace

Source: Photograph Susan Luckman

Or, perhaps even more wearingly in terms of its negotiations:

> A: So I put my son in childcare on a Tuesday so I have all day Tuesday to do work because he's only three and a half, nearly four so he's not at kindy or anything like that yet, so Tuesdays are my day but he's also pretty good actually, he's a pretty good kid so when I say Mummy has to go and do some work, why don't you watch some TV he goes okay Mummy; so he's really good like that, we do a lot of stuff in the mornings together so that I can do a little bit of work before my daughter comes home, usually ends up being about an hour and a half before she comes home; but in the mornings I get up early and if I need to I can do my designing sort of stuff in the mornings, so I would say I would go with let's see – and then on the weekends depending on what we've got on my husband's really good in that I can lock myself in my studio so if I do need to have those days I can do that, so I'd say it would vary; some weeks it would be eight hours Tuesday and some weeks it would be more like twenty hours, so it's nowhere near a full-time thing and it'd be awesome if it could be full-time but it's not, so it is what it is.
> ... despite the fact that I have an excellent husband who's really supportive of my work, it is still really hard because there are still

deadlines and there's still kids that get sick and there are still kids that don't want to go to childcare in the morning like this morning and it's like come on dude, mummy has to work, you need to go to childcare; it is really hard because he's I just want to stay home with you. ….. so I don't usually go into my studio at night time because it's kind of family time and it's quite hectic as well doing homework and tea and dishes and baths and all of that. But yeah, there's nights when I've just gone you need to do everything for the kids and I'm going in my studio, but that's Christmas time when it just gets really crazy or the orders come in from a person that's going to pay money for the work which is always awesome because cash is – it's really nice sometimes to actually see your work equated to money, like real money; so whereas when you're doing consignment it's like you do so much work and then you pretty much get a little bit of money, little bit of money, little bit of money.

(Female, Established Maker, South Australia)

With the few external demands and temporal frameworks, including the panopticonic disciplining gaze of co-workers in a collective studio space, needing to self-discipline oneself to ensure time is spent on income producing making comes to the fore in terms of our home worker's understandings of their work:

I work at home. I've got my own studio in the house. And on my days when I'm working at home I have a very regimented schedule. I wake up very – I wake up at 6:30 and I go to the computer right away, and often start working still in my pyjamas, unwashed hair. And I get going right away – the more I can do before 12 o'clock the better. Then I normally stop at about 9:30, eat a crumpet or have a cup of tea, keep working, and then I have a shower and what not before lunch. And after I've reached 12 o'clock then I think, "Alright, I can leave the house now if I need to." I might deliver stock – I live on Pulteney Street, so going into the CBD means that I would walk – I don't drive. So that does extend my trip a little bit. Then I'm home again. And I literally work all day. It's very, very strict. I've spoken to some people at work who say that they just went mad when they did freelance, and they just found themselves cleaning the house or getting distracted. But I don't see anything like that when I'm at home, I'm just really, really focussed. I'm happy not cleaning all day …. I don't see any dirty dishes, I wouldn't do a – yeah.

(Female, Emerging Maker, South Australia)

In a nutshell, for many of our makers the trade-offs remain worth it, but implicitly speak of the need to self-create a family-friendly workplace for themselves, when legislation and, importantly, also workplace culture, has not brought one into being. At least not one with as much flexibility around family as they may desire:

> [The cons of working from home are] that I work at 12 o'clock at night. And pros if my baby needs a feed I am right there.
>
> (Female, Emerging Maker, New South Wales)

What is evident here is home-based self-employment as a very clear instance of temporal 'presence bleed' (Gregg 2011). 'Presence bleed' refers to the ways in which digital communication technologies have enabled the further collapse of temporal as well as spatial boundaries between work and the rest of life, with the result that paid work often increasingly leaks into personal time, which results in longer hours of labour. Such leakage is also present for many of our makers who leave home to work in a studio, workshop of other space as a means by which to access the right equipment, community and/or to circumscribe physically their creative work time. Many of our interviewees in this category report going out to do their creative work but going home to do the (online) management, administrative and marketing work at home in the evening.

Boundary Work as Identity Work

In Ekinsmyth's research on mumpreneurs she reports that her respondents believe that they are not taken seriously when children can be heard in the background when on the phone, with the result being that they go to lengths to avoid this scenario in terms of how they spatially operate within and beyond the home (for example, making phone calls while waiting in the car for the school pick-up) (Ekinsymth 2013 & 2014). Taylor and Littleton (2016) have written more broadly about the difficulty of reconciling precarious creative work with the claims of others, especially given the 'other-directedness' of feminine identity (Taylor 2010). For these kinds of reasons, for many of our creative workers, the external, separate studio was an important marker of their serious identity as a maker, rather than someone making at home as a hobby. Ironically, while for some this was a personal thing, reflecting a long-held desire for a 'space of their own', dedicated purely to their creative practice, for many the significance of the studio space was more about how they felt others perceived them and their practice. That going out to work in this way somehow comes across as serious in the eyes of others, in ways working from home does not. They also reinforce other research findings around the time of one's work not being respected by others when people work from home; rather than seen as 'at work' that they are at home makes them drop-in-able, available to pop-out for lunch and so forth:

[Friends/family who know I work from home also caring for children] think it's a hobby thing and they don't think, well around the people in public service they don't comprehend it until when they come to my exhibition they realise how serious it is and there's more discussion about it.

(Female, Established Maker, Australian Capital Territory)

But I have to say, friends and family don't understand that you're working during the day and they'll just pop in and it's nice, it is nice to see them, but they don't understand that you might be busy, it's like, now you work from home you've got time for me.

(Female, Established Maker, Western Australia)

[Having a separate studio space] makes me feel more professional and it's much easier to take myself seriously. So, when I first started I worked from home simply because I couldn't afford not to, and it's really hard to separate the two. It's really hard to – and I just – I found it really hard to take myself seriously. I was working – we've got a really long kitchen so I was working down one end of the kitchen and screen printing in the backyard and – it's too hard. It's – because you don't – there's no – you're not going to work. You're not leaving. Unless you actually get dressed and go out the front door and walk around the block and then come back, which I've been known to do – because otherwise you don't feel like you're going to work so you kind of have to do those weird little things to get in the right frame of mind and go, right, yeah. It's just – it's really important to feel a bit, I guess, more professional, like I'm actually going to work. … if you're working from home then it's so easy to get distracted. You go off and do some washing or you do the dishes or – yeah, it's just – I kind of couldn't take myself very seriously.

(Female, Established Maker, Victoria)

Consistently, our makers with any experience of working from home report that it is not an unmitigated positive, for many reflect on the challenges. Even those supportive, or resigned to, the approach often find that working from home, especially with young children to care for, is far from a 'having it all' option. Indeed, they find that the spatial collapse of boundaries between paid work and the rest of life means that often neither gets the concerted attention it needs:

So yeah the idea was that I would work from home and be the stay at home parent and I would be able to work from home and in reality that is absolutely impossible because I'm mum and if your kid is around you it's just really not possible unless you expect to get interrupted every 20 minutes.

(Female, Emerging Maker, South Australia)

> Oh I thought it [having a child and working from home] would be really easy, I really did, I thought oh she's asleep, and it's true, I do stuff and she's a good sleeper, ...so that's good, I've still got 2–3 hours a day, which is when she's home it's good. [but in answering how easy/hard 'managing work/life balance is on a likert scale, I answered] very hard, ... it is a hard challenge because just personally it's, there's a lot of pressure and then you've got that mother guilt thing
>
> (Female, Emerging Maker, Victoria)

These experiences again parallel other research (Ekinsmyth 2014) which finds that, despite the potent myths of homeworking, the reality is it is difficult, if not impossible, to simultaneously undertake paid work while actively looking after children. Thus, makers working at home, as we heard above, tend to organise their business time around the time children spend in childcare and at school.

The makers in this study are drawn from the wide range of craft and design disciplines. Those who currently work from home or have experience of doing so are from a similarly broad range. For while some forms of creative practice tend to be inherently collective – glass-blowing for example tends to require large, expensive equipment and demands two people, one blowing the other to assist – regardless of the number of people required to translate ideas into craft product, people from all kinds of practice report benefitting from the creative stimulation and peer support of other makers. Shared studio spaces and workshops are just one way to cultivate these kinds of relationships, but they are a key and valued one. One understandable, though not necessarily beneficial, trend we noted among young, emerging makers was the desire for their own solo space. With many of them still living at home and accustomed to eking out their own corner for studio space in shared space in a training facility, this desire reflects a more general desire for independence, including spatial:

> I think a wise person once told me that when you have – because I guess when you start out you always think oh I would love to have my own studio and then I was told that as soon as you turn on the furnace you age 10 years immediately and I think having had more time in the industry the gloss has sort of worn off the idea of owning my own studio and I think you see having a communal studio is much nicer – less stressful sort of way of working. I think probably the best scenario for me would be a facility like the Canberra Glass Works with the kind of vibe of the Jam Factory.
>
> (Female, Emerging Maker, Australian Capital Territory)

But, ironically, early in one's career is probably the worst time to want to 'go it alone', separating oneself from invaluable networks which can enable the sharing of practice-based skills, business ideas and profile development. But not all emerging makers see things this way; for some the desire to work as part of a complementary collective is driving the creation of a new generation of artist-run spaces:

> [my dream workspace is] a studio which isn't at my home. A separate studio where there's a few people working in different fields, like furniture, perhaps.
>
> (Female, Established Maker, Tasmania)

Ultimately, what this sector and these experiences reveal are the ways in which traditional understandings of work-life balance simply do not make sense for these (mostly) women. Defined as "the relationship between the institutional and cultural times and spaces of work and non-work in societies where income is predominantly generated and distributed through labour markets" (Felstead et al. 2002: 56), work-life balance is a highly contested concept (see Gregory & Milner 2009; Ransome 2007). Our research findings parallel others which have found that working from home leads to higher levels of work-life conflict, especially around the reality of it leading to longer hours of work, and work's intrusion into family space (Gregory & Milner 2009: 8). We would argue that the contemporary design craft economy, especially as realised by (mostly women) working from home – as distinct from an external studio or co-working space – like other practices of home-based enterprise enabled by the internet entails, as Ekinsmyth has argued, not only a blurring of boundaries and the movement of paid work into the home,

> but the redefinition of the use-value of labour so that immaterial, emotional and affective labour become part of the capitalist labour arsenal. …. Blurring occurs because workers cease to realise where the boundaries are, when one is 'at work' and when one is 'at home', when one is 'working' or not. This brings centre stage, early materialist feminist arguments about redefining work and the value-producing nature of women's reproductive labour as well as arguments about the falsity of 'separate spheres'; in a sense, the economy has caught up and realised how to capitalise on such labour in such places.
>
> (Ekinsmyth 2014: 1232)

Collapsing the spatial boundaries between the work of mothering and of one's income generating work is a logical, largely middle-class coping response to the competing demands of contemporary hegemonic personal and professional expectations facing women. For regardless of how any individual woman and her community may define 'good mothering', across much of the industrialised world it involves a greater level of 'presentism' than is normally possible with a full-time paid job undertaken at a site outside the home. Wider shifts in white-collar work practices enabled by digital technology, increasing expectations and demands for mobility, as well as shifting workplace architectures which see hot-desking, co-working and open-plan spaces as increasingly normalised, have created a window of opportunity within which some workers can engage in 'unofficial' techniques and activities to take back some semblance of work-life balance (Sturges 2012). However, as we have seen, working from home is no magical fix to the pressures of expectations around intensive mothering, availability and engaging in paid work to both bring in an income and also help to secure one's own identity as a human being with a stake in wider society and not just the family.

Home-based design-craft micro-enterprise is clearly an instance of Jarvis and Pratt's extensification of work with the overflowing "experienced both in terms of *the nature of work* (a temporal overflowing) and *the location of work* (spatial overflowing)." (Jarvis & Pratt 2006: 337) Those who work from home have to themselves bear the costs associated with running their business: the space itself, equipment (both for the home making-space, as well as paying to outsource more expensive or niche production techniques), utilities, and even organising their own business accounts, superannuation, insurance and income protection (if they can even afford these costs). They are also unlikely to be unionised, effectively covered by industrial legislation and have to be their own occupational health and safety coordinator. As we are hearing in our interviews, negotiating the complexities of this 'new normal (Berlant 2011) of women's homeworking is no easy feat. Although often not made explicit many of our makers feel the pressure to be 'a good mother', whilst not losing their personal identity. We also too need to be attentive, as Duberley and Carrigan argue more broadly about home-based enterprise, to the irony of how the contemporary design-craft economy "reproduce[s] the discourse of intensive mothering by hiding the tensions between intensive mothering and entrepreneurship through self-exploitation and limiting business size" (Duberley & Carrigan 2012: 644). What is clear to us through our interviews is that sustaining a making practice that is economically viable, spatially appropriate and mentally rewarding is a personal challenge that requires creativity, compromise and commitment. Craft and the artisanal as 'labours of love', often underpinned by an ethos of self, family, community and environmental care and the exploration of economic alternatives is, ironically, custom-made to be an exemplar of these wider economic trends around not only the organisation of craft work, but contemporary middle-class labour more generally. Therefore, and importantly too, we need to acknowledge that "work-life boundaries are not only gendered but are also mediated by people's socioeconomic position" (Gregory & Milner 2009: 10). In keeping with other research into who is best served by entrepreneurial discourses (Gill 2014), middle-class women, especially those supported by partner or family income appear to be much more 'free' to make the kind of 'lifestyle entrepreneurship' choice to explore the possibilities of undertaking creative work from home. But even these relatively privileged practitioners are finding the reality of home-based micro-entrepreneurship frequently fails to live up to the promise, and in practice becomes a constant negotiation of trade-offs.

Acknowledgements

This research was supported under the Australian Research Council's Discovery Project funding scheme (project number DP150100485 'Promoting the Making Self in the Creative Micro-Economy'). We thank Belinda Powles and Kam Kaur for their invaluable input and assistance with the research project and, as always, the makers who have generously shared their stories with us. Susan would also like to acknowledge the support of the University of Leeds via the Cheney Fellowship which provided not only space to write the chapter, but also the ability to attend the June 2017 'Organization of Craft Work' workshop at the University of Birmingham.

References

Adkins, L. (2012) Out of Work or Out of Time?: Rethinking Labor after the Financial Crisis. *The South Atlantic Quarterly,* 111(4): 621–641.

Allen, S. & Wolkowitz, C. (1987) *Homeworking: Myths and Realities.* Basingstoke and London: Macmillan Education.

Allon, F. (2014) The Feminisation of Finance. *Australian Feminist Studies,* 29(79): 12–30.

Anderson, C. (2012) *Makers: The New Industrial Revolution.* London: Random House Business Books.

Baines, S. & Robson, L. (2001) Being Self-employed or Being Enterprising? The Case of Creative Work for the Media Industries. *Journal of Small Business and Enterprise Development,* 8(4): 349–362.

Beck, U. & Beck-Gernsheim, E. (2002) *Individualization: Institutionalized Individualism and its Social and Political Consequences.* London: Sage.

Berlant, L. (2011) *Cruel Optimism.* Durham, NC and London: Duke University Press.

Duberley, J. & Carrigan, M. (2012) The Career Identities of 'Mumpreneurs': Women's Experiences of Combining Enterprise and Motherhood. *International Small Business Journal,* 31(6): 629–651.

Ekinsmyth, C. (2014) Mothers' Business, Work/Life and the Politics of 'Mumpreneurship'. *Gender, Place and Culture,* 21(10): 1230–1248.

Ekinsmyth, C. (2013) Managing the Business of Everyday Life: The Roles of Space and Place in "Mumpreneurship." *International Journal of Entrepreneurial Behaviour & Research,* 19(5): 525–546.

Ekinsmyth, C. (2012) Family Friendly Entrepreneurship: New Business Formation in Family Spaces. *Urbani izziv,* 23(1): S115–S125.

Ekinsmyth, C. (2011) Challenging the Boundaries of Entrepreneurship: The Spatialities and Practices of UK 'Mumpreneurs'. *Geoforum,* 42: 104–114.

Felstead, A., Jewson, N., Phizacklea, A., & Walters, S. (2002) Opportunities to Work at Home in the Context of Work–life Balance. *Human Resource Management Journal*, 12: 54–76.

Gauntlett, D. (2011) *Making Is Connecting: The Social Meaning of Creativity, from DIY and Knitting to YouTube and Web 2.0*. Cambridge and Malden, MA: Polity.

Gill, R. (2014) 'If you're Struggling to Survive Day-to-Day': Class Optimism and Contradiction in Entrepreneurial Discourse'. *Organization*, 21(1): 50–67.

Gregg, M. (2011) *Work's Intimacy*. Cambridge: Polity Press.

Gregg, M. (2008) The Normalisation of Flexible Female Labour in the Information Economy. *Feminist Media Studies*, 8(3): 285–299.

Gregory, A. & Milner, S. (2009) Editorial: Work-life Balance: A Matter of Choice? *Gender, Work and Organization*, 16(1): 1–13.

Hochschild, A. & Machung, A. (1997) *The Second Shift*. New York: Avon Books.

Jarvis, H. & Pratt, A. (2006) Bringing it All Back Home: The Extensification and 'Overflowing' of Work – The Case of San Francisco's New Media Households. *Geoforum*, 37: 331–339.

Jurik, N. C. (1998) Getting Away and Getting By: The Experiences of Self-Employed Homeworkers. *Work and Occupations*, 25(7): 7–35.

Levine, F. & Heimerl, C. (2008) *Handmade Nation: The Rise of DIY, Art, Craft, and Design*. New York: Princeton Architectural Press.

Luckman, S. (2015) *Craft and the Creative Economy*. Cham: Palgrave Macmillan.

Luckman, S. & Andrew, J. (2018) Online Selling and the Growth of Home-based Craft Microenterprise: The 'New Normal' of Women's Self-(under)employment. In S. Taylor & S. Luckman (Eds.) *The 'New Normal' of Working Lives: Critical Studies in Contemporary Work and Employment*. Cham: Palgrave Macmillan, pp. 19–39.

Nel, P., Maritz, A. & Thongprovati, O. (2010) Motherhood and Entrepreneurship: The Mumpreneur Phenomenon. *International Journal of Organization Innovation*, 3(1): 6–34.

Parker, R. (1984) *The Subversive Stitch: Embroidery and the Making of the Feminine*. London: The Women's Press.

Pocock, B. (2003) *The Work/Life Collision: What work is doing to Australians and what to do about it*. Sydney: The Federation Press.

Ransome, P. (2007) Conceptualizing Boundaries between 'Life' and 'Work', *International Journal of Human Resource Management*, 18(3): 374–386.

Sturges, J. (2012) Crafting a Balance between Work and Home. *Human Relations*, 65(12): 1539–1559.

Taylor, S. (2010) Negotiating Oppositions and Uncertainties: Gendered Conflicts in Creative Identity Work. *Feminism & Psychology*, 21(3): 354–371.

Taylor, S. & Littleton, K. (2016) *Contemporary Identities of Creativity and Creative Work*. London and New York: Routledge.

Thompson, P., Jones-Evans, D. & Kwong, C. (2009) Women and Home-based Entrepreneurship. *International Small Business Journal*, 27(2): 227–239.

Wajcman, J. & Probert, B. (1988) New Technology Outwork. In E. Willis (Ed.) *Technology and the Labour Process: Australasian Case Studies*. Sydney, Wellington, London and Boston: Allen & Unwin, pp. 51–67.

5 Smells like Craft Spirit

Hope, Optimism, and Sellout in Perfumery

Nada Endrissat and Claus Noppeney

Introduction

Pamphlets and manifestos such as the "Craftifesto"[1] provide insight into what craft in contemporary society might mean. Craftifesto proclaims that craft is powerful, personal, political, possible. Accordingly, craft is open to anyone; engaging with craft makes a difference and can challenge and change the world. It encourages alternative economic modes of exchange and asks us "to rethink corporate culture and consumerism." As such, the contemporary craft spirit shows parallels to the political heritage of the Arts and Crafts movement of the 19th and 20th century. Notions such as "craftivism (craft activism)" "guerilla knitting" or "indie craft" reflect a "new energy" and willingness to re-engage with traditional crafts to protest and critique capitalism, exploitative labor practices and ways of living (e.g. Greer 2014; Hackney 2013: 170 – see also Atkinson (2006) on DIY and democracy). In addition, the missing opportunity for self-realization and the experience of meaninglessness at work haunt (knowledge) workers whose cognitive and creative work elements are increasingly subject to deskilling and standardization (e.g. Sennett 2008; Crawford 2009). The resurgence of manual work and do-it-yourself craftsmanship is seen as an opportunity to restore individual agency, autonomy, purpose, and meaning in work, as well as the need to be part of a community – often absent in conventional workplaces of the knowledge economy (Crawford 2009; Sennett 2008). All in all, contemporary craft seems to convey a positive spirit of optimism and hope by compensating for this loss of meaning and by providing a means to challenge and resist contemporary ways of living. As Deleuze (1995) put it, "creating isn't communicating but resisting" (Deleuze 1995: 143).

In this chapter, we critically discuss the meaning of craft in independent and artisanal perfumery. Perfumery is conventionally seen as a luxury commodity. However, it was not until the 1970s that the manual, and often intuitive, work of perfumers was replaced by quantitative calculus based on systematic consumer research and rational odorant

Figure 5.1 "Craftifesto"
Source: © Faythe Levine, reproduced with permission

design, leading to a stark commercialization of perfumes. In recent years, a "back to the roots" craft movement can be observed. Often frustrated by the "tyranny of sameness" (Dixit 2009: 12), professional as well as amateur and self-taught perfumers look for artistic and artisanal approaches to scent making that challenge the power and production approach of the big industry. This chapter focuses empirical attention on the Institute for Art and Olfaction (IAO) as an increasingly important player in the field of perfumery. Founded by Saskia Wilson-Brown in 2012 in Los Angeles, the IAO is part science lab, part conceptual art atelier, part classroom and community center. There is a strong sense of emancipation, empowerment and democratization in the air, signaling a comprehensive "new approach to the olfactory arts" (Wilson-Brown 2012). Wilson-Brown and the Institute fellows are passionate about spreading knowledge about perfume making among people who are interested in artistic expression. Their mission is to "democratize" the craft of perfumery in formats such as the "open sessions" where "first timers and professional perfumers alike learn and expand their craft through direct action" (http://artandolfaction.com/education/open-sessions/). Moreover, the IAO works hard to establish artisan and craft perfumery as an alternative to the commodified products of the big industry, for example, by annually giving out The Art and Olfaction Awards and emphasizing values such as transparency and inclusion.

Our findings suggest that while the idea of empowerment and hope for change is very present, it is only part of the story. As the craft label is adopted by the big perfume industry to market their products as "handmade" or "artisan," craft becomes a way of selling more expensive perfumes, feeding into consumer culture instead of challenging it. In addition, the craft movement provides innovative new ideas that the industry incorporates and capitalizes on without proper compensation for those who have developed the innovation. In other words, corporations are able to outsource the risk of product innovation to the craft movement. Finally, the meaning of craft as way of resisting and transforming big industry ignores the fact that alternative structures equally produce power and exclusivity.

The contribution of the chapter is first, to empirically outline the ambivalent meaning of craft in the context of artisan and independent perfumery. Second, by linking the findings to the debate around workplace enchantment (e.g. Casey 2004; Dutton 1998; Endrissat, Islam & Noppeney 2015; Jenkins 2000; Suddaby, Ganzin & Minkus 2017; Taylor & Bell 2012), and the characteristics of aspirational work in particular (e.g. Duffy 2017), the chapter contributes to understanding the ambivalent nature of craft in contemporary capitalism.

The Meaning of Craft – from the Arts and Crafts Movement to Contemporary Craftivism

The meaning of craft comes with various connotations. While some consider it irrelevant, or eye it skeptically as a home and hobby activity – "a distraction and leisure pursuit for 'ladies' with time and means" (Hackney 2013: 170), others see in craft a central practice for individual happiness and collective well-being in contemporary society. Engaging in craft work signals a willingness to get involved in everyday practices of "activism, agency, and ingenuity, and a desire to act independently" (Hackney 2013: 183), to resist and reject the givens and to find ways to make the world anew (Gauntlett 2011: 20). Craft stands for power, hope and optimism (e.g. Bratich & Brush 2011). Craft also expresses a choice: instead of consuming what big suppliers provide, it implies making something by yourself, which leads to new ways of perceiving and dealing with the world (Gauntlett 2011: 19).

Historically, the term craft was first used in the 18th century in a political context, to express "political acumen and shrewedness" (Dormer 1997: 5) – implicitly referring to power and secret knowledge – connotations that are still valid today (Greenhalgh 1997). Important for the understanding of craft and its meaning as a "politics of work" are two Victorian thinkers of the 19th century: John Ruskin and William Morris.

John Ruskin was the first to express the idea that creativity and craft are important aspects of everyday life and basic activities to build communities. Ruskin was known for his disdain of exploitative, laissez-faire capitalism and 19th century industrialism as well as his care for the common worker. His ideas can be viewed as a program for the future – and not just as an idealized view of a lost past (Gauntlett 2011: 26). He propagated the idea of communities, local-level organic production, care for the environment, and individual consideration of each worker – rather than seeing them as parts in a machine (Gauntlett 2011: 26). For Ruskin, the division of labor led to worker alienation. However, unlike the Marxist critique of capitalism, which emphasized the socio-economic aspects of the worker as wage-slave, Ruskin's concern was that the division of labor disabled the worker's creative voice and opportunity to put a creative mark on her work. If people cannot express themselves in their work, the system will degrade. While Ruskin did not offer a "simple manifesto for change," he established "individual autonomous creativity as a core value which society must nurture, not crush, if it is to retain any moral authority, or quality of life" (Gauntlett 2011: 33–34).

William Morris took the idea of individual creative expression to empowered creative communities. Similarly to Ruskin, Morris seems ahead of his time and is described by some as a "time-traveller from the future" (Pinkney 2005: 18–19), particularly with respect to his care for the environment and sustainability. While he acknowledged that the Middle Ages, which he considered a time of "real community of human beings," had its problems as well, it did not "aim at degrading the human spirit" like the profit-grinding society of Victorian England (Gauntlett 2011: 35). According to Gauntlett, Morris's legacy lies in modifying and disrupting things "by inserting finely produced material objects, and ethical working practices, into a society accustomed to 'shoddy' products and exploitative factories" to ultimately "prompt a transformation of society, via grand and revolutionary plans" (Gauntlett 2011: 37) This sense of hope and optimism in the production of cultural products is "much kinder" than the view of later critical scholars like Adorno who decried the enjoyment of the popular cultural industry (Gauntlett 2011: 38). But "instead of telling them how dumb their lives are, he [Morris] offers stories, manifestos, songs, and objects from a better future, to feed the positive aspirations which he believes still reside in human hearts" (Gauntlett 2011: 39).

The ideas of both Ruskin and Morris were taken up by the so-called Arts and Craft Movement, which was formed in the mid 19th century, with influence until approximately 1920. Alienated by industrialism, the movement propagated a reactionary "back to manual, creative work" which held the promise of connecting people with their own sense of self, with other people and nature (Greenhalgh 1997). Greenhalgh notes that by "uniting the work process directly to the demand for a higher quality of life, they had regenerated the idea that craft was synonymous with power" – "the crafts were to be a politicised form of work" (Greenhalgh 1997: 35). The movement had its "best moments" at the beginning of the 20th century. It was particularly active in Great Britain, Europe and the USA – where the idea of "control over one's own labor" was linked to American notions of self-reliance, individualism and community. Later, American inheritors of the Arts and Crafts Movement added the democratic elements of the do-it-yourself (DIY) culture (Gauntlett 2011). The problem of the Arts and Crafts movement was that it led to beautiful, handmade products that no-one could afford. The idea of "do it yourself" helped to overcome this paradox, for example by distributing working plans for furniture or needlework in magazines such as "the Craftsman" (Gauntlett 2011). Gauntlett concludes that the DIY culture is part of the original Arts and Crafts message, but "processed through American optimism, and communicated in a cheerful and unpretentious way" (Gauntlett 2011: 49).

The craft and DIY sentiment 'make do and mend' was particularly strong during World War II but ebbed away afterwards as people discovered the delight of manufactured goods. Suddenly, anything homemade was seen as cheap and embarrassing and of 'lower-class' (Gauntlett 2011). But since the 1960s the craft and DIY culture has gained influence again. Associated with alternative counterculture and new forms of resistance – see for example Rozsika Parker on embroidery as a *'weapon of resistance'* (Hackney 2013) – craft and DIY today represent a critical stance towards consumerism, economic growth and environmental issues. For example, the rise of Punk DIY culture is "characterized by a rejection of the glossy, highly produced, celebrity-oriented mainstream of popular culture ... and declares emphasis on content rather than style" (Gauntlett 2011: 53; see also Spencer 2008). Facing a multitude of "bland" and "empty" consumer goods, Spencer notices "an increasing amount of independent and creative minds who care enough to go against the grain and produce music, art, magazines and literature that is truly unique – whether it is likely to sell or not" (Spencer 2008: 11).

The resurgence of craft activity since the beginning of the 21st century is therefore both a continuation of the opposition to mass production, capitalism and alienated, meaningless work and also a 'new' phenomenon in that craft comes with a new energy and 'attitude' and political agenda including feminism, alternative modes of production, consumption and exchange (Hackney 2013; see also Atkinson 2006; Levine 2008; Gauntlett 2011; Greer 2008; Greer 2014; Spencer 2008). As Levine notes with respect to participating in the Renegade Craft Fair in Chicago, "there was this exhilarating energy throughout Wicker Park... I knew something big was happening... We were redefining what craft was ... we were creating an independent economy free from corporate ties" (Levine 2008: ix–x).

This optimistic sentiment is also found among other writers, such as Greer (2008), who argues in her manifesto 'Knitting for Good' that craft can create personal, social and political change. According to her, "the creation of things by hand leads to a better understanding of democracy, because it reminds us that we have power." (Greer 2014: 8). Craftivism – craft as activism – reflects resistance and a political choice as to what to produce and consume (Greer 2014). In a similar way, the Craftifesto (see above) expresses the personal and political meaning of the movement. It shows that craft has become "more than just individuals making nice things: there is now a sense of community and shared purpose" (Gauntlett 2011: 63). This new activism is a form of non-confrontational, quiet activism (Hackney 2013); it works through a changed attitude to life and small but important (subversive) acts (Greer 2014). In addition, craft work provides meaning, purpose and the possibility for agency, self-determination, and autonomy – aspects that are often absent from contemporary workplaces (Crawford 2009; Sennett 2008). Hence, contemporary craft continues to carry the meaning of hope that Morris had argued for: 'hope of product' – in the sense that the product is meaningful and worthwhile – 'hope of pleasure in the work itself' – the pleasure of working with one's hands – and the 'hope of rest' – the prospect of relaxing after finishing the work.

Overall, the visibility of the movement and its activities is supported by the internet. It also fosters the communication, collaboration, and coordination (the new crafter is super-connected – see Hackney 2013) as well as the demand and sale of craft products and supplies. As a consequence, the internet has helped to democratize the idea and accessibility of craft and DIY and made it less elitist than in the 19th or 20th century (Spencer 2008). Web 2.0 and social media are central aspects of craft work today.

Contemporary craft is a statement against contemporary consumer culture and advocates meaningful, whole experiences – at work and life in general (e.g. Sennett 2008; Crawford 2009; Gauntlett 2011: 64). As such, craft seems both "useful and pleasing, ethical and political" (Gauntlett 2011: 69). It shows strong ties to the values of the Arts and Crafts Movement and its influential thinkers Ruskin and Morris in that hope and optimism dominate the discourse. At the same time, scholars increasingly call attention to a more critical reading of craft. For example, Hackney (2013) cites research that bemoans the commoditized nature of consumer craft with its "readymade designs" that lead to deskilling and prevent people from exploring their own ideas (Hackney 2013 p.173). Black and Burisch (2010) worry about 'craftwashing' and the co-optation of craftivism by institutions to sell and advertise their own services and products. In order for craft to keep its radicalism, the authors call for 'unruly spaces'. Suddaby et al. (2017) call attention to the enormous economic success of craft products and craft's trajectory from "a hobby-work to a viable form of commerce" (p. 290). Online platforms like etsy.com or industries and products like craft beer have grown dramatically, making it difficult to believe that craft stands 'in opposition' to contemporary consumer culture. These examples illustrate the contested meaning of craft – the 'darker' discourse behind the optimistic hopeful one. In this chapter, we set out to explore the variety of meanings linked to craft work in perfumery.

The Field of Perfumery

Traditionally, perfumery has been considered a craft. Elusive to science, the making of perfume was based on 'secret' knowledge, which was passed on to the next generation of perfumers by working together (Roudnitska 1982). Personally developed recipes were based on manual, often intuitive, work and experimentation using traditional techniques. The human nose was so central to making a perfume that perfumers are still today called 'noses'. Perfumers had access to only a limited number of (natural) ingredients and they were considered artisan craftsman, sometimes even magicians, as scents and perfumes in particular were thought to have "an inexplicable, pseudo-magical force" (Classen, Howes & Synnott 1994: 187).

From Craft to Industrialization ...

With the advent of industrialization, the production of perfumes changed. Today, perfumery is a luxury commodity in most of the Western world. The making of a perfume is based on systematic consumer research and quantitative calculus of last year's bestsellers and consumer trends. Perfumers who work for big international fragrance houses execute precise briefs including the final production price, reducing the creative element of perfume making to a minimum. What seems to matter most is the packaging, the marketing and the branding – not the perfume, the former essence of the product. Consequently, the release of a new fragrance requires large marketing budgets. New releases "... smell of fear. The fear of being a flop," as Denyse Beaulieu, a pioneer of perfume criticism and blogging, says of many current mainstream perfumes (Beaulieu 2013). The perfumers remain anonymous and disappear behind the marketing campaign. And while perfume formulas have long been "well-kept secrets" (Calkin & Jellinek 1994), reflecting a deeply ingrained culture of confidentiality, advancements in analytical chemistry (e.g. gas cromatography, mass spectrometer) have undermined the traditional mindset of secrecy. Even complex formula can legally be acquired by anyone with access to a well-equipped laboratory (Briot 2011). In the 1980s, different forms of formula piracy – imitations, twists or copycats – became big business: "The perfumery profession was shaken" (Calkin & Jellinek 1994: vii) and became an "incestuous industry" (Guillemin 2016: 25). Hence, professionally trained perfumers analyze, describe, and formulate scents in industrial laboratories along a clinical and rationalized process that is "abstract from the outset" (Aftel 2001: 134). This commercialization and industrialization of perfumery sharply contrasts with the traditions of craft and artistry. The perfume industry has "taken over from art" (Ellena 1991: 345).

And Back to Craft ...

However, in recent years, a "back to the roots" craft movement and spirit have emerged. Often frustrated by the "tyranny of sameness" (Dixit 2009: 12), perfumers on the fringes increasingly look for conceptual approaches to scent making and reinvent the traditions of artistry and creativity in what has become known as "niche," "independent," "artistic," or "artisan" perfumery. The movement challenges mainstream industry in a number of ways. Referring to the notion of craft, some perfumers stress the selection of precious, rare and often natural raw materials that allow for a particular signature of the scent. Other perfumers emphasize the substantial manual work that is necessary in a low-tech and low-budget setting. However, the notion of craft also alludes to the idea of empowerment and resistance to "big industry," i.e. large perfume houses that dominate and control the field of perfumery not only by launching a massive number of new perfumes each year but also by supplying the necessary raw materials.

Democratization of Scent

Around the year 2000, basenotes.com, today the largest online database and interactive perfume community, helped to spread knowledge about perfumery and perfumes to a large community of perfume lovers. Numerous blogs, forums and platforms followed, providing easy access to perfume evaluations and critique. Moreover, the active fragrance DIY forums help to organize bottom-up peer support by providing knowledge and "behind the scenes" tips and tricks thereby making it possible to become a self-taught perfumer and granting access to formerly "secret" knowledge. The internet also provides a way to order raw materials in smaller quantities. In other words, the market that was formerly dominated by big industry with very limited access for independent perfumers (e.g. with respect to knowledge, support, access to raw materials, etc.) is democratizing. As Luca Turin, announcing the finalists of the Art and Olfaction Awards at Esxence Milan 2017, noted: "The gates of heaven have opened."

Culturalization of Scent

The rediscovery of craft in perfumery coincides with the trend to culturalize scent as an art form.

For example, in 2009, Christophe Laudamiel, an exceptional perfumer who was then still working at the international perfume house IFF, created the first scent opera for the Guggenheim Museum in New York. Subsequently, his olfactory creations (scent sculptures) have been regularly exhibited at trendy art galleries (e.g. Dillon Gallery, New York). At about the same time, the work of smell artist Sissel Tolaas was prominently featured in international media. And in 2012, the first major exhibition to recognize perfume as an art form at the Museum of Art & Design in New York was curated by Chandler Burr, the former New York Times perfume critic.

The Institute for Art and Olfaction

The Institute for Art and Olfaction (IAO) is a manifestation of the changing landscape and the "explosion of activity" in the perfume field as Saskia Wilson-Brown coins it in her founder's statement. While, on the one hand, the market for mainstream fragrances seems to be declining in popularity, the rise of niche perfumery with its focus on craft production goes hand in hand with the discovery of scent as a cultural form and the exploration of scent as a meaningful expression in creative practice. In this vibrant landscape, Saskia Wilson-Brown (SWB), an artist by training and professional in the film industry, founded the Institute for Art and Olfaction in 2012. The Institute is part creative lab, part conceptual art atelier, part classroom and community center. In fact, the institute stands out with its strong sense of emancipation, empowerment and democratization signaling a comprehensive "new approach to the olfactory arts" (Wilson-Brown 2012). One journalist describes Saskia as someone "looking to learn the rules solely in order to break them as soon as she possibly could" (Nys Dambrot 2013). Saskia and her team spread knowledge about perfume making among people who are interested in artistic expression. Their mission is to "democratize" perfume making in formats such as open sessions to provide an opportunity for "first timers and professional perfumers alike to learn and to expand their craft through direct action" (http://artandolfaction.com/education/open-sessions/). Moreover, the IAO establishes artisan and craft perfumery as an alternative to the commodified products of the industry, for example, by annually giving out The Art and Olfaction Awards that try to put into practice values of transparency and inclusion. Among its fellows are

Christoph Laudamiel and Andy Tauer, two established perfumers who have come forward with fragrance manifestos. While Christoph Laudamiel in his manifesto "Liberté, égalité, fragrancité" emphasizes the importance of democratizing scent and educating the public about opportunities to interact with scent (Laudamiel 2016), Andy Tauer speaks directly to the craft spirit in his 2010 Perfumism manifesto (Tauer 2010). He calls attention to the origins of the perfume craft: "Perfumism is the art of crafting aesthetical perfumes, which live on the image that their deliciousness provokes in the mind, rather than one suggested on the wrapping. It allows rediscovering low volume, slow and traditional perfumery." He also emphasizes the difference in attitude by declaring "We craft our creations with passion and share the joy of exploring scents (…) Everyone is niche. We are not. We are perfumers who care," hence stressing the importance of craft, care, community, and the focus on the scent per se (Tauer 2010).

In what follows, we explore the meaning of craft as it emerges around the Institute for Art and Olfaction, focusing on the two sides of craft: its hopeful, optimistic intention, and its more critical reading in contemporary capitalism.

Craft and Democratization: Access and Empowerment

The democratization of perfumery, which manifests itself on the internet in blogs and social media platforms, is carried forward by the Institute for Art and Olfaction through educational, promotional and field-building efforts, rooted in a political attitude:

> I was interested in science, art and education, but it was almost a political decision, too. I thought that the exclusivity of such an industry was part of everything that's wrong with the world.
>
> (SWB)

The IAO is dedicated to providing access to perfumery to anyone interested in it. By doing so, it tries to overcome the barriers that are set by the established industry for people who want to be part of this community. In fact, it was the personal experience of being excluded that motivated Saskia Wilson-Brown to establish new ways of learning in the context of an alternative community:

> I wanted to learn, but I couldn't learn. I found access to be extremely limited. […] My approach is, 'Let's all learn together,' so I gathered the resources.
>
> (SWB)

In weekly sessions that are open to the public one can use the well-equipped laboratory at the institute's space and experiment with an impressive selection of natural and synthetic molecules. The format of the open session provides an opportunity for newcomers as well as experienced perfumers to "learn and to expand their craft through direct action" (IAO website).

The program attracts a diverse crowd of people with backgrounds in education, beauty, marketing, journalism, business and artistic disciplines. Some of them come with a particular idea for a scent (e.g. searching for a particular composition of rose notes that they could not find on the market), others are dissatisfied with their careers and looking for alternatives (e.g. wanting to explore the possibility of launching a perfume brand) and others simply want to experiment with scent in their creative practice (e.g. using scent as inspiration for creative writing). The Institute's educational program is thus used for personal and cultural as well as commercial and entrepreneurial projects. What these projects have in common is the search for a new form of artistic expression that is made possible through the access that the IAO grants as well as empowerment with respect to providing the basic knowledge on how to work with scents, putting into practice the political agenda of the Institute:

> And our weekly open-session workshops, are part of our mission of creating access, welcome artists, designers, filmmakers, kids from East L.A., both men and women. I am not particularly fascinated with perfume as a consumption project. My interest relates to my arts background. The institute is based on the potential to subvert the industry in some way to change how we think about luxury and beauty.
>
> (SWB)

The atmosphere is always very friendly, casual and supportive. Ideas and impressions are shared and discussed openly.

> After three hours in this casual, friendly, social setting everyone left with a small spray vial of their new scent, their materials, a formula, and an elementary understanding of the basics of perfumery.
>
> (Participant Rose)

An article featured in L.A. Weekly aptly summarized the Institute's democratizing and empowering approach by stating:

> Anyone Can Make Perfume at this School in Chinatown.
>
> (Bartlett 2015)

Craft as Challenging the Rules: Hoping for a Better "Game"

In 2013, the Institute introduced the "The Art and Olfaction Awards." Inspired by the Independent Spirit Awards in the film industry, the awards attempt to promote scents in the artisan, independent and experimental category in an unbiased, objective way.

> The original intention with the award was to create something that was fair. I mean, there's an award that's out there that to my mind didn't seem fair. So for me it was a challenge of … How do we do this better or in a fairer way?
>
> (SWB)

The judging process is committed to the principles of transparency and integrity, contrasting with the mainstream perfume awards, which are known for their bias in selecting according to marketing budgets and sales expectations, thereby reproducing existing power structures and serving as yet another entry barrier to perfumery. The IAO awards are positioned in clear opposition to this:

> Our goals are pretty simple, they are not lofty, other than to celebrate artisan, independent, and experimental perfumers. We aim to treat their work with respect, regardless of marketing budgets.
>
> (SWB in Berlin 2017)

This message motivates a constantly growing number of submissions to the awards. In 2017, the fourth round attracted more than 260 submissions. A balanced mixture of more than 20 experts from distribution, perfume making, blogging and other related backgrounds were involved in two rounds of intensive judging. Mark Behncke, who runs the widely respected perfume blog Colognoisseur, acknowledges how the awards live up to their high values of transparency (with respect to process and criteria) and blind judging (with respect to anonymity of the submission), making it possible for anyone to participate and win the award – as long as the scent convinces the judges:

> The short history of this award has already shown that even the smallest brand can bring home the golden pear.
>
> (Mark Behncke)

Growing numbers of submissions and a steadily increasing media presence also raise awareness and contribute to the legitimacy of the perfumery craft, which was once "rudely referred to as housewife perfumery" (SWB). In addition, the awards promote the search for new aesthetic qualities. Luca Turin, who is widely known for creating the genre of perfume reviews in the early 2000s and is a judge in the awards, points out that some submissions exceed the market leaders and set new landmarks:

…last year on the prizes, there was a perfume from Kuala Lumpur called Miyako that I consider to be one of the greatest fragrances I've ever smelled. These two dudes, two [Asian] guys who look like electronics engineers, have produced something which is insanely great. And they can do that, and Guerlain [big perfume house] cannot do that. So this is the way the world is now actually working.

(Luca Turin)

The fact that anyone interested in perfumery has now access to the relevant knowledge and raw material changes the game for the better, fueling hope and optimism.

… the worst is over. And why is it over? It's over because perfume has become something completely different. Not in terms of sales, but in terms of spirit, something has happened.

(Luca Turin)

Craft as Gimmick

At the same time, the notion of craft in the perfume field is contested. Established brands refer to craft for promotional purposes, reducing craft to an empty rhetorical device. Increasingly, retailers advertise perfumes as "crafted" (e.g. Fragrance Outlet). Thus, even a Disney scent is promoted as "a beautifully crafted likeness of ice queen Elsa" (www. fragranceoutlet.com/products/frozen-elsa-figure-eau-de-toilette-spray-by-disney?variant=1128081434). Independent brands that started out with a commitment to craft production and alternative aesthetic ideals are acquired by major industry players (e.g. Estée Lauder) and grow into chains with numerous outlets. A new generation of trendy perfume stores and even duty-free shops is devoted to craft perfume labels for economic rational. The perfumism manifesto by Andy Tauer, in which he called for a return to craft and emphasized care and community (see above), is criticized for being nothing else but a new form of consumerism and marketing. For example, in a post on base notes, one community member cynically describes the perfumism manifesto as "mere marketing ploy" (www.basenotes.net/threads/246277-Perfumism-com-what-do-you-think), paraphrasing the manifesto as follows:

… We will create perfumes, yes. But more than that, we will churn out our own endless stream of flowery marketing gobbledygook to obscure meaning and create confusion. You think Creed is all marketing? Just wait 'til you see version 2 of the Perfumism Manifesto!

(www.basenotes.net/threads/246277-Perfumism-com-what-do-you-think, post submitted 18th February 2010, 11:11 PM)

And even the IAO Awards receive criticism for being "just a marketing campaign for unknown niche brands" (the critical www.fragrantica.com/news/2016-Art-and-Olfaction-Awards-Finalists-Announced-at-Esxence-7780.html). Saskia herself reflects critically on what the awards actually achieve for the field and individual perfumer. She notes that many perfumers seem to be primarily concerned about visibility and sales improvements:

> …most of the criticisms is stuff like,… you need to be bigger; you need to have more visibility outside of perfumery … it shouldn't be something that only the perfume industry knows about. Like the whole point for the finalists and the winner would be if Vogue magazine covered [them]… If Joe Schmoe in Dubuque decides to buy the perfume because it won the award, that's the important thing really.
>
> (SWB)

Craft and New Power Structures

The Institute for Art and Olfaction has contributed to changing the rules of the game. However, what started on the fringes to subvert the power structures of the industry has developed into new power structures of influence and exclusivity. Reflecting on the IAO as part of the larger craft movement, Saskia notes:

> I think if people refer to a movement, they'd probably be referring to a sort of a movement in every industry towards access and democratization and sort of dismantling power structures, which I think the IAO has done or does, tries to do. Well, ironically creating our own power structure, so the irony isn't lost on me.
> Interviewer: Ironically creating our own power structure, what do you mean by that?
> SWB: Well, the awards, that's a power structure.
>
> (SWB)

As the public recognition and awareness of the Awards has grown, the subversive engine of the IAO has also developed into a system of influence relationships that distributes authority. Members of the IAO community become judges whereas others are excluded from this role. In other words, even if the judging process is fully based on fairness, access, and democratic values, it generates a new form of exclusivity, granting the Institute power and influence. In addition, the value-based approach of the IAO Awards and the importance of care and community that the IAO puts forward intensify the relationships between the people involved with the Awards. The community resembles a tribe with strong links and shared values. Yet, besides solidarity and joy, sadness and other difficult emotions are part of the community life as well. For example, not everyone can be a winner of the awards, and rejections are also part of the "game." In other words, the craft spirit requires energy and emotional labor that is seldom talked about.

> Oh, and then the hardest part for me is writing the rejections. It's horrible. I try to write everybody a rejection letter and it takes me months, you know, I'm still doing it. … And then they have questions, you know, it's just a lot of correspondence really. And then it's also disappointing, they're upset and sad.
>
> (SWB)

Sellout

The last element of the contested meaning of craft spirit is whether craft actually intensifies the neoliberal ideology of responsibility and risk by helping big corporations to outsource the necessary resources and risks for innovative new products to independent craft perfumers. For example, Killian Wells, a finalist in the 2016 IAO awards critically remarked that "*The big brands carefully look at the niche brands and follow suit.*" The craft movement invests the necessary resources and bears the risk for innovative new products that are then incorporated by big brands and commercialized for profit. Hence, the IAO and its awards is thereby *supporting* big industry by providing innovative new ideas and drive.

> What do we do with it [the awards] at the end?… At this point I feel like it's really becoming promotional, I'm a promotional arm for perfumery with the awards.
>
> (SWB)

The craft movement generates creative ideas without being compensated for it. In economic terms, the craft spirit generates a public good that everybody (including the industry) can harvest for free. Ideas can be appropriated and exploited by mainstream brands. It is therefore not surprising that precarity is an overriding theme in the craft field of niche perfumery:

> I mean everybody wants to survive and a lot of people are in it for the money. You know, joke's on them because there's not much money. But I think for most people it's more about doing something of value and of beauty, you know. (…) I mean it's extremely precarious when people say I want to quit my job and be a perfumer I say don't do it, you're crazy. You know, do what I do, have a job and do this on the side. ….

I have actually two consulting jobs, yes. Oh yes, that's why I'm always so stressed. ... I had to be realistic you know. I can't live like I'm twenty-one ... anymore, it just doesn't work. ... So I guess I'm not an example of someone who's completely given up. But my hope is that the shift will eventually allow me to do this full, although honestly, I don't think that's very realistic. I think I'm always going to have a day job as long as I'm running the institute.

(SWB)

The possibility for agency, self-determination, and autonomy one can experience in the craft spirit hinges upon an economic life outside the craft activities. Even if perfumery offers opportunities for valuable and beautiful experiences, it hardly provides the prospects many hope for.

Conclusion

Our findings illustrate the meaning of craft in the context of niche perfumery. While the hopeful discourse around democratization, access, empowerment and resistance to power structures is palpable, the meaning is also contested. First, the economic success of craft products challenges the "alternative" notion of craft. As has been highlighted, the craft label is often adopted by perfume brands to market their products as "handmade" or "artisan." As such, craft becomes a way of selling more expensive perfumes, feeding into consumer culture instead of challenging it – a phenomenon well-known in cultural sociology. For example, the notion of authenticity or the "real" (e.g. Duffy 2013) has become ubiquitous in contemporary consumer culture and so have "hipster" or "alternative" products (e.g. Greif, Ross & Tortorici 2010).

Another important aspect of the craft spirit is that it provides "free labor" for the big perfume corporations. The craft movement develops innovative new ideas that the perfume industry is able to incorporate and capitalize on without having to pay the craft workers for it. In other words, the craft movement allows corporations to outsource the risk of product innovation to the craft movement. While the collaboration between craft skills and industry has been shown to be a positive driver of innovation for other industries (Crafts Council 2016), it seems important to acknowledge that these collaborations are often benefitting one party (industry) more than the other (craft workers). As Banks (2017) argues in his recent publication, cultural industries are far from being democratic arenas. Instead, discrimination, exploitation, stress and unequal pay dominate. If craft work is to have a future, issues of justice and fairness need to be addressed – especially in collaborations between cultural workers and "big industries."

Finally, the meaning of craft as way of resisting and transforming existing power structures ignores the fact that alternative "games" equally produce power and exclusivity – issues that the actors are not yet completely comfortable with. Overall, while the engagement with craft seems to provide opportunities for meaningful initiatives and sensual experiences, it does require high investments of time, energy and money. Initiatives and activities like those carried out by the IAO demand a great amount of energy and emotional labor that no-one is compensated for. As such, the craft movement is defined by "free work" – an aspect that is missing in the dominant discourse around craft but that has been discussed in the context of creative, cultural, or aspirational work (e.g. Banks 2017; Duffy 2017).

Looking at the wider appeal of craft, we would argue that craft has taken on the form of enchantment. In the literature, enchantment or re-enchantment is usually discussed as the counterbalance to the rationalization (disenchantment or loss of enchantment) of the industrial age (e.g. Casey 2004; Dutton 1998; Endrissat, Islam & Noppeney 2015; Jenkins 2000; Suddaby, Ganzin & Minkus 2017; Taylor & Bell 2012.) Max Weber used the term "disenchantment" to describe a "weary nostalgia" for the "displacement of tradition, myth and superstition by reason" (Suddaby, Ganzin & Minkus 2017). However, through the resurgence of craft, spirituality and religion, a return of "magic," "meaning" and "value" to work and life in general can be observed (Suddaby, Ganzin & Minkus 2017). However, we advocate a more critical reading of enchantment, one that draws together the hopeful emancipatory discourse with a more critical, reflective approach (Endrissat, Islam & Noppeney 2015). Accordingly, we see craft as enchantment in that it provides *meaning* and the experience of agency and control over one's skills, which is empowering. It also provides *hope* – a central element for cultural workers to keep going despite the fact that their working conditions are often precarious (Alacovska 2018). At the same time, the notion of enchantment also accounts for the fact that those who are "enchanted" become partly *blinded* (Ladkin 2006). Enchantment is able to divert attention from existing power structures, inequalities and precariousness. Craft as enchantment thus romanticizes the craft spirit by pairing meaning, value and control with the hope to be reimbursed for the investments at some point, making the existing conditions appear less strenuous. From a critical point of view, craft has taken on the status of a seductive ideology, the new "creativity" for those who are looking for self-expression and community through work. At the same time, we have seen in our analysis of artists who are working for a large U.S. corporate brand (Endrissat, Islam & Noppeney 2015) that enchantment is *not* either empowering workers or controlling them: it is a mixture of both that relies on the complicity of the workers themselves. Thus, the third element of craft as enchantment is the active participation of craft workers in the creation of enchantment. For example, founding the IAO and actively creating a community, establishing strong relationships with its members (see the notion of "tribalism" e.g. Suddaby, Ganzin & Minkus 2017) and celebrating each other in the context of the IAO Awards ceremony would not work without the active participation of the people. Craft as enchantment thus represents the ambivalent nature of contemporary work (e.g. Delbridge & Sallaz 2015). On the one hand, craft work creates "spaces of hope" filled with meaning, agency, and creative expression. On the other hand, it entrenches such expression within the entrepreneurial spirit and quasi-ideological imperatives, foreclosing opportunities for reflexivity and critique. Craft as enchantment incorporates various, partly contradictory, meanings within it.

In this chapter we have tried to account for the ambivalence of the meaning of craft within the field of independent and artisan perfumery, paying particular attention to the Institute for Art and Olfaction. We do not claim to have shown the "full picture." Our focus is necessarily a restricted one. But we hope that our illustration has been sufficient to sketch out the contours of what we have called "craft spirit" and its parallels to other work forms such as cultural or aspirational work – all emblematic of contemporary capitalism. Based on this, we conclude that the vivifying smell of the "craft spirit" might come with a bitter aftertaste for those who are enchanted by the hopeful discourse without accounting for the ambivalent nature of contemporary work.

Note

1 The Craftifesto was put forth by the makers of the DIY trunk show in 2008, http://indie-handmade.blogspot.ch/2012/07/craftifesto-power-is-in-your-hands.html (last accessed 25.01.2018).

References

Aftel, M. (2001) *Essence and Alchemy: A Book of Perfume*. London: Bloomsbury.

Alacovska, A. (2018) Hope Labour Revisited: Post-socialist Creative Workers and Their Methods of Hope, In S. Taylor & S. Luckman (Eds.) *The New Normal of Working Lives*. New York: Palgrave Macmillan, (Dynamics of Virtual Work), pp. 41–63.

Atkinson, P. (2006) Introduction: Do It Yourself: Democracy and Design. *Journal of Design History*, 19(1): 1–10.

Banks, M. (2017) *Creative Justice: Cultural Industries, Work and Inequality*. London: Rowman and Littlefield International.

Bartlett, J. (2015) Anyone Can Make Perfume at This School in Chinatown. www.laweekly.com/arts/anyone-can-make-perfume-at-this-school-in-chinatown-6338043 (last accessed 25.01.2018).

Beaulieu, D. (2013) *The Perfume Lover: A Personal History of Scent*. New York: St. Martin's Press.

Black, A. & Burisch, N. (2010) Craft Hard, Die Free: Radical Curatorial Strategies for Craftivism in Unruly Contexts. In G. Adamson (Ed.), *The Craft Reader*. Oxford and New York: Berg, pp. 609–619.

Briot, E. (2011) From Industry to Luxury: French Perfume in the Nineteenth Century. *Business History Review*, 85(2): 273–294.

Calkin, R. R. & Jellinek, J. S. (1994) *Perfumery Practice and Principles*. New York: Wiley & Sons.

Casey, C. (2004). Bureaucracy Re-enchanted? Spirit, Experts and Authority in Organizations. *Organization*, 11(1): 59–79.

Classen, C., Howes, D. & Synnott, A. (1994) *Aroma: The Cultural History of Smell*. London and New York: Routledge.

Crafts Council (2016) *Innovation through Craft: Opportunities for Growth*. London: Crafts Council. (last accessed 19.9.2017).

Crawford, M. (2009) *Shop Class as Soulcraft: An Inquiry into the Value of Work*. New York: Penguin Books.

Delbridge, R. & Sallaz, J.J. (2015) Work: Four Worlds and Ways of Seeing. Editor's Introduction to the Special Issue on New Worlds of Work. *Organization Studies*, 36 (11): 1449–1462.

Deleuze, G. (1995) *Negotiations 1972–1990*. New York: Columbia University Press.

Dixit, S. (2009). Fine Fragrance Business Trends. *Chemical Business*, 23(6): 11–26.

Dormer, P. (1997) The Salon de Refuse. In P. Dormer (Ed.), *The Culture of Craft. Status and Future*. Manchester: Manchester University Press, pp. 1–16.

Duffy, B. E. (2013) Manufacturing Authenticity: The Rhetoric of "Real" in Women's Magazines. *The Communication Review*, 16(3): 132–154.

Duffy, B. E. (2017) *(Not) Getting Paid to Do What You Love: Gender, Social Media, and Aspirational Work*. New Haven, CT: Yale University Press.

Dutton, G. (1998) The Re-enchantment of Work. *Management Review*, 87(2): 51–54.

Ellena, J. C. (1991) Creative Perfumery: Composition Techniques. In P. M. Müller & D. Lamparsky (Eds.), *Perfumes art, science and technology*. London: Elsevier Applied Science, pp. 333–345.

Endrissat, N., Islam, G., & Noppeney, C. (2015) Enchanting Work: New Spirits of Service Work in an Organic Supermarket. *Organization Studies*, 36(11): 1555–1576.

Gauntlett, D. (2011) *Making is Connecting. The Social Meaning of Creativity, from DIY and Knitting to YouTube and Web 2.0*. Cambridge: Polity Press.

Greenhalgh, P. (1997) The History of Craft. In P. Dormer (Ed.), *The Culture of Craft. Status and Future* (pp. 20–52). Manchester: Manchester University Press.

Greer, B. (2008) *Knitting for Good! The Guide to Creating Personal, Social, and Political Change, Stitch by Stitch*. Boston and London: Trumpeter.

Greer, B. (Ed.). (2014) *Craftivism: The Art of Craft and Activism*. Vancouver: Arsenal Pulp Press.

Greif, M., Ross, K. & Tortorici, D. (eds) (2010) *What was the Hipster? A Sociological Investigation*. New York: n+1 Foundation.

Guillemin, C. (2016) *Law & Odeur: Fragrance Protection in the Fields of Perfumery and Cosmetics*. Baden-Baden: Nomos.

Hackney, F. (2013) Quiet Activism and the New Amateur: The Power of Home and Hobby Crafts. *Design and Culture*, 5(2): 169–193.

Jenkins, R. (2000). Disenchantment, Enchantment and Re-enchantment: Max Weber at the Millennium. *Max Weber Studies*, 1(1): 11–32.

Ladkin, D. (2006) The Enchantment of the Charismatic Leader: Charisma Reconsidered as Aesthetic Encounter. *Leadership*, 2 (2): 165–179.

Laudamiel, C. (2016) *Liberté, égalité, fragrancité*: a Fragrance Manifesto. https://static1.squarespace.com/static/55882eade4b01ea9a58bf34d/t/5875308ba5790a35507d1688/1484075147515/Fragrance+Manifesto+07.pdf (last accessed 25.01.2018).

Levine, F. (2008) Preface. In F. Levine & C. Heimerl (Eds) *Handmade Nation: The Rise of DIY, Art, Craft, and Design*. New York: Princeton Architectural Press, pp. ix–xi.

Nys Dambrot, S. (2013). www.kcet.org/shows/artbound/smells-like-artistic-spirit-the-institute-for-art-and-olfaction (last accessed 26.02.2017).

Roudnitska, E. (1982) 'The Novice and his Perfume Palette', *dragoco report*, 29(1): 3–14.

Sennett, R. (2009) *The Craftsman*. New Haven, CT: Yale University Press.

Suddaby, R., Ganzin, M., & Minkus, A. (2017) Craft, Magic and the Re-enchantment of the World. *European Management Journal*, 35(3): 285–296.

Pinkney, T. (2005) Introduction. In T. Pinkney (Ed.) *We Met Morris: Interviews with William Morris 1885–1896*. Reading: Spire Books, pp. 18–19.

Spencer, A. (2008). *DIY: The Rise of Lo-Fi Culture*. London: Marion Boyars.

Tauer, A. (2010) Perfumism, manifesto. www.perfumism.com/manifesto.1.html (last accessed 25.01.2018).

Taylor, S., & Bell, E. (2012). The Promise of Re-enchantment: Organisational Culture and the Spirituality at Work Movement. In D. Boje, B. Burnes & J. Hassard (Eds) *The Routledge Companion to Organizational Change*. London: Routledge, pp. 569–579.

Wilson-Brown, S. (2012) IAO Founder's Statement. http://artandolfaction.com/about/a-note-from-the-founder/ (last accessed 04.04.2015).

6 Crafting Social Memory for International Recognition

The Role of Place and Tradition in an Italian Silk-tie Maker

Maria Laura Toraldo, Gianluigi Mangia and Stefano Consiglio

Introduction

This chapter focuses on the role of place and local history in building the brand identities of craft organizations. Recent research on craft organizations has focused on the local context as an important factor for identity recognition and distinctiveness. However, an important but understudied aspect of this relates to the organizational use of both the sense of place and history and how visions of the past are used to support and legitimate organizational operations. In this context, local history is not simply regarded as a timeline along which events come to pass, but as a symbolic and cultural artefact that organizational actors deliberately manage and construct.

Using the empirical case of an Italian high-end silk-tie maker, the chapter investigates how high prestige associated with ties draws from the past and the sense of place, which become salient components of the product brand itself. Drawing from the notion of social memory, we explore how material and cultural practices performed by the firm provide common cues for interpretation of the past. Our findings suggest the multifaceted and ambivalent ways in which the sense of place and tradition is deployed to create brand singularity, related to: 1) the specificities of the place – firmly embedded in the city of Naples, the image of the firm and that of the city become reciprocally reinforcing; 2) the family-owned tradition of the firm, particularly palpable in the sense of hospitality towards customers. We discuss the theoretical implications of our study in terms of understanding the ambivalence of the sense of place between creative context and chaotic or shabby site, and the ability of the firm to capitalize on a repository of social memories, commonly associated with local context specificities.

The renewed popularity of craft is increasingly marked by discourses that emphasize the sense of 'provenance' of handmade objects, and connection with makers and their stories (Luckman 2015). Partly in response to increasing mobile and delocalized manufacturing arrangements as well as an alternative to mass-produced products, the contemporary consumer economy is witnessing a revival of craft and handmade practices (Luckman 2015; von Busch 2010). Mixing a sense of authenticity and community support with a broader critique of standardized products made in delocalized industries (Dormer 1997), contemporary handmade craft appeals to an unprecedented sense of connection with the place of production (Gauntlett 2011).

Scholars have examined how the sense of place gives meanings to craft production, while simultaneously creating rich opportunities for brand narratives, opportunities that are rooted in local tradition, folklore and local mythical themes. The attempt to promote the connection with the sense of place responds to what Hede and Watne (2013) describe as *brand humanization,* where the place may evoke feelings of admiration, pride or satisfaction related to unique local stories or personalities, folkloric or mythical traditions. As suggested by Brown (2014), to humanize the craft enterprise and commerce, companies often turn to narratives that celebrate the role of production places and history. Within the context of craft brewing, Hede and Watne (2013) argue that the sense of place provides an anchor for differentiation from mainstream beer brands. Connection with the sense of place is further strengthened through personal brand biography, where prominent historical persons – being the enterprise's founder or more generic local heroes – provide coherent plotlines to narrate the organization. As this study shows, craft organization draws opportunistically upon a sense of place and local tradition, and simultaneously creates conditions for revitalizing brand identity to carve out a specific niche in the craft sector.

Recent research on craft organizations has also focused on the local context as an important factor for identity recognition and distinctiveness (Brown 2014; Crawford 2009; Gauntlett 2011;). However, an important but understudied aspect regards how craft organizations draw from the sense of place and history to build their craft identity. Interestingly, craft organizations often rely on collective memories about the local history and the place to construct a historicized company narrative. Organizational memory, and the management of memories, has increasingly interested organizational and management scholars (Rowlinson et al. 2014; Anteby & Molnar 2012; Nissley & Casey 2002; Rowlinson et al. 2014). Researchers have explored how organizations use historical images and narratives to reach their strategic objectives (Suddaby et al. 2010), as well as to foster collective memories (Feldman & Feldman 2006; Rowlinson et al. 2010) and selectively remember or forget aspects of their history (Nissley & Casey 2002). Classical studies on organizational memory (e.g. Walsh & Ungson 1991) recognized that organizations often rely on mastering their past to legitimate and support their operations in the present. As observed by Rowlinson et al.

(2014), in large part this research has focused on how memory is stored, retained, retrieved and instrumentally used to improve organizational performance, privileging a functional view of memory and the processes of collective remembering. More recently, other research has focused on the social aspects of organizational memory (Bell 2012), drawing upon various traditions including sociology and history. Although there has been an increased interest in how companies use organizational memory for identity and image development (Hegele & Kieser 2001; Nissley & Casey 2002), less has been done to explore how collective memories are used to create and foster specific representations of the past by mobilizing a plurality of collective memories.

This chapter examines how craft organizations enable the formation of collective memory that draws from local history and tradition, and how remembering is used to evoke specific social imaginaries. We do this by focusing on an Italian craft maker specialized in silk ties. This is a small family-owned firm located in the city of Naples, a firm in which the place of origin is one of the main markers of distinction, but which nevertheless has a global reputation, as shown by its high-profile customer portfolio. The remainder of this chapter will unfold as follows. First, we will briefly discuss existing literature on social memory in organization and management literature, framing our argument so as to contribute to understanding how memory assists craft enterprises in sustaining and reproducing their craft-based identity. Second, we describe our choice of setting for the study, giving background on the tie maker's, history and present-day activities. Finally, we discuss the implications of our findings, highlighting the importance of memory as a strategic asset for company identity formation.

Social Memory and the Politics of Remembering

A recent surge in interest in memory in management and organizational studies (Bell 2012; Nissley et al. 2002; Rowlinson et al. 2014) has focused on the social practices of remembering the past, exploring the way in which organizations actively manage memory to build their brand identity and image. Social memory studies have highlighted that the conditions for remembering are sensitive to the social context in which those conditions occur. For instance, Zerubavel (1996) shows that remembrance is experienced collectively, and that the way people reconstruct the past is socially mediated. As the author suggests, individuals' experiences take place within 'mnemonic communities' which consist of different 'remembrance environments' (such as family, workplaces, etc.) in which individuals learn the 'rules of remembrance' (Zerubavel 1996: 284). This point suggests that diverse (mnemonic) communities are likely to make sense of and recollect memories differently, but also participate in a process of commonly shared interpretation within that specific group.

Collective memories are more likely to occur through material culture media (Zerubavel 1996). Scholars have acknowledged the importance of material objects in recalling events via representation of the past (Bell 2012; Mistzal 2003; Nissley et al. 2002). In her account of social remembering, Mistzal (2003) observes that cultural artefacts are essential to establishing relationships with the past; social remembering, in this view, is a social experience that takes place interactively supported by material cues that are important both as reflections of and drivers of wider representation of the past. In a similar vein, Nissley and Casey (2002) show how corporate museums exhibitions use artefacts in conjunction with oral and written narration to construct and convey the company's history and image. Drawing from the notion of the 'politics of memory' (Yanow 1998), these authors show how objects are harnessed by a politics of 'exhibition of the organizational memory' that is focused on maintaining, fostering and controlling corporate identity. In particular, it is suggested that organizations deploy a politics of remembering as well as a politics of forgetting (deliberately choosing objects that are worth displaying and not exhibiting those that are not); at the same time, organizations also engage in a 'politics of imagining', which, according to Nissley and Casey (2002), has a temporal connotation. The politics of imagining is conceived as 'situated somewhere along the future-end of the continuum' (Nissley & Casey 2002: 41), whereas politics of remembering and forgetting are anchored in the past as an attempt to foster future imagining.

Thus, while companies can strategically use memory to encourage imagining, this appears to be primarily aimed at forecasting future experiences. Similarly, Johansson and Toraldo (2015) show that imagination and the imaginary constitute key resources of contemporary consumption, particularly when directed to fostering a sense of anticipation in the consumer. By suggesting certain types of experience, discursive representations are able to evoke imaginaries associated with specific feelings, sensations and social values. Although these studies recognize the importance of the imaginary for commercialization purposes, less has been done to explore how specific memories are mobilized drawing on the sense of place and history. In the next section, we turn our attention to the relationship between place and craft, and the engagement of craft organizations with local history and traditions of local making.

Place, History and Craft Organizations

Memories connect together experiences that refer to evocation of place and the remembering of place. Places are often used to facilitate remembering (Bell 2012) and one could argue that the formation of more perceptual memories is often embedded in place encounters and their evocation (Rodaway 1994). For instance, Rodaway (1994) shows how olfactory or visual memory often occur by means of association with specific environments, which provide – consciously or unconsciously – richer recall of the experiences. Because memory is often closely related to particular places, whether lived or imagined, and their emotional associations, we focus on how organizations are able to draw from a range of collective memories associated with place that engender interest in the artefact for the consumer.

The key role of place in stimulating memories has been acknowledged in a range of disciplines, including tourism studies (McClinchey 2016), urban and leisure studies, and marketing and management studies. Studies on craft have recognized the importance of place and sense of place but less has been done to explore how the sense of place can assist craft organizations to stimulate specific memories associated with the local context. The 'localist' spin in craft seem to be in tune with contemporary consumer culture, and the increased interest in authentic, small-scale and original objects with a local connection (Herzfeld 2015; 2004).

Craft tradition and craft makers may then be co-constituting and imprinting places. Along these lines, some recent experiments have focused on revitalizing urban and suburban settings, promoting regional craft-based traditions. 'Craft quartiers' have appeared in Manchester while 'craft towns' have been created, such as Farnham in Surrey, emphasising the local pottery tradition (Brown 2014). These initiatives show that the sense of place is increasingly used for promoting craft tourism, using authenticity and local craft skills as tools for destination management and place marketing. Furthermore, the promotion of place provides insights into the local production practices and methods and the history of materials; it is suggested that place provides site-specific inspiration (Brown 2014), influenced by the cultural and social milieu. As our case shows, designer-makers strongly root their practices in the urban pattern and are influenced by what is original, special, unique and of the place.

In parallel, local history may also be a source of influence for designers, production and commercialization. Ranisio, for example, argues that handmade craft cannot be disentangled from local history, as historical facts become prominent in the revitalization, establishment, and maintenance of craft makers and their brand identity (Ranisio 2014). Here, we explore the role of places and objects, such as cities, or family traditions – and the discourses around them – through a material focus, in which the crafted object constructs a relationship by evoking specific social memories.

Empirical Background and Method

The empirical focus of this chapter is a high-end tie producer located in the city of Naples. The firm is one the most prestigious handmade tie producers and tailoring brands in Italy, renowned for its use of high-quality raw materials and a hand-crafted process, as well as for its exclusive garments, which have contributed to positioning it among Italy's luxury brands. Through time, the original small boutique acquired an international reputation, especially after an Italian President, Francesco Cossiga, developed the habit of offering its ties during his official visits to (male) heads of state around the world. Founded at the beginning of the twentieth century, it is a third- generation family-owned company, currently managed by the owner, who is in charge of operations and the design process; he has also been the key person in building the brand identity in recent years. Originally, the boutique specialized in the production of nightshirts, importing exclusive products from England, at a time in which elegance for men was inspired by British fashion and style. The shop opened in Piazza Vittoria, on the elegant Riviera di Chiaia, becoming a '*small corner of England in Naples*'.

Over time, the owners have cultivated a distinguished 'Neapolitan production' image with a pronounced 'British connotation'. Elegance has become the main distinguishing feature associated with this brand. Today the boutique has a precise connotation, which in the owner's words translates into the formula of '*casual elegance*'. Despite increasing growth, the production process is still carried out in workshops in the Campania region, where a small team of highly specialized seamstresses work on manufacturing.

Although there is high demand for the product from customers, the firm has not been transformed into a big brand. It is still a small boutique, producing artisanal products. However, the company has several showrooms and small shops around the world: five showrooms in Milan, Lugano, London, Tokyo and Baku, and seventeen smaller shops elsewhere in the world. The ability to sustain the tradition of making, represented by handcrafted production and a spirit firmly anchored in past values and the city of Naples, with increasing international recognition, makes this firm an interesting site of analysis.

Our methodology is therefore analysis of a single qualitative case study. Two of the authors visited the production workshops and spent time there documenting the organization's daily processes by means of observations, fieldnotes and photographs. Semi-structured interviews were conducted with the owner and manager of the firm. Through these interviews, it was possible to understand the role of place in building the organizational brand, how the family tradition influences the company's identity, and how the past is remembered and recounted by the company to serve its company narrative. During the interviews, we guided conversation towards the history of the firm, with the aim of understanding the extent to which the past is used to give legitimacy to present-day company operations, and what the most recurrent memories of the firm's past and tradition are in that process. The interviews typically lasted about one hour and were tape-recorded.

In addition, archive documents – in particular, personal correspondence between the owner and celebrities, politicians and key figures – were consulted. To track the history and the present-day activities of the firm, websites and published materials were also consulted. These data provided further information on the origins and history of the firm that complemented the information elicited from the interviews.

Findings

Vachhani (2013) suggests that the global revival of craft is marked by the increasing presence of objects that evoke memories from the past. These contribute to underpinning the exceptional qualities of craft products, which act as a reservoir of historical and symbolic meanings (Crawford 2009; Dormer 1997). Our findings show that textual, material and oral memory assisted in constructing a sense of brand identity based on craft. As a response to standardized products and loss of tradition, the tie producer often promoted values of heritage and family, rooting his craft organization in local history.

The company identity was built by recalling memories of a local past, accomplished by referencing specific images or events, which elicited interest and commitment from different communities. The sense of place and tradition was deployed in ambivalent ways, using the rhetorical power of the 'past' (Zundel et al. 2016) to mobilize a plurality of social imaginaries. Our results suggested two key thematics linked to the firm's use of memories, related to:

- Historical and present-day episodes occurring in the local context
- The firm's family tradition and values

Analysis of these two themes led us to identify four primary repository of memories which are associated with historical and present-day episodes occurring in the local context:

1) the glorious past and local creativity, and 2) the local place as shabby and messy

These were anchored into the firm's family tradition and values, manifest in:

3) the practice of hospitality, warmth and openness, and 4) slow-paced selling and distribution.

Memories associated with these themes often revealed tensions. For example, memories relating to the local context revealed tensions about the city of Naples, as a place rich in history and heritage versus a context characterized by hidden powers and poor efficiency. These contrasting repositories of memories were differently mobilized and at times some emerged more strongly than the others.

Historical and Present-day Episodes in the Local Context

The firm tied its activities very closely to a sense of place, both conferring value on the specific qualities of the region and building its identity from that region's cultural image. The notion of place was considered both strategically important and imbued with a sense of non-economic value. The company being firmly embedded in the city of Naples, its image and that of the city seemed to be reciprocally reinforcing; the history and the glorious past of the city was often mobilized to foster representations of craft organization as built on local (historical) craft tradition.

> My grandfather used to say: the sartorial tradition is Neapolitan, but textiles have to be from England… the famous Grand Tour. The British were coming here to take drops of culture. Wherever I go in London visiting antique markets, I find images of Naples….

A key aspect that emerged from analysis of the interviews concerned the role of the handmade sartorial tradition of Naples. Several craft makers started their venture in Naples at the beginning of the 20th century (e.g. Gutteridge men's clothing). The city became renowned for producing tailored artisanal products and many Neapolitan boutiques specialized in the production of nightshirts and gloves. Accordingly, the firm engaged with the local by building a narrative based on the cultural and geographical expertise in making craft products.

> Here in Naples we have had this great tradition of craft since forever. Everything in Naples was tailor-made: ties, shoes, gloves, even tailored socks with the initials of the buyers' name or family emblem sewn on them… I remember when I was a child, I was eleven years old and my first job was to bring shirts to the 'cifraie'… there were several workshops where some ladies were sewing extraordinary things: little roses, crowns and every sort of personalized decoration…

A further connection with the city of Naples was made by using available historical resources from the city's past. The firm used visual images and visuality to mark a connection with that past; material objects and spatial arrangements sought to stimulate memories of a great past. In the upscale boutique, ties were not simply an item for sale exhibited in a transparent drawer, where it was possible to choose from among different types of tie. Instead, the ties acted as material cues through which to construct

Figure 6.1 The Tie Showcase Creates a Connection with the Past

a relation with the past, in this case associated with the cultural status of some star clients, such as Luchino Visconti, Aristotle Onassis and Kennedy.

A similar sense of history was conveyed by the display spaces in the boutique. Antique furniture in wood, lamps and decorations all made the small boutique on the Riviera di Chiaia a very unique place. When the customer enters, they have the feeling of jumping right back into the past. The small boutique of twenty square meters reminds the visitor of memories of Neapolitan high society members and their peaceful stroll along the evocative waterfront. Décor and furniture date back to the beginning of the 20th century and the boutique has gone through historical events:

> the two world wars, the decline of the ancient nobility and the appearance of the new middle class with the advent of the American products that bring substantial changes to fashion.
>
> (Official website 2017)

The firm deliberately refers to the history of its setting, bringing local values and traditions alive in the present. This is further strengthened by use of the Bourbon emblem, which is right on the front wall of the boutique. As objectified culture, the emblem reminds one of a specific historical time during the history of Naples. With the Bourbon dynasty, the Kingdom of Naples experienced an era of grandeur. Remembered as an enlightened monarchy, the Bourbons made Naples an important capital, marked by industrial advancement (e.g. metalwork, glass and porcelain production), erecting monumental architecture such as the Capodimonte Palace or The Royal Palace of Caserta. It is telling that the firm uses the emblem in its official communication and on tie packaging.

At the same time, the firm has been able to extract value from the sense of elegance associated with its craft objects. Not far from the main shop, there is an elegant showroom where customers find shoes, shirts, bags, foulards, jackets, scarves, wallets, belts, watches, cufflinks, perfumes, coats and many other iconic objects. The showroom was very carefully designed and all products displayed to recall specific ideas or contexts. A clear connection was established with the prestigious materials from other regions, such as the silks imported from the Macclesfield area in England that were used for producing ties. This connection is also manifest in other products such as shoes.

That was of great significance. During one of our visits to the showroom, the owner explained how he broke the long-standing relationship with one of his leading English shoe suppliers when the company was acquired by an Italian group:

> These shoes have lost their British associaations, replced by Italian design that gradually got the upper hand.

A further aspect that emerged from our analysis regarded how the firm sought to distance its identity from stereotypical images of the city. During our fieldwork, we noted that our respondents sometimes engaged in particular representations of the place in an effort to distance themselves from negative commonsensical attributes associated with the city (such as hidden, sometimes criminal, powers or a lack of transparent governance):

> Often Naples has been associated with the 'terra dei fuochi', the rubbish problem, polluted water. We are here in Naples, we want people coming to Naples.

The firm is clearly embedded in the local context, which is intimately related to a certain conception of Naples, a conception that sought to point beyond negative stereotypes and attempted to reveal a sense of sociality and the manual ability of local artisans. The firm was proud of the values associated with the place, such as passions, emotions and hospitality:

> We are a miracle, really. Twenty years ago, we [my family] just had this boutique, in Naples, a city where doing things is difficult ... we have a high demand for ties but we don't want to produce more ... Le Monde wrote an article on us ... 'the [company] miracle'.

Firm Family Tradition and Values

Various observations during the company visits showed that considerable effort was devoted to eliciting memories related to the family's history. Here narratives on the origin of the enterprise enabled reconstruction of the identity of the company, anchoring the present-day activities in traditional values:

> My grandfather created a workshop for shirt,s and in 1930 we had about thirty people in our workshop. In the 1970s we specialized in tie production and gave up shirts. This was a successful choice. When I was a child, I was destined to do this. At eight years old, my grandfather said: 'Now you are old enough to work in the shop with us'.

As emerges from this excerpt, the firm has a clear craft identity. Its handmade and workmanship identity is associated with the workshop where ties are produced. The small workshop in via Chiaia is staffed by twelve tie seamstresses who possess unique abilities in making a folded tie entirely by hand (and who are able to produce a tie in about ninety minutes).

The workshop also has a key role in the firm's ability to foster memories around warmth and hospitality. As observed during the visits, tie-makers work in a very family-like atmosphere. There is a fully equipped kitchen where they can relax; there is a cook who makes food once a week for all of the employees working there. It is into this context that customers are welcomed to the workshop. It is common for customers to visit the site of making, choose a textile, and receive a 'tailor-made' tie within a few hours. As the owner explained:

> We are in Naples. We want people coming here. We wish to offer a coffee, a sfogliatella. We don't want to convey sales volume, budget ... We want to communicate values, emotions, passion, hospitality and a positive Neapolitanness]napoletanità]...

As a sign of the centrality of place and family tradition, the owner explained in the interview that people could only buy the firm's ties directly from Naples or in dedicated shops. Buying the tie in Naples both gives a particular sense of embeddedness within local contexts that

Figure 6.2 Tie Workshop in Naples

emphasizes the singularity and uniqueness of the production, while also stressing the exclusivity and differentiated nature of the product:

> We are happily not technological. We don't do e-commerce.

To explain what being a craft organization means, a further association is made with the local place, with reference to a particular relaxed attitude in doing business:

> Once an executive from South Korea visited the shop and asked for a tie with a special silk that he saw here. He asked if we could ship it. I looked at him, asked him to sit and ordered a coffee and sfogliatella for him. Then I showed him the workshop and our steamers made the tie for him, live there. He was astonished, and I could have asked a fair amount of money for it ... he would have been happy to pay whatever price ... but we did not sell him a tie, we sold an experience!

If novel product distributions pathways such as online platforms (Luckman, 2015) are changing the way of marketing much handmade craft, our data also suggest a different story. Drawing on informality and a sense of closeness with clients, the firm was able to capitalize on an old-fashioned way of doing business:

> I've got my finger on the pulse of what people want. I don't do market research. When I look at a sample book, I know if customers want a yellow, red or blue tie. When I look at a samle book, I read it twice. First, it is my gut feeling… what I personally like. Then it is more rational. I ask myself: 'Do I like the white tie?' And at that point the customers' wishes come to mind …

Concluding Discussion

In an era of 'peak stuff', we are witnessing a rediscovery of meanings associated with consumption. Losing the appetite for standardized goods, some consumers are directing their attention to original objects that reflect an alternative ethos of consumption, based on distinctiveness and uniqueness (Herzfeld 2015). As argued by Claude Lévi-Strauss (2010), modern society has been marked by hypercommunication, a dynamic that encourages human beings to be constantly aware of what is happening in distant parts of the globe. For centuries, cultural differences secured originality and uniqueness among groups of people living at a distance from each other with little contact. Nowadays people are instead threatened by the risk of becoming mere consumers prone to adopt habits and artefacts disjointed from their context of origin (Lévi-Strauss 2010: 33–34).

In this chapter, we have argued that in this context some craft-oriented organizations emphasize the significance of the 'place' and local history in marketing their products and building their brand identity. Craft objects are increasingly praised for being evocative of place, history, and maker creativity (Vachhani 2013). We have examined how craft organizations enable the formation of collective memory drawing from local history and tradition, remembering in ways that are then used to evoke a specific set of memories. Through analysis of a well-known tie maker's working practices in the city of Naples, we examined how the sense of place and traditions are deployed to mobilize a repository of collective imaginaries.

As our findings have shown, the firm marked the connection with the city in multiple ways. The uniqueness of place is emphasized by recalling different moments of city history. First, the tie-maker dates its operation back to the artisanal local tradition prevalent at the beginning of the 20th century, a time in which small craft enterprises started to lay the ground for what would become the globally renowned label 'Made in Naples'. Evocation of a swarming city full of entrepreneurial vitality and with an unequivocal creative potential is key here. This idea of Naples transmits a deep sense of craftwork – artisanal, handmade, unique, emphasizing that the clothing and handmade textiles are prestigious items produced and commercialized by craft firms operating in the region.

Second, a strong link with tradition is created by establishing a connection with the provenance of materials, which in this case possess a clear British connotation. The tie-maker selects raw materials by cultivating relationships with British suppliers for silk provision, and the firm is able to mark its devotion toward tradition and sustain an association of the products with craft heritage.

However, the results of our analysis also suggest that there is an ambivalence in the collective memories associated with the city as a means of positioning its brand. On the one hand, narratives mobilize the creative potential and the long history of prestige and wealth usually associated with the city. But at the same time, its positioning is in opposition to a stereotypical image of the city: the firm brand identity was thus constructed by evoking very specific imaginaries of the place, through affirmation of a positive, as carriers of a positive *napoletanità* (Neapolitanness), and dissociation from a negative stereotypical image of a southern Mediterranean city marked by administrative problems.

The firm capitalized on its long tradition to enhance its reputation as a leading craft tie maker. As we have highlighted, the anchor of tradition was further reinforced by keeping technology at the margins. The entire tie production was hand-based, kept as traditional as possible. In the workshop scissors were the most sophisticated tools, and steamers shaped the ties as they always have. Thus, technology was not valued by the firm as such. It was, indeed, contrasted with the authenticity of social relations which were at the core of the firm's identity. The possibility of inefficiency, manifest in the absence of e-commerce was counterbalanced by the importance of human connections. Above all, the repository of memories associated with the sense of place made the organization's craft identity distinguishable by capitalizing on its history and tradition.

References

Anteby, M., & Molnár, V. (2012) Collective Memory Meets Organizational Identity: Remembering to Forget in a Firm's Rhetorical History. *Academy of Management Jnal*, 55(3): 515–540.

Bell. E., (2012) Ways of Seeing Organisational Death: A Critical Semiotic Analysis of Organizational Memorialization. *Visual Studies,* 27 (1): 4–17.

Brown, J. (2014) *Making it Local: What does this Mean in the Context of Contemporary Craft?* London: The Craft Council.

Crawford, M.B. (2009) *Shop Class as Soulcraft: An Inquiry into the Value of Work*. New York: Penguin.

Dormer, P. (1997) *The Culture of Craft: Status and Future*. Manchester: Manchester University Press.

Feldman, R. M. & Feldman, S. P. (2006) What Links the Chain: An Essay on Organizational Remembering as Practice. *Organization*, 13(6): 861–887.

Gauntlett, D. (2011) *Making is Connecting: The Social Meaning of Creativity, from DiY and Knitting to Youtube and Web 2.0.* Cambridge: Polity.

Johansson, M. & Toraldo, M.L. (2015) 'From Mosh Pit to Posh Pit': Festival Imagery in the Context of the Boutique Festival. *Culture and Organization*, 23(3): 220–237.

Hede, A. & Watne, T. (2013) Leveraging the Human Side of the Brand Using a Sense of Place: Case Studies of Craft Breweries. *Journal of Marketing Management*, 29(1–2).

Herzfeld, M. (2015) Artigianato e società: pensieri intorno a un concetto. *Antropologia*, 2.2 NS.

Herzfeld M. (2004) *The Body Impolitic. Artisans and Artifice in the Global Hierarchy of Value.* Chicago: The University of Chicago Press.

Hegele, C. & Kieser, A. (2001) Control the Construction of Your Legend or Someone Else Will—An Analysis of Texts on Jack Welch. *Journal of Management Inquiry* 10(4): 298–309.

Lévi-Strauss, C. (2010) *Mito e Significato. Cinque conversazioni radiofoniche.* Milano: Il Saggiatore.

Luckman, S. (2015) *Craft and the Creative Economy.* London: Palgrave Macmillan.

McClinchey, K. A. (2016) Going Forward by Looking Back: Memory, Nostalgia and Meaning-Making in Marketing for a Sense of Place. *Advancing Tourism Research Globally*, 23.

Misztal, B. (2003) *Theories of Social Remembering.* Maidenhead: Open University Press.

Nissley, N. & Casey, A. (2002) The Politics of the Exhibition: Viewing Corporate Museums Through the Paradigmatic Lens of Organizational Memory. *British Journal of Management*, 13: 35–45.

Ranisio, G. (2014) Ripartire dai territori: il ruolo dell'artigianato artistico napoletano. *EtnoAntropologia*, [S.l.], v. 2, p. 277–286.

Rodaway, P. (1994) *Sensuous Geographies: Body, Sense and Place.* London: Routledge.

Rowlinson, M., Booth, C., Clark, P., Delahaye, A. & Procter, S. (2010) Social Remembering and Organizational Memory. *Organization Studies*, 31(1): 69–87.

Rowlinson, M., Casey, A., Hansen, P. H. & Mills, A. J. (2014) Narratives and Memory in Organizations. *Organization*, 21(4): 441–446.

Suddaby, R., Foster, W., & Trank, C. (2010) Rhetorical History as a Source of Competitive Advantage. *Advances in Strategic Management*, 27: 147–173.

Vachhani, S. J. (2013) (Re)Creating Objects from the Past – Affect, Tactility and Everyday Creativity. *Management and Organizational History*, 8(1): 91–104.

von Busch, O. (2010) Exploring Net Political Craft: From Collective to Connective. *Craft Research*, 1: 113–124.

Walsh, J., P., Ungson, G., R. (1991) Organizational Memory. *Academy of Management Review*, 16 (1): 57–91.

Yanow, D. (1998) Space Stories: Studying Museum Buildings as Organizational Spaces while Reflecting on Interpretive Methods and their Narration. Journal of Management Inquiry, 7(3): 215–239.

Zerubavel, E. (1996) Social memories: Steps to a Sociology of the Past. *Qualitative Sociology*, 19(3): 283–299.

Zundel, M., Holt, R., & Popp, A. (2016) Using History in the Creation of Organizational Identity. *Management & Organizational History*, 11(2): 211–235.

7 Back to the Brewster

Craft Brewing, Gender and the Dialectical Interplay of Retraditionalisation and Innovation

Chris Land, Neil Sutherland and Scott Taylor

The significance of gender within contemporary craft work is frequently acknowledged but rarely analysed in empirical depth. In this chapter we explore the experiences of women working in the craft brewing industry, paying particular attention to how the recent expansion in craft-beer production and consumption is underpinned by a masculinised and patriarchal notion of retraditionalisation. This is made apparent in the masculinities evident in persistently reproduced structures, aesthetics, marketing and attitudes surrounding craft production in this sector.

Imprinting Patriarchy: Gender and Craft work

Although some of the craft practices discussed in this book are symbolically gendered as female, the dominant cultural image of the skilled artisan/craft worker remains predominantly male. The persistence of this masculine coding is integral to how craft has intersected with capitalism. In Cynthia Cockburn's (1983) classic study of technological change in the printing industry, *Brothers*, she highlighted the interactions between capitalism and patriarchy in shaping the practice and fate of skilled printers. In traditional printing, a *forme* had to be assembled by hand, with the printer selecting lead-block type from cases, and with printers assembling them according to the text but back to front. This required a high degree of literacy combined with an aesthetic sensibility for layout and when to split words. It also required a degree of physical strength to handle the final bound forms, as well as responsibility for maintaining the type. Proficiency in all aspects of this production process was what enabled the apprentice printer to lay claim to the identity of a master crafter.

Cockburn's historical account of change in the printing industry points to a number of attempts to break this unified practice, with employers taking on women or unskilled men to do parts of the work for lower pay. These moves were resisted by male guild members, and later by male-dominated trade unions, on the basis of the integrity of the craft. Women who had the literacy to work with type were kept from the job because they were positioned as lacking the physical strength to handle the forms.

Unskilled men had this strength but lacked the literacy and aesthetic sense to compose print. As such, the job of printer remained a position framed by masculinity and exclusive skill, reinforced through strong collective organization in the London Society of Compositors, whose chapters met in a 'chapel' (usually an upstairs room in a pub, which further excluded many women) and were headed up by the 'father'. Even when new technology was introduced, this patriarchal form of organisation, shored up against threat from both women and unskilled men, managed to keep the integrity of the job and control over apprenticeships that would accord skilled status to workers.

In Cockburn's account of printing, craft and skill are patriarchally legitimated achievements, connected to an integrated practice and the attainment of a specific social identity through apprenticeship. Historically, there is a wealth of evidence associating technological innovation in the workplace with deskilling. Division of labour has the potential to break down the integrity of a craft, enabling some work to be carried out by less skilled, and therefore cheaper, workers, such as women. This subdivision also breaks up control over the quasi-patrilineal system of apprenticeship that confers the status of skilled crafter (Braverman 1974; Noble 2011).

Behind this observation lies a broader question about the contingency of skill. As Lave and Wenger's (1991) concept of 'situated learning' suggests, the development of competence is not only capability of knowledge and skill, but also the development of a socially legitimated identity, initially through peripheral participation in a community of practice. Claims to skilled status depend on both this recognition by the community of practice and a wider social status. In most debate over deskilling and upskilling, the dominant definition of 'skill' is in terms of formal qualifications (Edgell 2012), but apprenticeships serve a similar purpose, with a legal-rational entity conferring skilled status on a particular worker (cf. Braverman 1974). Both processes reproduce gendered conceptions of skill that are dependent upon formal recognition by public institutions, rather than passed down within the family, and on more codifiable, technical forms of expertise, which predominate over forms of emotional skill, or practices significant in the domestic sphere. Sewing is a good example of the latter, and one that has had significant implications for the development of the garment industry. A skill that was traditionally passed from mother to daughter in the home, sewing is less commonly deemed to be a skilful practice (Cockburn 1981). This has meant that seamstresses have rarely been able to command the same kinds of salary bonuses for skilled work that male workers have, and automation has proven to be uneconomical, in large part due to the ready availability of very low-paid, mostly female workers (cf. Hammer 2015; Soldatenko 1999).[1]

We take brewing as our empirical site here, because it is so striking how the marketing and communications strategies of craft-beer production represent the industry in hypermasculine terms, connecting meaningful, masculine work to the authenticity of products. This framing of the industry suggests that women entering are clearly moving into a culturally coded 'man's world'. The later sections then examine how this positioning is experienced, negotiated and challenged by women brewers.

Gender, Marketing, Work and the New Craft 'Masters'

In the USA the 2015 merger of Anheuser-Busch InBev and SAB Miller saw a single brewing conglomerate control 80 per cent of all beer sales in the USA. In parallel, however, between 2007 and 2015, the number of breweries in the USA grew from 398 to over 4,000, and that growth was driven by micro-breweries. The situation in the UK is similar, with rapid growth in micro-breweries, especially in and around London, from just 142 in 1980 to over 1,400 in 2015 (Chapman et al. 2017: 1–2). Production by members of the Society of Independent Brewers (SIBA), the body representing small and craft breweries, grew by 16 per cent in 2014, at a time when overall alcohol consumption was falling (Smith Maguire et al. 2017: 19). Yet small independent brewers are flourishing around the world.

Marketers suggest this is because consumers are tired of mass production and standardised, homogeneous commodities differentiated only by a label or logo. That is the key marketing proposition of the UK-based craft-beer market leaders BrewDog. In a 2015 'welcome' video on their YouTube site, one of their brewers rolls a bowling ball into ten bottles of Stella Artois.[2] This image captures well the market proposition for craft beer, locating it in a masculine space of nostalgia, blue-collar work, bowling and beer and setting it against a world of large corporations who produce standardised, predictable commodities in order to make money. Anheuser-Busch InBev, the owner of the Stella Artois brand, is the largest brewing company in the world today. Its products are exemplified by Budweiser beer, a pale, innocuous lager targeted at mass markets with the goal of maximising profits. Against this instrumental capitalist logic, craft brewers like BrewDog have positioned themselves as David confronting Goliath: small upstarts motivated by a love of beer, not money, who are not afraid to offend and are out to transform the industry. BrewDog call out to a 'craft beer proletariat', heralding a revolution in both production and consumer taste. 'Craft' functions as a crucial signifier here, harking back to a pre-industrial, artisanal logic structured around craft as both skilful practice and passionate engagement (Sennett 2008). The promise is of an authentic and distinctive product, created by people who are genuinely 'passionate about craft beer', rather than just the corporate bottom line.

Using anachronistic ideals of masculine work to sell beer is not new. Budweiser's iconic 'This Bud's for you' advertising campaign from the

1980s 'paraded a collage of blue-collar workers from all walks of life, each of whom practiced his trade with consummate skill and enthusiasm... Bud saluted men who industriously pursued work as an intrinsically satisfying calling, men who applied their craft skills with good humor and determination' (Holt 2004: 99–100). Holt locates Budweiser's advertising success in their promise to resolve the contemporary crisis of masculinity. Under Reaganite neo-liberalisation, blue-collar workers (mostly men) faced an economic reality of deindustrialisation, unemployment and the rise of what they saw as feminised forms of post-industrial work. This reality was in stark contrast to a resurgent ideology of hard work and frontier self-sufficiency in the new enterprise discourse: 'Budweiser targeted this acute tension between the revived American ideals of manhood and the economic realities that made these ideals nearly unattainable for many men' (Holt 2004: 6–7).

If Budweiser's old advertising campaign offers a good example of a specific form of masculine work being used to anchor consumption-based identities, craft beer takes this a step further. Both hark back to an ideology of work far removed from paramount reality and promise to secure identity through consumption. With craft beer, however, authenticity is secured through a knowledge of the provenance of the beer, its ingredients, and a form of conspicuous consumption demarcated not only by premium pricing (craft beers are notably more expensive than either 'premium lagers' or real ales) but by a knowledge of the production process and ingredients, such as being able to distinguish styles of beer, hops, and yeasts. This knowledge is learned through consumption, with the new labour aristocracy of the service sector actively engaging customers in the education of their tastes (Ocejo 2017).

In his 2017 book *Masters of Craft*, Richard Ocejo reports on ethnographic research into the newly valorised work of high-end barbers, whole-animal butchers, cocktail bartenders, and artisanal, small-batch distillers. Like craft brewing, these professions are increasingly popular with college educated middle-class young men, who just a few years ago would have gone into a white-collar, office-based profession. More than skilled traders, the butchers, barbers and bartenders Ocejo researched also acted as arbiters of taste and culture, combining the embodied skill of craft with expert knowledge of their domain of consumption. As social identity construction has moved more towards consumption, those producers who can not only create valued goods, but also educate the tastes of high-end consumers, can command a social status well above the traditional blue-collar crafters of decades past. This change of status is founded on the centrality of knowledge in such work, but Ocejo also points to the intrinsic value of skilful practice and craft virtuosity. In an age dominated by immaterial labour and work that can be framed as feminised (cf. Gorz 2010; Hardt and Negri 2000; Huws 2014; Weeks 2014), the masculinised physicality of this kind of craftwork harks back to a golden age in which strength and skill were combined in a unified, knowledgeable, embodied practice that protected patriarchal privilege. As Ocejo puts it, these elite service workers 'are simultaneously respected knowledge workers and skilled manual laborers, and perform their work in public. Men are thus able to use these jobs to achieve a lost sense of middle-class, heterosexual masculinity in their work' (Ocejo 2017: 20). By anchoring craft, or artisanal, products in this promise of authentic masculine work, these jobs have become more attractive to young men seeking work, but this conception of craft also anchors the value, and authenticity, of their products in the regressive social structure of patriarchy.

Retraditionalisation, Masculinity and Craft Work

The combination of community and masculinity in contemporary images of craft and artisanal work in the gentrified spaces of post-industrial consumption thus anchors authenticity on a kind of legislated nostalgia for a sanitised, rose-tinted view of the past (Hatherley 2016). As well as being genuinely committed to a more grounded and ethical form of production, the new crafters are engaged in a kind of 'retraditionalisation' (Banks & Milestone 2011; Lash 1994) in which pre-industrial forms of craft are positioned as anchors of both masculine work-identities and community cohesion. As Ocejo (2017) notes, places like barbershops, butchers and bars were focal points for men in urban communities in the past, and retain that role in the contemporary imagination, even if not in reality. Although there are several women working in the butchers and barbers that Ojeco studied, and he does give over some space to considering their experiences, reporting on a female barber's experiences of learning to give a shave with a straight razor, but the overall sense is of an archaic set of very traditional values in service. Women and ethnic minorities are largely restricted to backstage jobs and do not reach the upper echelons where meaningful and long-term careers can be forged, at least partly because these workplaces are spaces where hegemonic masculinities are performed, which is precisely their appeal to consumers. This observation has already been made in relation to craft beer, and the specific whiteness of the masculinity being performed in that sector. Withers (2017) provides an acute analysis of the cultural and spatial racializing of craft-beer consumption. As he argues, the culture of craft beer is not only gendered, but also classed and raced so that 'the craft beer culture is informed and defined by whiteness' and dominated by college educated, white males (Withers 2017: 237).

This tension is most clearly evident in craft-beer marketing, where sexism and misogyny are frequently observed. Objectified women's bodies have long featured in beer advertisements – Budweiser has regularly used images of a doting female pouring a beer for a man, or swimsuit-clad blonde women lying on beach towels. Such objectified images of women appear designed to complement the more active working men, to present a couplet of desired-object and identified-subject. In many images of craft beer, and especially in BrewDog's promotions, a hypermasculine aesthetic of lumberjack shirts and big beards combines with extreme brewing (underwater brewing, very strong beers, or intense tastes like chilli beer) and a celebration of heroic entrepreneurialism (Watt 2016). Women often appear primarily as objects of derision, as in one advert mocking prostitutes, or with products like 'Trashy Blonde', a beer that was promoted with the following on the bottle label:

> A titillating, neurotic, peroxide, punk of a pale ale. Combining attitude, style, substance and a little bit of low self esteem [*sic*] for good measure; what would your mother say?
>
> You really should just leave it alone …
>
> …but you just can't get the compulsive malt body and gorgeous dirty blonde colour out of your head. The seductive lure of the sassy passion fruit hop proves too much to resist. All that is even before we get onto the fact that there are no additives preservatives, pasteurization or strings attached.
>
> All wrapped up with the customary BrewDog bite and imaginative twist. This trashy blonde is going to get you into a lot of trouble.
>
> (Reproduced in Atherton 2011)

Which, as Sophie Atherton (2011) noted shortly after the launch of the beer with remarkable understatement, made her 'uncomfortable' because 'even in the 21st century women are subjected to – and the subject of – far too much derogatory, degrading and violent treatment, behaviour and attitudes and anything that contributes to that ought to be considered unacceptable'.

This tension surrounding the retraditionalisation evident in contemporary craft work is, in some ways, at the heart of the contemporary craft discourse. Whilst the hypermasculine imagery of craft that is mobilised by Brewdog appeals to an atavistic ideal of masculinity, 'craftivism' politically revalorises traditionally domestic, feminised practices like knitting, crochet and quilting (Corbett 2013; Greer 2014; Rippin & Vacchani, this volume). This reframes what was, historically, a form of subsistence self-provisioning, or perhaps small-scale, petty commodity production for relatively localised consumption outside the household, to suggest a model for rethinking work beyond the capitalist, patriarchal employment relationship (cf. Friedmann 1986). Like many other domestic production processes maintained by women, brewing followed a trajectory from localised craft to industrialised production during the 19th and 20th centuries, with a massive increase in scale and formal employment in dedicated production sites outside the home. In the process domestic production was rebranded as a masculine hobby – 'home brewing'[3] – and the gender of brewing completed its shift from a highly skilled female-dominated profession in the 1300s, to a male-dominated, industrialised, deskilled form of mass production (Bennett 1996; Peyton 2013). Industrialisation brought profitability and efficiency, but at the cost of standardisation and oligopoly, reaching its apogee in the 1970s when the UK market was dominated by just a handful of large breweries, and relatively homogeneous, pale lagers had started their rise to eventually dominate the market (Brown 2010). Industrialisation thus combined a patriarchal and capitalist form of organising brewing, with standardised production for mass markets.

Whilst aspects of this mass production/consumption model had been problematised since the early 1970s by the CAMpaign for Real Ale (CAMRA) in the UK, small-scale brewing remained a male-dominated sphere, both in the production and consumption of real ales using traditional methods, such as cask conditioning (Thurnell-Read 2016). Whilst CAMRA has been relatively successful in putting the politics of production back into the pub and pump, it is first and foremost a consumer group and concerned with the authenticity of the product rather than production per se (Watson & Watson 2012). Craft beer, in contrast, mobilises the form of the labour process – 'craft' – as the core of the brand.

(Re)Introducing Brewsters

If brewing shifted from a female profession in the 1300s, to male-dominated, industrial mass-production by the 1970s, how do women working in the industry today fare, and how is the rise of craft brewing and retraditionalisation shaping women's experiences? Whilst Ocejo presents little data on women, he does hypothesise that 'women have greater representation in […] niche occupations than in their mainstream versions' (2017: 19). The lived experiences of women in these new craft industries, however, has so far largely been neglected. In his landmark study of craft brewers in the UK, Thomas Thurnell-Read (2014) included just one female respondent: 'One of a growing number of "brewsters" in the British brewery industry… Jane reflects how in spite of the male dominance of the brewery and pub industry she has confidence that her beers can 'speak for themselves' in acting as a clear and tangible demonstration of her skills and competence' (Thurnell-Read 2014: 52). Despite this, Jane clearly recognised that 'the main target for drinking beer is man' (*ibid.*). This tells us little about the gender dynamics of the sector, or the experience of working in it.

Brewing and alcohol consumption are peculiar contemporary cultures. The masculinity of drinking cultures means that women entering a profession such as brewing are expected to establish their legitimacy in a 'man's world' in a way that men never have to. As Ocejo notes:

Women in these new, elite, manual labor jobs ... experience threats to their pursuit of a professional identity in these male-dominated, masculine-coded jobs in spite of the lessened role emotional labour plays in them. These threats specifically come from male consumers who sometimes question their expertise.

(Ocejo 2017: 20)

Our analysis below suggests a great deal more ambiguity than Ocejo's passing comments suggest. Craft brewing has opened up a somewhat paradoxical space for innovation in product, process and identity, that is distinct from both industrialised mass production, and the more traditional, male-dominated, CAMRA scene. By challenging both tradition and mass industrialisation, the ultimately empty signifier of 'craft' in beer and brewing has created room for more diversity, with spaces for women to position themselves as doing something different. However, there is also clearly a continuation of sexism, misogyny, and exclusion on the basis of sex or gender.

Exploring the Experiences of Brewsters I: Women in a Man's World?

We began exploring the expanding world of craft brewing through gendered marketing materials such as those described above. Our intention was to gather data from brewsters to gain insight into why they were representing their beers in ways that could be interpreted as sexist or misogynist. Our attempts to gain access to companies like BrewDog were consistently unsuccessful over an extended period of time. During this process, we realised that there is a significant minority of women brewing in this sector, supported by networks such as the US-based but globally active Pink Boots Society. We therefore began to collect data from women working in the sector. In total, we conducted 17 interviews, with 15 women and two men (both men were partners and collaborators of the women being interviewed) in Europe and North America.

The interviews were semi-structured, to provide a high level of flexibility during the interaction. We chose this approach because the women worked in a range of positions: co-owner, head brewer, brewer, assistant brewer, marketing, and brewpub manager. Our intention was to gain a sense of how and why the women had chosen to work in a male-dominated masculine environment, whether they were experiencing change over time in the industry, and what they predicted as the future of craft brewing. Our analysis here focuses on representing those experiences as transparently as possible, within the analytical frame we have developed from the dataset. The following sections examine the concerning experiences of women working in the craft brewing industry, as well as covering their interpretations of how authenticity in craft brewing is anchored through a displaced homosocial fraternity as well as 'craft' skill.

Harassment and Discrimination

Despite innovation being used creatively to open up a space in the male-dominated brewing industry – which will be discussed later – discrimination remained an issue for our respondents. Interestingly, the predominant structure of the interviews began with an assertion that gender and sex discrimination was not an issue for them personally: that their beers spoke for themselves; and that quality would out, regardless of who the brewer was. Even though we recruited a significant proportion of brewsters through the generosity of a known feminist network, such associations did not generally personally resonate with the respondents. However, the interview narratives are striking in that initial disclaimers were often followed by a litany of discrimination or harassment. Indeed, a comment that 'I have never really had like any sexist comments to me ...' segued into:

> Actually I kind of had one today... this guy [from a company she applied for a job to] ... Wrote me a message, he goes, 'Hey hot stuff, are you still interested in applying?...'

This was followed by two further recollections of recent events of harassment:

> ... when we were hanging out [at a beer festival] he was kind of, I don't know, he was a little bit drunk and he was kind of poking me on my shoulders and on my sides ...
> ...at the brewery, we were just finishing up bottling and he kind of ... I just feel someone slap my [body] and I literally popped up and I go, 'What the fuck?' and I just looked at him and I was in such shock, and I just looked at [male colleague] and he didn't say anything and I just walked away, and I wish I had said something right there and then.

As we write this chapter, the revelations of sexual harassment of women in the Hollywood film industry are still making headline news, and being reinforced with reports from other sectors. One of our respondents, who worked in marketing for a brewery, had previously been in the music industry and drew parallels with similar experiences of harassment at pop concerts and award ceremonies. Common to both was male domination at the highest levels of the industry and the presence of alcohol:

I guess in industries where there's drinking involved ... I did myself, had to handle some unpleasant situations when there was actually a work-related event. But, we had a few drinks and stuff, and all of a sudden it wasn't a professional context any more.

In brewing, of course, alcohol is a constant part of the business. Brewers and other employees reported regularly visiting pubs where their beer was sold, either to check how it was being kept, or to further sales. In such a context, normal expectations of 'professional' conduct would often slide, as women engaged with sales reps (who had perhaps been drinking themselves) and with customers, who had almost certainly been drinking. Indeed, one of the key aspects of this industry is that much of the networking and 'social work' associated with a successful career straddles the boundary between work and leisure, and often involves intoxication, further eroding the self-regulation of behaviour that characterises formal workplaces. As several of the breweries we visited also had taprooms, where punters came to the brewery to drink, often excessively, on-site, even the brewery shop floor was not entirely separated from spaces of intoxication and excess, making inappropriate, sexualised behaviour even more likely than more in clearly delineated workplaces.

Work/life (Im)balance

Physical sexual harassment was the most direct and obvious form of discrimination reported by our respondents, but there are two other indirect forms of discrimination that were presented as significant. Both of these are built into the practices of brewing, structured into the workplace. The first indirect form of discrimination concerns the boundary between work and life, as described above. The overlap between work and leisure in the drinks business seems to have fostered an environment in which men hitting on women was fairly regular. The second example concerns the more conventional understanding of work and life as they pertain to domestic and familial responsibilities outside the workplace. It is well established that women continue to bear the primary responsibility for domestic and care work in the home, especially if children are involved. Even where work-family friendly policies are in place, these are rarely taken advantage of by men; simultaneously they can hinder women's career progression significantly if taken up as an option (Hochschild 1997). Brewing is not a very well-paid profession, especially working in London, where many craft breweries are based and where rents and the cost of living are some of the highest in the world. Despite this, working hours are long and often irregular. This had a significant impact on women who also had caring responsibilities outside work. As one brewster told us:

> We brew from five o'clock in the morning to like, 12 o'clock at night, sometimes 1 a.m. So, there are some, you know, sacrifices that have to be made ... and on the weekends ... I don't like to put women in a box and say: women are caretakers ... But if a person has children, I don't know a lot of brewers who have children. And if they do, they have a partner who's doing a lot of the caretaking.

Central to this was the inflexibility of the brewing process itself. Fermentation times vary with temperature and ingredients; in a craft brewery this is especially likely to be less predictable and standardised than in a larger, industrial producer. Similarly, a larger brewery might be able to employ shift patters of work to cope with the inflexibility of the brewing process, whilst still having regular working hours. For smaller breweries, however:

> ...the raw materials are in charge... I thought I was going to be home at a certain time, and it wasn't. We had to stick it out and, you know, baby-sit our beer and make sure that it was okay.

The use of the term 'baby sit' is telling here. For the women we spoke to, working as a brewster was difficult to imagine if they wanted a family, or even a social life. This work-life balance only became harder to achieve as brewsters became more established, moving on to head brewster and managing a team. As one head brewster, told us:

> [My partner] said, you never were brought up to think that you deserved to have a big job, and you're feeling guilty about this work-life balance thing. Like if your dishes aren't done, then you're a bad woman. But you could be running an organisation and still, if your dishes aren't done, then you're, kind of, not a good enough person.

She was only able to do the job because her partner took on much of the domestic work involved in maintaining a household. For women in a more traditional relationship, where they had primary responsibility for domestic labour and childcare, this arguably would not be possible. In summary, then, the materiality of the brewing process, with its inherent unpredictability, resulting from the process of fermentation and its dependence on yeast as a crucial non-human actant in production, combined with the wider gendered division of domestic labour, to suggest to women that this was a problematic profession – even those being successful within it.

Gendered Norms and Chivalric Sexism

Our final example of discrimination also derives from the conjunction of the materiality of brewing and gendered norms. As in Cynthia Cockburn's study of printers, the technology of brewing, and the unit sizes, tend to assume a large fully able-bodied person willing to be pushed physically. In order to lay claim to craftiness, the person is expected to accomplish all aspects of a craft, from the routine, mundane and dirty, to the more technical and conventionally skilful. This mastery of a complete skill set is crucial to becoming a crafter (Cockburn 1983; Sennett 2008). In brewing, the size of the vessels, the weight of raw materials and barrels, and the nature of the work involved in making beer, often seem to pre-suppose a very strong body of a size and shape more commonly found in men than women. As with printing, it is quite possible to find solutions, such as hoists and pulleys, that would enable a wider range of bodies to perform the task, but the norm was clearly established as large, male and fully able bodied. To give just one example, one head brewster in a small business told us the following story:

> We were taking a delivery … okay, we, I was taking in a delivery of nine pallets on my own. And … and the driver was being such an arse. He … he wouldn't help me in any way, like … like move any of these pallets. So I had to push nine tons' worth of goods into the warehouse … And you know one of those things where it's like physically too much for you; that was the only time I was just like: 'Oh, my God'.

This was presented as a gendered experience; other brewsters emphasised that no one should be expected to do work in this way, nor was it necessary given the technology and machinery available. This kind of experience did not prevent respondents from doing the job, but it suggest to them that they would find it more difficult than an average man to lay claim to full craft skill and status. Echoing Cockburn's (1983) findings, one head brewster told us:

> I think there would've been more opportunity, and it's nothing to do with sexism or anything like that. It's more of the production manual work. I think there's more opportunities for men to get stuck into beer, to be, to do a, you know, a good operator's role, really learn the plant and then move up that way … Whereas women are limited physically or don't choose to do that work. I think possibly it was a bit limited from the start … lifting, dirty work, you know. But dirty work can progress through to, you know, learning some good skills and progressing.

Whilst the account of unloading a truck suggests that the driver is an 'arse' for not helping out, the idea that doing the full range of work is necessary to be secure in the craft meant that men trying to help could also be a problem. One brewster, now well established, discussed this as a particular problem when she was just getting started in the business.

...there was ... a huge hurdle of getting over everybody's instinctual chivalry, which wasn't allowing me to do my job. There was never a problem about it, but I would go: 'Okay, I'll lift that,' and they'd be like: 'No, are you sure? I'll lift it.' And I'd be like: 'Yes, I'm really sure. I'm here to work.'... fortunately, up in Yorkshire they have a ... thread of farmers' wives, so there was an archetype there for me to sort of grab onto.

This kind of indirect discrimination, which we might tentatively call chivalric sexism, has some resonances with other highly gendered working contexts. In Spradley and Mann's (1975) *The Cocktail Waitress*, they note that whilst many men would sexually harass and grope the waitresses, there was often one man in a group who would tell the waiting staff to speak to him if any of his friends got out of line. Whilst this may be well-intentioned, the result is to further disempower the women, who are expected to call upon a man to help them do a job that is being made intolerable and unpleasant by other men in the group. It reinforces the sense that women can be positioned as out of place in a man's world, and always dependent upon men. In brewing, this dynamic placed female brewsters in a bind as they were trying to establish equality in a profession where the materiality of the brewing process was itself structured around a specific set of masculine norms. Offers of help both reaffirmed the normality of a man doing the job, and prevented women laying claim to the complete accomplishment of task that is required for becoming respected within the craft community.

Exploring the Experiences of Brewsters II: Reformulating Tradition?

Whist the above analysis paints a bleak picture of the experiences of the brewsters we interviewed, the overall message had a more hopeful flavour. If anything, experiences of harassment and discrimination were spoken of with more of a dull resignation – of practices and mindsets stuck in a bygone era that could be acknowledged, named and challenged– rather than something that should get in the way of future potentialities. Each interviewee was keen to discuss the more proactive part that they played within their 'scene'; the gradual erosion of gendered norms, expectations and stereotypes; and the innovative opportunities for women to participate in the industry that they are historically responsible for.

Indeed, 'it is almost certain that the earliest brewers were women, because food and drink preparation was their domain' (Peyton 2013: 15; Darwin 2017: 223). Historical research shows that this tradition continued until relatively recently, with frontier homesteaders in the Westward expansion of the United States still coding brewing as women's work. This provides the resources for respondents such as Jane in Thurnell-Read's (2013) study of micro-brewers to challenge men's domination of brewing by reviving the traditional term 'brewster', which harks back to a pre-industrial age when brewing was predominantly women's work (Bennett 1996).

Our respondents noted this, and their part in reviving the term to enable the construction of a historically legitimate social identity:

> Back in the day, brewers were women. Like, women were the first brewers. [in an article I wrote I mentioned a female brewer and said] she's a brewster. The old term for brewer. And apparently, it got changed to brewer.
>
> ...
>
> I think brewster has been out of use in British English for a long time. Like, there has not been brewsters around for the last 100 years, you know, it's been a long time. So, obviously, brewer is going to become the norm for people to say ... at the moment there are more male brewers than there are female brewers, but the female brewers are just as good as the male brewers, and they're recognised for that.

Direct references back to a bygone era were relatively rare, however, and more likely to be indirect. One respondent referred to the Yorkshire 'thread of farmers' wives', which provided 'an archetype there for me to sort of grab onto' when establishing her position in a Yorkshire-based brewery, early in her career.

These appeals back to a pre-industrial logic of domestic, petty-commodity production offered a means of legitimating women as brewsters, and clearly resonate with the pre-industrial idea of 'craft' and artisanal production as being somehow more authentic and grounded (Friedmann 1986). However many of our respondents preferred to emphasise discourses of innovation, experimentation and novelty to locate themselves in the industry. Female brewsters, in this account, were less conservative and more likely to take risks and innovate. Their aesthetic sensibilities and taste (sometimes linking to their experiences of cooking or baking) enabled them to challenge the conventional, industrial beers and real ales, by creating new tastes and styles, with the intent of shaking up what they experienced as a sclerotic and hidebound industry. For example, one brewster had twice been brought into quite traditional breweries to rejuvenate their product lines. Both breweries had well-established positions in the local area for their real ales but felt that they were missing out on the rapid growth in the craft-beer market and the changing tastes of consumers, who were turning to more heavily hopped beers, with a higher ABV:

> I met with the marketing last summer... and they did want new beer styles. And it's nothing new to most of the beer world, craft beer,

but they haven't done IPAs ... those kind of styles. So we've got [product name] that's just come out, which is just more adventurous with the hops, and our sourcing of different hops is tricky, but some different hops and different methods of hopping as well, which they haven't done.

Dry hopping or the use of 'hop rockets' (a contemporary flavour-infusing system) were radical innovations in a very traditional brewery. Whilst it upset the male brewers who had been working there for a while, the owners had brought a woman in to explicitly disrupt those traditions and reinvigorate the product range to appeal to changing tastes and market demographics.[4] This idea that women wished to be seen as more innovative and creative brewers was consistent across our interviews. For example, one well-established brewster noted that her brewery had a reputation for 'having a go at lots of different creative ... and taking ... an existing style and putting a twist on it... we never do anything that fits very well in a box'. Indeed, her desire for breaking with convention meant that the brewery, whilst commercially successful, often failed to qualify for awards because their beers failed to fit into the usual categories within which beers are judged and prizes awarded (cf. Wright 2014). This idea that women are more creative, and that men brew boring beers or 'brown liquids', was referred to in a third interview in which two female brewsters were discussing their practice together and how it was received by male colleagues:

Respondent 1: ...a definite and consistent trend that is the women who are doing interesting things ... [most English breweries are] doing the old-fashioned styles and English tweedy brown beers, and then you just, you know, flounce in with your poncy American art.

Respondent 2: For me, I was a scientist before I did this, so for me, different sort of, you know, chemistry and new hops, flavours, I find it so exciting. You know, and I think he should ... He doesn't. He just hates it. If I dry-hop, well, it's like the end of the world.

Respondent 1: Imagine if beer smelled of something other than mould?

As this conversation suggests, the female brewsters we interviewed present themselves as more creative than their male counterparts and less bound in 'traditional' modes of production. They were prepared to experiment and shake up the established practices in their industry. 'Craft' thus became a signifier that was future-orientated for them, suggesting change and disruption, rather than a nostalgic harking back to the good old days before industrialisation, as we might expect from a practice anchored in the discourse of craft (Land & Taylor 2014). Where post-Braverman labour process theory would suggest that innovation and change are often bywords for deskilling and the degradation of craft, these female craft brewsters understood their practices as both a continuation of pre-industrial craft traditions and as a contemporary, innovative practice. Although there were significant differences between the physical set ups in the breweries, even relatively small breweries used new techniques, ingredients and technologies. In the larger breweries, the production process itself was technologically controlled and cutting-edge technologies enabled nitrogen, rather than carbon dioxide, to be used to give beer a fizz. Fully automated canning lines enabled large-scale production for retail, as well as for bar sales.

However, there was no sense that contemporary technology was inimical to 'craft' production, or that it implied deskilling. If anything, it extended the range of craft skill, effectively upskilling the work of the brewers by demanding technological and scientific knowledge to use and maintain this equipment. Nor did it suggest a replacement of bodily senses, as the brewers spoke of the continued importance of embodied taste and smell in the production of beer, with brewers regularly sampling beer throughout its production, and tasting or smelling raw materials during the process. The real target when respondents discussed 'traditional' production was the established industrial forms of brewing, dominated by a fairly standardised set of beers, brewed using established technologies and ingredients, in a relatively standardised labour process dominated by men.

Women, Men, Craft Brewing: New World, Old Rules

From this, we would suggest that women in the contemporary craft brewing industry are still treated as 'women in a man's world'. Structural, cultural and social change during the Industrial Revolution and subsequently have encouraged the brewing and drinking of beer to be understood as a predominantly male activity, removing the female brewsters who brewed beer in the home and developed brewing processes over thousands of years (Bennett 1996). The materiality of the production process, both through units of design and in the unpredictability and temporality of yeast-based fermentation, intersects with a wider gendered division of domestic labour and bodily norms, to encourage us to think of women the exception, rather than the norm, in brewing – and by extension, in craft work. Add to this forms of direct sexism and even sexual harassment, possibly exacerbated by inebriation, craft brewing seems to be a very unwelcoming working world for women.

However, as we have also seen, the shifts in drinking cultures that craft beer has brought with it, alongside moves towards experimentation and innovation in brewing, have at least partially broken down the gendering of brewing, beers, and drinking, pointing to new opportunities for women to participate in the industry that they are responsible for historically. These two dynamics pull in different directions, and are still playing out in the craft brewing industry, but we expect that the progressive elements of craft, at least in craft brewing, hold out promise of greater equality and diversity, rather than leading towards a regressive, patriarchal retraditionalisation. The women we spoke to, whilst very clearly a minority still in the industry, enjoyed their work, position, status, and beer, and provide intriguing evidence of changing drinking cultures as opening up the future to greater gender equality.

Notes

1 This is not necessarily a stable configuration. London's mainly male Saville Row tailors have long maintained a specific skilled status in making bespoke suits and shirts for men. More recently companies like Hiut Denim have placed the 'craft master' status of their employees at the heart of their brand, using craft and the reshoring of manufacturing to justify denim jeans with a price tag over £200.
2 www.youtube.com/user/BrewDogBeer
3 It is worth noting that in the USA home-brewing was only made legal again, after prohibition, by the 1978 Home Brew Act, which some commentators have suggested led to a boom in home-brewing that created the conditions of possibility for the subsequent emergence of the craft-beer scene, and the rapid growth in micro-breweries across the USA since the 1980s (Chapman et al. 2017: 6). In many accounts of craft brewing, and in our own research, home-brewing is regularly cited as the starting point for craft brewers, with hobby becoming later recognized by friends and family, who encourage the brewer to upscale and professionalise (Chapman et al. 2017; Maciel 2017).
4 It is perhaps ironic that a hop-related innovation should be something that opens the gate for women to re-enter the brewing industry. As Judith Bennett (1996) notes in her history of women in brewing from 1300 to 1600, the shift from unhopped *ales*, to hopped *beers*, was central to the shift of brewing from women to men (1996: 11).

References

Atherton, S. (2011) 'Investing in Attitude. Will BrewDog's Brand Attract New Money?' Online blog at: https://afemaleview.net/2011/07/01/investing-in-attitude-will-brewdogs-brand-attract-new-money/ [accessed 10 February 2018].

Banks, M. & Milestone, K. (2011) Individualistion, Gender and Cultural Work. *Gender, Work and Organisation*, 18(1): 75–89.

Bennett, J. (1996) *Ale, Beer and Brewsters in England: Women's Work in a Changing World 1300–1600*. Oxford: Oxford University Press.

Braverman, H. (1974) *Labor and Monopoly Capital: The Degradation of Work in the Twentieth Century*. New York: Monthly Review Press.

Brown, P. (2010) *Hops and Glory: One Man's Search for the Beer that Built the British Empire*. London: MacMillan.

Chapman, N., Lellock, J. & Lippard, C. (2017) Exploring the Cultural Dimensions of the Craft Beer Revolution. In N. Chapman, J.S. Lellock and C. Lippard (Eds.) *Untapped: Exploring the Cultural Dimensions of Craft Beer*. Morgantown, WV: West Virginia University Press.

Cockburn, C. (1983) *Brothers: Male Dominance and Technological Change.* London: Pluto.

Cockburn, C. (1981) The Material of Male Power. *Feminist Review,* 9(Autumn): 41–58.

Corbett, S. (2013) *A Little Book of Craftivism.* London: Cicada.

Darwin, H. (2017) You Are What You Drink: Gender Stereotypes and Craft Beer Preferences within the Craft Beer Scene of New York City. In N. Chapman, J.S. Lellock & C. Lippard (Eds.) *Untapped: Exploring the Cultural Dimensions of Craft Beer.* Morgantown, WV: West Virginia University Press.

Edgell, S. (2012) *The Sociology of Work, 2nd Edition.* London: Sage.

Friedmann, H. (1986) Patriarchal Commodity Production. *Social Analysis,* 20: 47–55.

Gorz, A. (2010) *The Immaterial.* Chicago: University of Chicago Press.

Greer, B. (2014) *Craftivism: The Art of Craft and Activism.* Vancouver, BC: Arsenal Pulp.

Hammer, N. (2015) *New Industry on a Skewed Playing Field: Supply Chain Relations and Working Conditions in UK Garment Manufacturing.* Available online at: www2.le.ac.uk/offices/press/for-journalists/media-resources/Leicester%20 Report%20-%20Final%20-to%20publish.pdf/ [accessed 14 February 2018].

Hardt, M. & Negri, A. (2000) *Empire.* Cambridge, MA: Harvard University Press.

Hatherley, O. (2016) *The Ministry of Nostalgia: Consuming Austerity.* London: Verso.

Hochschild, A. (1997) *The Time Bind: When Work Becomes Home and Home Becomes Work.* New York: Metropolitan Books.

Holt, D. (2004) *How Brands Become Icons: The Principles of Cultural Branding.* Cambridge, MA: Harvard Business School Press.

Huws, U. (2014) *Labor in the Digital Economy.* New York: Monthly Review Press.

Land, C. & Taylor, S. (2014) The Good Old Days yet to Come: Postalgic Times for the New Spirit of Capitalism. *Management & Organizational History,* 9(2): 202–219.

Lash, S. (1994) Reflexivity and its Doubles: Structure, Aesthetics, Community. In U. Beck, A. Giddens and S. Lash (Eds.) *Reflexive Modernization.* Cambridge: Polity.

Lave, J. & Wenger, E. (1991) *Situated Learning: Legitimate Peripheral Participation.* Cambridge: Cambridge University Press.

Maciel, A. (2017) The Cultural Tensions Between Taste Refinement and Middle-Class Masculinity. In N. Chapman, J.S. Lellock and C. Lippard (Eds.) *Untapped: Exploring the Cultural Dimensions of Craft Beer.* Morgantown. WV: West Virginia University Press.

Noble, D. (2011) *Forces of Production: A Social History of Industrial Automation, revised edition.* London: Routledge.

Ocejo, R. (2017) *Masters of Craft: Old Jobs in the New Urban Economy.* Princeton, NJ: Princeton University Press.

Peyton, J. (2013) *Beer O'Clock: Craft, Cask and Culture.* Chichester: Summersdale.

Sennett, R. (2008) *The Craftsman.* London: Penguin.

Smith Maguire, J., Bain, J., Davies, A. & Touri, M. (2017) Storytelling and Market Formation: An Exploration of Craft Brewers in the UK. In N. Chapman, J.S. Lellock and C. Lippard (Eds.) *Untapped: Exploring the Cultural Dimensions of Craft Beer.* Morgantown, WV: West Virginia University Press.

Soldatenko, M. (1999) Made in the USA: Latinas/Os?, Garment Work and Ethnic Conflict in Los Angeles' Sweat Shops. *Cultural Studies*, 13(2): 319–334.

Spradley, J. & Mann, B. (1975) *The Cocktail Waitress: Woman's Work in a Man's World*. New York: McGraw-Hill.

Thurnell-Read, T. (2014) Craft, Tangibility and Affect at Work in the Microbrewery. *Emotion, Space and Society*, 13: 46–54.

Thurnell-Read, T. (2016) The Embourgeoisement of Beer: Changing Practices of 'Real Ale' Consumption. *Journal of Consumer Culture*, https://doi.org/10.1177/1469540516684189.

Watson, T. & Watson, D. (2012) Narratives in Society, Organizations and Individual Identities: An Ethnographic Study of Pubs, Identity Work and the Pursuit of 'the Real'. *Human Relations*, 65(6): 683–704.

Watt, J. (2016) *Business for Punks: Break All the Rules – the BrewDog Way*. London: Penguin.

Weeks, K. (2014) *The Problem with Work: Feminism, Marxism, Antiwork Politics, and Postwork Imaginaries*. Durham, NC: Duke University Press.

Withers, E. (2017) Brewing Boundaries of White/Middle-Class/Maleness: Reflections from Within the Craft Beer Industry. In N. Chapman, J.S. Lellock & C. Lippard (Eds.) *Untapped: Exploring the Cultural Dimensions of Craft Beer*. Morgantown, WV: West Virginia University Press.

Wright, S. (2014) *Accounting for Taste: Conversation, Categorisation and Certification in the Sensory Assessment of Craft Brewing*. Unpublished Ph.D. Thesis: Lancaster University.

York, P. (2017) *Peter York's Hipster Handbook*, broadcast on BBC4, Friday 23rd June, 2017.

8 'Craft' as a Contested Term

Revealing Meaning among Consumers in the Context of the Craft-brewing Industry from Authenticity Perspective in the UK

Nadine Waehning, Maria Karampela and Juho Pesonen

Introduction

This chapter analyses associations consumers attach to the 'craft' label in the context of the booming craft-brewing industry. Craft has long been employed as a symbol of distinct artisanship in this industry, but there are currently claims of a 'craft beer revolution'. The increasing number of craft breweries is in alignment with consumers' increasing need for authenticity (Kadirovet et al. 2014). Authenticity is becoming one of the cornerstones of contemporary marketing (Brown et al. 2003).

In this study, we analyse brewing industry definitions of craft, and argue that the term has been used and abused by both brewers and consumers to signify much more than the dictionary perspective of attachment to traditional methods and skills. Through 16 interviews, we reveal how the current ambiguity around craft is evident in its usage by consumers, and locate our findings within theoretical debates on authenticity.

We argue that this ambiguity is a challenge for the industry as the term is in danger of losing its original meaning. Without a clear definition of this signifier or clarity in its everyday use, it becomes challenging for stakeholders to even discuss the topic, or to plan sustainable growth. Ambiguity in the use of the term 'craft beer' also makes it impossible to define what is authentic and what it is not.

The rest of the chapter proceeds as follows. First, we examine existing conceptualisations of the term 'craft', focusing especially on brewing contexts. Then we review how authenticity and its different meanings link to consumer–product interactions before we articulate the objectives of our empirical work and its methodology. We then present our findings, and conclude with suggestions for future research.

'Craft' and 'Craft Beer': Diversity and Ambiguity in Production and Consumption

The terms 'craft' and 'craft beer' have witnessed growing interest recently from the academic community as well as practitioners and policymakers. This can be attributed to the increasing number of products claiming to be 'craft', as well as to craft products becoming trendy lifestyle choices (Gust 2016). In marketing, craftship[1] is also connected to luxury brands and products in consumer minds (Tynan et al. 2010), making it a valuable branding tool for many companies (Robinson 2017). However, consumer interpretations of the term, especially in relation to brewing, have been neglected. Industry definitions of craft (and craft beer) are also unclear (Pöllänen 2013). This lack of clarity creates risks for the sector's identity and quality standards. To achieve a better understanding, we turn first to scholarly understanding of the term 'craft', the focus of which is divided between perspectives of makers/producers and those of consumers; we review these separately below.

The official definition by the Oxford English Dictionary (2017a) adopts a producer-focused view, defining 'craft' as *"an activity involving skill in making things by hand"*. This aligns with Hanks's (1979) definition of craft as to *"make or fashion with skill, especially by hand"*. Campbell (2005) considers the term 'handicraft', of which 'craft' is a shortened version, as something that is produced 'by hand' or 'by foot' and is directly under the control of the worker. In this context, 'craft' is connected to an activity in which a product is designed and made by someone who *"invests his or her personality or self into the object produced"* (p. 27).

Research has examined handcrafters' motivations (Johnson & Wilson 2005), meanings of craft as experienced by home-based craftspeople (Mason 2005), makers' description of craft as an occupation (Dickie 2003; Pöllänen 2013), and the significant intrinsic values which drive them (Thurnell-Read 2014). All of these studies focus on the effects crafting has on the producers, starting from the position that crafting as a process allows makers to develop their personal identity (Johnson & Wilson 2005; Pöllänen 2013). Overall, this body of work concludes that products made by craftspeople are made with love and are personalised by the makers' personal history (Mason 2005).

Within these production-focused perspectives on the term 'craft', we observe disparities in its conceptualisation, as its meaning seems to be context-dependent. Similar ambiguities to those manifest in the craft beer industry are evident elsewhere. Craft souvenir makers have also had difficulties in finding a working definition (Peach 2007). In Scotland, the craft community has expressed concerns that the quality of product and design integrity may be reduced as demand from tourists increase (Peach 2007). Craft souvenirs are defined as locally produced, made by hand, and more expensive than mass-produced souvenir goods. However, mass tourism shapes the craft industry as the craftspeople orient production more towards volume, rather than quality or artistic experimentation (Peach 2007).

The aforementioned diversities and ambiguities associated with the term 'craft' are not surprising and we immediately see space for multiple interpretations. What exactly is the 'amount' of skill? How much needs to be done 'by hand' to be counted as craft? Most importantly for the context of this study, when we look at the Oxford Dictionary definition of a 'craft beer' as *"a beer made in traditional or non-mechanized way by a small brewery"* (The Oxford English Dictionary 2017b), confusion still remains. How 'small' must the brewery be, and in what ways exactly (brew strength, number of employees, turnover, etc.)?

This lack of clarity is evident in scholarly work and in definitions provided by industry representatives such as producers and policy/support bodies. In brewing, size seems to be a key point of conflict. In March 2014, BrewDog, one of the biggest players in the craft beer movement, proposed a definition that focused on four categories: authenticity, honesty, independence, and commitment. BrewDog excluded size and type of production specifically so that they themselves would be included in their definition of a craft brewery (BrewDog 2014), and unsuccessfully presented the definition at the Annual General Meeting of the Society of Independent Brewers (SIBA). In August 2016 SIBA also launched a new accreditation scheme to claim back the meaning of craft and offer a 'stamp of approval' to independent British breweries with a capacity requirement of less than 200,000 hectolitres annually that abide by SIBA's Manual of Good Brewing Practice (Woolfson 2016).

Industry definitions therefore seem to highlight that a craft brewery should be four things: 1. a certain size, 2. authentic – demonstrated for example through use of high-quality ingredients, 3. honest – ingredients and origin need to be listed on the labels, and 4. independent and committed to craft, in that at least 90 per cent of production must be craft beer. However, there is not a consensus that satisfies all parties. In addition, such producer-focused conceptualisations of craft ignore consumer interpretations. For that reason, we now turn to interpretations of 'craft' and 'craft beer' from a consumption-focused perspective.

In consumption, craft activity is considered as something to which a *consumer* brings skill, passion and judgement. Craft consumers are motivated by a desire for self-expression (Campbell 2005), and have a specific profile and attributes (Hu & Yu 2007). Hu & Yu (2007) identified three segments of craft consumers, differing from each other based on perceptions of the importance of craftwork, sensuous appreciation, cultural linkage, and ease of handling. The three segments are shopping enthusiasts, shopping lovers, and indifferent shoppers, and it was shown that the craft shopper or craft consumer segment is heterogeneous, with people interested in different dimensions of craft consumption.

Numerous studies have examined the craft beer consumer, with particular focus on three research areas: 1. choices between craft and commercial/industrial beers (Aquilani et al. 2015), 2. situational appropriateness and product familiarity (Giacalone et al. 2015), and 3. habits, attitudes and motives (Gomez-Corona et al. 2016). The constant comparison between craft and industrial beer permeates discourses around craft beer consumption. Donadini and Porretta (2017) report on an extensive study of craft beer in contrast to industrial beer. Similarly, Gómez-Corona et al., (2016a, 2016b) identified three clusters of consumers based on a number of dimensions, with one extreme being 'industrial beer consumers' and the other 'craft beer consumers'.

This body of work suggests that we should have a very clear understanding of what craft beer is and what industrial beer is, yet existing research fails to account for the exact meanings and interpretations that consumers attach to the term 'craft'. Indeed, research commissioned by SIBA presents some interesting findings (SIBA Admin 2016): 1. approximately 46 per cent of beer consumers expect craft beer to be made by small or microbreweries, hence size appears as a crucial dimension of craft beer for only half of respondents; 2. only 14 per cent of consumers expect craft to be produced locally; 3. 10 per cent of them are not certain about the actual meaning of the term. Therefore, consumers' interpretations of 'craft' in relation to brewing products lack clarity in similar ways to the lack of consensus amongst industry representatives.

In this study, we account for those multiple interpretations by adopting a consumer-culture theory perspective, through which craft consumption is viewed under the lens of consumers' search for authenticity. Authenticity is rarely adopted as an empirical perspective on craft consumption, yet it can provide a valuable perspective from which to examine consumer-based discourses and interpretations of 'craft' activities (Campbell 2005).

Authenticity

Authenticity has received significant multidisciplinary attention (Grayson & Martinec 2004). There may be as many definitions as those who write about it (Taylor 2001). This suggests it is best treated as a social construct, something observed rather than a property inherent in an object, person, or experience (Beverland & Farrelly 2010).

Authenticity and consumption are closely linked (Beverland & Farrelly 2010), as consumers actively seek authentic persons, products, brands, places, businesses, and experiences (Kadirov et al. 2014) to construct meaning (Emmons 2005). Postmodern market characteristics such as globalisation, hyperreality and deterritorialisation (Arnould & Price 2000) together with standardisation and homogenisation in the marketplace (Thompson, Rindfleisch & Arsel 2006) are key factors increasing consumers' interest in, and needs for, authenticity.

Wang (1999) distinguishes between two kinds of authenticity: the authenticity of objects and existential authenticity. Existential authenticity is activity-based, both intrapersonal and interpersonal. As an observed rather than inherent property, the authenticity of a concept, product, service, or experience lies in the minds of consumers and is not something that producers can build into it. Thus, while a craft worker is someone who designs the products, selects the production materials, and personally makes the object (Campbell 2005), authenticity is also dependent on the goals of the consumer (Beverland & Farrelly 2010).

What makes authenticity so crucial in consumption settings is that consumers' perceptions of authenticity in a product or experience can influence loyalty (Kolar & Zabkar 2010), thus providing important incentives to makers to associate their offerings with it. In addition, Lu et al. (2015) demonstrated that consumers' perceptions of the authenticity of ethnic restaurant brands is a critical determinant of brand equity, which in turn has a significant impact on consumers' brand choice intentions.

As a result, managers constantly seek to manipulate brands to appear more authentic and respond to consumers' expectations of authenticity (Kadirov et al. 2014). However, marketers should perhaps not focus on how to manipulate products and brands, but instead *"respond to citizens' quest for authenticity in the marketplace by a means of constructing authentic existence and practices"* (Kadirov et al. 2014: 73). Typical in this search for authenticity is consumers' quest to find something genuine, real, and true (Arnould & Price 2000; Beverland & Farrelly 2010; Thompson et al. 2006), suggesting this is where issues with the nature of authenticity, or defining what authentic is, lie. As Beverland and Farrelly (2010: 853) eloquently state: *"authenticity is impossible where common standards for what is real or fake are lacking"*.

In consumer culture theory, Campbell (2005) connects the search for authenticity to the craft consumer by proposing that craft consumption is regarded as a means of self-expression and authenticity in a world dominated by commodification and marketisation. For instance, uniqueness, technique, aesthetic and use, cultural and historical integrity, as well as the characteristics of the craftsperson and the shopping experience associated with craft souvenirs, are contributing factors to its authenticity (Littrell et al. 1993). Cohen (1988) nuances this, summarising three core viewpoints of the meaning of 'authentic' culture in tourism: commoditization, staged authenticity, and authentic experience, concluding that commoditization is not the end of an authentic experience. The tourism literature suggests that consumers do not seek in-depth knowledge and that a few core traits which are perceived to be authentic could be sufficient (Cohen 1988). Thus, we can conclude that we need to understand the elements that make craft beer authentic, especially the core ones.

In line with the above literature on authenticity and its relation to craft consumption, we can make some interesting observations about the term 'craft' in the brewing industry, and about the value of using authenticity perspectives to understand consumer interpretations of 'craft' beer. First, as craft breweries are predominantly locally based businesses that mainly cater for their relatively confined regional markets and raise sentiments of local pride, it is natural that they (and their products) are regarded by consumers as opposing forces to a globalising world. This places craft breweries very clearly within the authenticity debate (Campbell 2005). Second, craft breweries are often differentiated from larger, multinational beer producers in terms of the culture of production and customers. Yet in recent years we observe a rising number of larger breweries tapping into the craft beer market via takeover of craft breweries or via developing their own 'craft' beers. This further challenges the notion of authenticity, and what is meant when academics, practitioners, and consumers refer to 'authentic' craft beer products and experiences.

In sum, then, we have argued that there is a lack of a broadly accepted definition of those terms, but that the most crucial matter is the neglect of consumers' interpretations, which could inform further the ways employed to communicate about those products and experiences. This lack of understanding is significant for both academics and practitioners. The next section outlines the aims of this study, and its theoretical and practical value.

Purpose and Value of the Study

Given the little in-depth information in existing literature regarding consumers' perceptions of the term 'craft' when it relates to beer products and experiences, and given the value consumers attach to this signalling term, the current study seeks to explore consumers' interpretations of the term 'craft' in relation to beer products and experiences via adopting authenticity as its theoretical lens. We argue that this perspective can uniquely inform discourses on craft (beer) consumption, as it can lead to further understanding of what 'authentic' craft beer experiences are and how they are represented in consumers' minds.

Conceptually, this research provides unique in-depth insight into consumers' interpretations of the term 'craft' in relation to craft beer products and experiences, by exploring how perceptions might differ for different groups of consumers, as recommended by previous literature (Ihatsu 2002). In particular, we capture diverse connotations associated with 'authentic craft experiences' by consumers of different age and gender groups, as well as of varying levels of self-proclaimed beer knowledge. This is significant in enriching broader scholarly understanding of the term 'craft', and in clarifying the relative importance of perceived attributes of craft beer in consumers' minds.

Practically, we provide insight to practitioners, industry associations, and policy/support bodies with regard to consumers' interpretations of the term 'craft', and what they perceive to be authentic craft experiences in relation to brewing products. This is crucial, given that existing efforts to define those terms have been constrained to debates within the supply side. In this phase, where the craft beer industry is booming, ensuring that all key stakeholders' perspectives are accounted for is vital in order to reach a joint understanding of those terms, and, most importantly, to establish and maintain quality standards.

Methodology

We adopt a subjectivist perspective, in that reality is effectively created by social actors, actions, and perceptions (Geertz 1983; Ortner 1984; Von Krogh & Roos 1995). Meaning is created through the interaction of social actors, which is the result of adjustment to the unique external environment and to other individuals (Arbnor & Bjerke 2008; Earley & Singh 1995; Watkins 2010). We used an inductive approach to develop our analysis, via discovering empirical patterns, themes, and categories (Vaismoradi et al. 2013).

Face-to-face, semi-structured interviews with 16 consumers were conducted (Merriam 2014; Myers 2013), as interviews can provide novel insights into a topic compared to quantitative data collection, which was the approach of earlier studies in this area (Donadini & Porretta 2017; Gómez-Corona et al. 2016a, 2016b). The applied sampling technique here was non-random judgment sampling. More precisely, convenience and snowball sampling approaches were followed, something often used in qualitative research (Pesonen et al. 2015). It was crucial that the respondents represented different age groups, genders, and varying levels of beer knowledge, because it is more important to generate interviewees who represent various voices than to achieve a specific sample size (Myers & Newman 2007). Table 8.1 presents the profile of the respondents.

Data were collected until theoretical saturation was achieved (Marshall 1996). All interviews were recorded and transcribed and supplemented with researchers' notes. We applied thematic analysis to identify core constancies, meanings, and recurring words and themes, according to the stages proposed by Fereday & Muir-Cochrane (2006) (see Figure 8.1).

In the first stage, a code manual was developed, and codes were written with reference to Boyatzis (1998) as follows: 1. Naming/labelling the code; 2. Defining the theme, 3. Describing how the theme might occur. After developing the initial code book (the first nine codes in Table 8.2), those codes were applied to the first set of data from eight consumers. Then, the same codes were applied to the next eight interviews. Through this reliability test, the first set of codes was confirmed to apply to the dataset as a whole. However, four additional codes were identified (highlighted as 'NEW' in Table 8.2). Finally, for stages 5 and 6, discussion amongst co-authors helped to combine and retest the coding.

Table 8.1 Respondents' Profile

Interviewee code	Gender	Age	Self-claimed frequency of drinking beer	Place of interview
C1	Female	30	Casual drinker	Brewery tour
C2	Male	30	Regular beer drinker	Brewery tour
C3	Female	28	More a wine drinker but interested to learn more about beer	Brewery tour
C4	Female	22	Does not drink beer often	Brewery tour
C5	Female	40s	Works for CAMRA (Campaign for Real Ale)	Brewery tour
C6	Male	60s	Beer enthusiast, works for CAMRA	Brewery tour
C7	Male	60s	Beer blogger, rather knowledgeable	Brewery tour
C8	Male	21	Casual beer drinker	At home
C9	Male	22	Regular beer drinker	At home
C10	Male	22	Occasional beer drinker	University
C11	Male	42	Casual beer drinker	At home
C12	Male	45	Casual beer drinker	At home
C13	Male	59	Casual beer drinker	At home
C14	Male	23	Drinks often, works in the tap room	Student union
C15	Female	21	Works in a pub, required to try ales for the job	Student union
C16	Female	29	Works in a pub and every Friday and Saturday gets a range of beers to try	Pub in York

Findings and Discussion

Some of the attributes of what consumers understand by the term 'craft beer' have been previously identified (e.g. the importance of the size of the brewery). Such associations are confirmed in our data. However, these attributes appear to have emerged from comparison of 'craft' beer with beer labelled as 'industrial', and it seems this comparison has acted as a barrier to scholarly research to account for the exact meanings and connotations that consumers attach to the term 'craft'. As our interviews reveal, there are associations that consumers make about 'craft' beer products and experiences that have not been previously identified, such as the importance of variety of beer products. Figure 8.2 presents an illustrative representation of the different meaning categories which our analysis revealed.

A close observation reveals that there are attributes associated with 'craftiness' in brewing contexts that relate to the producing firm (brewery), the producer (brewer), the method of and approach to

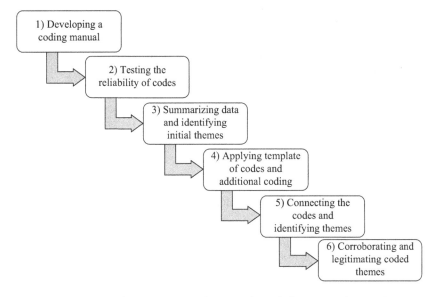

Figure 8.1 Stages of Thematic Analysis [Adapted from Fereday and Muir-Cochrane (2006)]

production (brewing), and the final product (beer). While this could have been employed as a way to structure the presentation of our findings, we have opted to establish first the ambiguity of the term 'craft beer' as experienced by consumers and subsequently to organise our findings using the prominence of each association as the guiding structure. In this way, our results provide indications about the relative importance of certain attributes of craft beer. The next sections present those findings in more detail.

Craft Beer as an Ambiguous, Diverse, and Abused Term

Our analysis reveals a lack of consensus and diversity of views about what 'craft' in relation to brewing products and experiences represents, or should represent, that was materialised independent of, and across, all levels of self-proclaimed knowledge of craft beer. This diversity further emphasises that the need to reach a deeper understanding of the term 'craft' in this specific context is imperative, in order to inform the discussion around the development of a definition that will take into account all key stakeholders' perceptions.

Interviewees readily admitted lack of knowledge or understanding about the term, which demonstrates that 'craft' can be attached to any beer products and experiences without clear standards. The majority of

Table 8.2 Coding Manual

Code 1

Label	Positive: Quality
Definition	Referring to the quality of the product/process/ingredients
Description	The label term could be specifically named in an overall description of the meaning of craft (by a consumer) and refer to the actual product, the process or the ingredients used.

Code 2

Label	Positive: Size of the brewery/production
Definition	Referring to the size of the company producing the beer
Description	The label meaning can refer to the size of the brewery, the batches the breweries produce, small overall company and small independent brewery.

Code 3

Label	Positive: Flavours
Definition	Referring to variety of flavours, unique flavours
Description	The label meaning includes nice taste, bigger variety, more flavours, etc.

Code 4

Label	Positive: Art/skill
Definition	Referring to specific skill, creating something, unique brewing style
Description	The label meaning includes the emphasis of it being a unique product, and how each brewery varies in their production processes and end products.

Code 5

Label	Positive: Packaging
Definition	Referring to keg
Description	The label meaning includes the emphasis that craft beer comes in kegs or certain- sized bottles (generally smaller ones).

Code 6

Label	Positive: New modern brands
Definition	Referring to non-tradition brand, pioneering
Description	The label meaning includes craft beer is more modern, up-and-coming, not old or traditional.

Code 7

Label	Negative: Distribution channels
Definition	Referring to what is being distributed in supermarkets not being craft
Description	The label meaning includes craft beer should not be in big supermarket chains or pub chains but instead it should be in craft pubs, local farmers' shops, etc.

Code 8

Label	Negative: Marketing ploy
Definition	Referring to it is a misused/hijacked term by multinationals, as a marketing ploy
Description	The label meaning includes craft is now a buzz word, the mass producers are taking over small breweries, it seems to be a way to sell more poorly produced beer.

Code 9

Label	Negative: Consumers as victims
Definition	Referring to consumers increasingly being warier of falling victim to the term 'craft' being misused by large organisations.
Description	The label meaning includes the specific fear consumers have of buying something they assume to be a craft product but it turns out to be just a small brewery which was bought by a large brewery or a large brewery calling their beer 'craft beer'.

Table 8.2 (Cont.)

Code 10

Label	Positive: Stage 4 **NEW**: It is local
Definition	Referring to the location where the brewery is situated
Description	The label meaning includes anything participants describe as local, but does not specify how far the distance need to be for a brewery to be still called local to that person.

Code 11

Label	Negative: Stage 4 **NEW**: Price
Definition	Referring to a comparison between craft and non-craft beer and the implication that craft beer costs a bit more.
Description	The label includes any words describing or implying a higher cost for this product in comparison to non-craft beers.

Code 12

Label	Neutral: Stage 4 **NEW**: 'I don't know'
Definition	Referring to comments where participants claimed no knowledge of craft beer or a specific probing question.
Description	The label covers participants who might be claiming to lack knowledge in parts of the interview or if the topic was overall an area they did not feel knowledgeable about.

Code 13

Label	Positive: Stage 4 **NEW**: It is new/innovative
Definition	Referring to the association with craft and newness and/or innovation.
Description	The label is specifically focused on the terms of new and/or innovation linked to craft beer.

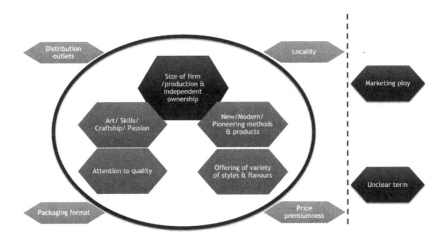

Figure 8.2 Overview of Meaning Categories

our respondents appeared confident that they had great awareness about craft beer as a product category and had quite strong and passionate personal views, both positively and negatively inflected. In other words, consumers were either unclear of what the term refers to, or expressed very strong and diverse opinions about what it entails. This mix of ambiguity and diversity highlights the blurred boundaries of the term 'craft', and jeopardises the industry's ability to safeguard quality and continue legitimising premium prices for craft beer consumption in the long term.

However, while most consumers have strong (albeit different) views about what the term should represent, that does not preclude them from recognising that the term has been abused, with many considering that we will perhaps never reach a common understanding of it:

> The most misused and misunderstood term in the whole beer industry. It is generally used to mean keg but to me it should not mean keg, it should be about the way it is produced, but it is never going to be defined like that because the multinationals have taken on craft as a term … it is never going to be defined. So, I find it is a marketing ploy and nothing more.
>
> (C5)

> But that *[the term craft]* has been hijacked by bigger producers who are saying they are producing craft although they producing beer left right and centre. It's been replacing the authentic breweries. I am still falling back to it and I am still drawn to it but you are warier of it, falling victim to it. You might be 'yea ah right I take that away' but then you find out that it's made by a big brewery.
>
> (C1)

Most illustrative of the ambiguity of the term is that, even in those passionate statements where consumers agreed on the term 'craft beer' being hijacked or abused, there are still multiple connotations assigned to it. Craft was associated to the style of beer or the type of container it is enclosed in, or directly connected with the size of the brewery and its production. Having illustrated therefore the lack of consensus around the term, we now proceed to examine the various connotations consumers assign to it.

Craft Beer Linked to Size of Brewery and Production

As shown, consumers consider the term 'craft' to have been appropriated and misused by 'big' breweries or multinationals. In theory, there is nothing that stops large, established breweries making similar beers to those of microbreweries: they can build similar facilities, hire people with the necessary skills, buy the same ingredients, and make similar beer.

Yet, from the consumers' perspective, beer made by larger companies is a marketing ploy and is not in line with their understanding of the term 'craft' beer.

For the vast majority of our participants, the size of the brewery is a key criterion for considering a certain beer or brewery as 'craft'. It was widely observed that 'craft' is a type of beer produced by small-sized breweries, which can only produce in small qualities or batches each time:

> ... for me craft means small, unique, [...], it's small batches, quality.
>
> (C1)

> Small batch, it's up-and-coming, its more definable; the same with authentic and provenance.
>
> (C2)

> Ahm ... anything that is probably new or ... what microbreweries are making. It is important to me. I would prefer it over mass-produced beer.
>
> (C10)

> ... making a smaller batch ...
>
> (C11)

Moreover, consumers suggested that archetypal craft beer products and experiences are not simply those offered by small-sized breweries, but more specifically, those provided by small-sized breweries that are independent from multinational beer companies. This distinction introduces a new dimension to our understanding of consumers' perceptions of craft: that of brewery and production size (micro or small) being interdependent with the nature of brewery ownership (independence from multinationals or bigger players), as indicators of authentic 'craft' beer products and experiences. These indicators could therefore be regarded as primary factors taken under consideration by consumers during their decision-making processes. Our respondents also referred to the frustration they feel when realising that a beer they purchased considering it was craft is in reality made by larger producers. This feeling of deceit suggests that consumers have certain expectations about craft beer products and wish for greater control in making informed purchasing decisions.

As mentioned earlier, the size of the brewery and production have been identified as an important factor in beer industry efforts to define the term 'craft' (e.g. in SIBA's seal of craft beer). Brewery size and independence from larger players are also included in official definitions of the term established by associations in other countries. In the USA, the world's largest craft beer producer (Craft Brewing Business 2017), craft beer is defined by two criteria: 1. the brewery needs to be independent,

2. annual production should be of six million barrels of beer or less (Brewers Association 2017). The second criterion however, the introduction of a numerical value as an upper limit of production size, can be considered controversial, as it has been steadily increased in the previous years (CNBC 2013), and critics seem to suggest that this has purposely been done to keep certain breweries within the 'craft' category (e.g. Boston or Sierra Nevada). This is an indication of the power that larger brewers have on key decision-makers in the industry.

That larger or multinational players are trying to push into the growing craft beer market is common knowledge among brewers and consumers alike, as demonstrated during the interviews. Indeed, as shown earlier, consumers often perceive the term 'craft', at least in this context, to be a marketing ploy. However, our analysis has also made very clear that consumers consider the small size of the brewery and of production in conjunction with independence from larger or multinational beer companies as a crucial attribute of 'craft' here, and this is a key factor taken into consideration when making 'craft' beer purchase decisions. The fact that consumers are very passionate about craft beer not being produced by larger players, including multinationals buying up smaller breweries, is also evident from recent examples of consumer boycotting 14 'imposter' beer brands (Business Insider UK 2017). Overall therefore, both small size and ownership independence will need to be linked to definitions of craft beer to ensure consumers' viewpoints are accounted for.

Attention to Quality, Art, Passion, Innovation, and Variety as Key Attributes of Craft Beer

Our analysis also revealed that there were many additional key connotations relating to the producer, the method of production, and the final product. In consumers' minds, these attributes were crucial in order for them to consider a craft beer truly authentic.

First, our interviewees considered that craft beer products stand at the end of a process permeated with continuous attention to quality, in relation to ingredients used and processes followed:

> …as long as it is produced with top quality ingredients and is done properly, it is a craft beer.
>
> (C7)

This aspect is covered by SIBA's 'seal of craft', as it is stated that in order for a craft beer to be authentic, it should always use high-quality ingredients, which should all be listed along with beer origin on the label in order to ensure transparency and help consumers make informed decisions (SIBA Admin 2016). However, our interviews highlighted some additional relevant connotations that have thus far not been covered in industry attempts to define the term. Participants considered that it was not only the high-quality ingredients or the attention to the process of brewing that made a beer worthy of the label 'craft', but also the art behind the production process, the expertise and skill involved in timely and appropriate combination and addition of the right ingredients:

> Each brewery varies, how they decide when to add the ingredients. I can see the art behind it a lot more.
>
> (C3)

> What I assume from what I heard they are taking different bits and make something new.
>
> (C4)

The 'art' and 'expertise' that are instilled in the brewing process refer to the ability to uniquely combine ingredients, and to the continuous and passionate creativity and experimentation that always leads to new products, and new experiences for the consumers:

> Craft in beer ... ahm yea I guess small not even small ... breweries making, perhaps experimenting with different styles of beer and making a smaller batch, and then when it goes well making it commercially. Sort of experimenting to see what they can do and offering more experiences for their customers. That is better than the mass- producers.
>
> (C11)

Artistic expression, skills, and continuous experimentation and innovation in production processes were considered to be the source of novelty and differentiation in regard to the range of beer styles that were offered by 'craft' breweries. Those elements were considered as the differentiating points of craft beer in comparison to industrial, mass-produced beer, but most importantly, they were perceived as part of a pattern that guides everything in the craft brewery's presence and purpose. Experimentation and novelty were seen simultaneously as continuous processes detrimental to a brewery's craftiness and as the brewery's raison d'être. As C11 above states, experimentation is a process that *"when it goes well,"* then its products are exploited commercially; yet, this clearly shows that consumers recognise that experimentation does not always lead to good results, and entails risks for the brewer. Consumers' interpretation of the term 'craft' here is that, despite its success or failure, continuous innovation must be a key element of any brewery claiming to be craft.

This continuous effort, in conjunction with artistic expression and expertise, is perhaps why consumers perceive craft in brewing contexts to be synonymous with notions of variety and flavour. Our interviewees highlighted that craft breweries produce a variety of different styles of beer, different flavours, and different levels of strength in the end product:

> I would tend to choose a craft beer taste over a sort of old traditional brand because there is a bigger variety of flavours there and they pioneer the interesting brews. Hijack by bigger breweries, same with distilleries. For me craft means small, unique, more flavour, it's small batches, quality.
>
> (C1)

> Ahm… anything that is probably new or ahm… what microbreweries are making. It is important to me. I would prefer it over mass-produced beer, because of the nice taste, bigger variety of hops and bitterness and percentage.
>
> (C10)

What is worth observing here is the obsession of consumers with the ability of the brewery to continuously produce a wide range of new beers. Such ability is perceived as the means to offer consumers unique taste experiences. To consumers' eyes this uniqueness is, again, linked with size: uniqueness can be achieved via small batches of carefully and artistically crafted products that can only be experienced by 'few'.

Overall, continuous attention to quality, innovation, and creativity along with ability to produce a range of styles and flavours of beer products are fundamental attributes of 'craft' breweries and brewing processes, yet, surprisingly, these have not been addressed or accounted for in any industry attempts when defining craft beer.

Peripheral Associations of Craft Beer: Price Premium, Acceptable Forms of Packaging and Distribution, and Locality

We now turn to more peripheral, less prominent connotations that consumers in our study related to craft beer. These associations move beyond the actual production processes and final core products, and touch upon other aspects of the marketing mix deployed to establish the role of craft beers in the contemporary marketplace.

As mentioned earlier, consumers associate craft beer with uniqueness and variety. These characteristics have implications for the price range in which craft beer is marketed:

> We had a discussion recently … and I think the real ale is always from a hand pump and craft from a pressure pump, from cans and bottles, and costs a bit more. I certainly choose a craft beer over that of a large brewery.
>
> (C12)

C12 further considered that this price premium is a positive association for craft beer products: craft beer is considered to be worthy of a price premium because it provides the customer with extra value. Allegedly, with the brewer's higher attention to quality and instilment of creativity and effort, craft beer is a product of better quality, hence a moderate price premium in comparison to industrial beers is interpreted as good value for money. This matter can also be interpreted through an authenticity lens: consumers might consider that truly authentic craft beers are more expensive than industrial due to the artistic expression of the producer, their hands-on approach, and the meticulous processes of production followed in comparison to the mechanised forms of production employed by industrial beer producers.

Similarly, the associations of 'uniqueness', 'quality', and 'premiumness' attached to craft beer appear to have implications for the acceptable forms of packaging and distribution:

> It [craft beer] is generally used to mean keg but to me it should not mean keg, it should be about the way it is produced, but it is never going to be defined like that.
>
> (C5)

Equally, selection of appropriate distribution outlets appears to also add to consumers' perceptions of a beer product as 'craft'. In line with its unique and artistic nature, consumers seem to consider that beer distributed or sold in mass-retail environments is not craft:

> Personally, it was a term I imagine by small producers, as a way to differentiate themselves from the large mass-producers, but unfortunately the mass-producers are taking it now and it's changing ... now there is a craft section in the supermarkets, so it is dead to me personally.
>
> (C2)

Price premiumness, packaging in kegs and small bottles as well as distribution in outlets such as brewery shops and specialised stores are thus symbolic representations of authentic 'craftiness' in brewing contexts.

Finally, perhaps the most surprising finding of this study was the (lack of) role of locality and origin of the beer products. Only one of our consumers contemplated, in a quite uncertain mode, that for him a beer can be considered 'craft' if it is locally made:

> I would say it's a local, I don't really know to be honest, made by a smaller brewer.
>
> (C9)

None of the other interviewees mentioned or even implied that local origin matters when considering whether a beer is 'craft'. This is surprising because brewers often credit the expansion of the craft beer movement in general, and the success of their individual breweries and products in particular, to their linkage with their local communities (Mintel 2013). In fact, highlighting local origin is a widespread strategy for breweries across the UK. Clear signals of origin, including place of production or of sourcing of ingredients (mainly water), as well as symbols associated with certain locales are actively embedded in marketing communication strategies and packaging. Hence, breweries evidently consider their locality as a key part of their 'craft' identity, yet consumers do not seem to share this view.

Conclusions, Implications, and Areas for Future Research

The starting point of this study was the diversities observed in research, among industry representatives and consumers with regard to the meaning of the term 'craft'. Existing discussions in the literature are heavily supply-side oriented, and the phenomenon has not been closely examined from the consumers' perspective. This study therefore sought to explore consumers' interpretations of the term 'craft' in relation to beer products and experiences via adopting authenticity as its theoretical lens. In particular, the current research aimed to provide further understanding of how 'authentic' craft beer experiences are represented in consumers' minds.

Our analysis revealed a range of meaning categories associated with the term 'craft', and provided insight into their relative importance in consumers' minds. Consumers predominantly associate authentic craft beer contexts with small size and independent ownership of the producing brewery, attention to quality, artistic expression and expertise instilled into the production process, as well as continuous innovation. Other, more peripheral elements, such as price premiumness, packaging and distribution formats, and connection to locale and origin appear to be less straightforward. These peripheral elements can potentially reinforce the authenticity of a craft beer product or experience but are not necessary conditions. In other words, it is possible that different consumers may not 'settle' for a beer being labelled as 'craft' unless, besides the core elements, it is also produced locally, it comes in a certain container, it is sold at certain places, and to a higher price in comparison to mass produced beer.

In terms of practical contribution, by providing insight to practitioners, industry associations, and policy/support bodies with regard to consumers' interpretations of the term 'craft', and what they perceive to be authentic craft experiences in relation to brewing products, the study adds understanding of the demand side to efforts to define 'craft' in those contexts. This is important because representation of all stakeholders' perspectives in this critical phase of development for the craft beer industry is crucial in order to safeguard quality standards and ultimately ensure its sustainability.

At the moment, amidst continuous debates on what this highly contested term represents, efforts by industry bodies such as SIBA to define craft beer cannot be assumed to reliably capture the meanings associated with craft beer, unless all stakeholders' views, including those of consumers, are represented. Understanding what consumers perceive as authentic craft beer products and experiences may be the key to designing an official seal of 'craft' in this context that allows for the most important stakeholder, the consumers, to voice their views. At the same time, industry representatives can ensure that this new seal would be one that consumers do not associate with a marketing ploy, which is challenging, as this kind of approach would actually be a marketing approach (Holt 2002).

Nonetheless, the findings have provided clear indications of the core elements that a new or relaunched 'seal' of craft in brewing contexts should entail. What is real, true, and genuine is not the actual product itself: it became very clear throughout our analysis that craft beer products are something that global breweries can imitate. However, what they cannot imitate are the brewers' entrepreneurial passion, artistic expression, and personal touch that they extend to the production process and the final product, from start to finish, that is, from creatively designing the product and unique and timely combinations of ingredients to attaching labels by hand and making personal deliveries. This is reflected in Campbell's (2005) work; he argues that craft producers invest their personality or self into the object produced and that the ownership of the craft product is with the producer.

There are therefore some key practical implications emerging from our findings. First, it seems that craft breweries centre their marketing efforts around their products, yet this approach cannot provide any kind of competitive advantage when a similar product can be made by companies owned or supported by large breweries. Instead, craft brewers might differentiate their products through the idea that they are made not by mechanised equipment, but by people who are personally vested into the brewing process through participating in its every stage and by assuming the risks of experimentation. An official seal of 'craft' should therefore account for the ways in which consumers in our study regarded craft beers: as something brewed with love, with unique flavour varieties, and made in small, experimental batches by a skilled and creative artist. As a result, such a seal should incorporate ideals of entrepreneurship, enthusiasm, passion, and the personalised spirit of products.

Second, the craft brewing industry should adopt a more macro-marketing perspective in its pursuit for authenticity. Kadirov et al. (2014) encourage businesses to be authentic through the promotion of common good, community welfare, and mutually beneficial outcomes. In a similar vein, the craft-brewing industry could use such an approach as a platform to clearly position itself societally. In particular, the industry could more actively focus on its substantially different culture of drinking (Cohen 1988), by aligning craft-beer consumption with a 'consuming less, consuming better' standpoint, a positioning strategy that clearly differentiates it from binge-drinking. Consumers perceive the brewer as the artist who experiments and introduces them to new flavours and experiences; craft beer could be positioned as a culture of experimentation with new tastes that are socially enjoyed and consumed. By connecting itself with overall lifestyle consumption habits, the craft-brewing sector could gain a competitive advantage over larger actors in the beer industry.

Our study has revealed a number of areas where further research is needed, given that the craft-brewing industry is in constant flux and at a very dynamic phase of its lifecycle. First, we have made a distinction between core and more peripheral meaning associations that consumers attach to the term 'craft' in brewing settings; further research is needed about the conditions where some of those peripheral meanings assume more prominence (e.g. they might emerge as more important for different types of consumers). Second, the role of locality needs to be explored further. Localism and origin may be more important in selecting among different craft beer brands than in perceiving a certain beer as craft in the first place. It is also crucial to examine the marketplace from various viewpoints. A larger-scale study that systematically compares consumers' and brewers' perspectives of the term 'craft' would allow for a clearer identification of the core attributes of authentic craft beer products and experiences, hence enhancing opportunities for reaching a broader consensus. Finally, we note that craft beer production and consumption touch upon numerous topics such as entrepreneurial business practices and broader alcohol consumption. There are many opportunities for exploring the extent to which previous research findings in other sectors extend to this context as well.

Note

1 We consciously use the term 'craftship' and 'workship' in lieu of the more gendered terms 'craftmanship' and 'workmanship', for the reasons set out in the book introduction.

References

Aquilani B., Laureti T., Poponi S. & Secondi L. (2015) Beer choice and consumption determinats when craft beers are tasted: An exploratory study of consumer preferences. *Food Quality and Preference*, 41, 214–224.

Arbnor I . & Bjerke, B. (2008) *Methodology for Creating Business Knowledge.* 3rd edn., London, Sage Publications Ltd.

Arnould E. J. & Price L. L. (2000) Authenticating acts and authoritative performances: Questing for self and community, in S. Ratneshwar, David Glen Mick & Cynthia Huffman (Eds.) *The Why of Consumption: Contemporary Perspectives on Consumer Motives, Goals, and Desires*. London, Routledge.

Beverland M. & Farrelly F. (2010) The quest for authenticity in consumption: Consumers' purposive choice of authentic cues to shape experienced outcomes. *Journal of Consumer Research*. 36, 838–856.

Boyatzis R. (1998) *Transforming Qualitative Information: Thematic Analysis and Code Development*. Thousand Oaks, CA: Sage.

Brew Dog (2014) Defining craft beer at SIBA. Available at: www.brewdog.com/lowdown/blog/defining-craft-beer-at-siba. Accessed at 29/04/2017.

Brewers Association (2017) Craft brewer defined. Available at: www.brewersassociation.org/statistics/craft-brewer-defined/. Accessed at 08/08/2017.

Brown S., Kozinets R. V. & Sherry Jr J. F. (2003) Teaching old brands new tricks: Retro branding and the revival of brand meaning. *Journal of Marketing*, 67(3), 19–33.

Business Insider UK (2017) Craft brewers are calling for the boycott of these 14 'imposter' beer brands. Available at: http://uk.businessinsider.com/craft-brewers-boycott-brands-acquired-by-anheuser-busch-2017-5?r=USandIR=T/#1-goose-island-1. Accessed at 16/08/2017.

Campbell C. (2005) The craft consumer: Culture, craft and consumption in a postmodern society. *Journal of Consumer Culture*, 5(1), 23–42.

CNBC (2013) Sam Adams and the data defining craft beer. Available from: www.cnbc.com/2013/09/13/sam-adams-and-the-data-defining-craft-beer.html. Accessed at 08/08/2017.

Cohen E. (1988) Authenticity and commoditization in tourism. *Annals of Tourism Research*. 15, 372–386.

Craft Brewing Business (2017) World of beer craft: Craft beer market in Europe to grow 11 per cent 2017–2021. Available at: www.craftbrewingbusiness.com/news/world-beer-craft-craft-beer-market-europe-grow-11-2017-2021/. Accessed at 08/08/2017.

Dickie V.A. (2003) Establishing worker identity: A study of people in craft work. *American Journal of Occupational Therapy*, 57(3), 250–261.

Donadini G. & Porretta S. (2017) Uncovering patterns of consumers' interest for beer: A case study with craft beers. *Food Research International*, 91, 183–198.

Earley P. C. & Singh H. (1995) International and intercultural management research: What's next? *Academy of Management Journal*, 38 (2), 327–340.

Emmons R. A. (2005) Striving for the sacred: Personal goals, life meaning, and religion, *Journal of Social Issues*, 61 (4), 731–746.

Fereday J. & Muir-Cochrane E. (2006) Demonstrating rigor using thematic analysis: A hybrid approach of inductive and deductive coding and theme development. *International Journal of Qualitative Methods*, 5(1), 80–92.

Geertz C. (1983) *Local Knowledge: Further Essays in Interpretive Anthropology*. 3rd edn., Michigan, Basic Books.

Giacalone D., Frøst M. B., Bredie W. L., Pineau B., Hunter D. C., Paisley A. G. & Jaeger S. R. (2015) Situational appropriateness of beer is influenced by product familiarity. *Food Quality and Preference*, 39, 16–27.

Gómez-Corona C., Escalona-Buendía H. B., García M., Chollet, S. & Valentin D. (2016a) Craft vs. industrial: Habits, attitudes and motivations towards beer consumption in Mexico. *Appetite*, 96, 358–367.

Gómez-Corona C., Lelievre-Desmas M., Buendía H. B. E., Chollet S., & Valentin D. (2016b) Craft beer representation amongst men in two different cultures. *Food Quality and Preference*, 53, 19–28.

Grayson K. & Martinec R. (2004) Consumer perceptions of iconicity and indexicality and their influence on assessments of authentic market offerings. *Journal of consumer research*, 31(2), 296–312.

Gust G. (2016) *Tapped: An Inside Perspective on the Craft Beer Movement.* Available at: https://sc.lib.muohio.edu/bitstream/handle/2374.MIA/5927/Gust_ProjectColor.pdf?sequence=2andisAllowed=y. Accessed at 02/01/2018.

Hanks P. (1979) *Collins Dictionary of the English Language*. London, Collins.

Holt D. B. (2002) Why do brands cause trouble? A dialectical theory of consumer culture and branding. *Journal of Consumer Research*, 29(1), 70–90.

Hu B. & Yu H. (2007) Segmentation by craft selection criteria and shopping involvement. *Tourism Management*, 28(4), 1079–1092.

Ihatsu A. M. (2002) Making sense of contemporary American craft. Academic dissertation. University of Joensuu, Publications in Education.

Johnson C.J. & Wilson L. E. (2005) 'It says you really care': Motivational factors of contemporary female handcrafters. *Clothing and Textiles Research Journal*, 23,115–130.

Kadirov D., Varey R. J. & Wooliscroft B. (2014) Authenticity: A macromarketing perspective. *Journal of Macromarketing*, 34(1), 73–79.

Kolar T. & Zabkar V. (2010) A consumer-based model of authenticity: An oxymoron or the foundation of cultural heritage marketing? *Tourism Management*, 31(5), 652–664.

Littrell M. A., Anderson L. F. & Brown P. J. (1993) What makes a craft souvenir authentic? *Annals of Tourism Research*, 20(1), 197–215.

Lu A. C. C., Gursoy D. & Lu C. Y. (2015) Authenticity perceptions, brand equity and brand choice intention: The case of ethnic restaurants. *International Journal of Hospitality Management*, 50, 36–45.

Mason R. (2005) The meaning and value of home-based craft. *International Journal of Art and Design*, 24, 261–268.

Marshall M. N. (1996) Sampling for qualitative research. *Family Practice*, 13(6), 522–526.

Merriam S. B. (2014) *Qualitative Research: A Guide to Design and Implementation*. San Francisco, John Wiley and Sons.

Mintel (2013) Provenance in food and drink – UK – March 2013. Available from: http://academic.mintel.com/display/657918/. Accessed 02/02/2014.

Myers M. D. (2013) *Qualitative Research in Business and Management*. London, Sage.

Myers M. D. & Newman M. (2007) The qualitative interview in IS research: Examining the craft. *Information and Organization,* 17(1), 2–26.

Ortner S. B. (1984) Theory in anthropology since the sixties. *Comparative Studies in Society and History,* 26(1), 126–166.

Peach A. (2007) Craft, souvenirs and the commodification of national identity in 1970s Scotland. *Journal of Design History*, 20(3), 243–257.

Pesonen J., Komppula R. & Riihinen A. (2015) Typology of senior travellers as users of tourism information technology. *Information Technology and Tourism*, 15(3), 233–252.

Pöllänen S. H (2013) The meaning of craft: Craft makers' descriptions of craft as an occupation. *Scandinavian Journal of Occupational Theraphy*, 31(2).

Robinson N. (2017) How far will mainstream lager makers take craft? Available at: www.morningadvertiser.co.uk/Drinks/Beer/Mainstream-lager-brands-versus-craft. Accessed: 26/05/2017.

SIBA Admin (2016) Independent brewers take back craft beer. Available from: www.siba.co.uk/2016/08/10/independent-brewers-take-back-craft-beer/. Accessed: 29/04/2017.

Thurnell-Read (2014) Craft, tangibility and affect at work in the microbrewery. *Emotion, Space and Society*, 13, 46–54.

Taylor J. P. (2001). Authenticity and sincerity in tourism. *Annals of Tourism Research*, 28(1), 7–26.

The Oxford English Dictionary (2017a) Available at: https://en.oxforddictionaries. com/definition/craft. Accessed: 25/04/2017.

The Oxford English Dictionary (2017b) Available at: https://en.oxforddictionaries. com/definition/craft_beer. Accessed: 25/04/2017.

Thompson C. J., Rindfleisch A. & Zeynep A. (2006) Emotional branding and the strategic value of the doppelganger brand image. *Journal of Marketing*, 70(1), 50–64.

Tynan C., McKechnie S. & Chhuon C. (2010) Co-creating value for luxury brands. *Journal of Business Research*, 63(11), 1156–1163.

Vaismoradi M., Bondas T. & Turunen H. (2013) Content analysis and thematic analysis: Implications for conducting a qualitative descriptive study. *Journal of Nursing and Health Sciences*, 15, 398–405.

Von Krogh, G. & Roos, J. (1995) *Organizational Epistemology*. London, MacMillan.

Wang N. (1999). Rethinking authenticity in tourism experience. *Annals of Tourism Research*, 26(2), 349–370.

Watkins L. (2010) The cross-cultural appropriateness of survey-based value(s) research: A review of methodological issues and suggestion of alternative methodology. *International Marketing Review*, 27(6), 694–716.

Wollfson D. (2016) *Craft marque? SIBA launches accreditation to reclaim "craft" beer.* Available at: www.morningadvertiser.co.uk/Article/2016/08/09/SIBA-launches-accreditation-to-reclaim-craft-beer. Accessed 02/01/2018.

9 Making Livelihoods within Communities of Practice

The Place of Guild Organisations in the Craft Sector

Nicola J. Thomas and Doreen Jakob

This chapter interrogates the place of professional networks as communities of practice (COPs) for craft practitioners who live in remote, rural locations and make their livelihood from their creative practice. The South-West region of Britain has a significant population of craft makers working in a highly distributed manner. Some makers work in small clusters (Harvey et al. 2012) but many work in their own homes or individual workshops. Through in-depth qualitative analysis, this chapter locates the ways in which makers develop or join organisations to support their livelihoods, particularly those that distinguish the quality and value of the skilled labour that makes hand-crafted work. Specifically, it explores the role of regional craft guilds for their members, what members value about these organisations, the politics of belonging, and the role they play in the life of current members and their livelihoods.

The organisations we address in this research serve craft practitioners in rural areas who are looking to gain access to peer support, develop their practice and gain the benefits of networking, despite their lack of geographical proximity. While clusters are often valued for the benefits of networking and spillover effects of co-working (Storper & Venables 2004), many craft practitioners find isolation from other makers to be part of their creative life. Although urban-based craft makers may find themselves similarly isolated, rural practitioners are likely to be faced with greater barriers to participation in a creative network, through high costs or lack of availability of transport, or by living in remote places that have a weak creative infrastructure (see Bell & Jayne 2010; Gibson et al. 2010).

The challenge of enabling the positive benefits to dispersed makers that arise from social connection has been recognised within UK rural policy initiatives since the 1920s. The UK Government established the Rural Industries Bureau in 1921 and put in place officers tasked with supporting the agricultural and rural industrial sector (Bailey 1996). At the time, craft industries in rural areas ranged from those who served agricultural industry, such as wheelwrights and blacksmiths, to industrial commercial crafts, including potteries, and craft practitioners inspired by the aesthetic dimensions of decorative and functional craft. The aim of the Rural Industries Bureau was to support diverse rural craft workers and improve their livelihoods, encourage businesses to modernise or respond to new markets, offer professional support and business development and encourage new businesses to locate in the countryside. The Rural Industries Bureau supported the development of regionally based craft organisations that brought together similarly high skilled professional crafts practitioners intent on supporting each other to sell their work through new retail opportunities (Thomas 2018).

These networked organisations were often called 'guilds', drawing on the established medieval craft membership structures that the Arts and Crafts Movement had revived. The Rural Industries Bureau encouraged development of county-wide craft guilds that were craftsperson-led, with the support of a local officer employed by the Bureau. Early examples in the South-West were the Gloucestershire Guild of Craftsmen, founded in 1933 and the Devon Guild of Craftsmen established 1955 (Thomas et al. 2012; Thomas 2018). These guilds encompassed a range of materials-based practices of craft making including blacksmiths, basketmakers, potters, weavers, silversmiths, boatbuilders and printmakers. The organisation of these guilds revolved around exhibitions of members' work that were offered for sale, showing the makers' work together in a diverse display. A distinctive feature of these guilds was the quality of work, undertaken by people who were highly skilled, made their income from their craft practice and were considered to be designers as well as craft practitioners.

Given that rural guilds were developed to enable members to access new retail markets, it is important to note the change in retail environment that has evolved in the craft sector over the last 80 years, and to consider this in relation to the ongoing value of the guild organisations. In the 1930s retail outlets for design craft were scarce, often found in larger cities, such as the Red Rose Gallery in Manchester. The Rural Industries Bureau identified a lack of local markets and encouraged the guilds to develop local patronage through seasonal 'pop-up' retail exhibitions. This practice continues today. Such fairs and festival now take place across the UK and continue to diversify and grow in number. Direct selling to the public has a long tradition within the craft sector. This includes via the Open Studio movement where clusters of makers and artists advertise studio openings and tours. Crafts practitioners also work with galleries who offer boutique retail experiences. Alongside these face-to-face retail markets, online selling has transformed the craft sector with online platforms such as etsy.com, and niche craft online platforms like madebyhandonline.com offering makers the opportunity to sell direct to customers.

Given all these retail opportunities, it is important to consider why craft guild organisations continue to be viable given that they were originally formed to enable access to retail markets when there were few alternatives in rural areas. Although the range of retail opportunities open to makers has increased, it often continues to be a struggle to make a viable livelihood. The market for handcrafted items remains niche, particularly in challenging economic times. Makers often depend on a portfolio of teaching or other employment to supplement their income from selling their work. Locating customers who want to invest in quality, hand-crafted items means makers need to seek out organisations that attract these consumers. Identifying and supporting quality craft practice has been the remit of the regional guilds since their inception.

This chapter focuses on the Devon Guild of Craftsmen and the Gloucestershire Guild of Craftsmen. These guilds have around 400 members between them and are steadily growing. Between 2012 and 2015 the authors undertook an Arts and Humanities Research Council-funded research project that utilised mixed qualitative methods to interrogate the reasons why these guilds have survived throughout the 20th century and explore, with current members and staff, the importance of these organisations in the contemporary creative economy. Through 40 in-depth interviews, a survey of guild members (167 responses), participant observation at guild events, and discourse analysis of guild archives, we examined the place of geographically organised craft guilds in the UK's creative economy, past and present.

The two guilds were chosen as case studies because they share similarities but have slightly different trajectories of development. Both are membership organisations serving professional designer-makers. At time of writing the Gloucestershire Guild of Craftsmen has around 80 members and The Devon Guild of Craftsmen has around 270 members. Until 1985 both guilds were similar in scale and activity, functioning as maker-led networks, managed by a committee of members. The Devon Guild's increased size dates from a decision in 1985 to invest in a formal headquarters which incorporates a large exhibition space, retail gallery and cafe. In recent years, it has received core funding from the Arts Council as one of its National Portfolio Organisations. It is known as an exhibition space for contemporary craft and touring exhibitions, has a well-developed craft education and community crafts programme, offers a programme of maker development support, commissions new work when supported by grant funding, all enabled by a professional staff who drive the organisation. The Gloucestershire Guild of Craftsmen retains the spirit of the maker-led guild, organised by the guild's committee, with the help of a paid administrator and retail manager. The guild has always had some form of retail gallery space, at time of writing, 'The Guild at 51', situated within The Wilson, a gallery and museum in Cheltenham. Highlights of the guild year are the regular seasonal pop-up exhibitions which take place over a few days to a couple of weeks and bring guild craft out to the market towns for local audiences to purchase.

The Gloucestershire Guild supports craft education through regular workshops and demonstrations organised by members.

We start the chapter by spending time with Susan Early, a basketmaker, working in willow and foraged hedgerow materials. This attention, first and foremost, to the individual members, echoes the process of our research. To understand the importance of the guild in a maker's life, we used an ethnographic approach, spending time with makers, sitting in their studios, talking with them as they worked. As they talked, their 'guild life' unfolded, allowing us to see the small ways in which deep associations with the organisations were made. It has been important to keep individuals like Susan centre stage in our research, recognising that each member in a guild has these rich stories and associations. We contextualise the themes of Susan's stories by considering how guilds might be regarded as communities of practice, drawing on the extensive literature inspired by the work of Lave and Wenger (1991). We then go on to draw on survey data to explore the elements of this community of practice, the processes of joining, how members participate in the guild, the senses of belonging that this engenders and the process through which the guilds have changed over time.

Making a Livelihood

Susan has been a member of the Gloucestershire Guild of Craftsmen since 2007. She developed her interest in basketmaking as a recreational pursuit while her children were young, and then deepened her skills and interests through continued practice, taking further courses and completing a degree in Visual Arts in 2005. An unexpected request to run basketmaking workshops at the Victoria and Albert Museum (V&A) in London, shortly after her graduation led Susan to focus her attention on how she could make a livelihood from her craft practice:

> I finished my degree, was busy looking for a job when a friend of my sister's, a curator at the V&A, saw one of my baskets and asked if I would do a demonstration at the V&A, which threw me a bit but because I was looking for a job, I said yes without thinking really because I'd done basketmaking for a long time. […] [I] set up some classes in the village, [and] started teaching on a weekly basis so I'd know all the answers [to questions V&A visitors might ask]. […] The classes went well, I started being asked to do more classes, started making more baskets, did sales at the village hall and then Annie Hewitt from the guild saw my baskets and asked if I'd be interested in being a member of the guild. So, I joined the guild and it's gone on from there really.

Susan now has a wide portfolio of work: making public commissions, functional baskets, abstract forms, and teaching basketmaking to others.

She joined the guild as an Associate member, a scheme that enables emerging professional makers to gain access to the guild network, whilst developing their practice. This two-year period gives members the opportunity to settle into their work and get support and advice from a mentor in the guild. For Susan, this time as an Associate allowed her time to develop her livelihood and professional identity:

> You continue to progress and improve and take your work further and actually, it was just what I needed, just at the right time because it really, really focused my thoughts and I thought 'I've got to be focused and make something beautiful, as well as useful.

The relationship between mentor and Associate member is one that can create a powerful and long-lasting relationship. Susan's mentor was furniture maker Paul Spriggs, whose respect and understanding of the Arts and Crafts traditions of the Cotswolds infused his own work.

Susan is a modest maker, who might not have applied to the guild had she not been encouraged: 'I probably felt, it was lovely that Annie asked me, and it was perfect timing for me, but I think I was slightly insecure about my own ability… I certainly wouldn't have approached them'. The importance of the guild being open to new members and encouraging creative talent was important for Susan's own career. When talking about the guild, Susan often returns to discuss the standard of work and the reputation of the guild. Susan could remember going to the guild exhibitions as a child:

> I was brought up around here and my parents used to take us to the Gloucester Guild of Craftsmen's Exhibition every year in Painswick … I remember being quite in awe of the quality of the work, so in fact when I was asked to be in the guild, I was quite concerned I wasn't good enough.

Alongside her mentor, other guild members affirmed that her work was improving through her years as an Associate:

> I found other members very helpful, nobody has ever said a negative as such, but it's the positives that come through: "Those look really good" [they] notice a change or something, which is just very, very nice … [a] positive affirmation. I think it is just the quality, constantly trying to improve quality.

Alongside the positive affirmation that she was producing good-quality work when she joined, guild membership for Susan emerges as a driver to keep improving the quality of her work: 'It makes you keep or attempt to keep standards up, I think you put those on yourself by being a member'.

The process of reflecting on her professional practice is something that Susan has undertaken, working with other master basketmakers and she views her guild membership as a key element in the ongoing pursuit to continue improving the quality of her work: 'I've since been to a number of master basketmakers and gradually really, turned round and looked at my baskets thoughtfully and mindfully and the guild has helped that incredibly'.

For many makers, the diversity of skills required to run their business is challenging. Alongside making their work, crafts practitioners often need to be able to take professional quality photographs of their work; organise the sale and marketing of products; run social media promotions; keep accounts in order; maintain studio space; manage a website, which increasingly includes an online shop; manage client relationships; locate and supply galleries and retail outlets; apply for exhibitions, commissions, and grant-funded projects; prepare and deliver teaching or projects to different publics; and order materials and maintain stock levels. These tasks require a diverse portfolio of skills which can stretch a maker's abilities and knowledge base. It is common for professional makers to be sole traders in their business, possibly supported by a family member, but often individually responsible for securing the success of their business. Susan is no exception and looked to the guild as a way of accessing support for the wide portfolio of activities that she needed to become accomplished at as a new professional maker. Susan was able to get help with elements of the business skills portfolio that she needed to be on top of to maintain her livelihood:

> Nick Ozane, who's the administrator, he's been brilliant … he has given me I think three mornings' computer help, just helping me set up things as basic as invoice things, to speed things up, mailing lists, which has made a huge difference.

The guild offers a permanent retail sales outlet for Susan's work: 'It's a great place to have one's work displayed', particularly as she is 'not terribly computer-literate or interested in that business side of things'. The guild shop becomes a place

> where I've always got work, so people can ask me about my work, and always beautifully displayed. I've always got somewhere to put it which is really very helpful, alongside other people's work which I think is a great standard and you wouldn't want to let each other down.

Susan sells her work in different outlets, but the guild shop and exhibitions are a regular part of her portfolio. Developing her work to sell at the guild as an Associate meant Susan had to learn how to price her work:

The other thing the guild has been very helpful about is costing because although we give a percentage to the guild, that's to us really because we're all part of it, you can learn where to price things or how to price things.

Being a member of the guild and visible on their website is again about being recognised as producing work to a certain standard, which is important on applications for grants, fellowships and commissions: 'Being a part of the guild, does imply a certain standard'. Susan indicates that she is not dependent on sales through the guild but sees the investment as 'a hugely brilliant place to advertise myself'. In February 2018 this was taken literally, as she set up her workshop in the window of the guild's shop for a week, allowing passers-by to see her demonstrating and making new work, alongside a special exhibition of her work for sale in the shop.

For many individual makers who work in isolation, whether by choice or by necessity, joining a guild offers access to peers and the potential for conversations that support a livelihood. Susan found unexpected friendship through the guild:

Having lived here for years, I certainly wasn't joining the guild to try and get to know people, but I have found getting to know other makers, who actually then end up being in a similar situation to yourself, it's been really, really good actually, I've been surprised at how lovely it's been.

The companionable element of the guild emerges through planning meetings, putting up exhibitions, delivering work to the shop and attending member events. The guild appears to become gradually woven into people's lives, the rhythms of the guild year creating associated rhythms of social connection. Susan's integration within the guild was shown in the 80th Anniversary year when she co-designed the Summer Show, placing her at the centre of the key selling event for the guild. Susan recently worked with another maker, Sarah Cant on a collaborative project 'Two Make' which was curated to support members' continued professional development. As a new mother, Sarah brought her baby to the development days, where she and Susan worked on their joint project. Throughout the research the idea of a 'guild life' emerged, with long-standing members lives becoming interwoven with other members, through the exchange of objects used on a daily basis, skills shared and companionship gained.

The Guild as a Community of Practice

Listening to members like Susan and witnessing the activities of the regional craft guilds through the research pointed us to consideration of the communities of practice literatures. Communities of practice have been the subject of considerable analysis and debate since the publication of Lave and Wenger's (1991) sociological theorisation of communities of practice as self-organising structures, followed by Wenger's (1998) thesis presenting communities of practices as 'social learning systems' that 'explain mutual learning and knowledge exchange' (Bolisani & Scarso 2014). When one considers the key characteristics of a community of practice identified by Wenger (1998: 125–6, cited in Roberts 2006: 625) one can immediately see the attraction of placing craft guilds within this frame of analysis. The act of selection creates a strong bond between members; practices of governance that have evolved over time enable the resolution of conflict and smooth running of the group; exhibitions that have an annual cycle with a well-oiled machinery to make them happen based on clear divisions of labour; friendships between members spill out beyond the guild; long-serving committee members report their service with pride; there are reports of ease of participation for new members from those who are admitted; members share mutual admiration for work of a similar quality; there is an easy exchange of help, materials and skills; members know stories of past members and activities, and these histories of the guild endure through oral traditions and create a sense of shared belonging. All these characteristics chime as productive examples of a community of practice. Indeed, Wenger thought his approach to understanding situated learning, and how communities of practice acted as the mechanism through which knowledge was held, transferred and created, was well witnessed in third-sector and voluntary contexts.

There is however a danger of reifying this community into a warm, homogeneous group, that is positive, experienced and valued equally by all. One of the critiques of the communities of practice literature is that it doesn't account for power and the messy politics of social relations, the difference that spatial diffusion makes, and a detailed attention to the practices that underscore the practices of the communities as they evolve (Amin & Roberts 2008; Handley et al. 2006; Roberts 2006). Attending to the fissures that emerge in these organisations has been important in exploring how guilds function and the role they play in makers' lives. In addition, if these long-standing guilds are to be seem as good models of peer support that could be replicated, understanding these challenges and how they have been navigated is critical.

These two organisational case studies enabled us to collect data from a large cohort of professional designer-makers who have successfully forged their livelihood in rural areas. Understanding their motivations for joining a membership organisation, and their reasons for supporting it enabled us to learn about the professional needs of crafts practitioners in the contemporary creative economy. Paying attention to the way in which makers value their guild membership and the practices of the guild enabled us to consider what makes these organisations robust communities of practice.

We should guard against over-romanticising such organisations simply because they have been sustained over long periods of time. Instead we should use them to understand how organisations might serve the needs of contemporary craft workers, and the challenges for enabling dispersed rural creative workers to gain the advantages of working together in mutually supportive ways.

The original impetus to undertake this research was recognition that for several decades guild organisations had successfully served a growing membership and navigated the challenges of sustaining a grass-roots, volunteer maker-led network. Each guild had followed a slightly different path with varying degrees of professional administration but maintained their status as member-led organisations. For a sector that is dominated by sole practitioners, the organisations offered something that makers valued, and wished to invest in, year after year. The creative industries sector often overlooks the crafts, as a sector of limited economic value; however, craft guilds, as modes of organisational support, may in fact offer much to the wider creative economy (see also Luckman (2015: 27 and 63) for an acknowledgment of the place of craft guilds in the creative economy). They have shown how it is possible to sustain and improve the livelihoods of dispersed creative workers who wish to connect to their peers, gain validation, receive recognition and ensure that the outputs of their creative labour are appropriately placed in the market.

Achieving Membership within a Craft Community of Practice

To join the Gloucestershire Guild of Craftsmen or the Devon Guild of Craftsmen a maker must put forward an application including examples of their work and a written explanation of their craft practice. Both guilds have committees which meet to discuss prospective members' work and to judge it against their collective understanding of what makes up 'guild quality'. This takes into account the skill of the maker, their individual style and design qualities, quality of the product and attention placed on the finish of the work. A maker is expected to have a style that is recognisably theirs, not derivative, and individual elements are expected to make up a coherent portfolio of work. Both guilds accept makers who have professional standards, with Associate membership being available for those who are starting out on their career path.

The ongoing work of maintaining the standard of the guild is seen by some as a collective effort: 'It is up to present members to ensure this excellent standard and good presentation of work continues'. This journey starts when a prospective new member applies, and the selection and election committee judge the quality of their work. In both guilds, the selection and election committee is constituted mainly from the current membership, with the Devon Guild of Craftsmen also having an external member with expertise in contemporary craft practice. Serving on the selection and election committee is seen as a responsible job which is much sought after by members. It offers a form of professional development as committee members use the experience to reflect on their own practice, and to learn from the critique that they exchange with other members. As one member noted, they felt they actively took part in shaping the guild:

> by supporting the guild ... election/selection committee which helps me to keep me informed about makers, other disciplines, and in touch with other members, and helps me question what standards and criteria should apply to incoming work and how that reflects upon my own.

The processes of gaining entry to a community of practice are a key element of the organisational dynamic of a community of practice (Amin & Roberts 2008: 357). How a community of practice opens itself to new members, who is admitted, on what basis, and how they get inducted into the cultures of the organisation is critical. Going through the selection process was noted by members to be a challenging process. The preparation of a portfolio of work for consideration by peers with the associated judgement of success or failure placed members at emotional risk. How this process was managed and communicated clearly left its mark on some members, who used the research survey to recall their experiences of going through the selection process. Some chose to draw attention to what they perceived to be the subjective judgements of the committee members, and noted that when they reapplied 'The membership had changed and they successfully admitted with the same portfolio to a different section panel'. Others recalled the reasons they were originally rejected: 'that the work didn't show enough range of ambition technically and artistically'. In response to this feedback the same member told us that 'time and experience' resolve this weakness; 'I reapplied a number of years later and showed a wider range [of work]'. Care is taken by the guild to ensure that a discipline-specific maker is part of the judging panel for a prospective maker's work: this allows specific feedback to be received on a failed application: 'I received a letter from the jeweller on the interview board'. Another member who was rejected as a full member was accepted as an Associate: 'I had only just started my own business after leaving college – so they felt it needed time to develop ... a long-standing member of the guild became my mentor'. For some prospective members, the selection committee drew attention to parts of their work where the quality of finish might be improved such as the use of a handmade catch to a necklace over a machine-produced component. Attending to such small but important feedback resulted in a successful membership application.

Being granted membership is by no means certain; indeed, the archives of both guilds have letters and emails written to unsuccessful applicants telling them why their work was not deemed to be of 'guild quality'. Some unsuccessful members take considerable umbrage and harbour hurt pride and sever their desire to join the guilds. This is a site where power plays out. The criteria for membership are challenging to maintain, where applicants' work is expected to be unique, show personal style and originality, whilst being of the highest quality standard. As craft practices change and greater use of technology is incorporated (such as laser-cutting and 3D-printing), the responsibilities of the selection and election committee need to move with the current practice to ensure that the guild does not stagnate. As one member suggested, there is a 'danger in the respected guild system becoming an anachronism'. Here members noted that the guild 'has to adapt to new ways of practice, become relevant to younger members' and to ensure that they are 'adapting to current models, younger makers, the traditional with the new, waking people up to contemporary making without denying the craft tradition'. Such reflections on the discourse of handwork, and the importance of craft traditions alongside the incorporation of new technology and contemporary techniques were seen in both guilds. Both openly supported and encouraged new practices to be showcased within the guilds, which was noted within the research project as a marker of these membership guilds as sites which supported innovation and change. Here we see the community of practice needing to shift its terms of entry as the meaning of craft changes in response to new technologies, aesthetics and the demands of the market.

Those who do make the bar of membership are aware of the positive value of the mark of distinction that guild membership brings to their work. Members report that guild membership means that they have received the 'kite mark for quality' or been admitted to a guild that has established a 'tradition of excellence and bar of standard'. Joining a long-established guild is important for some who note 'The history gives guild status and kudos'. The longevity of both guilds and the reputation they have forged over time was marked in many members' responses. For members in Gloucestershire this was particularly important. In this region, the weight of the late nineteenth and early twentieth century Arts and Crafts Movement looms large, which places additional significance on the regional craft guild maintaining standards of excellence. A Gloucestershire Guild member noted, 'It is a standard of enduring excellence which provides reassurance to clients of the guild and a sense of belonging to culture inheritance'. For another member, the 'illustrious history validates one's own work' and for another the 'prestigious' nature of the organisation and importance for 'quality assurance' were key motivations for applying to join.

Sustaining a Community of Practice: The Value of Membership

The attraction of joining the guild encompasses many different elements. An open-response questionnaire to all guild members elicited varied responses which reflect the range of ways makers look to the guild for support. For many, guild membership was about achieving 'recognition for skills I had accumulated'. For another member 'to get the recognition that my work was good enough to be a member'. This recognition might be a personal affirmation in a field where individuals don't receive regular reviews and appraisals of their work. It also, however, acts as a public affirmation of their quality, with a respondent noting they joined the guild 'to have the backing of a guild as a form of quality control'. Being seen as an equal amongst peers often emerged as an important reason for joining the guild, with responses like this being common: 'to exhibit my work with others whose work standards I admired'. Gaining recognition associated with a certain standard was a key driver for many respondents, as explained by one member: 'to increase my profile in the quality craft world' and 'reach the public from a respected platform'. In a crowded market place, where quality is difficult to judge, the idea of the guild as a place that holds up standards is attractive. This is also true for galleries, particularly where they may not have expertise in craft disciplines. One member explained that they joined the guild in response to 'peer pressure from a couple of galleries I supply'. Here the guild may be seen to act as a clearing house, affirming the quality of a makers work, which is used by external organisations in their decision-making process to stock their work.

For many members, the opportunities provided by the guild to enable them to make money from their craft were central, as one member summarised: 'There is substantial financial pressure on members to make a living and the guild can play an important part in that'. Many makers were clear that the guild opened up 'exhibition opportunities' and the ability 'to sell work, have status, contacts, advertising'. In these terms, joining the guild is a business transaction to improve their livelihood, particularly important for some in the early stage of their career as they shared that they joined the guild 'to develop my career when I was getting established'. For those with a livelihood already established, reaching new audiences for their work was a reason to join. A respondent noted their membership enabled them 'to expand the commercial reach of my business'. Both guilds were originally created to support the selling of rural craftspersons' work within an organisation that protected quality and standards. These driving forces remain central to members, with members finding categories such as access to new customers, mark of quality, marketing and promotion, exhibition spaces and gallery shop sales being very important to the way in which they gain benefit from their guild membership.

The role of peer mentoring and as a trusted place to gain hands-on advice was witnessed throughout the research. The attraction of being 'part of the support group of local craftsmen' motivated one member to join the guild. Another member articulated the same sentiment: 'to gain the opportunity to ask questions about specific problems that might arise with various aspects of my craft'. For others, the attraction lay in the organisational structure: 'I am also keen on being part of a well-established cooperative'. The recognition of the guild as a space of mutuality was frequently noted through the research, with members often giving value to the spirit of collective action that the guild ethos signals: 'It's important that craftspeople joined together to create the guild. They also created a spirit of support which is still very much part of the guild'. The importance of this collaborative spirit emerged in different ways for different members. The work that the guilds do in advocating for makers and campaigning for craft played a role in this member's decision to join the guild 'to have a voice in issues affecting makers'. This reason draws attention to the challenge for sole practitioners of making their voices collectively heard. Seeing craft development organisations like the guilds as a way of enabling a collective voice to be heard is reminiscent of the role of medieval guilds in protecting the labour rights of the members (see, for example, Richardson 2001).

Developing Practices of Mutuality within a Community of Practice

The ethos of mutuality that underlined the founding of the regional craft guilds has continued to exist in the way in which guild members discuss their sense of belonging. The research undertaken went on to interrogate if members did actually participate in the guild and receive benefits of mutuality. Many members had different ways of participating, reflecting the diverse ways in which a member might interact with a networked organisation. A more transactional response to the question: 'How do you participate?' generated the response 'I pay my subscription and supply stock [for the retail shop]'. Other responses indicate the way in which a member might take part in the rhythm of guild activities: one member reported they 'attend exhibitions, meetings and social gatherings', and another 'I attend talks, workshops and private views'. Others draw attention to their work being employed as facilitators on workshops and outreach projects, and for others supporting the guild's cafe was also seen as support 'eat cakes in the cafe!' Such support is important as the cafe profits provide a key source of income for the Devon Guild. Others demonstrate that their participation runs deeper, participating in the organisation and management by being a 'Board member, trustee' and 'serving on the selection and election committee'.

As Susan's experiences highlight, the social and peer support elements of guild membership were raised by many members as reason to join and maintain membership of the guild. Despite the growing use of social media for peer support, the importance of local face-to-face relationships was cited as an important reason for membership. For others, the critical role of peer dialogue in helping them to improve their work was central. It is notable that 54% of the Devon Guild of Craftsmen membership indicated that they met other guild members whom they identified as personal friends regularly each year (44% a few times a year, 15% at least once a month). Members also reported using their guild connections to routinely support professional collaboration (28%) and selling their work (41%).

Some members, when asked about their participation, provided apologetic responses: 'I don't really', 'not enough', 'I have not been a great member', 'afraid I don't'. Some of these responses explained their absence and noted 'I live too far away, when I am free of kids there may be more time and I can commit more. Sorry!'. For some this lack of participation was associated with guilt: 'I feel grateful for what I see being done on my behalf and feel a little guilty I do not participate more'. It was notable that more members from the Devon Guild of Craftsmen evoked feeling of disconnection, which some of the responses connected with distance: 'Being far away I miss out on local events and companionship'. The Devon Guild opens its membership to makers who live across the South-West of Britain region. Given the dispersed rural nature of the region, some members might be a three-hour drive from the guild's headquarters. For some members, this distance has an impact of their ability to participate: 'I live a distance away… I used to attend meetings and forums. Price of fuel escalated, [I] can no longer afford to take part'. The guild has tried, with varying success, to find ways to overcome these inter-regional challenges with local events taking place and members organising their own meet-ups.

Growing Pains: Professional Challenges to the Community of Practice

When discussing members' sense of ownership and bonds to their guild, there emerges a difference between the responses to the different guilds in the study: the Devon Guild of Craftsmen and the Gloucestershire Guild of Craftsmen. These differences relate to the size, scale and management of the organisations. The Devon Guild now has a professional staff who take on much of the day-to-day running of the guild, with much less reliance on the grass-roots activity and participation of members that defined the early decades of the organisation's existence. The Gloucestershire Guild continues to have a strong member-led ethos, with members undertaking regular activities like organising retail exhibitions and stewarding in the shop alongside the paid retail manager. Some Devon Guild members feel that the professionalisation of the guild organisation has diminished the way in which members can take part: 'The membership are not as involved with the everyday organisation, there are now paid staff for everything!!' or another member noted that the guild had transformed 'from DIY members helping to paid staff doing all the jobs'. For some the professionalisation of the Devon Guild into a crafts development organisation which received public funding has resulted in a loss of connection and ownership for members: 'By taking large amounts of money from funding bodies, guild policy is now largely dictated by them rather than the members'. The members who draw attention to the historical change in feeling from a grassroots organisation to a professional body are often aware of the history of the Devon Guild members' decision to buy its own premises in the mid-1980s. Their feelings of loss are the result of a decision made by the guild members as they learnt to manage their new capital investment. The membership quickly realised that their cooperative efforts were a risk to the guild and they started to employ professional arts organisers to manage the new enterprise. The Devon Guild retains its constitution as a membership organisation; however, the decision to buy a building alongside the work that it takes to maintain this investment did fundamentally change the ethos of this organisation. This issue raises the potential threat that comes from introducing professional staff into a community of practice, and the way in which this changes the social bonds and connections that build over time.

The voices which express a sense of loss about a feeling of belonging linked to the Devon Guild are not seen in the more grass-roots orientated Gloucestershire Guild. It would, however, be wrong to overclaim craft practitioners' desire to be taking a significant role in managing and undertaking organisational work. When asked the direct question 'Would you like to take on an official role?', 87 per cent of the Gloucestershire Guild and 91 per cent of the Devon Guild members responded negatively. One member who did not want to be part of a grass-roots guild summarised their view saying: 'I want it to be run by properly paid employees, not volunteers'. Members' reasons for not wanting to get involved included: 'My time will be spent on admin and not making'; 'I dislike committee meetings'; 'I'm too busy'; 'I was not looking for this from the guild'; 'I am burnt out of enthusiasm for committee politics'; 'I would not fit in'; 'I live too far away'. The negative feeling about greater involvement suggests that both guilds are negotiating a fine balance between enabling members to feel connected while not making membership too onerous. For the Devon Guild, this means ensuring the members know that their voices and opinions matter and are listened to. Many members consider that the staff have judged this well, reporting that 'The bulletins send a clear message that involvement is welcomed' and another member noting 'I feel I can be as involved as I want to be, which gives me a greater sense of ownership'. The negative desire to get more involved is a more testing management challenge for the Gloucestershire Guild, which is more dependent on some paid staff supported by the considerable voluntary labour of committees and working parties, alongside all members stewarding in the shop rota.

The decision in 1985 by the Devon Guild to change the structure of the organisation by establishing a permanent headquarters raises the issue of whether organisations like guilds are causes of stagnation or forces for innovation within the creative sector. In the 1980s the Devon Guild wanted to do more for its members, and the shift to a more commercial orientation was a signal of the desire to innovate. Over time the professional staff have maintained this forward momentum through new capital development programmes (such as the decision to extend the building with a new exhibition space) and through curatorial programmes and exhibitions. One member noted the role of the leadership in driving this moment 'Exciting curatorial decisions come from the directors, not the membership', with another noting the importance of 'strong and clear leadership'. In many ways, the decision by the Devon Guild to bid for Arts Council funding work as a nationally recognised development agency for the craft sector means that the organisation is now geared towards a pathway that encourages innovation, expects the organisation to serve the professional development of the crafts sector, and to find creative ways to reach to wider and diverse public audiences.

The Gloucestershire Guild of Craftsmen has, in recent years, also received Arts Council support, with a deliberate aim on the part of of the funding body to support the development of the guild to ensure it continues to serve its members' interests and to increase the organisation's ability to work with members of the public. For many years the Gloucestershire Guild had a retail shop in the Gloucestershire village of Painswick. Over time this village suffered from reduced footfall, and the retail sales from the guild plummeted. The retail shop became a quiet place where members went to fulfil their stewarding duties, knowing it would be a quiet day to complete their accounts. With the redevelopment of the nearby museum in the bigger population centre of Cheltenham came the opportunity for the guild to take over a retail space and close their failing retail shop in Painswick. At the time of the research this move was being planned and grants applied for to support the move. The full force of the guild's skill base was exploited, particularly those makers for whom craft was a second career, whose first career skill set proved valuable; those with accounting, fundraising and grant-writing expertise were brought into working parties.

Discussions about the move to Cheltenham at social events, annual general meetings, at exhibitions and in private conversations were all about the exciting potential, set against the awareness that this was a move that would force the guild to raise its profile and ensure that the members were able to supply a shop that might have a larger turnover, and to provide a regular customer base with a changing display. Key members of the Gloucestershire Guild committee were heavily invested in enabling the move to go smoothly. The voluntary nature of their roles meant they were giving considerable unpaid labour to the guild, sometimes with gritted teeth and a sense that the extra work needed to be endured. The successful hiring of a highly skilled and experienced retail manager whose expertise in the craft sector was widely known and respected was a cause of great relief. As time has gone on, the new retail shop, the Guild at 51, has proved to be a great boon to the Gloucestershire Guild, raising its profile within the national contemporary craft scene and attracting new members who further rejuvenate the membership. Retail sales have increased, the partnership with the Museum means that more workshops for the general public have been possible, and the guild has been able to open its energies towards providing greater opportunities for increasing the professional development to members.

Conclusion

Regional craft guilds have had an enduring place in the lives of designer-makers in the South-West of Britain for more than 80 years. As the accounts of makers in this chapter have revealed, despite unprecedented access to retail opportunities and the social connections with other makers through online fora, the role of regional communities of practice which are organised to support the retail and professional development of a maker's work remains of great value. The craft membership networks in question offer makers routes to market, the means to connect with other peers, opportunities for professional development and recognition that their work is of high standard.

Craft guilds can also be considered as a community of practice; much of this literature in recent years has focused on knowledge management and business contexts. By looking at craft guilds, we return to the spirit of Lave and Wenger's 1991 work, which paid attention to craft practice such as tailors and butchery. The qualitative approach taken in our research emphasises the importance of exploring the situated nature of communities of practice. These craft guilds are not sites where makers routinely and predominantly share their craft skills with each other; their making skills have already been honed by the time they join the guild. Instead, following Lave and Wenger's (1991) original discussion of communities of practice as sites of situated learning, these guild communities of practice emerge through the sharing of specific knowledge and expertise, and from a shared desire to secure a livelihood.

Who can become a member of a community of practice, and the routes to membership, are key markers in many typologies (Amin & Roberts 2008). In an otherwise unregulated sector of the creative economy, the ability for makers to gain guild membership, with the associated stamp of a quality threshold that is trusted by external parties, is vital. The importance of the shared understanding of craft skill cemented through membership is a key marker in establishing and maintaining this community of practice. There is a strong shared understanding of this discourse of craft, based on making high-quality, handmade products within the guilds, as can be seen from the ways members talk about their experiences of joining this elite group of makers.

Members of the guilds recognise each other's skills and qualities, share a sense of commonality and cement this through local interactions that play a distinctive part in securing a livelihood. Successfully joining this community of practice and gaining membership to organisational bodies that judge quality according to certain standards allows makers to gain a level of distinction, which in turn enables them to charge appropriately for their work based on their expertise. Indeed, being able to retail products alongside other skilled designer-makers offers security in terms of pricing appropriately for the hours of labour invested. In addition, for makers who have formal training and educational qualifications, but largely gain their skill and expertise over time by working with their materials, the lack of formal professional career structures and progression routes can result in feelings of disorientation and not knowing if one's work is good enough or valued by others. These peer-reviewed organisations offer a means of professional development and recognition.

As Roberts (2006: 625) notes, 'Communities of practice are not stable or static entities'. The original motivation for the Rural Industries Bureau to supportive development of regional craft guilds in the 1930s was to enable makers to collectively find routes to markets and gain mutual support. The cooperative nature of the guilds continues to attract contemporary makers, even though the organisational ethos has changed over the years. Guild sociality reveals many of Wenger's characteristics of communities of practices: guild spaces recognise the division between professional makers and recreational enthusiasts who may make a living from their craft, but not to the perceived 'standard' set by guild gatekeepers. The responsibility of these gatekeepers in maintaining openness to change and allowing new generations of makers with different processes, techniques, materials and requirements to enter the organisation is important.

The challenge to these communities of practice emerges in relation to increased professionalisation and the distancing of members from the day-to-day operations of the organisation. As Wenger notes, the characteristics of communities of practice are found in the small acts of bonding between people (Wenger 1998: 125–6). In the context of the guild, members meeting to discuss the organisation of an exhibition, or volunteering time to clean up after an unfortunate flood, are the activities that lead to shared stories, memories and practices. The rise of professional staff has led to the undermining of these small acts of connection at the Devon Guild, creating some tensions that have the potential to erode the strength of the community of practice. In the case of the Devon Guild of Craftsmen and the Gloucestershire Guild of Craftsmen, this challenge to the community of practice has not yet been fully realised.

This is perhaps because the membership recognises that, while some small practices have fallen by the wayside, their organisation is stronger for the skills and experience that the professional management brings, and this enables members to spend more time in their studio, creating new work to sell to the public. This suggests that the original vision of the Rural Industries Bureau, to support rural makers by collectivise their efforts, continues to bear dividends.

Acknowledgements

We acknowledge the financial support of the AHRC for the project titled 'Situating Craft Guilds in the Creative Economy: Histories, Politics and Practices' (AH/I001778/1) without which this research could not have been undertaken. We would also like to acknowledge the project partners, The Devon Guild of Craftsmen and the Gloucestershire Guild of Craftsmen, who welcomed us into their organisations to undertake the research.

References

Amin, A. & Roberts, J. (2008) Knowing in action: Beyond communities of practice. *Research Policy*, 27: 353–369.

Bailey, A. (1996) Progress and preservation: The role of rural industries in the making of the modern image of countryside. *Journal of Design History*, 9(1): 35–53.

Bell, D. & Jayne, M. (2010) The creative countryside? Policy and practice in the UK rural cultural economy. *Journal of Rural Studies*, 26(3): 209–218.

Bolisani, E. & Scarso, E. (2014) The place of communities of practice in knowledge management studies: A critical review. *Journal of Knowledge Management*, 18(2): 366–381.

Gibson, C., Luckman, S., & Willoughby-Smith, J. (2010) Creativity without borders? Rethinking remoteness and proximity. *Australian Geographer*, 41(1): 25–38.

Handley, K., Sturdy, A., Fincham, R., & Clark, T. (2006) Within and beyond communities of practice: Making sense of learning through participation, identity and practice. *Journal of Management Studies*, 43(3): 641–653.

Harvey, D.C., Hawkins, H., & Thomas, N.J. (2012) Thinking creative clusters beyond the city: People, places and networks. *Geoforum*, 43(3): 529–539.

Lave, J., & Wenger, E. (1991) *Situated learning: Legitimate peripheral participation*. Cambridge: Cambridge University Press.

Luckman, S. (2015) *Craft and the creative economy*. Basingstoke: Palgrave Macmillan.

Richardson, G. (2001) A tale of two theories: Monopolies and craft guilds in medieval England and modern imagination. *Journal of the History of Economic Thought*, 23(2): 217–242.

Roberts, J. (2006) Limits to communities of practice. *Journal of Management Studies*, 43(3): 623–639.

Storper, M., & Venables, A.J. (2004) Buzz: Face-to-face contact and the urban economy. *Journal of Economic Geography*, 4(4): 351–370.

Thomas, N.J. (2018) Modernity, crafts and guilded practices: Locating the historical geographies of 20th century craft organisations. In Price, L. & Hawkins, H. (Eds), *Geographies of Making, Craft and Creativity*. London: Routledge.

Thomas, N.J., Harvey, D.C., & Hawkins, H. (2012) Crafting the region: Creative industries and practices of regional space. *Regional Studies*, 47(1): 75–88.

Wenger, E. (1998) *Communities of practice: Learning, meaning and identity*. Cambridge: Cambridge University Press.

10 The Cordwainer's Lair
Contingency in Bespoke Shoemaking

Robert Ott

Introduction: Into the Subterranean Space of Craft

Turning the pages in a glossy magazine featuring luxury products, one likely will come across an image of a craftsperson carefully cutting a suit, trimming the thread on a handbag, or polishing a shoe. Invariably they will be portrayed as wearing clean and tidy clothes in a carefully staged and pristine workshop deemed worthy of producing uniquely handcrafted artefacts made of exquisite materials. However, in reality, these artefacts may begin their life in lowly spaces never intended to be seen by future owners. These workshops often are hidden away, subterranean spaces that protect those who work in them from prying eyes while toiling at their craft.

These spaces can be understood as craft 'lairs'. A lair is a secluded or hidden place, a secret retreat or base of operation. Such workspaces belie the common representation that craftspeople systematically employ a perfected process to make perfect specimens. In fact, the opposite is true. I am suggesting craftship—specifically bespoke crafting—is secretive and messy, a journey of mitigating tensions between materials, tools, makers, and clients. There is no single right way of doing things. The workshop is a place of carefully managed predicaments, where the optimal course of action is dependent (contingent) on internal and external situations, and as Niklas Luhmann suggests (1984), neither necessary nor impossible, always potentially otherwise.

This chapter explores the organizational structures and processes of craft through the concept of contingency. According to Luhmann, contingency is

> something that is neither necessary nor impossible; which can be as it is (was, will be), but is also possible otherwise. The term thus designates the given (experienced, expected, thought, fantasized) with regard to possible otherness; it denotes objects in the horizon of possible modifications. It presupposes the given world, and does not designate what is possible in the first place, but what is otherwise possible from the point of view of reality.
>
> (1984: 152, author's translation)

It is an ethnographic account of a workshop, craftspeople, materials, and tools. Here, contingency suggests experimentation as a key factor that guides craftspeople from the known to the unknown, minimizing errors and avoiding irreparable damage during the making of bespoke shoes.

Craft Fashion and Fast Fashion

In modern life, the consumer's relationship with craft as a means of production has been both detested and exalted. Social desires to imitate and conform with inferior products, and a simultaneous desire for the fashionable and prestigious, are manifest in proud ownership of hand-knitted scarves, or hard-wearing shoes, while differentiation is also sought through the most ephemeral of fast fashion (Entwistle 2015).

Craft brings connotations of something handmade, avoiding the implication of cheap labour associated with 'factory-made'. Paradoxically, through much of modernity, factory-made items were more expensive and hence more prestigious. Factory-made artefacts could stand for consumer desire to conform, and not be individualistic. The reaction of children to hand-knitted sweaters rather than store-bought exemplifies this desire to fit in. This is likely a phenomenon of the mid-twentieth century, perhaps a reaction to wartime limited resources and rationing of materials. We now have come full circle, as we witness people proudly wearing clothes and shoes that display the marks of handwork.

Technological advancements and continuous changes in what the consumer prefers affect how fashion is produced and consumed (Bell 1976, Wilson 2013). The mechanisms employed in production and consumption are a set of interconnected activities that include makers, materials, tools, equipment, practices, processes, buildings, ships, trains, trucks, sellers, supply, demand, and buyers (Joshi, Barnes and Eicher 1992, Leopold 1993, Wills et al. 1973). Within this, different mechanisms exist for different approaches to production for different markets (Fine and Leopold 1993). Women's fashion is organized differently from men's and children's; clothing, accessories and footwear utilize different materials and processes; luxury fashion attracts a different consumer than mass-market apparel (Entwistle 2015). Consequently, a number of mechanisms—fashion systems—coexist at any given time and change continually. The study of fashion systems is beginning to be recognized as a rightful discipline with its own frameworks (Gully 2009, Smith and Whitfiel 2005a). Research on fashion systems tends to fall into six broad and overlapping categories: 1) fashion design and business strategies (see, e.g., Choi 2003, Malem 2008, McRobbie 2004a); 2) profiles and characteristics of fashion designers (see, e.g., Choi 2003, McRobbie 2004b); 3) fashion design processes and techniques (see, e.g., Aage and Belussi 2008, Rantisi 2004); 4) fashion design and pedagogy (see, e.g., Au et al. 2004, Bailey 2002, Drew et al. 2002, Greenberg 1994, Gully 2009); 5) consumer behaviour and public perceptions of design and designers (see, e.g., Smith and Whitfield 2005b); and 6) fashion and culture (see, e.g., Crewe and Forster 1993, Entwistle 2015, Forster 2009, Sparke 2004). This expansion of the idea of fashion systems, particularly in the late twentieth century, has consistently pushed manufacturers to do things faster, more productively, and cheaper through increased use of innovation, mechanization, and scale of economies (Gunasekaran 2001).

The momentum for manufacturing advancements in fashion is currently focused on mass-production in general and 'fast fashion' in particular. Fast fashion was pioneered by Inditex, the Spanish multinational organization behind retailing giant Zara in the 1990s, reducing the lead times that govern the processes of development to selling of product from the nine-month industry average to as low as one week, dramatically increasing the introduction of new styles (Burgen 2012). Zara's business model was quickly adopted by competitors and new entrants to the fashion market, including H&M, Topshop, Aeropostale, Forever 21, Next, Primark, and Uniqlo. Their success has not been without controversy, raising concerns with conditions that significantly compromise the health, safety, and fair treatment of workers. This was most recently exemplified by the 2013 collapse of the Rana Plaza building in Bangladesh, killing 1129 and injuring more than 2500 garment workers producing for Primark, Benetton, and many others. Other concerns point to practices that compromise the environment by diverting harmful effluents into river systems, and the ethics of producing excessive amounts of clothing and footwear. Concerns about workers, environment, and overproduction point to signs of disenfranchisement among a growing number of consumers who question the high social and environmental cost of producing fast fashion, and the low perceived value of the products. These consumers may look for alternatives in how they consume fashion.

Today's consumer can be overwhelmed by product choices available between brick-and-mortar stores and the round-the-clock convenience of on-line shopping. However, there is evidence that some modern-day consumers will reject inexpensive, throwaway fashion items in favour of well-made, durable objects. Some consumers are protesting the social and environmental impacts attributed to fast fashion by shifting decision-making from extrinsic (materialistic) to intrinsic (value-driven) characteristics. Moreover, it may be as cost-effective purchasing one pair of higher-priced, high-quality shoes as it is to buy three pairs of low-cost, low-quality shoes. 'Slow fashion' (Fletcher 2007), a countermovement to fast fashion, may signal a return to craft values and the process of making goods.

This is supported by suggestions from the British Crafts Council that a newfound interest in crafted things is also a reaction to an 'ever more screen-based entertainment culture, [where] there is a hunger for the authentic and the handmade' (Crafts Council 2012: 11). Crafting—possibly in the popular (and perhaps homely) imagination associated with scrapbooking and making eggcups out of toilet paper rolls—is again becoming socially desirable. Some people are drawn to the nostalgia of being both maker and consumer. They form knitting groups to make sweaters using home-spun woollen yarns from backyard sheep, reserve a weekend to fashion leather sneakers, forage in pastures and woodlands for native vegetables and herbs, and devour content served up by television programmes, magazines, websites, blogs, and social media platforms. As Christopher Frayling in his book *On Craftsmanship* points out: 'Craftsmanship has again become fashionable in high places' (2011: 7), suggesting that the intrinsic qualities of handmade artefacts are gradually growing in appeal compared to the extrinsic characteristics of fast-fashion brands.

In *The Craftsman* (2008), Richard Sennett investigates the history of craftship and the relationship between material, worker, and organization. He observes, 'Craftsmanship may suggest a way of life that waned with the advent of industrial society—but this is misleading. Craftsmanship names an enduring, basic impulse, the desire to do a job well for its own sake' (p. 9). Crafting encompasses the economic, political, and socio-logical consequences of making things. By looking at the process of making, the role of industrialization, and the evolution of crafts, Sennett claims that crafting has become the bridge between the challenges of the industrial revolution and the successful adoption of mechanizing work done traditionally by hand. However, definitions of 'old-world' crafting processes are surprisingly divergent. For example, while Sennett offers that craftship is 'the skill of doing things well' (p. 8), Frayling defines craft as 'an activity which involves skill in making things by hand' (2011: 9). Making sense of craft is a more complex and diverse issue than is apparent at the outset, depending on the academic frame of reference: in anthro-pology, it might be the making of artefacts for personal use; in sociology, it might be the making through skilled manual labour; in economics, it might be the precedent to capitalism; in marketing it might be consumer product differentiation; and in art, it might be the tension between intent and outcome. For the purposes of this chapter, I will define craftship as 'the skill of doing things well by hand' within the context of organiza-tional structure and processes.

While contemporary craft embraces the benefits of technology, my narrowed definition emphasizes handwork; that is, hands manipulating tools and materials to fashion an artefact. Even mass-producing fashion goods still involves a significant amount of manual-labour positioning, guiding non-rigid components through machines, despite continual advancements in automation, suggesting that a definition of craft as process is not sufficient. Craftspeople working in fashion (particularly tailoring and shoemaking) draw on established fashion systems to differ-entiate their position in relation to process, customer, and artefact. Mass-produced suits and shoes, 'off-the-shelf' or 'ready-to-wear', offer the consumer no input into materials and fit. 'Custom' generally allows the consumer to select materials; 'made-to-measure' allows the consumer to select materials and adapt fit. Custom generally does not include fittings and made-to-measure may only include a fitting at the end of production to allow for minimal alterations. 'Bespoke', the approach analysed here, engages the client and craftsperson to create a unique, one-of-a-kind artefact, in design, materials, fit, and finish. It is not only time-consuming, but also the most expensive approach.

The approaches of fashion craft are not always readily discernible by the average consumer and often lead to the misuse of terms for the purposes of marketing and differentiation. If one were to consider the term 'bespoke' to represent the most prestigious form of fashion craft, it is conceivable that a made-to-measure maker might borrow the term 'bespoke' in attracting a potential client with a promise of lower cost and quicker delivery than a competitor. Attempts have been made to legally define and protect the term 'bespoke', emphasizing the sensitivity and code of conduct important to fashion craftship, and the continued onslaught by fast-fashion operators on craftspeople whose livelihoods hinge on the pride and reputation of defining their craft. Understanding and appreciating the complexity of bespoke craft resides in the relationship between client, craftsperson, process, and product; and the contingencies which an individual needs to consider when handcrafting an artefact.

Contingency and the 'One Best Way'

As noted earlier, contingency is predicated on the idea that there is no single right way of doing things. In fact, there are many ways of navigating internal, external, and emerging factors when addressing a given problem. Contingency is a way of dealing with the known and the unknown in order to identify a problem, propose solutions, allocate resources, organize work, make decisions, lead people, mobilize knowledge, and adapt learning. While contingency has been described as a 'principle for organizing knowledge in a given area of study' (Umanath 2003), common notions of 'there is no single right way of doing things' and 'it depends' underestimate its possibilities as a concept. Luhmann's definition of contingency as stated at the outset suggests a multiplicity of views, each different and neither necessary nor arbitrary, an important extension to earlier understandings of the concept.

In organization studies, contingency suggests there is no single structure that is appropriate and applicable in all circumstances, and no single process that is effective and desirable in attaining organizational goals. A substantial number of quantitative and qualitative studies conducted since the 1960s (e.g., Burns and Stalker 1961, Chandler 1966, Child 1972, Donaldson, 1996, Donaldson 1999, Drazin and Van de Ven 1985, Galbraith and Lawler 1993, Lawrence and Lorsch 1967, Mintzberg 1983,

Mintzberg 1994, Tidd 2001) identified size, strategy, technology, complexity, and uncertainty as contingency variables that influence organizational structure, process, and performance. Here, my task is to find the appropriate fit between the workshop and contingency.

Tidd specifically defines uncertainty as 'a function of the rate of change of technologies and product-markets' and complexity as 'a function of technological and organizational interdependencies' (2001: 175). Although these two factors are independent of each other, in some cases the potential interactions increase. The resulting four combinations Tidd describes are: 1) low complexity/low uncertainty: product differentiation focus, marketing competency, multi-divisional organizational structure; 2) low complexity/high uncertainty: technological focus and competency, functional organizational structure; 3) high complexity/low uncertainty: project management focus and competency; professional organizational structure; and 4) high complexity/high uncertainty: multiple foci and competencies, flexible, adaptive, and learning organizational structure.

In applying Tidd's complexity/uncertainty model to footwear, mass-market casual shoes fall into the low complexity/low uncertainty quadrant. Manufacturers compete on brand names, fashion-appropriate design and styling, materials, and price in multi-segmented distribution channels including mass merchants, off-price retailers, and department and specialty stores. Athletic shoes are an example of low complexity/ high uncertainty products driven by high-performance features and technological advancements. Footwear manufacturers representing brands that are distributed through both their own store network and third-party retailers can be described as high complexity/low uncertainty organizations. These companies focus on manufacturing a broad range of footwear styles including sandals, casual shoes, dress shoes, boots for men, women, and children. Lastly, high complexity/high uncertainty characterizes entrepreneurial organizations including the workshops of bespoke shoemakers. These organizations often rely on a small group of workers making one-of-a-kind objects.

Contingencies of structure and process include some internal to the organization and some that are external (Donaldson 2001). Complexity and uncertainty relate directly to the work being performed and consequently are situated within the workshop. Organizational size—the number of individual people working—is considered by some researchers to be an internal factor (Child 1975). However, I suggest—based on my assertion that organizations have access to external resources, including labour, materials, and space, to meet operational demand—workers are contingent. Hence, the number of people employed is an external factor as operational demand is generally driven by consumer demand over which an organization may have limited control. Donaldson (2001) contends that external factors directly and indirectly influence intra-organizational contingencies, thus shaping organizations to fit their environment. The next section outlines how I approach this argument empirically.

Places, Spaces, Things, and Faces

To gain a deeper understanding of the dynamics involved in the making of a pair of shoes, I conducted an ethnography of shoemakers who are masters in their trade earned through either formal schooling or by practice (achieved after 10,000 hours or five to seven years of work) and apprenticeship. The fieldwork was conducted in a workshop located in Toronto, Canada, from August 2016 to February 2017 and resulted in 97 hours of observation, 84 hours of audio recordings, 59 hours of video recordings, and over 1000 photographs.

My preconceived image of the shoemaker formally dressed in a stately showroom outfitted with antique fixtures showcasing their work was mostly taken from visiting modern shopping centres with large display windows and a salesperson standing just inside the shop door. These shopping centres are the Mecca of consumerism, cathedrals of consumption (Ritzer 2010), drawing faithful followers worshipping at the altar of fashion within glorious spaces. Indeed, makers of luxury fashion goods are aggressively shifting their focus to how they are perceived by their customers. Gabriel (2005) argues that organizations, once preoccupied with efficiency and rationality of production operations, are turning to the consumer as the measure of organizational competency. The consumer not only wants products to be functional, but also desires an experience that is magical, fantastic, and alluring. Thus, organizations are finding themselves increasingly preoccupied with the emotional capital they need to invest in their customers; that is, what is required for the consumer to develop a loyalty to a brand, return, and buy more. Fashion is a powerful medium in marrying the product and the aspirational expectations of the consumer, leading to accelerated changes in the choices of product offered and the element of surprise in how the product is offered. There appears to be more emphasis on the experience of making a purchase rather than the product itself. This ambiguity is of concern and therefore a recalibration of the relationship between organization, product, and consumer is of interest.

However, my preconception of the workshop was misplaced. I did not enter it by striding up marble steps; instead, I stepped down worn concrete stairs to be greeted by a nondescript solid steel door. With no doorbell in sight, I was relegated to knocking on the door, following up with increasingly loud bangs. Figure 10.1 shows the fortified, unmarked entrance suggesting that there is nothing of importance beyond. The workshop might be perceived initially as unwelcoming; however, visitors quickly adapt to the notion that the surroundings have little connection to the product created therein, feeling they have exclusive access to a

Figure 10.1 The Entrance into the Cordwainer's Lair

secret world. The physical attributes of the spaces in which the crafts-people work are situational, depending on operational requirements and how the craftspeople interact, collaborate, and solve problems. These are spaces that allow for experimentation, activities that accept mistakes and corrective resolution as part of the creative process in the production of a bespoke pair of shoes. These are spaces of mystery.

Once the metal door opened, I was greeted by the chemical aroma of glue, the pungent tang of burning leather, and the friendly grin of the lead shoemaker. Within a workshop measuring a mere eleven square meters, five craftspeople go about their work. Cramped spaces evoke historical accounts of workshop conditions during early nineteenth century England—the moment when more shoes were made entirely by hand than at any other time—where the smaller workshops were often in an upper floor garret, or in a dismal basement lit only by a pavement light, boosted—when allowed—by a candle or oil lamp (Salaman 1986). The lighting of the contemporary workshop, however, is quite different and provided by overhead fluorescent fixtures.

The main workbench was occupied by three craftspeople engaged in various stages of hand-making shoes, and a fourth person sitting at the design desk. The tiny space is stuffed with equipment, materials, tools, and supplies. The craftspeople are focused on their work, only responding to intermittent comments from the lead craftsperson (and owner of the workshop). The whirring of grinders and pounding of hammers are superseded by music pumped from a mobile phone to small speakers. Previously, songbirds in cages kept the craftspeople company (Swann 2003) and provided similar audio entertainment. The music in the contemporary setting is varied and upbeat, but decidedly chosen to the taste of the lead cordwainer.

In this study, I am interested in understanding what embodied skills, materials, and tools inform contemporary practices of craftship, specifically how the body and materials interrelate, how work is organized, and what factors influence the making of bespoke fashion artefacts. The tiny workshop requires the people within it to carefully manoeuvre in a premeditated dance to avoid bumping into each other. This close proximity of bodies focused on their individual tasks also allows the lead shoemaker to survey the work being done from the proximity of his seat. Comments on why something is being done a certain way or corrective instructions are immediate and unobtrusive. Communication is as much done by body language as by direct verbal interaction. There are no formal meetings; instead, daily instructions of tasks greet the workers most mornings as they arrive at the workshop. The hours are varied, driven by meeting a hard deadline or getting lost in time while pushing to finish something to no one's urging other than their own.

It becomes clear that each craftsperson is in the workshop for their own personal reasons. They are twenty or thirty something, all having abandoned studies or professional careers in media production, economics, and science that left them both professionally and personally unfulfilled. They each had a yearning for working with their hands, continually working on perfecting a skill, and taking pride in creating a physical artefact. For some, a hobby has turned into a calling to train in shoemaking, despite the financial hardship that accompanies the departure of a well-paid professional job. As the lead shoemaker professes: 'I am in the eleventh year of a self-imposed life sentence', after quitting his job, moving to Italy to study and apprentice, and return to Toronto to open the bespoke shoe workshop. He finds satisfaction in what he does with his hands, but admits that running the organization presents challenges—not the least of which is dealing with customers. 'Life would be great, if it were not for the customer', he says with a sigh and a laugh. Working as a shoemaker is precarious, and the craftspeople the master employs are apprentices sourced through an informal international network of aspiring shoemakers looking for an opportunity to work with a craftsperson for a few weeks or months in order to practice their craft, learn new skills, and gain experience. Therefore, the organization's existence is contingent on supply of both work and people at a given time and location, neither necessary nor unattainable.

This precariousness subjugates the shoemaker to financial obligations, often deferring capital investments in the workshop, and assuming higher risks. It therefore is not surprising that the non-essential components of the workshop are found objects. The workbench was already in the space when the shoemaker rented the basement, the chairs were found on the side of a residential street, collected candy tins hold nails, and decorative jars hold tools. Yet it appears that this limitation of resources is a motivation for resourcefulness, driving innovation through contingency. As a result, improvisation, the ability to draw on available material, cognitive, affective, and social resources (Pina e Cunha et al. 1999), takes advantage of adapting an object for some other use than that which is was designed for. Figure 10.2 shows the contrast in the tools themselves, such

Figure 10.2 Shoemaking Tools and Supplies on the Workbench

as hammer, pliers, knives, and awls, which are the best in their class, while secondary tools and supplies are often found and repurposed objects.

The making of handmade shoes is a skilled operation involving not only the use of leather with its variable qualities and peculiarities, but also the covering of the asymmetrical human foot, which is even more variable than leather (Salaman 1986: 20). Shoes are a functional item that must respond to the wearer's need for support and comfort. In describing the process of making shoes, I will limit the parameters of bespoke footwear as a leather object that fully envelops the foot. In this context, an Oxford is a formal lace-up shoe, typically worn by men. It has a vamp (the front of the shoe) attached to the quarters (upper sections that covers the sides and back), a tongue, eyelets and laces, a toecap, a backstrap, a low heel and often a welt construction. The upper consists of the components seen above the sole when the shoe is worn. The sole is comprised of the insole, the part closest to the bottom of the foot; the outsole, the material on the bottom and exterior that comes into contact with the ground while walking; and bottom filling, the material filling the space in between. The welt is a strip of leather that runs along the perimeter of the sole. The sole is then attached through stitching, adhesive, or a combination of both. The benefit of sewn welt construction is that a shoe can be fitted with a replacement sole as long as the upper part of the shoe not damaged. Welted shoes are significantly more time- consuming and expensive to make due to additional hand sewing than mass-produced shoes that primarily rely on glued or moulded soles. In the workshop I observed, a pair of shoes with glued soles typically takes about 27 hours to produce, whereas welt soles can command up to 40 hours of highly skilled labour.

The process of building a handmade shoe is usually a set of linear steps that transform materials—with tools and a healthy amount of elbow grease—into an artefact. It is important to understand that the composition of a shoe is an organic process whereby materials are cut, ground, heated, hammered, honed, layered, bonded, shaped, and poked, rather than assembled from pre-made components. Therefore—apart from geographic variations—craftspeople's training, and personal adaptations, the process follows the following stages: measuring, design, pattern making, cutting (clicking), sewing (closing), preparation, lasting, making, and finishing. This is consistently evidenced by a number of how-to books over three centuries, such as de Garsault (1767), Rees (1813), Devlin (1839–41), Leno (1885), Plucknett (1916, 1922, 1931), and Thornton (1970). While the process of shoe construction was mechanized during the Industrial Revolution, the steps have largely remained the same as if done by hand.[1] Figure 10.3 provides a view of the underside of a shoe during construction. At this stage—making—the upper section has been stretched over the last with the heel and mid sections nailed and glued to the insole. The toe section has been temporarily secured to prepare for

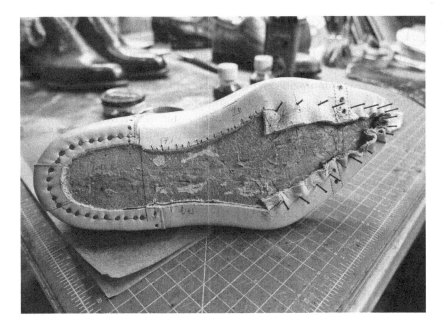

Figure 10.3 A Partially Constructed Shoe

the removal of excess leather from the toe point before the outsole can be attached.

In order to relate the effects of contingency on bespoke shoemaking, it is important to understand how complexity and uncertainty shape a bespoke artefact. Mass manufacturing focuses on developing a prototype which serves as a model of a product for replication. Depending on whether the product is a new development or an existing product adapted for new materials, the process of prototyping is iterative until the manufacturer is satisfied with the final sample. The purpose of prototyping is to articulate, code and draw technical specification sheets of the components and processes required to minimize, even eliminate, problems during production. Consequently, prototyping is an exercise of precision and engineering to ensure components fit together. Solving problems associated with diverse materials often used in shoes is paramount in meeting production quotas, delivery schedules, and costs. Shoes are produced in different standard sizes and often several colours—it therefore is not uncommon for this one prototype to derive dozens of variations. Inherently, the value of the finished artefact lies in the near limitless, perfect replications—identical siblings—of the prototype. Consequently, whether producing ten, one hundred, or one hundred thousand specimens, each will be identical to the prototype.

In contrast, in bespoke shoemaking, the final artefact is effectively the first and only prototype. This prototype eludes replication, as attempts to make multiples effectively creates new prototypes which would be cousins as opposed to identical siblings. Therefore, the craftsperson making a bespoke object only has a single attempt at achieving perfection, while simultaneously minimizing errors and avoiding irrevocable disaster. And if that is not pressure enough, the craftsperson needs to make a mirror image duplicate, effectively a brother or sister to the original. While a bespoke shoe may appear to be an object made entirely of leather, there in fact are multiple and, in some cases, seemingly incompatible materials on the inside hidden from view. A bespoke pair of shoes is one of the highest complexity artefacts and extreme cases of craftship available to us.

Apprenticing to become a shoemaker and subsequent master crafter requires the individual to be able to construct a shoe from the beginning, from making a pattern to finishing, with the exception of design. In practice, lead shoemakers often delegate tasks to specialists or apprentices. Stitching the uppers is considered an especially difficult task as mistakes can only rarely be corrected. Conversely, mundane jobs such as fastening the insole to the last, even if done imperfectly, have no material effect on the look and function of the shoe and therefore may be left for apprentices to do. While lead shoemakers are expected to be able to superbly execute each step of making a shoe, they also need to embody many skills that are often crafts unto themselves, including cabinet making when customizing a last, surgery when dissecting animal skins, and material science when bonding diverse materials. The traditional idea of a shoemaker is that of a solitary individual who works alone. This remains largely relevant existentially for the hand sewn maker at work today (Salaman 1986: 20), but that individual usually works in a small community at the same time.

The practice of working alone existentially and the inherent self-reliance of the maker imposes unique conditions. Problems that arise during the process can be difficult to articulate, given the fact that a bespoke pair of shoes is both the prototype and final artefact. Hence identifying and resolving problems is largely tacit, with knowledge building over many years. The solutions to the problems are rarely recorded on paper or electronically because it is unlikely that a similar problem will be encountered in the future. Knowledge is embodied in the maker; transfer of knowledge is more likely to happen through learning how to work through problems independently than through teaching by an experienced maker. Notwithstanding, the learning is contingent on the solutions applied to problems in previous steps that may have been unnecessary or improbable.

In Figure 10.4, the apprentice has been tasked to attach the sole to the uppers and then attach the heel to the sole. On the left, he dry fits three layers of cattle hide that usually make up the heels and visually inspects the balance of the shoe. The sole and heel of the shoe must sit flat on the

Figure 10.4 Balancing the Shoe: the Case of the Wedge

floor with the regular heel. However here, the apprentice needs to make a counterbalancing adjustment to the heel by inserting a wedge. The wedge will be noticeable in the final product, but it will not necessarily be seen as a mistake—it may even be considered a design detail. This is a case of experimenting with an unknown outcome, dealing with a previously unencountered problem that could have been avoided at an earlier stage in production. The contingency here is both unnecessary and improbable, in Luhmann's terms.

While inserting a small wedge in the heel—where the edge might be dyed dark and consequently minimize the appearance of individual layers in the building of the heel—has no particular aesthetic implications on the final product, the shoemaker might encounter very different situations. Sometimes uppers contain a decorative element of 'broguing', small holes punched through the leather and edged with two rows of stitching. When moulding the upper over the last, the maker must engage with the inherent elastic properties of the leather, coaxing the material over the last, eliminating sags and wrinkles to create a smooth surface. The foot is a complex shape, described by one maker as 'an elliptical hemisphere with hyperbolic paraboloid characteristics'. This step therefore requires not only experience, but also anticipation, to understand the cause and effect that stretching a material has on an artefact. Distortion of shape and spacing, and inconsistent distance between the two stitched lines, is a common unintended consequence of the maker's focus on stretching the upper to the last, a delicate dance between the strength of the body and the fragility of the material. The maker at this stage has few options: unmount the upper from the last and re-stretch, leave as is and continue with the possibility of the distortion of the broguing to correct itself, or start over again. From Luhmann's perspective, this is a case of an indeterminate situation brought about by not necessary and not impossible processes.

Experimentation is a process of contingency that mitigates the possibilities of the known with the probabilities of the unknown, as theorized by Luhmann. I suggest that experimentation draws on previous knowledge and its application to different situations. Thomke points out that 'experimentation matters because it fuels the discovery and creation of knowledge and thereby leads to the development and improvement of products, processes, systems, and organizations' (2003: 1). Cannon (2005) suggests that failure is a predisposition of experimentation to discover successes, to maximize the opportunity for learning from failure, and minimize costs. Consequently, experimentation involves failure to achieve success. All too often the value of experimentation in organizations is neglected because it is seen as taxing existing resources, counterproductive to established operational processes, and expensive (Cannon and Edmondson 2005, Desouza et al. 2009).

While the failure of experimentation is intended to help an organization learn and reduce overall costs, the implications on craftship may have the opposite effect. In the cordwainer's workshop, pushing the limits on experimentation can have a detrimental outcome. The maker must attach the sole to the upper and prepare for finishing by cutting off excess material from the sole and heel before using an electric sander to smooth the edges. Using a knife to cut is faster than sanding, but improvisation of this kind, intended to hasten the finals steps in completing the shoe, easily leads to disastrous results: the knife can easily slip off the sole and gash the upper. Such an event is a 'moment of death' for the artefact. The action is irreparable, and the maker has to make a new shoe.

However, experimentation and improvisation in themselves and as part of the process of innovation are critical and failure is to be expected. As noted years earlier in a rare convincing passage in the book *In Search of Excellence*:

> The most important and visible outcropping of the action bias in the excellent companies is their willingness to try things out, to experiment. There is absolutely no magic in the experiment. It is simply a tiny completed action, a manageable test that helps you learn something.... But our experience has been that most big institutions have forgotten how to test and learn. They seem to prefer analysis and debate to trying something out, and they are paralyzed by fear of failure, however small.
>
> (Peters and Waterman 1982: 134–135)

Research on the role and benefits of experimentation have centred on large organizations as part of a larger innovation agenda (see Desouza et al. 2009, Cannon and Edmondson 2005, Edmondson and Nembhard 2009, Gupta et al. 2007, Lee et al. 2004, Sonenshein 2014). However, based on my observations in the workshop, I would suggest that experimentation and improvisation are entrenched practices of craft, in the sense that these practices are not optional—in fact, experimentation is unavoidable even at the expense of becoming catastrophic in the workshop.

Conclusion: Bringing Craft out of the Lair

In this chapter, I situated contingency not only as a process of experimentation unfettered by a single, right way of doing things, but also through the argument that actions are not always necessary, possible, or determinate. Handcrafting a pair of shoes is complex and rife with uncertainty. While theories of contingency tend to focus on large organizations, Luhmann provides an appropriate lens through which to explore craftship as practiced by individual makers. Further, he conceptualizes contingency as possibilities to explore the unexplored and acknowledges choice of possibilities as integral to experimentation. This is significant to the re-emergence of craftship, its traditions and practices, and its implications for contemporary fashion systems.

My characterization of a singular cordwainer's workshop as a lair is unapologetically narrow, but not limited. The approach developed here differentiates our current understanding of contingency in organizations and suggests that craftship requires new ways of theorizing. In this study, the otherness of making things is precipitated by the otherness of the process where bespoke craftspeople develop both the prototype and the finished artefact at the same time. Therefore, the understanding—and acceptance—of the messiness shaped by experimentation in the process of contingency in craftship and its apparent opposition to the organizing of fast fashion is of great importance. Contingency in organizations involves a multiplicity of views, each different and neither necessary nor arbitrary.

Note

1 The steps of making a welt construction pair of leather dress shoes (both the left and right shoe are made in tandem) are as follows:

> **Measuring:** As a shoe is, foremost, a functional object of comfort and fit, and it is important for cordwainers to have a thorough understanding of the anatomy of the foot. As Leno (1885, p.25) points out, feet differ not only in proportion and size, but how they resist and conform to pressures of walking, sitting, and standing. It is not uncommon for the foot to elongate a full size when the arch of the foot is pressed.

Therefore, the art of measuring does not lie in capturing measurements, but instead the shape and dimension of the foot the measurements define and making allowances accordingly. For measuring bespoke shoes, the client is seated, knee at right angle, and the socked foot on a piece of heavy paper. A line is drawn around the foot that serves as markers for its critical dimensions. In addition to the length of the foot, the circumferences of the root of the toes, joints, past joints, instep, heel, ankle, and the height of the ankle bone are transcribed to the outline. This process then is repeated for the other foot.

After measuring the foot, a three-dimensional model of the foot—a 'last'—is created. Made traditionally from wood and more recently from plastic, the last may be created from scratch or modified from an existing last. The last is used for both design and construction, which will transform the last from a rough counterpart of the foot to the final form of the shoe.

Design: The client is invariably an active contributor to the design of the shoe, helping to select a style, materials, details, colour, and finishes. A sketch of the design is produced and the last is modified to reflect the design elements, most commonly the shape of the front of the shoe. At this stage the purpose of design of the shoe diverges from function of fit to expression of aesthetic. That is, from the back of the heel to the joints of the toes, the shoe must cradle the foot to provide support; from the joints to the tip of the toes few such restrictions exist as the shoe's toe shape is influenced by trends in fashion whether that be a square, round, or pointed toe. With the last now representing the shape of the finished shoe, fabric, paper or masking tape is placed on top of the last and, using the sketch as a point of reference, the design is transferred. The resulting 'mask', which captures the three-dimensional nature of the design, is removed from the last and flattened into a two-dimensional representation which serves as the blueprint for creating the pattern.

Patternmaking: The mask is used to identify the parts of the top sections of the shoe, including the inside lining, and working patterns are produced.

Clicking: 'Clicking' is a traditional cordwaining term used to describe the sound a knife makes when cutting leather on a hard surface. This step of the process includes the cutting of the leather for the top sections of the shoe, called the 'upper' as suggested above, and the lining. At this stage a mock-up of the shoe may be made to ensure that the pattern accurately reflects the design and—most importantly for the bespoke client—that the shoe fits. At this stage changes to the design and the last may be made. Past this stage, it is not possible to make further changes to fit or the shape of the toe. The mock-up or 'fit shoe' stage may undergo as many iterations as necessary to satisfy both the client and the maker.

Closing: 'Closing' refers to the preparation, fitting, and stitching of the various parts of the uppers. In the case of multiple parts of the uppers, components are 'skived', which involves the bevelling of the edges of the leather pieces to reduce the bulk of overlapping layers of material, before they are sewn together.

Preparation: Before the shoe can be constructed, the preparation of the bottom parts includes the cutting of the insole, welt, and heel. The insole is then attached to the bottom of the last, ensuring that the arch of the foot is maintained.

Lasting: 'Lasting' involves the stretching of the uppers over the last. Various materials are inserted between the uppers and lining during lasting to increase stability and shape the final form. These components include 'counters' placed at the heel and the sides of the shoe to address rigidity through select applications of resin or glue and a 'toe puff' to maintain the shape of the shoe toe.

Making: The attaching of the sole to the uppers is the final, major step in construction a shoe. In a welted construction, two methods of attaching the sole are currently practiced. Both involve the placement of a thin strip of leather —the 'welt'—around the perimeter of the upper and sole. The difference between the two methods is that one uses glue and the other hand- stitching. Apart from the additional time and skill required, the key benefit of the hand-stitched welt construction is that a worn sole can be replaced thus extending the life of the shoe as long as the uppers are in good shape. The last step is attaching the heel to the bottom of the sole.

Finishing: The finishing of the shoe includes the trimming, colouring, and burnishing of the edges of the sole and heel. At this stage, final repairs and the removal of stains are conducted before colouring or applying a patina to the uppers. Burnishing, polishing, waxing, inserting of laces and insole liners complete the final act of shoemaking.

References

Aage, T. & Belussi, F. (2008) From fashion to design: creative networks in industrial districts. *Industry and Innovation*, 15(5): 475–491.

Au, J. S., Taylor, M. G. & Newton, E. W. (2004) Model of design process of Hong Kong fashion designers. *Journal of Textile and Apparel Technology Management*, 4(2): 1–14.

Bailey, S. (2002) Student approaches to learning in fashion design: a phenomenographic study. *Art, Design & Communication in Higher Education*, 1(2): 81–95.

Bell, Q. (1976) *On human finery*. London, UK: Hogarth Press.

Burgen, S. (2012) Fashion chain Zara helps Inditex lift first quarter profits by 30%. The Guardian. www.theguardian.com/business/2012/aug/17/zara-inditex-profits [Last accessed 2015-07-3].

Burns, T. E. & Stalker, G. M. (1961) *The management of innovation*. London, UK: Tavistock.

Cannon, M. D. & Edmondson, A. C. (2005) Failing to learn and learning to fail (intelligently): how great organizations put failure to work to innovate and improve. *Long range planning*, 38(3): 299–319.

Chandler, A. D. (1966) *Strategy and structure*. Cambridge, MA: MIT Press.

Child, J. (1972) Organizational structure, environment and performance: the role of strategic choice. *Sociology*, 6(1): 1–22.

Child, J. (1975) Managerial and organizational factors associated with company performance. *Journal of Management Studies*, 12(1–2): 12–27.

Choi, Y. (2003) Understanding ICT adoption from the SME user centred approach: views from the boutique fashion SMEs and the Australian government. Presented at the Small Enterprise Association of Australia and New Zealand 16th Annual Conference, Sept. 28–Oct. 1, 2003.

Crafts Council, Creative Scotland, Arts Council of Wales, Craft Northern Ireland (2012) Craft in an age of change.

Crewe, L. & Forster, Z. (1993) Markets, design, and local agglomeration: the role of the small independent retailer in the workings of the fashion system. *Environment and Planning D*, 11: 213–233.

Desouza, K. C., Dombrowski, C., Awazu, Y., Baloh, P., Papagari, S., Jha, S. & Kim, J. Y. (2009) Crafting organizational innovation processes. *Innovation*, 11(1): 6–33.

Devlin, James (1839) *The guide to trade: the shoemaker.* London, UK: Knight.

Donaldson, L. (1996) *For positivist organization theory.* London, UK: Sage.

Donaldson, L. (1999) *Performance driven organizational change.* London, UK: Sage.

Donaldson, L. (2001) *The contingency theory of organizations.* London, UK: Sage.

Drazin, R. & Van de Ven, A. H. (1985) Alternative forms of fit in contingency theory. *Administrative Science Quarterly*: 514–539.

Drew, L., Bailey, S. & Shreeve, A. (2002) Fashion variations: student approaches to learning in fashion design. Presented at the Learning and Teaching in Art and Design Conference, April 11–12, 2002.

Edmondson, A. C. & Nembhard, I. M. (2009) Product development and learning in project teams: the challenges are the benefits. *Journal of Product Innovation Management*, 26(2): 123–138.

Entwistle, J. (2015) *The fashioned body: fashion, dress & modern social theory.* 2nd edn. Cambridge, UK: Polity Press.

Fine, B. & Leopold, E. (1993) *The world of consumption.* London, UK: Routledge.

Fletcher, K. (2007) Slow fashion. *The Ecologist*, 37(5), p. 61.

Forster, S. V. (2009) Connections between modern and postmodern art and fashion. *The Design Journal*, 12(2): 217–241.

Frayling, C. (2011) *On craftsmanship: towards a new Bauhaus.* London, UK: Oberon Books.

Gabriel, Y. (2005) Glass cages and glass palaces: images of organization in image-conscious times. *Organization*, 12(1): 9–27.

Galbraith, J. R. & Lawler, E. E. (1993) *Organizing for the future: the new logic for managing complex organizations.* San Francisco, CA: Jossey-Bass Inc. Pub.

de Garsault, F. (2009) *Art of the shoemaker: an annotated translation.* Lubbock, TX: Texas Tech University Press.

Greenberg, E. (1994) The importance of autonomy in encouraging creativity: managerial implications from a study in fashion design. *Creativity and Innovation Management*, 3(3): 167–176.

Gully, R. (2009) Cognition and process vs. design artifact in fashion design pedagogy. In: *Cumulus 38° South.* Swinburne University of Technology, 1–11.

Gunasekaran, A. (2001) *Agile manufacturing: the 21st century competitive strategy.* Oxford, UK: Elsevier.

Gupta, A. K., Tesluk, P. E. & Taylor, M. S. (2007) Innovation at and across multiple levels of analysis. *Organization Science*, 18(6): 885–897.

Joshi, O. P., Barnes, R. & Eicher, J. (1992) *Dress and gender: making and meaning.* Oxford, UK: Berg.

Kambil, A., Eselius, E. D. & Monteiro, K. A. (2000) Fast venturing: the quick way to start web businesses. *Sloan Management Review*, 41(4), p. 55.

Lawrence, P. R. & Lorsch, J. W. (1967) Managing differentiation and integration. *Organization and environment*, 2(2): 267–274.

Lee, F., Edmondson, A. C., Thomke, S. & Worline, M. (2004) The mixed effects of inconsistency on experimentation in organizations. *Organization Science*, 15(3): 310–326.

Leno, J. B. (1885) *The art of boot and shoemaking.* London, UK: Crosby Lockwood and Co.

Leopold, E. (1993) *The manufacture of the fashion system.* London, UK: Pandora.

Luhmann, N. (1984) *Soziale systeme.* Frankfurt am Main, Germany: Suhrkamp.

Malem, W. (2008) Fashion designers as business: London. *Journal of Fashion Marketing and Management*, 12(3): 398–414.

McRobbie, A. (2004a) A mixed economy of fashion design. *The Blackwell Cultural Economy Reader*: 1–14.

McRobbie, A. (2004b) *British fashion design: rag trade or image industry?* London, UK: Routledge.

Mintzberg, H. (1993) *Structure in fives: designing effective organizations.* Englewood Cliffs, NJ: Prentice-Hall, Inc.

Mintzberg, H. (1994) Rethinking strategic planning part I: pitfalls and fallacies. *Long Range Planning*, 27(3): 12–21.

Peters, T. & Waterman, R. (1982) *In search of excellence: lessons from America's best-run corporations.* New York, NY: Harper & Row.

Pina e Cunha, M., Vieira da Cunha, J. & Kamoche, K. (1999) Organizational improvisation: what, when, how and why. *International Journal of Management Reviews*, 1(3): 299–341.

Plucknett, F. (1916) *Introduction to the theory and practice of boot and shoe manufacture.* London, UK: Longmans, Green and Co.

Rantisi, N. (2004) The designer in the city and the city in the designer. *Cultural Industries and the Production of Culture*, 33, p. 91.

Rees, J. (1813) *Art and mystery of a cordwainer.* London, UK: Gale, Curtis, and Fenner.

Ritzer, G. (2010) *Enchanting a disenchanted world: continuity and change in the cathedrals of consumption.* Thousand Oaks, CA: Pine Forge Press.

Salaman, R. A. (1986) *The dictionary of leatherworking tools, c. 1700–1950 and the tools of allied trades.* Lakeville, MN: The Astragal Press.

Sennett, R. (2008) *The craftsman.* New Haven, CT: Yale University Press.

Smith, G. & Whitfield, T. (2005a) The professional status of designers: A national survey of how designers are perceived. *The Design Journal*, 8(1): 52–60.

Smith, G. & Whitfield, T. W. (2005b) Profiling the designer: a cognitive perspective. *The Design Journal*, 8(2): 3–14.

Sonenshein, S. (2014) How organizations foster the creative use of resources. *Academy of Management Journal*, 57(3): 814–848.

Sparke, P. (2004) *An introduction to design and culture: 1900 to the present.* New York, NY: Routledge.

Swann, J. (2003) *Shoemaking.* Buckinghamshire, UK: Shire Publications Ltd.

Thomke, S. H. (2003) *Experimentation matters: unlocking the potential of new technologies for innovation*. Boston, MA: Harvard Business Press.

Thornton, J.H. (1970) *Textbook of Footwear Manufacture*. 3rd edn. London, UK: Butterworth & Co Publishers Ltd.

Tidd, J. (2001) Innovation management in context: environment, organization and performance. *International Journal of Management Reviews*, 3(3): 169–183.

Umanath, N. S. (2003) The concept of contingency beyond "It depends": illustrations from IS research stream. *Information & Management*, 40(6): 551–562.

Wills, G., Midgley, D. & Christopher, M. (1973) *Fashion marketing*. London, UK: Allen & Unwin.

Wilson, E. (2013) *Adorned in dreams: fashion and modernity*. London, UK: I. B. Tauris.

11 Craft as Resistance

A Conversation about Craftivism, Embodied Inquiry, and Craft-based Methodologies

Ann Rippin and Sheena J. Vachhani

Introduction

Craft and making cultures have enjoyed a recent resurgence, with sociologists, philosophers and social theorists arguing that a 'back to basics' culture is socially connective. As Gauntlett argues (2011: 2), making is connective because 'acts of creativity usually involve, at some point, a social dimension and connect us with other people'. In addition, in the act of making things 'we increase our engagement and connection with our social and physical environments' (*ibid.* 2). Cultures of making, sharing and organizing through craft have hitherto been marginal in studies of management and organisation. The increased popularity of everyday creativity, do-it-yourself cultures and forgotten craft activities has much to teach organisational scholars and deserves closer attention (Vachhani 2013). These are also sites of resistance that serve as innovative strategies to challenge inequalities, and this chapter explores the tensions between craft and academic work. We expose the tensions and contradictory dynamics of academic publishing that may promote innovative methodological and writing practices but under the weight of standardisation and competition are still unable to adequately accommodate craft-based methodologies. Building on the theme of craft as resistance, we also examine the meaning and potential of 'craftivism' as a critical resource that can be used to challenge organisational oppression and exploitation (see Agosin 2014; Parker 1996). The term 'craftivism' has been coined recently (Greer 2008) and fuses 'craft' and 'activism' to denote craft practices that form explicit political activism, such as knitting placed in public spaces as in the case of yarnbombing (Moore & Prain 2009). Craft practices become sites of resistance, and we discuss themes around craft-based methodologies, resistance and embodied inquiry through a dialogue with Ann Rippin whose fascinating work employs textiles and craft-based methodologies using practices of quilting to explore the materiality of the text, foundation myths and leadership (Rippin 2007).

As a practitioner and academic, Ann makes textile art, especially large, heavily surface-decorated and embroidered quilts, as part of her research and teaching on work and organisation. Ann has researched organisations such as Marks and Spencer, The Body Shop, Starbucks and Nike and also made art dolls as a way of exploring the Laura Ashley brand and its place in the hearts of British quilters.[1] Ann's cutting-edge and multiple-media work uses techniques of juxtaposition and is heavily influenced by the work of Walter Benjamin. In our dialogue we reflect on our experiences of working at the intersections of craft practice, organisation and academia and explore the potential and challenges of using non-traditional, arts-based methods to act, resist or speak out as a means of challenging organisation. We further this discussion by connecting personal experiences with the role of craft in a global political context and address the relationship between craft and academia.

We begin the chapter by setting the scene and situating craft and craftivism in recent discussions of everyday creativity and craft as a force for social connection and challenge to mass-production-driven consumer culture. We continue by drawing on Ann's personal history and academic work as a way of unearthing a number of intellectual and conceptual concerns in the use of craft practices and arts-based methods for understanding organisations. We take a rather unusual approach by developing a biographical conversation to explore and reflect on the practices Ann employs in her academic work. Thus, our aim is to interweave personal history and conceptual arguments that extend the ways in which craft practices and resistance are conceived. We then provide some critical reflections on craftivism and its subversive potential. The chapter is shaped around a number of personal themes that engage different modes of craft-based resistance, namely: the relationships between the intellectual and the haptic; the sensory basis for textile work; resistance and utopian notions of craft; generosity and scarcity in producing craft objects such as the abundance of materials for use in textiles workshops; and the influence of De Certeau and Benjamin in the conceptual thinking behind some of the projects and pieces Ann has produced.

Situating Craft and Craftivism

Craft has long been considered part of identity-making projects involving socially connective activities. This consolidates the somewhat romantic notion that craft can bring people together (Dissanayake 1995; Dormer 1997) through communal, group-based activities. Dissanayake (1995: 41) explores the inherent pleasure in making, the *joie de faire*, in using 'one's own agency, dexterity, feelings, and judgment to mold, form, touch, hold, and craft physical materials', which insinuates a more vibrant, grass-roots pride grounded in everyday nature associated with craft.

Discussions of craft have inevitably led to defining its position in relation to art and other forms of creative expression. As Gauntlett (2011: 22–3) cogently summarises:

> The term 'craft' is further complicated by its relationship with 'art'. Somehow the two concepts have become separated, so that 'art' tends to mean the truly creative transformation of ideas and emotions into visual objects (or texts, or performances, music, or whatever), whilst 'craft' – having been shoved out of that space – ends up indicating the less prestigious production of carvings or pots, by less creative people who just like making carvings or pots.

The political terrain in which the divisions between art and craft have long been contested and have led to the separation between 'having ideas' and 'making objects' (Dormer 1997). The split between art and craft has also led to the marginalisation of women's work (Parker 1996) as women have been traditionally associated with craft work, and men with art. Craft continues be positioned and constructed in different ways depending on whether one focuses on artisanal, factory-based craft, recreational crafters, or craftspeople whose work is more akin to fine art. An instructive case example is the work of Grayson Perry. We can see his work through the lens of Bourdieu (1980): Perry makes work in ceramics and textiles, both associated with women and with craft, but it is coded as art by an elite, culminating in a Turner Prize in 2003.

For writers such as Gauntlett (2011), making and sharing are already political acts which, whilst small, cumulatively challenge larger social institutions such as popular media or giant supermarkets. In contrast, craftivism is considered part of the gentle revolution away from mass-production-driven consumer culture towards a conscious effort to make and overtly resist the strictures of capitalism, not least the appropriation of public spaces by large companies through their advertising and occupation of urban properties. Craftivism gently but firmly critiques the homogenisation of the high street.

However, craft-based activism is not a new idea, something Greer (2008) acknowledges. The idea that the decorative can become subversive is well-worn. In *The Subversive Stitch*, Rozsika Parker (1996) explores how the art of embroidery has been used both to educate women into the ideals of femininity but also as acts of resistance to the constraints of femininity. Homecraft as well as financial recession both led in different ways to the rise of embroidery as a skill and decorative practice. Parker writes that the context for embroidery practice has changed since the backlash against feminism following its Second Wave. Rejecting women's traditional crafts became a moment of feminist resistance that led to an ambivalence of embroidery as a source of creative satisfaction but also an emblem or instrument for oppression. Feminism is part of both authors' academic practice and this ambivalence has long since fascinated us. The discussion of the subversive potential and political construction of craft culture serves to situate recent theoretical debates around the development of craft activities in contemporary Western society and how craft has been historically associated with resistance. The chapter now turns to Ann's work as a way of reflecting and drawing out themes of craft-based resistance.

SV: '*Let's start with your history and discuss how you got into using textiles as a way of understanding organisations.*'

AR: 'I think I have to start at my university days. I went to a brilliant set of schools, but it was at university that I was confronted with the growing nostrum that knowledge is always incomplete and temporary. At school it was still pretty much about getting to the right answer. It was at university that this was questioned and problematised. Someone unfortunately now forgotten by me said, 'Always admit the possibility that you might not have the monopoly on truth'. I don't think I was constitutionally ready to hear this, but it certainly made a huge impact on me. Much of my degree was in French, just before it became saturated in Post-structuralism but at the right time for Existentialism to have permeated everything, and *le nouveau roman* to become influential. I was interested in the new novel with its repetitions of scenes and truths as seen and experienced by different characters. There is no one single truth, everything is open to interpretation and reinterpretation.

This might seem a long way from textiles, but it isn't. They are wonderful for showing two sides of something (such as a cushion with a front and back showing different aspects of a social phenomenon, which several students have produced over the years) or a piece which shows its workings – that it is something constructed and not a single finished item descended from some epistemological heaven. And it can be bold. One of the earliest pieces I made was my Nike Doll. I was teaching the Nike case to Business Strategy students, and, funnily enough, at twenty years old they wanted to talk about globalisation and its impacts. The case, though, did not admit this. It was about the marketing genius and business strategy of Phil Knight. The students wanted to talk about child labour and the impact of global branding, but there was no room for this in the seminars. I was frustrated by this and went home and made a doll. This was how a lot of my early textile work started. I was upset or angry and went home and put all this pent-up emotion into cloth. I made a very traditional doll called a topsy turvy or upside-down doll which has a different doll at each end separated and united by a skirt which obscures one while revealing the other. An example would be Red Riding Hood at one end and the Wolf at the other. Mine had the all-American girl with blonde plaits and a shiny polyester stars and stripes frock at one end and a rag doll representing the factory worker in Indonesia making the shoes. The further away you position yourself from the site of production, the easier it is to salve your conscience about working conditions.

However, this epistemological approach raises tensions of craft-based methodologies and their ambivalent relationship to academic work. The role of curiosity, intuition, imagination, tentativeness and creativity become diametrically opposed to the desire for certainty the Academy rewards, especially in positivist approaches. The irony is that the positivist approach and the craft or studio-based practice approach start from the same place: curiosity and intuition. The positivist starts from a hypothesis based on an intuition, applying a selection of tests to prove or disprove it. The art-practice researcher begins in a similar place: curiosity about a phenomenon. The difference is in the choice of research instrument – the self, with little concern given to validity and replicability, and the disposition, mentioned above that there can be no final definitive account of a social phenomenon.

It should also be noted that art-practice researchers have a different way of listening to their data and engaging in embodied inquiry. Positivists sometime describe their coding procedures as listening to data, but generally they mean paying very close attention to patterns which emerge in, say, interview transcripts. There is seldom an admission that these are produced from the *habitus* of the researcher, the mental universe of class, education, ethnicity, political affiliation, nationality and so on. Art practitioners, on the other hand, are explicit that they listen to their work, waiting for it to talk to them, possibly months or years later through the comments of others viewing the final product. Studio practitioners like Barrett and Bolt (2010) make this an explicit part of their process, describing an 'exegesis' as they seek what their paintings have to tell them (Barrett & Bolt 2010). This notion that matter, in the form of paint, fabric, clay, steel or similar, can have a voice and that matter can be vibrant is now gaining respectability though the work of new materialists such as Jane Bennett (2010) and has been explored through perspectives such as actor network theory in management and organisation studies (Law & Hassard 1999).

Virtually all makers report the phenomenon of entering into a dialogue with the art piece, many reporting that the piece tells the maker when it is finished, something that comes up at almost every workshop I have attended. At one level, we instinctively understand this approach, so that we understand Sophie Strong, an embroiderer when she writes:

> To allow the stitches to speak, [I] work with plain, hardwearing fabrics in muted tones, applying colour with thread.
>
> (Perry 2014: 83)

Again, the conversation is informed by the maker's *habitus*. The difference is that this is made explicit, and in some cases celebrated. The maker's point of view, or personal style is often highly valued.

The debate about whether art is useful or useless (as Oscar Wilde would have us believe: 'All art is quite useless' – in the Preface to *The Picture of Dorian Gray*), is as fraught as the debate about the difference between art and craft, as described above. Art has a fine tradition of the political, from satire to political cartoons. In contemporary art in the UK, as we have seen, Grayson Perry has crossed the divide between the high art world, winning his Turner Prize in 2003, and Banksy has refreshed the visual lampoon with his spray cans. Although Perry now has a studio with assistants, both he and Banksy are largely heroic, individual actors. Their form of resistance is effectively authored'. Having explored the divides and tensions in using craft-based methodologies, we turn now to a less individualised, more collective form of resistance through craft.

Reflections on Craftivism

SV: 'We have spent time thus far discussing craft-based methodologies. Let's turn to less individualised forms of resistance. What are your thoughts on craftivism as a way of bringing ostensibly overt and group-based forms of resistance and craft together?'

AR: 'I once scored a tremendous hit at a conference where I described myself as a scholar activist. This was extremely popular with other academics. I think they liked the idea of being revolutionaries in the spirt of '66 hurling paving stones metaphorical or otherwise. My activism, however, is of a rather quieter kind. Johnella Bird describes looking for 'talk that sings' when she interviews people, by which she means the words that really resonate in telling a story and bring it to life (Bird 2004). This is what I am looking for in my work: imagery that sings, that draws people in and makes them want to engage with the thoughts behind the piece. I do not want to shock or confront people, but I do want them to hear the mermaid's song and be drawn in. Beauty as much as horror can change the world, and new materialist thinking, such as Bennett (2010), that focuses our attention on the agency of materials and objects, is a good place to start to think about craftivism.

I was brought up in primary school as a very small child with myths from the Greeks and Romans. I read them in the versions written by Rosemary Sutcliffe, Roger Lancelyn Green and Geoffrey Treece. One of the entrancing things about the stories was the illustrated versions from the artists Janet and Anne Grahame Johnstone which had warriors of Modigliani-like proportions and gracefully arching feathers in their sparkling helmets. Later on, I moved onto the faintly ridiculously scholarly versions by Robert Graves as the anthropologists really got their teeth into what these myths were all about. I received an early lesson in aesthetics which has stayed with me, as well as a fundamental human truth, Amazons aside, that men go out and do the heroic things and women stay at home making sure the hero has a home to return to. In fact, in biology lessons it was pointed out to the all-girls class that the medical symbol for men was a circle with an arrow pointing to the heavens while the one for female was a circle on a cross, the woman sitting waiting for his return. It was the early days of the Second Wave of feminism so at least the teacher had the grace to apologise and roll her eyes.

The point I want to make here is that for most of the planet now, and for most of history, men have been dominant and women have been suppressed. Being suppressed is a tricky position. You have little or no power, a contrast to the arguments made by post-feminists around the control and agency of women in modern society (cf. Gill & Scharff 2011). I cannot think of a better way of putting it than if you are oppressed or suppressed, you have to learn to hint.

Craftivists rely on a sense of niceness. They do not bomb or set fire to things. They even soften the notion of bombing by prefixing it with soft yarn. Yarn, again, has always been associated with women and with women organizing in the domestic sphere. You cannot produce woven cloth without a group effort in a settled location. You need to grow linen or farm sheep and you need a range of skills from treating the raw fibre to spinning it, weaving it, cutting it and stitching it. Communities, to return to the theme of social connectedness, are necessary to produce textiles. Textiles form a buffer against the hardship of life. Elaine Scarry (1985) suggests that creativity is a response to and alleviation of suffering, and textiles are a good example of this. They protect the wearer throughout life. Craftivists play with this notion. They soften and buffer the urban world, which can be cruel and dehumanising. Thus, they make small-scale interventions such as knitting a cuff for a tree or embroidering tiny banners to hang on metal fences or wrapping up defunct petrol stations with quilts to protest against urban degeneration. These threaten no one. They are not permanent like graffiti. Eventually they will degrade back into the earth. They wait patiently to catch the eye; they hint. Their form of resistance is gentle, sometimes tacit. This is a long-established tradition, as can be seen from those Greek myths which are full of fibres, threads and textiles. Agamemnon and Achilles were farmers when they weren't being warriors and their wealth came from agriculture, part of which was spinning and weaving the production of an exchangeable item. Their tunics and cloaks were made of wool, not cotton. Textile production was vital to the ancient economy.

In this context, we can think about Penelope, wife of Odysseus, sitting at home waiting for his return from the Trojan War. Penelope had twenty years of waiting for her husband to return. During this time, she is repeatedly pestered by men wanting to marry her. The patriarchy in action, if you will: a woman cannot live unclaimed by a man. Penelope tells them that she will choose a new husband when she has finished either weaving or embroidering depending on the source, a shroud for her father-in-law, Laertes. For three years she weaves in the day and then at night undoes the work. To a practising textile artist, this is clearly nonsense. The constant undoing and redoing would produce a rather tatty piece of work, dirty and with fraying support threads, but there is no mention of this. What matters is that Penelope is skilled with textiles, which makes her economically useful in this agrarian society. She also remains sexually chaste and thus above reproach as the mother of legitimate children. I mention her because she is powerlessness and yet she survives on her wits and through the work of her hands. What she produces seduces men into respecting her and allowing her to live her own life. I expect that there has been speculation about what she was weaving or embroidering into her work. Penelope survived, it seems to me, because she could seduce by her economic utility.

Moving forward to Victorian times, little girls were taught to sew to improve their economic prospects. Poor girls could become seamstresses, or go into service, which at some point would have included marking linen for the laundry and hence the rise of the sampler, an educational device which has been rendered into a decorator icon. Rich Victorian girls were taught to produce fine needlework as part of their list of accomplishments to get a good husband. Needlework was plain or ornate, and instruction manuals reflected this well into the twentieth century. Once again, like Penelope, after whom a brand of tapestry wool used to be named, women showed their worth with their textile skills. There was very little sign of resistance. There is one nineteenth-century American sampler with an unusual sentiment. Generally, sampler quotations are about early death or reflect the maker's piety. The one I am thinking about, however, said something like: 'Mary Smith made this and hated every stitch she did'. Generally, the samplers showed Christian virtue, women's sinfulness through the strangely frequent Adam and Eve and the Tree of Knowledge motif, and expertise with the needle. Once again, for the stitcher, seduction was achieved through textile skill.

Craftivism takes on this tradition. A great deal has changed for women in the two hundred years since Seneca Falls and The Pankhursts, but genuine and full emancipation has yet to be achieved. Craftivists have noticed this. In my understanding, most craftivists are women. They do not identify themselves as artists, who have produced subversive works for centuries. They identify as 'crafters'. There is a distinction here between 'crafters', 'craftivists' and 'craftspeople'. Crafters practise a variety of handicrafts, for example: knitting, embroidery, macramé, patchwork and quilting, paper crafts and weaving. Cardmaking, in particular, has undergone an explosion of interest in the last ten years. Cards are generally made for special occasions such as birthdays, weddings, engagements, new babies and new homes. They are very elaborate and often three-dimensional but almost always made from pre-formed elements which are largely just assembled by the crafter. The other crafts are also about home- and family-making.

They promote social coherence and community- making and are often associated with traditional milestones in women's lives. Quilts are made to mark births and marriages and deaths. Making a quilt from a dead partner's shirts remains a socially sanctioned way of mourning the death of a spouse in the quilting world. Quilts are also made for significant birthdays and children leaving for university. Increasingly quilts are made to mark retirement from paid employment, and there is a significant rise in the number of quilts made to celebrate divorce. Craftivists on the other hand, tend to engage more with the outside world. As mentioned above, they represent an attempt to reclaim the high street by placing hand-made, one-off items in public, often urban areas to protest different causes, such as the environmental impact of global brands or the corporate colonisation of public space.

Craftivists are usually committed to recycling or upcycling materials. Their banners are likely to be made from salvaged curtains, for example (see Greer, 2008, for particular examples). To buy special materials would be seen as contributing to the mounds of overproduced materials going into landfill and thus to the problem of global consumption which they challenge. 'Crafters', on the other hand, have recourse to a whole selection of commercial resources frequently looked down on by craftspersons. They have almost 24-hour television channels dedicated to selling them the materials to practise their crafts, along with big box stores in retail parks and sprawling enterprises on the internet. These are all sold as promoting women's creativity. However, what is produced is a different combination of the pre-formed elements on offer. The 'sentiments', as they are called, are prepared for crafters to stick onto the handmade card, cupcake or cushion.

Craftivists aim to subvert this. What matters is the message. Recycling is positively encouraged rather than buying new and pristine 'supplies'. Group endeavours rather than the meek, single woman sewing with her neck bent and head down in silent contemplation, are a central feature of craftivism. Craftivists aim to critique the 'man-made', and I use that term deliberately. This can include the perfect body form demanded by the fashion and beauty industry, the effects of globalisation on the high street, the pressure for land which forces out local people in favour of expensive housing for incomers, and all other effects of capitalism, globalisation, the industrial-military complex and any other effects of the masculine hegemony we have omitted. The method is to use craft, particularly knitting, in yarn-bombing activities, but also sewing, particularly patchwork and quilting, so closely associated with the domestic, the comforting and the protective. Hence craftivists will produce small tie-on samplers protesting about an issue while simultaneously quoting the implicit oppression in the sampler form. They will cover a redundant petrol station in patchwork to draw attention to the environmental degradation of the petrol economy. They will knit and crochet tubes to attach to trees or benches in public areas as an act of reclamation of public space.'

SV: '*These practices of gentle resistance can have unintended consequences, or not quite achieve their aims. Do you have any reservations with craftivist approaches to resistance?*'

AR: 'I am broadly in favour of these subversive acts. I know that I would thoroughly enjoy the adrenaline rush of wrapping a tree in the dead of night, trying to avoid the surveillance cameras that capture so much of our life. I have certain reservations, or indeed questions:

> Firstly, is this another form of oppression? If we see objects having agency in the landscape of craftivist practice, we need also to consider that no tree ever asked to be wrapped in knitting, no derelict petrol station asked to be further humiliated by being wrapped in a patchwork cosy.
>
> Secondly, we have discussed the use of materials and recycling in craft-based resistance and a purist might consider the use of unnatural acrylic fibres antithetical to the core purpose of craftivism, such as yarn bombing (Moore & Prain, 2009). I can see that this juxtaposes the natural and the unnatural. I understand that craftivism and thrift go together, and that acrylic yarn is cheap and plentiful and virtually indestructible, therefore making a strong statement about biopolitics and environmentalism. This is a taste judgement of course, but the use of unnatural, acrylic fibres forgets the rich history of yarn and wool that is part of the culture of knitting and crocheting.
>
> Finally, I am aware of the tensions that it might reinforce the links with women and powerlessness, domesticity, stealth and hinting. It is a matter of perspective as to whether it brings about social change of any persistence, is largely seen as a spectacle or that it does much to raise the consciousness of young women. Craftivism is associated with women organising, often feminist organising that is facilitative or galvanises feminist community and communality. This may well involve discussion of feminism as participants work together, for example. It also draws on prescribed feminine values. In a recent *New York Times* article by Wollan (2011), Jessie Hemmons, at the time a 24-year-old artist, emphasises the femininity of yarn bombing, stating, "Street art and graffiti are usually so male-dominated …Yarn bombing is more feminine. It's like graffiti with grandma sweaters".'

SV: '*We have explored different moments in women's organising thus far. Drawing on feminist and feminine values seems to feed into your work as an embodied inquirer. Do you recognise some of the themes in, for example craftivism, in your own textile work?*'

AR: 'Having said all this, I can move on to consider my own work in these terms. First, I can clearly state that I do not think that it has any impact at all. I do it largely for myself. I hope that what I sew occasionally causes someone to see the world differently for a moment, but I don't think it compares with, say, Guernica or Goya's Disasters of War. I do it because I have to. I do it because it is my voice. And I do it for pleasure. This last point is possibly the most subversive of all. One of the most damaging things about the commodification and monetisation of academic work and higher education more broadly is that it has ceased to acknowledge the pleasures of scholarship. My work insists on this and refuses to let it be expunged from what is valuable. My pleasure in my work is entirely sensory. I love the feel of the various fabrics I use: linen, cotton, silk, wool. I love the sound of the needle going through a piece of cloth as I stitch it. I love the crunchiness of layers of embroidering stitches encrusting a surface. I love the sparkle of beads and sequins. I love the way one stitch can affect the success or failure of the whole piece in terms of balance, rhythm and repetition. I love the smell of paint and of pure cotton. I love to feel really sharp scissors slice through cloth. This is an example of what Audre Lorde called 'the erotic' (Lorde 2007). It is a form of the life force which courses through our bodies, and that is the key point here. This is an embodied response to the world and learning about it. And it is one of pleasure. Hence Lorde says that there is no difference to her between painting a fence, moving against her lover's body or writing a poem except the degree of the erotic. This is now almost entirely absent from academic work. To admit to seeing beauty in something and responding to it bodily would be considered quite suspect. To write about the (admittedly rare) joy in seeing a company that is run on love working beautifully would be to open oneself to accusations of a loss of objectivity and critical thinking. And yet there is always something of Lorde's erotic in academic work. Seeing a pattern in data, suddenly understanding something previously mystifying, finding a missing element in an argument, discovering something or constructing the text when writing up a piece of research can surprise us with joy, joy which is felt in the body.'

SV: '*You can feel this sense of the erotic in your work and the pleasure that is derived from it. What kinds of techniques does this involve?*'
'My work is quite deliberately excessive. I have always worked in layers. I will stitch an area on a piece of work and then put fabric over it and stitch again. I like the idea of secrets in the work. Only I know they are there. It is a covert relationship with the work even when it is out of my hands and out in the world. The notion of layers and gaps and holes brings me to De Certeau in his essay on Jules Verne and the impossibility of ever really saying anything with any great certainty. De Certeau talks about knowledge as being an amassing of holey layers, fissures and lacunae. As De Certeau points out, this all looks solid from a distance.

Figure 11.1 'Detail of a Quilt about The Body Shop and Identity' by Ann Rippin
Source: © Ann Rippin, reproduced with thanks

Our research looks valid and verified and testable, but actually, it is a pile of gappy accounts which we hope will convince a reader. My textiles make a virtue of this.

This is detail of a quilt I made about the Body Shop and identity. I was heavily influenced by Anita Roddick when I was growing up in Nottingham, and the piece which was ostensibly about Roddick, turned into an exploration of my association with the Body Shop brand and how it shaped my identity. Anita Roddick was an activist and entrepreneur. I am a disappointed romantic who regrets the fact that the world could be a much better place but never actually does anything about it. In the above panel, I was thinking about the Body Shop and geographic locations. I encountered and fell in love with the brand in Nottingham. I did a long research project and met Roddick in Littlehampton. I began a long period of reflection and research on the company in Bristol. The Nottingham piece has three almost standing- stone pieces of Nottingham lace, stitched and dyed, over another piece, over a piece of crimson silk. Identity has to be constructed. It appears as a monolith but it's an illusion. What we have are layers, and the layers are incomplete, like lace. The bits that are missing, the negative form is what makes lace lace. Good handmade lace is one thread according to the Bristol lacemakers. If you undo the knot and pull the end the whole thing unravels. Which is an interesting metaphor in itself (we are reminded of the ball of thread in the myth of Ariadne and Theseus). But the lace here is tough, machine-made lace in artificial fibres. What looks like a fairly dense, solid panel is anything but. It is machine-made and handmade. It is delicate, and it is tough. It is expensive, and it is cheap. It is made of lace, the fabric of the virginal and the vampish. The whole piece is ambiguous and capable of any number of readings, like identity, like Roddick, like a brand.'

Thoughts on juxtaposition

SV: 'I remember coming to one of your talks which was to a women's group of embroiderers and knitters in Ystradowen in South Wales. In the talk you explored the Laura Ashley project and the idea of juxtaposing techniques of embroidery, embellishment and the insertion of images to invite different interpretations. Could you elaborate on this practice and how what you produce for pleasure differs from your academic textile pieces?'

AR: 'One of the elements that distinguishes my academic quilts from my pieces made purely for my own pleasure, is a desire to get people to look again and to look more closely, and to make up their own minds. Heather Höpfl and Steve Linstead wrote about the baroque quality of organisational life, the way that we are bombarded with material objects to keep us docile and compliant through sheer deluge (Linstead & Hopfl, 2000). Corporate branding and authorised imagery are good and ever-growing examples of this. Advertising and the internet add to this baroque piling on of detail to stun us into awed silence and to overpower any impulse to resistance that we might have. Höpfl and Linstead advocated resensitising ourselves to this subliminal invasion by looking again. Benjamin, in his last great, unfinished 'Arcades' project, added an overtly pedagogic element to this, and John Berger took it up and illustrated it particularly clearly in *Ways of Seeing*. Benjamin was interested in the dazzle of merchandising, particularly in luxurious shops, and through plate-glass windows filled with lovely shiny things that we feel we absolutely must have. He decided that to make his point about the seductiveness of capitalism he would let his readers work things out for themselves in a kind of early action learning, through juxtaposing images and letting people make up their own minds. By placing two elements together people are invited to compare and contrast and thus draw conclusions without being preached at. Berger does this brilliantly with a nineteenth-century reportage picture of a child in abject poverty on one page juxtaposed with a painting of a poor child from the 'big-eyed' school of art. The sentimentalisation of the painting shows us how we allow ourselves to absent responsibility for the urban poor. It holds a mirror up to human behaviour where we may

Figure 11.2 'Image from Textile Project on Starbucks' by Ann Rippin
Source: © Ann Rippin, reproduced with thanks

put the painting on our walls, but we wouldn't let the actual child over the threshold.

This juxtaposition takes us to my textile project on Starbucks. In the piece above, I juxtaposed all sorts of images: luxurious cups of coffee with women picking the beans on subsistence wages; the individuality of local cafés compared with the corporate uniformity of Starbucks; the romance of Italy with the reality of boxy shops in rainy Bristol and so on. I don't make any direct judgements in the piece itself. I just put the pictures together and let people make their own minds up.'

SV: '*How else do you think your work addresses issues of resistance?*'
AR: On two main levels, I think. If I think about management practice, and what I used to teach, and train in before that, I think it challenges the lean, efficiency, target- setting agenda. Doing more with less is a mantra that seems to be the epitome of the management message, not least in universities. Business Process Reengineering, Total Quality Management and Lean thinking were all about eliminating waste and stripping out the surplus. My own work is excessive, as I have already described, but I found that in workshops people respond ridiculously positively to having lots of

materials, being able to take what they want without asking and to waste and make mistakes.

Writers on creativity do talk about this in rather abstract forms. Eliminate the fear culture. Allow people to make mistakes and so on, but I have discovered that providing people with a lot of material in my workshops enables them to establish rapport with me and to go into a space they rarely experience. From a psychodynamic perspective, this makes me the all-providing mother, the nurturer they never had, or did have and now miss, and that might well be true, but at another more mundane level, I think they respond well to being given a gift. You have to do things, if you want people to be creative, which says to them: "You matter. I have brought this material to you and for you. I want you to have everything you could possibly need and you can take it all and use it in any way you like to make you feel good". Adults in my workshops appreciate this generosity, and it feels countercultural. I can provide a number of examples, but at the end of the workshop someone always says, 'I can't believe you brought us all this stuff'. In conventional gift theory, they reciprocate by doing the task, but I also think that they respond to generosity at a really fundamental level.

Allied to this, I get asked quite often where I get my ideas from and if I know how something is going to turn out before I make it. I don't always know where ideas come from. They come from my *habitus*, and what Barthes would call my image repertoire, so they come from me, my life and my experience. I never know how a piece will turn out before I make it. If I did, I wouldn't need to make it. I let it evolve and let it tell me what it wants to be. Again, this is antithetical to traditional academic work. Applying for grant funding you are expected to know your outcomes, have a research plan and well thought-out research design. The idea of listening to the materials, channelling their needs and ambitions is not appealing to funding bodies. You have to be brave and self-sufficient to do this sort of work.

The other level is more philosophical and concerns the importance of the made. There is much media coverage about making, from the wild success of the *Great British Bake Off* to Japanese designated National Treasures making sword blades, to a crop of painting shows, to *Robot Wars*. We seem to be surprised by our own delight in our ability to make things ourselves. What I am interested in here, and we both are, is the way in which you cannot make something without leaving a trace of yourself on it or in it. One of the more bizarre episodes of my professional life was being invited to have a look at an advanced level Japanese embroidery workshop in the Cotswolds. I was expressly not allowed to breathe on the work in progress. The embroiderer would fold back a piece of covering cloth and I could have a look at what was revealed as I held my breath. What was at stake was my polluting the maker's bodily connection with the work. As an embroiderer myself, I know that my body is transferred into my work at a mundane level. Mary Douglas's dirt that is matter out of place (Douglas 1966): skin oil, saliva from threading needles, fibres of various sorts and tiny flakes of skin work their way into the textile. Plus, no stitcher will ever make and place stitches in exactly the same way, just as experts can tell reproductions from the original by looking at an artist's brush strokes. All this matters because it insists on the personal and the embodied, what we are often exhorted not to include in our published work. Insisting on the embodied and personal is a defiant act of resistance to the disciplinary regimes that are unable to accommodate craft-based methodologies. I am an embodied inquirer, and, I suppose, I matter.'

Concluding Thoughts

Talking through the themes of this chapter and writing it together has enabled us to reflect on the histories and processes at the intersections between craft, textiles and academic practice. We have developed this discussion to consider ways in which resistance and craft meet, such as craftivism, and have drawn on Ann's extensive experience as a practitioner and academic and the tensions between craft and academic work. It is hard not to be struck by the textures achieved in her work through layering and juxtaposing different materials and techniques. This serves to highlight the opportunities that arise from using craft-based methods to convey complex organisational issues and histories, such as the Laura Ashley and Starbucks projects explored in our dialogue (see Taylor & Ladkin, 2009, for a discussion of arts-based methods and managerial development). Moreover, using craft as academic practice brings to the fore epistemological questions regarding legitimate knowledge and embodiment as a means of resisting and challenging organisations, what we have termed becoming an embodied inquirer.

Even with a critical mass of organisation scholars writing with their bodies and advancing the understanding of embodiment both theoretically and empirically, it is still rebellious to think beyond the text for the majority of management and organisation studies. Layers of stitching, embroidering secrets into the work or how the negative form of lace forms a voice in the text become ways of foregrounding the haptic and sensual elements of craft and provide an invitation to further consider how the body relates to organisations and research methodologies. Decades of writing that demonstrate the dark sides of organisation and how disembodied employees have become in their work and whether they matter at all is testament to the idea that neglecting the body and the imagination, both vital in craft and making, is leading to dystopia which we can still avoid.

As scholar activists we have a role to play in insisting on the danger of this imbalance and denial of embodied resistance. The contradictory dynamics of academic publishing, which may promote innovative methodological practices but succumb to the weight of standardisation, are unable to adequately accommodate craft-based methodologies. Using craft and making practices to represent, transform or unearth different dimensions of organisations insists on self-reliance and support as well as resilience and self-motivation. *Showing* through making rather than *telling* through the generation of text or numbers might be our bravest act of resistance.

Note

1 See www.accessart.org.uk/i-am-accessart-ann-rippin/

References

Agosin, M. (2014) *Stitching resistance: women, creativity, and fiber arts.* Tunbridge Wells: Solis Press.

Barrett, E. & Bolt, B. (2007) *Practice as research: approaches to creative arts inquiry.* London: Tauris.

Bennett, J. (2010) *Vibrant matter: a political ecology of things.* Durham, NC: Duke University Press.

Bird, J. (2004) *Talk that sings: therapy in a new linguistic key.* Auckland: Edge Press.

Bourdieu, P. (1980) *The logic of practice.* trans. Richard Nice. Stanford: Stanford University Press.

Dissanayake, E. (1995) The pleasure and meaning of making. *American Craft,* 55(2): 40–45.

Dormer, P., ed. (1997) *The culture of craft.* Manchester: Manchester University Press.

Douglas, M. (1966) *Purity and danger: an analysis of concepts of pollution and taboo.* London: Routledge.

Gauntlett, D. (2011) *Making is connecting: the social meaning of creativity, from DIY and knitting to YouTube and Web 2.0.* Cambridge: Polity.

Gill, R. & Scharff, C. (eds) (2011) *New femininities: postfeminism, neoliberalism and subjectivity.* Basingstoke: Palgrave Macmillan.

Greer, B. (2008) *Knitting for good! A guide to creating personal, social, and political change, stitch by stitch.* Boston, MA: Shambhala Publications.

Law, J. & Hassard, J. (eds) (1999) *Actor network theory and after.* Oxford: Blackwell Publishing.

Linstead, S. & Hopfl, H. (eds) (2000) *The aesthetics of organization.* London: Sage.

Lorde, A. (2007) *Sister outsider.* Berkeley: Crossing Press

Moore, M. & Prain, L. (2009) *Yarn bombing: the art of crochet and knit graffiti.* Vancouver: Arsenal Pulp Press.

Parker, R. (1996) *The subversive stitch: embroidery and the making of the feminine.* London: The Women's Press.

Perry, J. (2014) *The sewists.* London: Lawrence King.

Rippin, A. (2007) Stitching up the leader: empirically based reflections on leadership and gender. *Journal of Organizational Change Management,* 20(2): 209–226.

Scarry, E. (1985) *The body in pain: the making and unmaking of the world.* Oxford: Oxford University Press.

Taylor, S. & Ladkin, D. (2009) Understanding arts-based methods in managerial development. *Academy of Management Learning & Education*, 8(1): 55–69.

Vachhani, S.J. (2013) (Re)creating objects from the past – affect, tactility and everyday creativity. *Management & Organizational History*, 8(1): 91–104.

Wollan, M. (2011) Graffiti's cozy, feminine side', New York Times, 18th May 2011. Available at: www.nytimes.com/2011/05/19/fashion/creating-graffiti-with-yarn.html?hpw. Last accessed 1/2/18.

12 Being Maker-Centric

Making as Method for Self-Organizing and Achieving Craft Impact in Local Communities and Economies[1]

Fiona Hackney, Deirdre Figueiredo, Laura Onions, Gavin Rogers and Jana Milovanović

Craft, Community and Economy

Urban planner Susan Silberberg (2012: 19), writing about making as a means to collectively imagine public space, observed that

> in making, we learn, mentor, design, question, act. Making involves a community of individuals, spaces, organisations and institutions over a length of time; it requires a higher level of human contact, a higher level of intent, community awareness and connectedness.

The result, in her view (*ibid.*), is a 'deeply inclusive approach' and a 'community that is nurtured, that builds social and political capital, through a process that engenders trust'. This chapter explores making, and its associated values, through the lens of Maker-Centric, an Arts & Humanities Research Council-funded project that works with stakeholders and community groups to explore how arts and crafts, hand-making and digital fabrication methods might build community, social and cultural change, and, longer term, economic assets and agencies. The project was funded through the Connected Communities programme, designed to respond to non-academic user and stakeholder needs, extending findings from existing research to new audiences and building capacity through public engagement and knowledge exchange (https://connected-communities.org/). Understanding craft affordances within a broadly conceived notion of craft in an 'expanded field' (Shales 2017), valuing anonymous and amateur crafting, and making as a mode of engagement are central concerns.

Maker-Centric builds on learning from the project Co-Producing CARE: Community Asset-based Research & Enterprise (CARE) (https://cocreatingcare.wordpress.com/the-project/), which was led by Professor Fiona Hackney and Deirdre Figueiredo, Director of Craftspace in Birmingham. While CARE examined how collaborative community crafting might serve as a means to resolve differences, raise consciousness, and build affective relationships, Maker-Centric applies this work with stakeholders, community groups, small businesses, and creative organisations in a specific region, the English Midlands and the Black Country. The geographical focus responds to Craftspace's location and its remit to employ craft to strengthen and revitalise communities (http://craftspace.co.uk/). New stakeholder Creative Black Country joined, building on their work with the '100 Masters' initiative, which showcases the range and quality of creative practice in the region (www.creativeblackcountry.co.uk/). The English Midlands is a highly diverse multicultural region; working with crafting groups and crafts-related entrepreneurs and small businesses recognises the skills, knowledge, expertise, competencies and capabilities embedded in these communities (Hackney 2013b). The region also has a long history of industrial innovation and radical thinking in arts, sciences and manufacture, manifest in the work in metal and enamels showcased at the Bilston Craft Gallery, ironwork at Ironbridge, Staffordshire ceramics, and textiles in Nottingham and Hereford, for instance. Engaging diverse communities with this rich heritage through creative making activities provides space to imaginatively inhabit, respond to, interpret, and develop contemporary perspectives on the past, as a catalyst for future-thinking about who we are, how we live, work, and relate to one another in prescribed place-based communities.

The conceptual framework underpinning Maker-Centric was prototyped at the Connected Communities Research Festival: Community Futures and Utopias (2016) (https://cocreatingcare.wordpress.com/maker-centric-2016/). Ruth Levitas's (2013) conceptualisation of utopia as method to imagine alternative ways of living through the Imaginary Reconstruction of Society (IRS) was central. We examined how co-creative making might provide a platform for community co-speculation as a form of 'living heritage', broadly defined as heritage driven by activities rather than simply the possession of assets. A group of participants, many of whom had contributed to CARE, met for a series of workshops at Soho House Museum in Handsworth, Birmingham. This building was the home of industrialist Matthew Boulton and site of his Soho Manufactory, which employed the latest 18th-century technology to produce decorative metalwork such as ormolu and silver plate. It also served as a meeting place for the Lunar Society: men, such as Erasmus Darwin, James Watt, and Josiah Wedgwood, who laid the groundwork for the industrial revolution. Soho House is an ideal place in which to conduct speculative future-thinking informed by the consequences of the industrial past.

The project team worked with storyteller Gauri Raje and artist Melanie Tomlinson, who manipulates sheet metal – draws into, prints on, cuts and shapes it as a central component of her work. The group used artefacts from Boulton's house: an ormolu mirror, a silver-plate sugar spoon, and an engraving depicting a balloon flight, as inspiration for telling their own utopian and dystopian stories of remembered pasts and imagined futures of making and craft. Emerging themes of migration, health, and ecology, among others, formed the basis of a process of collaborative making that translated into work with Fab Lab West Bromwich and a collectively crafted Praxinoscope (Figure 12.1). Based on an early form of moving-image technology, this object serves as a catalyst to provoke conversations about craft, migration, health, ecology, heritage, agency, place and community futures.

Figure 12.1 Utopia/Dystopia Praxinoscope

We also brought together participants from three projects under the Utopia as Method rubric (Making Centric, Life Chances, and Prototyping Utopias), which foregrounded differences and commonalities in projects that, as Katerina Alexiou observed, approached the subject of utopia from different disciplinary perspectives: heritage and making, design and dreaming, social science and creative disruption. All involved a re-examination of the past, paid attention to place and the specificity of local context, and focused methodologically on processes of making and acting as a means to engage people from diverse communities in utopian thinking (Figueiredo 2018). The past (heritage), along with place and creative process (craft and making), shaped the Maker-Centric focus on taking a material place-based approach to prototyping a method and toolkit for community agency and future-thinking. This is based on the premise that 'making in place', with all the historical, geographical, cultural, political and economic specificities that it entails, and critically re-imagining place through creative 'place-making', are vital to engaging and connecting communities to develop and build on existing assets, abilities, and agencies.

Partnership working is at the heart of this work. It is essential to embedding research in communities, gaining trust, minimising risk, and building legacy. Internationally, Maker-Centric also involves knowledge exchange with the Terra Vera Association, in Kostanjevica na Krki, Slovenia, a grassroot initiative dedicated to creating opportunities for interpersonal solidarity, anthropological research, environmental care and ethical economy. Working with refugees, Terra Vera supports community resilience and sustainable development through praxis, especially a network supporting women handcrafters as local entrepreneurs. The organisation's remit to work with low-income communities, encourage intergenerational dialogue, provide new opportunities for vulnerable social groups, and promote creative re-use of material and clothes, parallels our research with place-making, making exchanges and maker spaces. We report on all of this work here, in a way that is consistent with our collaborative ethos: this chapter has been written by a number of those involved in Maker-Centric and represents a range of voices and perspectives on the aims, experiences, and outcomes that shaped and were shaped by the project. Hackney has written the framing and contextual sections, Figueiredo details research activities conducted in Birmingham from a Craftspace perspective, and project artists Laura Onions and Gavin Rogers discuss working with groups Petals of Hope and Gatis Community Space in the Black Country reflecting on how the experience of community engagement might inform arts courses in Higher Education. Finally, Jana Milovanović from Terra Vera describes some of this organisation's activities, setting the scene for future collaborations to disseminate and develop a collaborative Maker-Centric method. In that sense, the chapter shows how the approach we've developed can also be applied to academic work as collaborative process.

Craft and the Creative Industries: A 'Bottom-up' Approach through Co-produced Community Engagement

Susan Luckman (2012: 9–10; see also this volume) cited Katherine Gibson's call for a return to 'the grass-roots work of engaging the community and being open to developing new economies'. In this she advocated that creative industries reconnect with cultural workers in rural, regional, and remote locations. Such a shift, she argues, offers a way to see 'vernacular creativity, local strengths, and community wishes' and the affective relationship with, and affordances of, place or 'edge-places of creativity', as she terms them. While Luckman's focus is non-urban localities, her thesis about paying attention to overlooked creative places, craft heritage and activities that involve the 'affective messiness of trying to live well' (Luckman 2012: 1–2) is equally applicable to the amateur craft groups, community organisations, and independent businesspeople that Maker-Centric works with in deprived inner city areas with a rich cultural heritage of decorative arts and crafts in an industrial context (Adamson 2013).

Critical engagement with 'living heritage' as a means of place-making – heritage driven by activities rather than simply the possession of assets – is a central discursive thread of our Maker-Centric work. A walking tour of the Black Country enamel trail run by craftsperson John Grayson, for example, used the visual and material language of the decorative arts to comment on contemporary news stories and, ending in the Bilston Craft Gallery, showcased his political satirical pieces alongside the 18th-century enamels that inspired them. The importance of this, living heritage in fostering identity, well-being, and revitalising civic agency, is underscored by the Royal Society of Arts (RSA) Heritage Index, a digital tool that maps the use of heritage in local areas, and is purposely inclusive and future-focused: foregrounding 'anything that is inherited from the past, which helps us interpret the present and plan for the future' (Schifferes 2015: 10).

Such conceptions of cultural work and workers are very different from the clusters of technologically savvy, networked professionals, and urban creatives who conventionally populate creative industries discourse (Florida 2003). Operating on smaller, more individual scales, these groups and individuals are freer to experiment and explore alternative modes of production. At a time when the structures of capitalism are under severe strain and alternative, countercultural values and ways of living move into the mainstream, a new breed of amateur makers unburdened by professional demarcations, but connected through social media, resourced and informed, might be in a position to challenge, reassess and re-imagine cultural work, how it operates, and its meanings or rewards (Hackney 2013a: 171–6; Hackney et al. 2016b). Such thinking shifts the focus away from considerations of how governments and other key local agencies can introduce 'top-down' strategies to develop local creative industries, and towards the 'bottom-up', co-produced initiatives which inform the creative ecology of the Maker Movement (Levine and Heimerl 2008). It is an approach that, working alongside partner community organisations, can be driven by arts research and teaching in higher education.

The revival of craft production amongst amateurs, artisans, small firms, and enterprises as a 'prominent feature of late-modern life' invites us to pay attention to the 'enigmas of experiential variation, personal subjectivity and human agency in everyday work contexts', something that has been largely ignored in academic debate on cultural work (Banks 2007: 123, 28). Craft provides a rich source for exploring the experiential, as well as subjectivity and agency at work. Researching user experiences on the digital craft platform Etsy, the RSA identified social connection and a sense of emotional fulfilment as major motivations for those selling and buying over the site (Dellot 2014). Exploring affect and emotion particularly with regard to the value of place within the creative process, at the point of making as well as consumption, is central to Luckman's research with cultural workers, and underpins her more recent work on craft and the creative economy (2015). Questions of experience, emotion, subjectivity, and agency were also fundamental to the CARE project in our examination of the sewing circle as a model of reflexive, affective labour, which supports distinct forms of engagement and communication (Hackney & Maughan 2016a). The affective values of making emerged again in relation to caring for a parent with early stage Alzheimer's in research conducted with the artist and researcher Mah Rana (Rana & Hackney 2018).

Being attentive to the experiences of making, the affective relationships involved, and spaces and places occupied is essential to any understanding of the organisation and value of craft work. Capturing these elements, however, like working with craft and community, is an inherently untidy, sometimes difficult, and always challenging process. Methodologically, Luckman underlines the importance of hearing the voices of participants. Maker-Centric sought to capture the conversation and interaction involved in collaborative making through photography, film and the artefacts produced. Our methodological framework is informed by two key theoretical approaches that address the complexities of community cooperation and creative practice. Alison Gilchrist (2009), an expert in community development and advisor to our project, draws on complexity theory to argue for a model of 'community' as an integrated and evolving system of networks comprising diverse and dynamic connections. She extrapolates an 'edge of chaos' model where communities occupy an intermediate zone between rigidity and randomness, in which what she terms 'untidy creativity' operates (Gilchrist 2000). Her insights help us think about the messy process of interaction and engagement within groups, and how they might better operate in relation to wider infrastructures, networks, processes of knowledge construction and identity formation. In *Together: the Rituals, Pleasures and Politics of Cooperation* (2012) sociologist Richard Sennett, meanwhile, argues for creative practice as a powerful means of cooperation because it enables people to respond to others on their own terms. Involving such skills as the ability to listen well, behave tactfully, find points of agreement, manage disagreement, and avoid frustration, cooperative making can achieve interactions that are 'knitted together' through exchanges of difference (dialogic cooperation) or the location of common ground (dialectic cooperation) or, most often, a combination of the two.

Ezra Shales, exploring the value of craft in our daily lives, writes about what he terms 'anonymous craft', 'craft commons', 'collated', 'multihanded' or 'commonplace craft' where 'human necessity and empathy for materials flow together' to help us cope with everyday challenges such as earning a living or managing fear and anxiety (Shales 2017: 20, 16). Invoking the wood turner and educator David Pye, he describes craft as 'types of workmanship', replacing nostalgic notions of the hand as the defining value with a version of craft that is located in quotidian making, something that applies equally to industrial manufacture and amateur practice (Adamson 2013; Knott 2015). This understanding of the everyday affectiveness of craft work and the craft worker suggests a version of cultural work that, grounded in the messiness of everyday life, has the potential to critically respond to it and shape a better future. As Alexiou put it in her reflections after our 'Utopia as Method' workshop: 'We dream the same dreams of peace, equality, diversity, opportunity and respect for each other and for the planet but we strive to realise them differently in our locations and contexts through, mostly, small steps'.

A Toolkit for Deviation: Making Method from Mess in the Black Country

Drawing on social design theory (Armstrong et al. 2014), Levitas's concept of IRS, and the heritage of the West Midlands metalwork industry, Maker-Centric aimed to develop a flexible process of connected do*ing* activities: walking, mapping, talking, exploring, researching, making, sharing, reflecting, and applying, that together constituted an imaginative reconstruction of society from the shared perspectives of the groups involved. Discussions with collaborator Creative Black Country (CBC) helped establish the project method: to fabricate 'stamps' and stencils inspired by the decorative heritage of metalwork manufacturing in the Midlands, and put researchers in touch with groups linked to the Wolverhampton Voluntary Sector Council (WVSC). Representatives attended a taster session at Wolverhampton School of Art to find out about the project, participate in mapping and printing activities, and share stories about their histories of making. Two groups, Petals of Hope, facilitated by Michelle, and Gatis Community Space, facilitated by Maria, agreed to participate in the project. They worked with the project artists and a group of students to devise weekly idea development workshops over a three-month period, with key points of interchange where the groups came together to fabricate their ideas and share their work or experience, at a final knowledge exchange event at Soho House Museum.

From the start of their 'making journeys', the groups responded with very different place-based mapping activities that resulted in two distinct sets of artefacts, framed by the interests, enthusiasms, and skills of their members. Gatis Community Space, showing interest in the ecology of place and environment, looked outside to the fabric of the surrounding community in Whitmore Reans, finding faces in the urban landscape that inspired emoji stamps; stamps for T-shirts and telephone cases based on street signage; and a branded logo which, fixed to the base of a boot or employed as a graffiti stencil, could be stamped (in an environmentally friendly manner) into the surrounding landscape to direct people to their community space. Arun Bector and his colleague Nick from the Asian Men's Mental Health group joined Gatis to create stamps from photographs of Wolverhampton high-rise council flats, which Aron vividly remembered from childhood, subsequently torn down to make way for new housing. This resulted in a set of digitally fabricated stamps with grips made from 1960s style door handles that Arun uses to engage communities in discussions about housing and the environment, raising funds for a community Fab Lab in Wolverhampton. Petals, in contrast, focused on stitching and home crafts, making stamps that reflected the diversity of participants and their shared identity as a women's sewing group. Whilst several women have impressive craft skills, at least one had little English. Crafting became a shared language to facilitate communication and early discussions about food, place, home and families explored commonalities and differences, resulting in the decision to collectively make a tablecloth with embroidered place settings displaying flowers from each woman's country of origin.

The knowledge sharing event was an important moment for reflecting on, synthesising, and prototyping a 'Maker-Centric Method' with common elements and a shared ethos that could be customised by other groups and organisations. The 'messiness' of the Maker-Centric process seemed to reflect inherent complexities in communities and community working, and became a defining aspect of the project.

We sought to chart a journey through and unravel a method from the 'mess', establishing a series of propositions, proposals and situations for making and thinking, and thinking through making, which convey a sense of repetition and alterity. Finding key words and images that emerged during Maker-Centric, researchers noticed that words such as 'invite', 'map', 'place', 'support' can be read as verbs and nouns: doing *and* naming words, something that nicely encapsulates a method that is grounded in process (making/doing) and results in identifying (naming/understanding) new knowledge about participants and groups. Designed on a grid like a board-game, the toolkit can be cut up, rearranged, and customised. It is intended to be playful, open-ended, and adaptable, to reflect the fact that working with and in communities is not linear, nor should it be.

Following Grant Kester (2005: 2), researchers were mindful that conversation can serve as an important tool if 'reframed as an active, generative process that can help us speak and imagine beyond the limits of fixed identities and official discourse'. For Maker-Centric participants and researchers 'making in place', with all its associated activities and experiences, served as the reframing process that helped imagine alternative futures and identities in the community. In one participant's words, 'I come to be with others, they are like my family, we chat, make, gossip'. The series of iterations described below and pictured (Figure 12.2) aims to move towards a community method that builds upon rich, local, everyday practices, and can be adopted and adapted by those looking to foster projects in their own communities. It provides a model for further reflexive work to be undertaken with the project groups, partners, researchers, and participants to use, modify, adapt, and contribute to, in an ongoing iterative process of community knowledge generation.

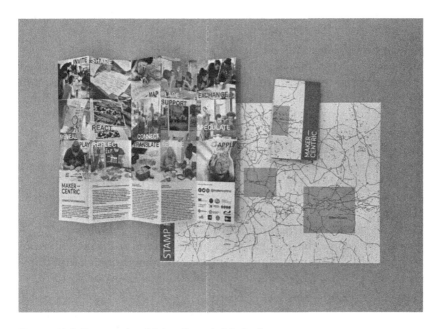

Figure 12.2 Prototyping Maker-Centric Method

Invite: *find, locate and connect with communities*
Groups meet face-to-face to gauge interests and expectations, and ensure project will be of benefit. Identify key contacts who already coordinate community initiatives, invite them to taster sessions to spark their imagination and catalyse involvement. Be clear about intentions, ideas, and processes.

Share: *facilities, resources, time, and knowledge.*
Gifting and sharing of ideas, materials, and companionship is key. To share is to give, to give is to actively participate. The momentum of sharing keeps a project moving forwards, and can be a major catalyst for knowledge acquisition.

Place: *ground the project in a location*
Situating a project in a location that is already part of a group's core identity and activities makes it easier for people to take part. Existing community groups often have their own safe spaces; take time to understand these settings and how group activities shape them.

Map: *exploring groups and participants.*
Mapping exercises and activities enable participants to physically and conceptually explore the terrain of their community in terms of place, needs, skills, expectations and, most of all, potentials.

Exchange: *knowledge and experience.*
Enable time and space for conversations where unexpected connections, shared experiences, knowledge, and skills could emerge. Exchange can become the foundation for moving a project forward, in an empowering approach led by the community.

Reveal: *participant values and virtues*
Unveiling your practice can allow participants to connect with you and encourage them to reveal things about themselves, their abilities, and aspirations. This should be done in an inspiring, non-threatening, and enabling way. Project facilitators should become ambassadors of knowledge and discovery.

React: *to needs, history, politics, and ideas*
Flexibility is essential to allow a group to formulate ideas and decide how they wish to develop and resolve them. Keep time free for reaction-based events and activities such as accessing research materials, trying a different process, or walking. Reacting keeps the project live and responsive.

Connect: *people, opportunities, ideas, processes, skills, problems.*
Connecting people, things, ideas, skills, processes, and problems will create a 'circuit board' of potentialities for making, thinking, and reflecting, and spark engagement. Also connect with stakeholders to ensure legacy.

Play: *allow time for play and failure.*
Time in a safe space to tinker, explore, experiment, deviate, and make mistakes is crucial for learning because it promotes chance and risk.

The opportunities that craft offers to engage with textures, colours, and processes is a great way to give permission to play.

Reflect: *iterative feedback and reflection.*
Form creative strategies for gathering ongoing reflection about participants' experience: what they think and how they feel, to gauge project affect as a process of ongoing evaluation. This should be embedded in project ethics.

Translate: *materials, experience, and language*
While making involves handicraft skills, it also encompasses associated skills that can be translated into problem-solving in a range of settings. Working with a multilingual group where English might be a second, third, or even fourth language we found that making together enabled the acquisition of language skills in an informal, everyday environment.

Realise: *process, outcome, and potential*
The process of becoming cognisant (to realise) is bound up with the process of giving material formation (realisation). Realisation through making can result in a process of wider realisation about self, other, situation, potential, and agency, among other things.

Apply: *skills, knowledge, and legacy*
The application of craft, from process to outcome, provides a model for approaching other challenges in the community. Self-realisation strengthens the wider application of skills, aptitudes, and abilities, to apply for funds, run a group, teach skills, develop a business or community initiative, and build project legacy.

Craftspace: Mapping Craft assets and Agencies in Handsworth, Birmingham

Craftspace is a craft development organisation based in Birmingham with a thirty-year track record. It supports curation, production, and research, devising projects which actively demonstrate the progressive role of makers and craft in civil society. Its programme is underpinned by socially engaged, participatory, collaborative and co-created approaches to engaging communities through craft and making. It works in the belief that craft is not just a commodity, but has an important role to play in building social, cultural, economic and human capital, as well as strengthening and revitalising communities.

Maker-Centric enables Craftspace to take an enquiry-based approach to work towards its strategic goals. Soho House Museum was an ideal setting to explore industrial and material heritage as a site for innovation and engagement with alternative forms of craft entrepreneurship. Surrounding the house, the district of Handsworth is a very ethnically diverse community that has been shaped by generations of inward migration. As an organisation, Craftspace supports the idea of situated research through practice, craft in place-making, and hyperlocal methodologies. Craft and the act of making together as a means to produce knowledge and experience – including unique forms of embodied knowledge – also feed into and are of benefit to the wider ecology, a concern that framed the CARE project and continues to inform Maker-Centric.

Place-based heritage as an inspiration, and sometimes a provocation, was central to the creative work undertaken by one specific group of participants. This group, all aged over fifty, used craft as a vehicle and lens to investigate the idea of purposeful work in later life as a means to take stock, reskill, plan ahead, connect with others, and live more healthy and enjoyable lives. Making prototype souvenir products for the Soho House shop in Birmingham and bespoke banners in Dublin Castle, groups learnt skills that transitioned them from hand-making to digital production (see Hackney & Figueiredo forthcoming). The project demonstrated how purposeful and collectively practised craft work offers real benefits of social interaction, well-being, connectivity, and emotional and cognitive stimulus, combating the negative effects of isolation. Taken further, it can have economic benefits; one member of the group now runs a successful independent business, while others have taken up further training, set up an informal making group, and are regular attendees and volunteers at the Fab Lab. The stability of the group and the process of collective making were essential elements in this process. In these community contexts, craft enterprise facilitated a range of things through democratic forms of making: skills exchange, collective or co-operative making, co-created and authored methods of production, all providing a different 'return on investment'. Profits or benefits based on a holistic accrual of agency and social capital resulted in productive, connected, resilient, and healthy communities. Participants were enacting a valuable contribution through cultural citizenship and stewardship of skills after they were no longer fully economically active. This is a generative way of working that challenges some of the dominant notions and modes of craft production, commerce, and consumption. If we view these participants as cultural workers, not laboring for immediate financial gain, this process begins to encompass and articulate a collective, community driven form of 'social work' and 'cultural responsibility'.

Maker-Centric Birmingham takes this learning about materialising craft as a community asset through purposeful, connected working another stage, by using it to uncover and potentially support otherwise 'hidden' cultural workers: craft communities, individual makers, and small businesses, which operate in what might be considered 'edge-places of creativity' (Luckman 2012:1). Furthermore, it aims to employ this method to raise consciousness about such creative community and interrogate the extent to which local decisionmakers, policymakers, and other agencies take them into account. A number of seasoned community participants from the CARE and Utopias projects took on the role of creative ambassadors to apply and further realise their skills as community researchers (Facer

& Enright 2016). Together with professional maker Melanie Tomlinson, and equipped with a materials-based, creative toolkit that was developed from the Utopia praxinoscope, they went out to groups and public spaces to map the craft skills of people in and around Handsworth. The group visualised the collected data and stories into a co-created artwork, that will form the basis of the Birmingham Maker-Centric toolkit and act as a catalyst to engage stakeholders in discussions about how to mobilise these assets for social and economic good in the locality, and beyond.

The mapping revealed many stories and assets. Some craft activists had a long-term anchoring effect within the community. The Cannon Street Memorial Baptist Church craft group of African Caribbean women of different generations has been active for several decades. They meet weekly to make knitted and embroidered products which they sell at local events. Whilst gaining from the social connection and mutual support, the economic purpose is to fundraise for the church to maintain its beautiful historic building and charitable activities, thereby ensuring continuity of a vital community facility, resource, and network. Although unpaid, putting their skills and resourcefulness to purposeful and organised use identifies these women as cultural workers engaged in 'work', which has mutually beneficial outcomes that need to be recognised.

Individuals are also asset hubs around which a flow of exchange and productivity takes place. Professor Black has run a Caribbean carnival workshop in a community centre for over thirty years (see Figure 12.3). His embodied skill of specialist making and an incredible archive have kept

Figure 12.3 Carnival Costume Workshop

this craft alive. His mission has been to teach young people skills and support their associated cultural traditions. The project also involved working with a retired blacksmith with such specialist skills as arc welding, who works peripatetically with his mobile anvil and equipment. Commissions include repairing balustrades on the motorway, cannons and guns on army tanks, and making the 30-foot-high ornamental gates for London's Kensington Palace. His father was a farmer; from the age of 11 he was helping to weld and repair trailers. He still tinkers with metal in his shed and fixes things for people locally.

Other traders like Kamal Sewing Machine Ltd were hubs of knowledge and interwoven connections. They sold all manner of materials and tools, and ran a workshop that mended domestic and industrial machines bringing together the world of hobbyists with that of manufacturers. The Perry Common Shed project, inspired by the national men's shed movement, is a volunteer run community resource where people can learn woodwork skills. They keep costs down through a partnership to source free wooden transport pallets which are re-purposed by members for their projects. Financial donations help to sustain the group in a socio-economically deprived area, enabling older people to learn new woodwork skills – perhaps equipping them to take on other work in the future.

This project revealed groups wishing to extend, increase or formalise their craft activities, such as a Somali women's sewing group who practice dress making and were looking for space to rent in Handsworth, and a group of volunteers restoring a historic building who wanted to build craft activity into the life of their community space. There were individuals who expressed a desire to learn a new craft skill but wanted to access it locally, and others who had been practising that skill privately for years who were willing to share it more widely. Part of this work in the future will be to build a toolkit to help realise these cultural workers' aspirations by connecting groups with each other, external agencies, resources such as the Fab Lab, and other means of support. Our creative ambassadors and new participants have enhanced their skills, both in terms of fabrication and social agency, gaining in confidence to go out into the community, facilitate conversations, learn new skills, and pass on existing ones. One ambassador has become motivated to set up a creative enterprise and two have become regular volunteers at the Fab Lab helping to develop it as a community resource. The premise and outcomes of this research also allows us to reflect on the ways in which we as a development agency might link micro-assets to the macro-environment for greater impact.

Spaces of Welcome: The Value of Craft for Migrants and Refugees in Slovenia

> I would like to run a workshop. I have so many ideas for making handmade goods. Not only from leather, but also from wood. I would

like to live and work in the same place, have a room to sleep in and a workshop nearby. I would like to make everything myself, from the toilet to the kitchen. I would like to create mosaics, wire up the electricity, make my own bicycle.

(Erfan, 25, Iran)

Invention in craft and responsiveness to social need cannot be taught; it must be found. Responsibility to social needs can be taught – and should be more often.

(Shales 2017: 95)

The village of Kostanjevica na Krki is located in the Schengen region on the border with Croatia, an area that witnessed a regular flow of refugees and asylum seekers through the 'Balkan Route' between September 2015 and March 2016. For a large majority Slovenia was, and remains, a transit country, yet new enterprises started to appear. Terra Vera is a grassroot initiative in this area. Consisting initially of cultural anthropologists, it has grown as an informal network of young creatives, hand-crafters, artists, artisans, designers, start-up entrepreneurs, hubs, and art institutions looking for ways to address the situation. Shales observes how historically craft has 'developed in response to demand, inventing itself anew wherever and whenever there was patronage' (2017: 95). Terra Vera identified a demand and a social need seeing craft as an important means to frame a response to migration in ways that build on individual and collective skills and resources, so that people might better locate themselves, build resilience, and find ways to visualise and 'make' a future (sometimes literally, as twenty-five-year-old Erfan suggests).

Members undertook scoping activities, visiting camps and detention centers, talking to people and gauging their knowledge and talents, both formal and informal. Professional achievements were less important than skills, potential, experience and enthusiasm. Weekly social gatherings at Ziferblat – a homely social venue in the heart of town, in stark contrast to the asylum center – involved ten participants: a poet, cook, economics student and musician from Syria, an electrician, carpenter, construction worker, and student of marketing from Cameroon, a henna painter and a handcrafter from Iran, and an Afghani boy with artistic skills. Beginning with art therapy and storytelling, the workshops progressed to handcrafts as the group grew and became even more diverse. Local independent creatives and organisations joined from the Fashion Department at Ljubljana University, jewellery designer Martina Obid Mlakar, ceramic artists Dragica Čadež and Hana Karim, young interior design team Prostor Vmes, and visual artist Samira Kentrić, as well as film-makers. Social networks were established alongside the training and workshops.

Palmas, who became a mainstay of the workshops, emphasised the importance of creative making for integration and knowledge exchange through a reciprocal gifting process between cultures and societies:

> It has to do with integration. Finding yourself in a new society, learning new ideas … From the workshops I have learned that the deeper you go, the more creative you are, and you become increasingly integrated … there is an exchange of cultures. The ideas I consider come from within me, they are a part of my culture. My design or idea grows and enriches the society.
>
> (Palmas, 34, Cameroon)

For forty-two-year-old Houda from Syria, the benefits of the workshops were more basic and fundamental than that: 'Today's workshop made me like Slovenia, for this was the first time I felt like a human being'. For others, it was the material properties and collective processes involved in craft that had the most memorable effect. The experience of working in clay motivated Sveta from Russia to take an educational route:

> As we held hands in clay I felt that the barriers were washed away. We played, joked and laughed in the most universal language, we were connected as humans from a single planet, a single earth, now creating together out of this earth. It was a beautiful experience, which inspired me to enroll into a research program in the psychology of cultural diversity and inclusion, which I am studying at right now.
>
> (Sveta, 25, Russia)

The experience of creative making and skills exchange built trust in the group, and personal stories were exchanged. Uncovering the human narratives of migrants, particularly refugees, provides counter narratives to prevailing migration discourse, even if 'stereotypes are obviously present and cannot be ignored and this can cause a problem within the community' (Janža, 24, Slovenia).

Anthropologist Kathleen Stewart (2010: 340) developed the twin concepts of 'worlding' and 'bloom spaces' to explain how we can operate affectually in the world. Worlding refers to the condition of being in the world, something that is understood and lived through the senses and is particularly sharp at times of individual and communal tension and transition. It involves the emergence of bloom spaces where the senses come to the surface, new lessons are learnt, different priorities emerge, connections, and adjustments are made, and where we can understand ourselves and others with new depth, clarity, and calm, despite the circumstances. Refugees and migrants, habitually forced into unknown and often terrifying situations, might experience 'worlding' more intensely than other groups. In such circumstances craft workshops can become bloom spaces in which life becomes a series of daily, lived minute adjustments as participants draw on their resources, learn new skills, address challenges, survive, and even thrive, despite the circumstances. The workshops became a means of promoting solidarity models built on participatory work as a method for collective empowerment and social cohesion. The group designed a social inclusion program where people could meet on equal terms in 'Spaces of Welcome', spaces of co-creation, knowledge sharing, and skill transfer, where identities could be explored and formed in collaboration and in a safe place, as an immediate response to the current needs. The group explored a hybrid mix of traditional, contemporary, technical, and professional skills developed through synergies between newcomers and local creatives. Co-designing and skills exchange enabled the development of a shared purpose, common values, and respectful intercultural dialogue as participants paid attention to one another and listened purposefully. Taking advantage of the fashion for buying local, Terra Vera is currently developing a craft-entrepreneurship initiative leading to the creation of an ethical marketing brand, from idea to the final product, for ethical, sustainable crafts.

In October 2017 the group curated 'Living Room' in collaboration with the Slovene Museum of Architecture, an exhibition of their products including decorative items, jewelry, graphic design, and furniture. Like Maker-Centric, 'Spaces of Welcome' develops personal contacts, enables new co-operations to emerge, and provides a space in which existing assets can be optimised through education, employment, and business start-ups, something that can inform policies in these areas in the context of migration. Focusing on collaborative making, it fosters aptitudes and affordances that come to the fore as a consequence of migration. Less than two years after the project launch, the Terra Vera team now involves Palmas and Erfan as two of their most active members. They and many others who reached the country as refugees and were mobilised as trainees are now becoming trainers and mentors with the ability to link traditional technologies to contemporary design approaches. Optimism is high; as Moutez from Syria's says, 'I hope to do so much more. I want to make bags from waste material. I am a person who truly likes his job and products'.

Maker-Centricity in the Future

The thinking that informs Maker-Centric is grounded and embedded in the history and practice of craft work. Silberberg details the value of creative making for individuals, organisations, and institutions in forging spaces, connections, raising levels of intent, and awareness: a version of community craft in an 'expanded field'. Luckman, in her critique of creative industries discourse focuses on cultural workers, paying attention to vernacular creativity, local strengths, community wishes, and the affordances of edge-places of creativity. Levitas's utopian method draws on the history of the Arts and Crafts Movement to critique and re-imagine the social, political, and economic structures of society, while Sennett argues that the processes involved in *doing* art and craft cooperatively can help us put this re-imagining into practice in small, incremental, yet fundamental ways. Together these ideas, coupled with the team's learning from the CARE project, lay the foundation for a co-produced Maker-Centric method (or methods) that builds on the affordances and agencies of craft working but can be shaped by communities *in* communities and, as such, responds to their needs.

Maker-Centric to date has supported two very different place-based community craft journeys with Gatis Community Space and Petals of Hope in Wolverhampton; unearthed and mapped an unexpected, and largely hidden, group of cultural workers in and around Handsworth, Birmingham, including Professor Black, the Somali women's sewing group, and the Perry Common Shed project; examined the value of Fab Labs for connecting people and building community assets; and undertaken knowledge exchange with Terra Vera in Slovenia, learning about their work with Erfan, Palmas and their colleagues. Working with partners Craftspace and Creative Black Country, the project will continue to build resources based on the value of place-based craft work to optimise community assets and the organisation of cultural work in communities. Making, for instance, might provide a means for re-imaging work in a future society funded by universal basic income.

Craft, however, is no magic panacea for all social, cultural, and economic ills. Petals of Hope is located on the Heath Town estate in Wolverhampton, which houses 700 asylum seekers and refugees from 46 nations in a city that voted overwhelmingly for the UK to leave the European Union. While the women cooperated to sew their tablecloth, pressures in the form of entrenched views from local residents, on occasion, emerged. Signaling the underlying challenges and contradictions that those living in such complex circumstances face on a daily basis, future research will consider how 'being Maker-Centric' might enable craft and cultural workers to move beyond such tensions.

Note

1 This work was funded by the Arts and Humanities Research Council (AHRC) under Grant number: AH/P009638/1: Maker-centric: building place-based, co-making communities.

References

Adamson, G. (2013) *The Invention of Craft*. London: Bloomsbury.
Armstrong, L., Bailey, J., Julier, G. & Kimbell. L. (October, 2014) *Social Design Futures: HEI Research and the AHRC*. University of Brighton and Victoria and Albert Museum.

Banks, M. (2007) *The Politics of Cultural Work*. Basingstoke & New York: Palgrave Macmillan.

Dellot, B. (2014) *Breaking the Mould: How Etsy and Online Craft Marketplaces are Chainging the Nature of Business*. www.thersa.org/discover/publications-and-articles/reports/breaking-the-mould. Accessed 12.02.2018.

Facer, K. & Enright, B. (2016) *Creating Living Knowledge: The Connected Communities Programme*. University of Bristol and AHRC Connected Communities Programme.

Figueiredo, D. (2018) *Utopia as Method Exchange Project. Community Futures and Utopias*. Connected Communities Report. https://connected-communities.org/wp-content/uploads/2016/04/Creating-Living-Knowledge.Final_.pdf. Accessed 10.01.2018.

Florida, R. (2003) *The Rise of the Creative Class*. New York & London: Routledge.

Gilchrist, A. (2000) The Well-Connected Community: Networking to the "Edge of Chaos". *Community Development Journal*, 35(3): 264–75.

Gilchrist, A. (2009) *The Well-Connected Community: A Networking Approach to Community Development*. Bristol: Policy Press.

Hackney, F. (2013a) Quiet Activism and the New Amateur: the Power of Home and Hobby Crafts. *Design and Culture: The Journal of the Design Studies Forum*, 5(2), July: 169–194.

Hackney, F. (2013b) CAREful or CAREless? Collaborative Making and Social Engagement through Craft. *Engage 33*: Critical Craft, 23–37.

Hackney, F. & Maughan H. (2016a) Stitched Together: Community Learning, Collaborative Making'. *Futurescan 3: Journal of Fashion in Higher Education*. Helena Britt, Laura Morgan, Kerry Walton (Eds): 194–206.

Hackney, F., Maughan, H. & Desmarais, S. (2016b) The Power of Quiet: Re-making Affective, Amateur and Professional Textiles Agencies. *Journal of Textile Design Research and Practice*, 4(1): 33–62.

Hackney, F. & Figueiredo, D. (forthcoming) Better Together': Co-Creating *Living Heritage, Community Assets & Enterprise* In Thomas, N. & Luckman, S. (Eds) *The Craft Economy: Makers, Markets and Meaning*. London & New York: Bloomsbury Academic.

Kester, G. (2005) Conversation Pieces: The Role of Dialogue in Socially-Engaged Art. In Kucor, Z. & Leung, S. (Eds) *Theory in Contemporary Art since 1985*. Blackwell: London.

Knott, S. (2015) *Amateur Craft: History and Theory*. London & NY: Bloomsbury.

Levine, F. and C. Heimerl (2008) *The Rise of DIY Art, Craft and Design*. New York: Princeton Architectural Press.

Levitas, R. (2013) *Utopia As Method*. Basingstoke & New York: Palgrave/Macmillan.

Luckman, S. (2012) *Locating Cultural Work: The Politics and Poetics of Rural, Regional and Remote Creativity*. London & New York: Palgrave Macmillan.

Luckman, S. (2015) *Craft and the Creative Economy*. Basingstoke & New York: Palgrave Macmillan.

Rana, M. & Hackney, F. (2018) Making & Material Affect. From Learning & Teaching to Sharing & Listening. In Prior, R. (Ed) *Using Art as Research in Learning & Teaching: Multidisciplinary approaches across the arts*. Bristol: Intellect.

Schifferes, J. (2015) Mapping Heritage. *RSA Journal*, Issue 3.

Sennett, R. (2012) *Together: The Rituals, Pleasures & Politics of Cooperation.* London & New York: Penguin Books.

Shales, E. (2017) *The Shape of Craft.* London: Reaktion Books Ltd.

Silberberg, S. (2015) The Common Thread, *RSA Journal*, Issue 3.

Stewart, K. (2010) Worlding Refrains. In Gregg, M. & Seigworth, J. (Eds). *The Affect Theory Reader*, Durham, NC & London: Duke University Press, pp. 339–53.

13 Reflecting on the Relationship between Craft and History

Perspectives, Resources and Contemporary Implications

Richard K. Blundel

Introduction

This chapter examines some of the more prominent features of the complex and often highly contested relationship between contemporary forms of craft and their earlier incarnations. It responds to a persistent conceptual challenge that also has significant practical implications. As Adamson (2013: 210) puts it:

> This false choice of modern craft, between present and past, complicity and detachment, is a discursive trap. Only by traversing that dialectic can craft be a powerful agent of change, both morally and economically.

The chapter considers how craft researchers might draw fresh insights from historical studies in order to bridge this temporal divide. I hope that the examples might also prove helpful to practitioners as they seek to incorporate and transcend the legacies of previous generations.

The chapter is divided into three sections. First, I summarise the main themes identified in the existing body of research and illustrate how historically informed studies have shed new light on craft practice and modes of organisation in the modern era. The second section is concerned with the different ways in which craft practitioners and others, such as market intermediaries and connoisseurs, have enrolled historical narratives and associations as a resource, typically with the aim of either promoting or defending particular craft products, practices or values. The third section offers some concluding remarks on the scope and limitations of historical research methods, and how they might contribute to future work in this area.

These reflections are coloured by my attempts, as a social science generalist, to engage in more historically informed research on craft practice in a variety of organisational contexts, ranging from farm-based cheesemakers to small-boat builders, furniture designer-makers and brass musical instrument manufacturers (e.g. Blundel & Tregear 2006; Blundel & Smith 2018).[1] It is not possible to present a comprehensive overview of such a diverse and extensive literature,[2] but I have made a conscious effort to illustrate my argument by referencing an eclectic mix of studies that span the visual arts, design and craft-based production. One of the key lessons I have learned is that the more tangible, surface-level variations between different domains of craft practice can mask important commonalities and connections. I hope that these extracts will encourage others to engage with this wider literature, extending beyond their own specialism, and that the sources cited might offer some useful entry-points for new research projects.

Craft in Historical Perspective

Writing two decades ago, the British art and design curator, Paul Greenhalgh, argued that the crafts had, 'not been well-served' by historians during the last century, and that this inattention had contributed to, 'a contemporary crisis of confidence' in the field (Greenhalgh 1997: 21). Since that time, we have witnessed a further 'craft revival' and a considerable flowering of research on the crafts, much of which has revolved around its organisation, practice and meaning (cf. Dormer 1994; Ferris 2016). Many of these studies address the interplay between the growth of craft-based enterprises and broader processes of industrialisation, enabling researchers to chart the practical consequences, both for individual practitioners and for the wider socio-economic and cultural landscape. In the following summary, I have assembled three broad themes that may be of interest to readers of this volume: common trends; alternative interpretations; and lived experiences. Each theme is illustrated with extracts from empirical studies that draw on a diverse range of disciplinary backgrounds, including the history of science, business and economic history, anthropology, and cultural studies.

Common Trends

Historical theorising plays an essential role in locating the surface phenomena that we observe in contemporary craft in relation to the deeper currents of cultural, technological and socio-economic development. For example, Sabel and Zeitlin (1997: 2–3) have pointed out how craft practices have both borrowed from and become integrated with the logics and strategies of industrialisation, thereby exemplifying a phenomenon that the authors characterise as the 'recombinablility and interpenetration' of different forms of economic organisation (cf. Scranton 1997). Carnevali's (2003) account of the Birmingham jewellery quarter in the period after 1945 is a striking contribution to this literature. This business-historical study comprises a detailed examination of discrete episodes in a particular local setting in which the researcher is also acutely aware of their relationship to much longer-term processes:

> The history of jewelry making in Birmingham in the postwar period is merely a detail of a complex tapestry (in a dynamic, time-rich sense, a sort of tapestry *à la Bayeux*), and to do it full justice it should be told as a *Bildungsroman*, starting from the adventurous beginnings of inventors and craftsmen in the late eighteenth century.
>
> (ibid. 274)

Carnevali's study investigates the evolution of the production methods of small artisanal firms in this industrial district with the aim of gaining a better understanding of the underlying logics and the strategies of the actors involved. Her findings challenge prevailing accounts of industrialisation by reasserting the role of such firms as repositories of craft knowledge and skills, while also (in some instances) acting as a catalyst for product and process innovation. This leads the author to question the long-term prospects of jewellery manufacturers supplying the mass market, in contrast to those that combined traditional hand-working with contemporary design and a selective use of mechanisation:

> The designer-makers and firms that have specialized in high-quality jewelry and that have used flexible methods of production, however, will be able to capitalize on the distinctive features of the industrial district: the skilled workers, the design culture of the School of Jewellers, and the institutional structures for the promotion of innovation.
>
> (ibid. 295–296)

Historical research can also track changes in the *meanings* attributed to core terms such as 'craft' and 'craftsman'. This is exemplified by the case of artisan cheese in the United States, which has undergone three major changes over the last two centuries while remaining wedded to a largely unchanged body of knowledge and skills – the 19th century 'cheese factories' referred to in this quotation employed hand-working and craft practices that were broadly similar to their farm-based counterparts:

> [C]ontinuity in artisans' *know-how* and fabrication methods – over time and across factory and farmstead practices – is obscured by changes in artisanal *production* over the past century. After being introduced as a farm chore whose responsibility fell to colonial and pioneer women, making cheese by hand in the United States was

transformed into a blue-collar factory job, a rural alternative for men to farming. It shifted again in the twentieth century to a life-style choice pursued, among others, by professionals escaping office-bound careers and urban or suburban backgrounds. The meaning of making cheese by hand has moved from being a chore to a skilled trade to an expressive endeavor.

(Paxson 2013: 98)

Greenhalgh's (1997) argument also revolves around changes in meaning. In common with a number of later contributors, he suggests that much of the difficulty lies in the word 'craft', which he sees as an 'unstable compound', due to the way it has formed over the last two and a half centuries, underpinned by three distinct sources: the separation of 'fine' and 'decorative' arts; a re-valuation of 'the vernacular'; and the 'politics of work'. The essay elaborates on the different intellectual origins and ideological potential of each element, and how they were pulled together at a particularly opportune 'historical moment' in the late 19th century in countries such as Britain, Germany and the United States, which adopted the principles of the Arts and Crafts movement (*ibid.* 36–40; 51 n.56). By unpacking the antecedents and legacy of such developments, historical research can help us towards a deeper understanding of current tensions and contradictions in the craft world.[3]

Alternative Interpretations

Historical research can uncover evidence that leads to new views on the role of earlier generations of craftsmen. For example, Adamson (2013) poses a direct challenge to the conventional narrative on the role of craft, and the fate of craftsmen, in the period of the industrial revolution. He adopts a broadly chronological framework and constructs an elaborate argument around four main themes: the changing nature of 'manipu-lation' or control of craft activity in the workplace; the persistence of craft's 'mystery' in the face of efforts to systematise knowledge; the rela-tionship between craft and the 'mechanical'; and lastly, how 'memory' – characterised here as craft's, 'deep connection to materiality and cultural continuity' (*ibid.* xii), has influenced its capacity to engage with progres-sive movements. Hilaire-Perez's (2007) analysis of scientific and indus-trial developments in eighteenth-century Europe addresses this point and argues that, '[o]ur understanding of the role of artisans cannot simply be reduced to that of routine and resistance' (*ibid.* 139), and that they played a key role in forming the increasingly complex technical culture of this period. Constructed with reference to numerous examples, including gunmakers, locksmiths and carpenters, the research indicates that many craft guilds promoted knowledge-sharing, helped inventors to secure financial rewards, and incentivised the dissemination of new inventions (*ibid*. 139–146).

While research on ancient and exotic craft practices might appear divorced from most contemporary (Western) practice, it can also provide valuable insights. For example, Dilley's (2009) anthropological study includes an account of the traditional practices of Senegalese artisans. It depicts the successive stages of learning in a weaving apprenticeship, from mere instruction to, 'dreaming and other forms of spirit contact' (*ibid*. 58), which for master weavers becomes a potent source of ideas for new designs or inter-lacings. In this instance, we see how mysticism can become a source of, 'domain-specific knowledge power' (*ibid*. 53–54), which draw on Ancient Africa's more profound, holistic understanding of the crafts (Hampâté Bâ 2010).

Lived Experiences

My final theme begins from the perspective of the craftsperson, both as an individual and – in many instances – as a member of a social group. Research into these lived experiences often takes the form of a biographical account or an oral history (Thompson 1997). For example, the work and life of the engraver, David Kindersley (1915–1995) is celebrated in a volume co-authored by his wife and fellow-engraver, Lida Cardozo Kindersley, along with Lottie Hoare, a writer on craft, and family friend, Thomas Sherwood, an academic who had previously commissioned engravings from the workshop (Cardozo Kindersley, Hoare & Sherwood 2013). While biographical writing is sometimes derided as little more than hagiography, there are many examples of scholarly studies that locate the lives of individuals in a wider context, indicating how their subjects interact with other people and with the technologies, cultures, institutions and economic conditions in which they lived (Stager Jacques 2006). There are a number of ways in which historical writing of this kind has the potential to enhance our understanding of craft. For example, it can help researchers to recognise, and to clarify, *technical* issues that have a bearing on their practice, such as the attention given to spacing of letters. In a similar way, it can draw attention to *organisational* issues that might otherwise be overlooked, such as the subtle distinctions between the self-perceptions of the 'designer-craftsman' and other members of the workshop, and how such distinctions appear to dissolve when they are working collaboratively on larger projects. Sensitive biographical writing can also provide a glimpse of how an individual's work is infused by a particular spiritual or ethical quest, while oral histories provide opportunities to introduce 'unknown voices', such as studio assistants, and explore 'hidden spheres', such as the relationship between craft practice and domestic life (Thompson 1997: 44).

One of the commonly recorded narratives in craft biographies is of practitioners seeking creative inspiration by engaging with their peers, who may be working in similar or even unrelated areas:

> Kindersley did not see his workshop as the only place where he would learn. During holidays with the ceramicist Bernard Leach he had moments of wondering whether to go and spend time at St Ives learning pottery techniques from him. He liked the idea of single-mindedly applying himself to another craft in order to expand his understanding of working with natural materials. However, responsibilities to his family and clients came first and he did not find time for his imagined education.
>
> (Cardozo Kindersley, Hoare & Sherwood 2013: 52–53)

This opens up the possibility of pursuing references to other craftspeople, across different biographical accounts, which may reveal both shared experiences as well as some notable contrasts. Comparative work of this kind is sometimes extended into a collective biography,[4] such as Friend's (2017) finely woven depiction of the interconnected lives of a circle of friends that included the artist and wood engraver, Eric Ravilious, and contemporaries such as Paul Nash, Edward Bawden, Helen Binyon and Enid Marx. The narrative and accompanying images trace the working out of the inherent tensions highlighted by Greenhalgh (1997). By shifting the focus between the individual and the collective, the narrative probes the way that people have negotiated between craft values and commercial imperatives, and managed the, sometimes fraught relationship between crafts, fine art and industrial design.[5]

It is also possible to examine how the working practices, values and lifestyles of craftspeople have been reproduced across time, by combining interview evidence from contemporary practitioners with historical evidence about previous generations, including their teachers, and mentors. For example, I am involved in a collaborative project with the furniture designer-maker, Philip Koomen (Figures 13.1 and 13.2), which combines interviews with long-established practitioners, looking back at their own formative experiences, paired interviews with their former apprentices, and historical evidence from a number of sources, including observation, biographies, archives and oral histories (Koomen & Blundel 2018).

Historical Narratives and Associations as a Contemporary Resource

It has long been recognised that many organisations deploy the 'rhetorical power of "the past," through which actors might better elicit emotive commitment from different audiences' (Zundel, Holt & Popp

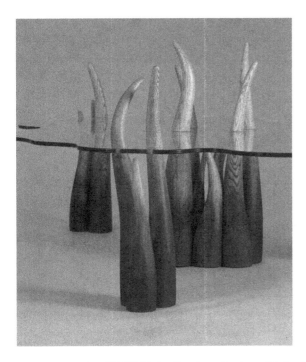

Figure 13.1 'Pondlife' Table by Furniture Designer-Maker Philip Koomen
Source: © Philip Koomen, reproduced with permission

2016: 214). Craft-based enterprises are no exception and are well-versed in redeploying historical narratives to address present-day concerns. Indeed, as Glenn Adamson has pointed out, the inherent properties of craft products and practices imbue such organisations with a particular capacity to engage in a proactive dialogue with history:

> Craft's relationship to time is complex – rather like a novel set in the past but written in the present. When the potential of this temporal structure is realized, craft can be a powerful mediator between the present and the past, and therefore between the individual and the collective.
>
> (Adamson 2013: 210)

History is a resource that can be used – and in some cases abused – by organisations, whether the aim is to establish or reinforce their legitimacy, or to engage in other forms of identity work. This tendency, which has surprisingly long-standing antecedents, has given rise to numerous hagiographic accounts and 'creation myths' over the years, which pose

Figure 13.2 Sculptured Chairs by Furniture Designer-Maker Philip Koomen
Source: © Philip Koomen, reproduced with permission

additional explanatory challenges. For example, a recent feature article on, 'Craft's identity crisis', included this striking comment on the negative effects from Raoul Shah, chief executive of the agency that created the 'Craftworkers' advertising campaign for Levi's[6]:

> [W]ith the resurgence of heritage brands, words like authenticity and craft became jumbled up and overused. "Craft" became so throw-away that the value inherent in the word became hard to believe.
>
> (quoted in Walker 2016: 42)

This concern is echoed by Christopher Frayling, former Rector of the Royal College of Art. He applies the cultural writer and educator Raymond Williams's notion of an unbroken chain of 'retrospective regret' to successive (English) craft revivals, not in order to dismiss them out of hand, but rather to examine more closely the assumptions that underpin many accounts of craftsmanship. Having challenged the notion of the contemporary craft potter as an inheritor of a (largely imagined) independent workshop tradition, he concludes:

> The myth of the happy artisan – like the "artist craftsman", craft guilds to which select potters could belong, and the confusion of rural workers with guild craftsman – did not exist until the nineteenth century, when it became part of a romantic reaction against the spread of industrial capitalism. And the history which underpins much of the 'craft revival' is, in fact, nostalgia masquerading as history.
>
> (Frayling 2011: 66)[7]

How are we to respond to this kind of critique? The obvious implication is that we need more rigorous analysis of the past. However, it is also important to recognise the implicit value judgements that are being exercised when today's craftspeople seek to locate themselves in a broader historical narrative: one person's honest attempt to engage with an 'authentic' tradition might be dismissed by another as at best a misrepresentation or at worst a 'selling-out' of the past.[8] In the rest of this section, I seek to probe this thorny issue by drawing on concrete examples that illustrate how historical resources have been appropriated by a variety of actors in the craft sector.

The appropriation of craft heritage is addressed in a number of the contributions to this volume, including Maria Laura Toraldo and colleagues, whose empirical case of an Italian silk-tie maker illustrates how craft organisations engage in the formation of collective memories, drawing on local histories and traditions to foster distinctive representations of the past (Toraldo, Mangia & Consiglio 2018). As the authors note, this is an important phenomenon for contemporary craft, where the recourse to distinctive historical imaginaries has a particular relationship with industrial capitalism and the homogenising tendencies of modern production, distribution and communication technologies. However, the deployment of provenance and associated (histories) as a source of value also has its own history, which can be traced back to the pre-industrial era. For example, in the first century CE, when Greek cheese was exported to Rome, one of the best-known varieties was called *Cynthos*, after the island on which it was produced:

> Pliny described it as being made from ewes' milk and considered its good quality to be largely dependent on the shrub *cytisus* [...], which was extremely palatable to sheep and produced especially good milk.
>
> (Cheke 1959: 63)

Stories of this kind are typically co-created by members of craft communities, market intermediaries and connoisseurs. There is also a common pattern in which accounts that have previously enrolled a relatively small niche audience are, under certain circumstances, reproduced and disseminated on a larger scale, influencing popular tastes and prompting adoption in higher-volume markets.

While these historical narratives depend to some degree on a grounding in reality, it is important for researchers to read them, 'against the grain' in order to unpack the underlying influences and causal relationships. As a consequence, it may even be necessary to abandon conventional approaches to historiography in favour of more creative alternatives. Consider, for example, the challenge of explaining the origins of Camembert, 'the flower of French cheeses' (Boisard 2003). Having examined the wide variety of partial and often contradictory accounts that are available in the archives, the author concluded that, 'Rather than attempt to establish the true story of Camembert, [...] *I chose to write the story of its myth*, to try to situate it in its time and place, and to understand the context in which it had emerged, the better to understand its message' (*ibid*. xii – emphasis added).[9] Industrial-scale production of this cheese variety has brought its own variant of the tradition-based discourse, in which the continued use of craft-related practices by smaller makers, such as the use of simple ladles in the moulding process, serves to enhance the image of the large industrial-scale producers who have automated the process (Boisard 2003: 187–195).

Another illustration from the world of cheese, is the case of 'Red Cheshire', an English cheese, which remains popular to the present day.[10] The origins of this particular type can be traced to the 18th century, when improvements in agricultural production methods, the road network and newly emerging system of canals, opened up new marketing channels for a regional variety that was already well sought-after beyond its immediate area of production. A thriving trade had emerged, supplying (white) Cheshire cheese to coach travellers on the transport artery between London and Holyhead, on the North Wales coast. Local farmers attempted to take a share of the business by 'passing off' their products as Cheshire. This prompted a regulatory intervention, with unintended consequences:

> Pressure was applied to make the Welsh farmers colour their product red so as to distinguish the inferior cheese from true Cheshire, but, just to show how contrary customers can sometimes be, the red colouring proved so popular that the Cheshire makers found themselves obliged to add it to their cheese.
>
> (Smith 1995b: 35–36)

Zundel, Holt and Popp (2016) provide a useful framework for operationalising the ideas discussed in this section. The authors begin by contrasting the historian's approach to history, which is oriented towards rigorous narrative reconstructions of the past, with that of organisations seeking to deploy their own histories, and those of their local contexts, as a resource. They then distinguish two ways in which organisations make use of history: 'for outward commitment' (i.e. 'to build identities to help foster commitment among external audiences') and for 'inward commitment' (i.e. 'providing inspiration to employees about what the organization can be'). Examples of both categories can be found in the contributions to this volume. For example, 'outward commitment' is evident in Jennifer Smith Maguire's (2018, this volume) examination of the fine wine field, where craft is represented to an 'authenticity taste regime' through notions such as *terroir* and provenance – representations of the soil, climatic conditions and cultural heritage of the wine- producing region. Similarly, the quest for inward commitment is apparent in Robin Holt's account of the extended master–apprentice relations and conservative practices that form the *shokunin* (Sushi chefs), and which in their turn yield skills that appear incompatible with 'conveyor-belt' sushi (Holt & Yamauchi, 2018, this volume). It is clear that craft products, processes and contexts provide a rich seam of storytelling, typically constructed around the more evocative and vernacular elements of the relevant historical narrative, that is capable of promoting both 'inward' and 'outward' commitment. However, the authors go on to identify another way in which organisations can make use of history, a way which would appear to have a particular significance for contemporary craft. This third use, which the authors describe as, 'being historical', has a somewhat less instrumental character and involves organisational actors gaining insights into contemporary challenges by drawing on past experiences, such as earlier ways of working. They frame the concept of 'being historical' around Edith Penrose's ([1959] 2004; 1960) quasi-evolutionary insight that an organisation's historical hinterland is not *simply* a pliable resource, which managers reconfigure in an unreflective way to yield specific 'productive services' (i.e. capabilities). As she pointed out when reflecting back on her original argument, 'history matters' (Penrose 1995: xiii): an organisation's growth process is shaped by a cumulative process of collective learning. In practice, 'being historical' in this sense can have both a constraining and an enabling effect. Penrose's own historical analysis of the Hercules Powder Company indicated how the past was, 'forcing it down certain paths, and at one and the same time acting as a wellspring for the imaginative use of resources to yield different products and services' (Zundel, Holt & Popp 2016: 228–229). Whilst there is ample evidence of a recursive Penrosian learning process operating in a variety of organisational types, it appears plausible that today's craft-based entrepreneurs and innovators might be especially open to the influence of this third use of history where:

[H]istory is no longer a matter of resuscitating a desired past from a current stand-point, and thus with future ends in mind, but one where through immersion in past one gains a sense of the constraints and (open) possibilities existing for people in that period.

(ibid: 229)[11]

History as Method: Directions and Limitations

In the preceding sections, I have summarised a varied selection of historically informed research and discussed how the past is used to defend and promote contemporary craft practice. To conclude, I consider the scope and limitations of historical research methods, and how they might contribute to future work on craft practice and organisation. I hope that these comments and suggestions may prove helpful to readers who are interested in embarking on historical research in one of these areas.

Historical studies are generally written up as structured narratives, illustrated and substantiated with frequent references to archival sources.[12] However, the 'historical turn' in management and organisation theory (Clark & Rowlinson 2004) has problematized what critics see as an endemic 'universalism and presentism' (i.e. the assumption that organisations are similar irrespective of the local context and historical background) (Booth & Rowlinson 2006). For example, efforts to 'explain' growth-related phenomena tend to become myopic when overly simplified temporalities are combined with an unreflective focus on a 'decontextualized, extended present' (*ibid.* 6). Causal explanations can be undermined because researchers place undue emphasis on proximate, readily quantifiable and relatively short-run factors. One of the major challenges in constructing these narratives is to combine 'immersion into the history of the industry being studied' with the necessary analytical clarity (Jones 2001: 918). We have seen how craft practice and organisation is best understood through multi-level accounts, spanning individuals, social groups and broader contextual settings. Given the specialised and often elusive nature of craft practice, unpacking the resulting interactions is likely to require a profound understanding of a range of influences, including: source materials (e.g. wood, clay, textiles); embodied knowledge and skills; and socio-economic influences, values and cultural norms.

The requirement for in-depth, multi-level approaches is particularly acute when researching organisational growth processes, an issue that has continuing resonance for today's craft practitioners. Research in this area has been constrained by a continuing lack of consensus over the meaning of core concepts such as 'business growth' (Leitch, Hill & Neergaard 2010), coupled with an unreflective use of biological metaphor (Clarke, Holt & Blundel 2014), which can engender naïve and erroneous assumptions (Achtenhagen, Naldi & Melin 2010: 289). Craft-based ventures are characterised by hybridity, or the presence of multiple, often conflicting institutional logics (Mair, Mayer & Lutz 2015). This will typically take the form of inherent tensions between commercial, creative and other values-based imperatives. However, structured historical narrative approaches may prove helpful in addressing the issue of hybridity, and thereby aiding our understanding of the growth process in craft-based organisations.[13]

So perhaps the most obvious starting point for historical research on craft is to examine the lived experience of those engaged in these activities. However, it is also important to recognise that some aspects of craft may not be amenable to examination through conventional historical research methods, as a consequence of the embodied and often deeply personal nature of craft working practices, including the ways in which countercultural values infuse the work[14]. With appropriate modifications, tried-and-tested biographical approaches, of the kind undertaken by business historians and other specialists, could provide new insights into the development of craft-based enterprises. A new generation of collective biographies would shed more light on the internal dynamics of craft communities and organisations, though the depth and quality of the analysis would, to a large degree, depend on the researcher's ability to access suitable archival material, and to complement it with other relevant sources, such as craft artefacts and documentary evidence. Oral histories and collaborative writing could also make a distinctive contribution.

Notes

1 While the usual caveats apply regarding my responsibility for any errors and omissions in this chapter, I would like to acknowledge the insights that I have gained over the last two decades from: my co-authors on several of these projects, including Peter Clark, Jean Clarke, Robin Holt, Philip Koomen, Fergus Lyon, Anja Schaefer, David J. Smith, Michael Thatcher, Angela Tregear and Aqueel Wahga; 'regular' business historians, including Andrew Godley, Andrew Popp and Michael Rowlinson; and many craft practitioners who have kindly shared their time and experience over the years. I am also indebted to the editors for their comments on an earlier draft.

2 It is difficult to locate a comprehensive overview of this diverse literature. Adamson's (2010) 'craft reader' provides a useful starting point by assembling extracts from a wide variety of researchers and commentators, past and present.

3 For example, debates over the relative merits of bespoke items that combine hand-crafting with digital technologies, or between craftivists and more conventional practitioners, can be seen as a present-day working out of the contradictions between the same three elements: 'decorative arts', 'the vernacular' and 'the politics of work' (Greenhalgh 1997).

4 The term, 'collective biography' has undergone a number of re-interpretations. I am referring here to a traditional approach, described recently as a distinct methodology that 'self-consciously retains a focus on the individual even when it sits within work which aims to use individual lives to explore

collective experiences, or within studies of communities (geographically, socially or culturally defined)' (Cowman 2016: 85).

5 For example, the Kindersley and Ravilious biographies both demonstrate how 20th-century craft practitioners were able to combine a strong attachment to traditional practices – engraving in wood and stone – with an active engagement with modern technologies and institutions: David Kindersley created new fonts with the Monotype Corporation and Letraset, amongst others; Eric Ravilious produced novel designs for Wedgwood ceramics; and Enid Marx created innovative seating fabrics for the London Underground.

6 In these advertisements members of the new generation of 'makers' are depicted, wearing the company's products while engaged in their craft work.

7 While the text of this chapter, 'Skill: a word to start an argument', carries the date '2011', it is worth noting that the author based it on material that he had published as long ago as 1982 and 1990 (Frayling 2011: 20).

8 See, for example, the anthropologist and popular broadcaster Alexander Langlands's idiosyncratic text on traditional crafts (Langlands 2017). Having enrolled historical evidence in pursuit of normative goals – 'I get angry over the lack of basketry in our lives' (*ibid.* 340) – the author is at risk of undermining an otherwise interesting analysis.

9 In practice, his account *does* address historical developments that saw this local, farm-produced artisanal cheese variety becoming a national symbol, produced on an industrial scale. The analysis ranges from the rationalizing impact of science (e.g. pasteurisation, which in the case of Camembert was undertaken directly by students of Louis Pasteur) to the role played by technology (e.g. the expanding rail network) and nationalism (e.g. the symbolic role that this cheese variety played in the First World War).

10 Examples include a farm-produced cheese, Appleby's, which is still made in small batches using unpasteurized milk and traditional methods, including calico bindings (www.applebyscheese.co.uk).

11 In this respect, it is interesting to note that the authors' examples of 'being historical' include French aircraft engineers who produced traditional handwritten ledgers, 'as they did in times where craft production meant that each product bore the mark of its maker' (Zundel et al. 2016: 230).

12 While much of this material is qualitative in nature, the analysis of quantitative data also plays an important role in some historical writing, including seminal works such as Braudel's (1981–1984) trilogy *Civilization and Capitalism* (Stager Jacques 2006, 43).

13 In a previous article, we addressed the issue of analysing the growth process in another type of hybrid organisation, the social enterprise (Blundel & Lyon 2015).

14 See, for example, the dialogue with the weaver, Ann Rippin, which appears elsewhere in this volume (Rippin & Vachanin 2018)

References

Achtenhagen, L., Naldi, L. & Melin, L. (2010) 'Business growth': do practitioners and scholars really talk about the same thing? *Entrepreneurship Theory and Practice*, 34 (2): 289–315.

Adamson, G. (2010) *The craft reader*. London: Bloomsbury.

Adamson, G. (2013) *The invention of craft*. London: Bloomsbury.

Blundel, R.K. & Lyon, F. (2015) Towards a 'long view': historical perspectives on the scaling and replication of social ventures. *Journal of Social Entrepreneurship*, 6 (1) 80-102.

Blundel, R.K. & Smith, D.J. (2018) 'Imagined outcomes': contrasting patterns of opportunity, capability, and innovation in British musical instrument manufacturing, 1930-1985. Enterprise and Society, (in press).

Blundel, R.K. & Tregear, A. (2006) Artisans and 'factories': the interpenetration of craft and industry in English cheese-making, c1650–1950. *Enterprise and Society*, 7 (4): 1–35.

Boisard, P. (2003) *Camembert: a national myth*. University of California Press: Berkeley CA [trans. R. Miller from Le Camembert: mythe nationale. Calman-Levy: Paris, 1992].

Booth, C. & Rowlinson, M. (2006) Management and organizational history: prospects. *Management and Organizational History*, 1 (1): 5–30.

Cardozo Kindersley, L., Hoare, L. & Sherwood, T. (2013) *Cutting into the workshop: celebrating the work and life of David Kindersley*. Cambridge: Cambridge University Press.

Carnevali, F. (2003) Golden opportunities: jewelry making in Birmingham between mass production and specialty. *Enterprise and Society*, 4 (2): 272–298.

Cheke, V. (1959) *The story of cheese-making in Britain*. London: Routledge & Kegan Paul.

Clarke, J., Holt, R. & Blundel, R.K. (2014) Re-imagining the growth process: (co)-evolving metaphorical representations of entrepreneurial growth. Entrepreneurship & Regional Development, 26 (3-4): 234–256.

Clark, P. & Rowlinson, M. (2004) The treatment of history in organisation studies: towards an 'historic turn'?. *Business History*, 46 (3): 331–352.

Cowman, K. (2016) Collective biography, in S. Gunn & L. Faire (Eds.) *Research methods for history*. Edinburgh: University of Edinburgh Press, pp. 83–100.

Dilley, R. (2009) Specialist knowledge practices of craftsmen and clerics in Senegal. *Africa*, 79 (1): 53–70.

Dormer, P (1994) *The art of the maker: skill and its meaning in art, craft and design*. London: Thames and Hudson.

Ferris, M. (2016) Making Futures: crafting a sustainable modernity – towards a maker aesthetics of production and consumption. *Making Futures*, 4 (n.p.).

Friend, A. (2017) *Ravilious & Co: the pattern of friendship*. London: Thames & Hudson.

Frayling, C. (2011) *On craftsmanship: towards a new Bauhaus*. London: Oberon.

Greenhalgh, P. (1997) The history of craft. In P. Dormer (Ed.) *The Culture of Craft: Status and Future*. Manchester: Manchester University Press.

Hampâté Bâ, A. (2010) Where the hand has ears. *Resurgence,* 263 (November–December): 42–44.

Hilaire-Pérez, L. (2007) Technology as public culture in the eighteenth century: The artisans' legacy. *History of Science* 45 (2): 135–153.

Holt, R. & Yamauchi, Y. (2018) Craft, design and nostalgia in modern Japan: the case of sushi. In E. Bell, G. Mangia, S. Taylor & M. L. Toraldo, *The organization of craft work*. Routledge: Abingdon, pp. 20–40.

Jones, C. (2001) Co-evolution of entrepreneurial careers, institutional rules and competitive dynamics in American film, 1895–1920. *Organization Studies,* 22 (6): 911–944.

Koomen, P. & Blundel, R.K. (2018) Developing craft practice within and between workshops: an inter-generational comparative study, *Making Futures*, 5 (in press).

Langlands, A. (2017) *Craeft: how traditional crafts are about more than just making*. London: Faber & Faber.

Leitch, C., Hill, F. & Neergaard, H. (2010) Entrepreneurial and business growth and the quest for a 'comprehensive theory': tilting at windmills? *Entrepreneurship Theory and Practice*, 34 (2): 249–260.

Mair, J., Mayer, J. & Lutz, E. (2015) Navigating institutional plurality: organizational governance in hybrid organizations. *Organization Studies*, 36 (6): 713–739.

Paxson, H. (2013) *The life of cheese: crafting food and value in America*. Berkeley, CA: University of California Press.

Penrose, E. T. [1959] 2004. *The theory of the growth of the firm*. 4th ed. Oxford: Oxford University Press.

Penrose, E.T. (1995) 'Foreword to the third edition' in E.T. Penrose, *The theory of the growth of the firm*. 3rd ed. Oxford: Oxford University Press, pp. ix–xxi.

Penrose, E.T. (1960) The growth of the firm—a case study: The Hercules Powder Company. *Business History Review*, 34 (1): 1–23.

Rippin, A. & Vachhani, S. (2018) Craft as Resistance: a conversation about craftivism, embodied inquiry and craft-based methodologies. In E. Bell, G. Mangia, S. Taylor & M. L. Toraldo, *The organization of craft work*. Routledge: Abingdon, pp. 217–234.

Sabel, C.F. & Zeitlin, J. (eds.) (1997) *World of possibilities: flexibility and mass production in western industrialization*. Cambridge: Cambridge University Press.

Scranton, P. (1997) *Endless novelty: specialty production and American industrialization, 1865–1925*. Princeton, NJ: Princeton University Press.

Smith Maguire (2018) Wine, the authenticity taste regime and rendering craft. In E. Bell, G. Mangia, S. Taylor & M. L. Toraldo, *The organization of craft work*. Routledge: Abingdon, pp. 60–78.

Stager Jacques, R. (2006) History, historiography and organization studies: The challenge and the potential. *Management and Organizational History*, 1 (1): 31–49.

Thompson, P. (1997) The potential for oral history and life story research on the crafts movement. In: T. Harrod (Ed.) *Obscure objects of desire: reviewing the crafts in the twentieth century*. London: Crafts Council, pp. 42–50.

Toraldo, M.L., Mangia, G. & Consiglio, S. (2018) Crafting social memory for international recognition: the role of place and tradition in an Italian silk-tie maker. In E. Bell, G. Mangia, S. Taylor & M. L. Toraldo, *The organization of craft work*. Routledge: Abingdon, pp. 118–133.

Walker, D. (2016) Craft's identity crisis. *Crafts*, 258 (January–February). London: Crafts Council.

Zundel, M., Holt, R. & Popp, A. (2016) Using history in the creation of organizational identity. *Management & Organizational History*, 11 (2): 211–235.

Index

Printed in the United States
by Baker & Taylor Publisher Services